KING *of all* BALLOONS

MARK J. DAVIES is an Oxford local historian, public speaker and guide with an especial interest in the history and literature of the non-university aspects of the city. The life of James Sadler involves both the 'Town' of Oxford and the university 'Gown' side of the city's history, and is one reason why it appealed to the author. Mark is considered an authority on the historical and current roles of Oxford's waterways, having lived on a residential narrowboat on the Oxford Canal since 1992. He has appeared in various television and radio documentaries about *Alice in Wonderland*, the waterways of Oxford and Oxford Castle. For more information please see www.oxfordwaterwalks.co.uk.

SIR RICHARD BRANSON, Founder of the Virgin Group, is a businessman, investor and entrepreneur. He holds Guinness World Records for crossing the Atlantic by hot-air balloon in 1987 and crossing the Pacific by hot-air balloon in 1999.

DON CAMERON MBE is a Scottish balloonist and founder of Cameron Balloons, the largest manufacturer of hot-air balloons in the world.

KING *of all* BALLOONS

The Adventurous Life of James Sadler, the First English Aeronaut

MARK DAVIES

Foreword by Sir Richard Branson
Afterword by Don Cameron MBE

AMBERLEY

ACKNOWLEDGEMENTS

The author wishes to acknowledge the support of the Greening Lamborn Trust, whose objective is to promote public interest in the history, architecture, old photographs and heraldry of Oxford and its neighbourhood by supporting publications and other media that creates access to them.

First published 2015
This edition published 2018

Amberley Publishing
The Hill, Stroud
Gloucestershire, GL5 4EP

www.amberley-books.com

Copyright © Mark J. Davies, 2015, 2018

The right of Mark J. Davies to be identified as the Author of this work has been asserted in accordance with the Copyrights, Designs and Patents Act 1988.

ISBN 978 1 4456 8286 0 (paperback)
ISBN 978 1 4456 5309 9 (ebook)

British Library Cataloguing in Publication Data.
A catalogue record for this book is available from the British Library.

Typesetting and Origination by Amberley Publishing
Map and table illustration on pages 12–13, 14 and 18 by Thomas Bohm, User Design, Illustration and Typesetting.
Printed in the UK.

CONTENTS

PREFACE

In the late 1920s, a shiny metal object was spotted during the demolition of some dilapidated buildings in a dingy alley in one of the poorer parts of Oxford. It proved to be a medal. On one side was the profile of a man identified as 'James Sadler: First English Aeronaut'; on the reverse, with a date of 7 October 1811, the words 'Ascended from Birmingham. Traversed Upwards of 112 Miles in 1 Hour 20 Minutes' were circumscribed around an image of a balloon and basket containing two men.[1]

That discovery was symbolic, since at the time the many achievements of James Sadler, even in his home city of Oxford, had been virtually expunged from memory. Yet that feat of travelling at a preposterous 84 mph and of being the first Englishman to fly provides only a glimpse of a long and hugely productive life far removed from his more likely career choice as a pastry cook and confectioner in the family business. Instead, as well as two distinct periods as a professional balloonist, he devoted himself to inventing many kinds of chemical apparatus; to improving guns and cannons; building patented engines; and filling a unique role for the Navy during a turbulent period of European hostilities. He also fathered two sons who followed in his aeronautical footsteps. James Sadler's was a life which brought him much enjoyment and much anguish, much praise and a little ridicule. It also brought him passing fame, yet even before his death in 1828, aged seventy-five, his name had largely faded from memory.

Yet the very fact that he had reached such an age, after indulging in such a hazardous pastime for so many years, is in itself somewhat remarkable: his first pioneering flight had been made in October 1784, in Oxford, at the age of thirty-one. On that occasion, he had become the first English, arguably British, aeronaut. In order to do so, he had overcome educational disadvantage, financial constraints and apparent class bigotry and professional jealousy to achieve his dream. Yet he finished his days in impoverished near-anonymity. Even in Oxford, the only public reminders of James Sadler, one of its most ingenious, courageous and inspiring home-grown sons, are a plaque near the location of that historic first ascent; his gravestone (in what is no longer a public cemetery); and, recently, his adoption by the Museum of Oxford as one of its ten most significant Oxford personalities.

This book is an attempt to redress that neglect, to pay tribute to a 'most ingenious, but unfortunate man', a 'perfect prodigy in mechanics' and a 'true philosophical genius' whose unique combination of vision, practicality, determination and bravery enabled him 'to prepare, make, form, and confine that surprizing Volatile Æther by which he ascended into those Regions almost beyond human Thought'.

*

My intention in writing this book was to honour a neglected Oxford hero, a man who, had he been associated with an Oxford college, rather than being a mere Oxford tradesman, might have become a household name. Or indeed, as one contemporary commentator put it, even if he had done what he did in Cambridge, where the sciences have always been held in higher repute. I had thought to concentrate solely on his achievements within Oxford itself, to make this a truly *local* history book. The more I learned about this intriguing character, however, the more I felt that his wider successes deserved – if you will excuse an addition to the plethora of laboured, flight-inspired, contemporary puns which populate this book – a wider airing. He did, after all, make ascents from a dozen different British towns and cities, and his son Windham from twice that many. Nearly twenty of these were the first ever known from these places, and Windham's ill-fated career included the first ever crossing of the Irish Sea. Yes, these were accomplishments of national importance, the first fledgling flutters of a technology which has seen men on the moon and journeys of millions of miles into space, most recently to uncover some of the secrets of Pluto. A detailed account was, surely, long overdue.

A biography has been written about the first Scot to fly, the first Irishman, and the first man ever to pilot a balloon in Britain, an Italian. Yet there was nothing specifically about the first Englishman. One reason for this glaring omission, perhaps, is Sadler's enigmatic character. It is possibly an overused adjective, applied too readily to historical characters. In Sadler's case it is particularly apt, however, because although he achieved brief fame, and became known personally to many influential figures within the fields of science, literature, politics, the military, the aristocracy and even the royal family, clues to his true character are rare, and he himself left little by which to gauge it: no diary, virtually no letters, and even the first-person accounts of his exploits were evidently written for him by more erudite hands. In the words of Hugh Torrens, author of the *Oxford Dictionary of National Biography* entry (2004), 'Sadler's life was of deeds, not words, and left great problems for any biographer.'

I have also taken the opportunity to include appendices relating to some other largely ignored heroes (and heroines) of early ballooning, partly for context and partly to shed new light on their exploits. With the advantage of modern computer search techniques, I have been able to add to what is already known about the doggedly persistent Scot, James Tytler; Harper, the Birmingham man who used Sadler's original equipment to fly farther than anyone else had, yet whose achievement has registered so little that even to this day his first name cannot be stated with certainty; and Mrs Sage, the first Englishwoman to fly, with James Sadler's help, as well as some other women 'balloonarian' pioneers. These intrepid women, whose bravery was often downplayed at the time and has been little acknowledged ever since, included the French Simonet sisters, who were the first to fly in Britain; the Sadlers' family friend, Miss Thompson, the first woman to fly in Ireland; the accident-prone yet ultimately unscathed Margaret Graham, the first Englishwoman to fly solo; and Jane Stocks, who was back in the air only a fortnight after surviving a crash in which her male companion was killed.

In other words, from the starting point of Sadler's probably impetuous decision to launch himself skywards on a crisp, clear, October morning in Oxford in 1784, the book developed with much of the wayward unpredictability of those early balloon flights, leading me in unexpected directions, both fruitful and unhelpful, both thrilling and discouraging, both rewarding and costly, taking me to rather different places than those originally intended! On that journey I have been helped, as well as by staff in libraries, museums and archive centres too numerous to mention, by the following: William Acton, Clive Bailey, Tamara Bennett, Sir Richard Branson, Clare Brant, Don Cameron MBE, Sharon Cure, Robin Darwall-Smith, Peter Deller, Nick Fox, Nic ap Glyn, Richard Holmes, Derrick Holt, Eliza Howlett, Stephanie Jenkins, Phil Marston, James Middleton, Valerie Petts, Miriam and Steve Pullinger, Catherine Robinson, Graeme Salmon, Susie Shutt, Tony Simcock, Marty Smith, Richard O. Smith, Hugh Torrens and Joanne Wilson.

I have opted to include many contemporary quotations, some quite long, rather than try to rephrase the information to present my own interpretation. This may make for a less smooth narrative but will, I hope, avoid the common trap of allowing imagination to overtake the facts, and allow readers some scope to form their own opinions.

In terms of sources, I have quoted freely from the letters and diaries of contemporaries and also from newspapers, for which, because these are nowadays easily found via digital archives, I did not feel it was necessary to cite the page and column numbers in every case. It may also be worth noting that because of widespread plagiarism of newspaper accounts, the source cited may not necessarily always be either the only one or the first (or indeed, of course, the most accurate!). Almost all quotations from *Jackson's Oxford Journal* come from its third page, where items of local news generally featured. Much biographical information relating to Sadler's contemporaries has been gleaned from the online *Oxford Dictionary of National Biography* and, for those with Oxford University associations, from the multi-volume *Alumni Oxonienses*.

Mark Johnstone Davies
Oxford, August 2015

FOREWORD

As the first English aeronaut, James Sadler is one of those early pioneers who has had an enormous influence on all who have followed in his footsteps.

He was born and lived in Oxford, only a few miles from Kidlington, where I lived for many years. His first manned flight, a historic first by any Englishman, ended just a few miles away from the city.

Sadler was also a family man. I know from my own balloon crossings the additional pressure that brings. I remember in 1997, as myself, Per Lindstrand and Alex Richie prepared to make the first non-stop balloon flight around the world, I wrote a heart breaking letter to my children just in case I didn't return. The goodbyes never got any easier but like Sadler I've always had an urge to live life to its fullest.

On two occasions, Sadler came down in the sea. It's an experience with which I can empathise, but I had the reassurance of knowing that others were aware of my exact location. Sadler had to rely on the willingness and skill of others to come to his rescue.

But above all, what I think I admire most about Sadler is the range of his interests and talents. He could easily have selected a safe career, running the family business in Oxford, but chose instead a far more challenging course, overcoming a lack of privilege to realise his dream.

I am fascinated by how things work, how things are done and how things might be done differently. It seems to me that James Sadler – balloonist, engineer, inventor and scientist – had a similar outlook. I hope that this book helps his name and his achievements to become much more widely known. His contribution to the noble causes of adventure and exploration deserves much greater recognition.

Sir Richard Branson, Virgin Group Founder

CHRONOLOGY

* = first ever manned balloon flight from this location. Windham Sadler made the first ascents from several more: Cork, Derby, Doncaster, Exeter, Hull, Pontefract, Rochdale, Sheffield and Wigan. Distances are point to point, rather than actual; altitudes as reported at the time.

27 Feb. 1753
James Sadler baptised St Peter-in-the-East, Oxford

5 Nov. 1775
Marriage to Mary Harper, Abingdon, as 'cook'

23 Nov. 1777
First child Mary Ann baptised, Abingdon

9 March 1779
John, first son, baptised

7 July 1779
Made freeman of Oxford as cook

23 July 1780
James, second son, baptised

1 March 1782
Thomas, third son, baptised

9 Feb. 1784
First launch of hydrogen balloon from Dr. Sibthorp's, Oxford

15 May 1784
Balloon 'with an Animal suspended' launched from Botanic Gardens, Oxford

4 Oct. 1784
* First hot-air ascent from Oxford (travelling six miles)

12 Nov. 1784
First hydrogen ascent from Oxford Botanic Gardens (travelling twenty miles)

5 May 1785
From Moulsey Hurst, Surrey with William Windham MP (thirty-five miles)

12 May 1785
* Manchester (from Long Mill Gate, renamed Balloon Street; fifty miles and two and a half miles altitude)

30 May 1785
Eliza, second daughter, baptised

24 June 1785
Col. Richard Fitzpatrick's ascent from Oxford in Sadler's balloon

29 June 1785
Assisted Mrs Sage to become first British female balloonist

25 Aug. 1785
* Worcester

19 Oct. 1785
* Stroud

March 1793
To Bristol with Thomas Beddoes

24 Oct. 1795
Second marriage to Martha Hancock, Bristol
1795/1796
Appointment as Barrack Master, Portsmouth Harbour, then Chemist to the Navy
17 Oct. 1796
William Windham Sadler, youngest son, born London
27 Nov. 1798
Martha Maria Sybella, second and youngest daughter, born London
7 July 1810
Oxford ascent (first for twenty-five years) with son John (travelling fifty miles)
24 Sept. 1810
Bristol as far as the South Wales coast (ditching in Bristol Channel after 100 miles)
3 July 1811
    * Cambridge
7 Oct. 1811
Birmingham to Lincolnshire: 112 miles in eighty minutes
29 June 1812
Manchester (altitude of three miles and 640 yards)
1 Oct. 1812
Dublin to near Liverpool (ditched in sea; 130 miles linear distance after total journey of 237 miles)
7 Sept. 1813
Windham Sadler's first ascent at *Cheltenham
1 Nov. 1813
    * Nottingham
1813/1814
Manufacturer of soda water, London
15 July 1814
James and Windham together from London, being probably his last ascent (to an altitude claimed to be five miles, though could not realistically have been higher than about three)
29 July 1814
Windham Sadler and Mary (?) Thompson, London
1 Aug 1814
John Sadler (second and final ascent), London
22 July 1817
Windham Sadler's crossing of Irish Sea from Dublin to Wales
26 Nov.1817
Death of James Sadler, son of James, in India
1824 to 1828
Resident at Charterhouse hospice, London
29 Sept. 1824
Windham Sadler's death on his thirty-first flight, from Bolton
27 March 1828
Death of James Sadler in Oxford

Map A. Map of British Isles showing relevant locations, those in capitals being places where either James or Windham Sadler made the first ever balloon ascents.

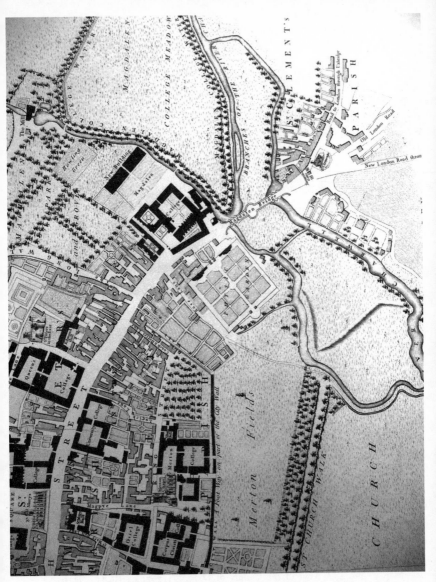

Map B. From 'A Map of the County of Oxford' (1797) by Richard Davis, surveyed 1793 and 1794 (reproduced by Philip Riden, 1975).

Note (north of the High Street): Queen's College and St Peter-in-the-East church; (south of the High Street): St Mary Hall Lane (near the top of which was No. 104, the Sadlers' nineteenth-century confectionery), University College (to the right of which is the Sadler's home of No. 84 and the Angel Inn) and the Physic Garden. The Sibthorps' Cowley House is among the cluster of buildings to the south-east of the River 'Charwell' and James Sadler's 1810 ascent was from the western end of Merton Field.

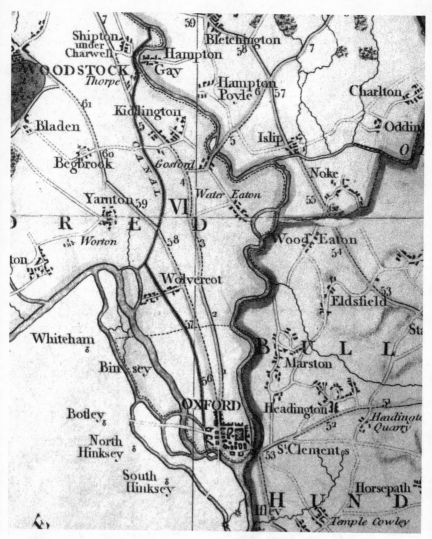

Map C. From 'A Map of the County of Oxford' (1797) by Richard Davis, surveyed 1793 and 1794 (reproduced by Philip Riden, 1975).

James Sadler's historic first six-mile trip of 4 October 1784 landed on 'a small Eminence betwixt Islip and Wood Eaton'. Note too Woodstock, which he had hoped to reach; Headington, where the cat parachuted from their balloon by James and John Sadler in 1810 landed; and Kidlington, where Thomas Warton's fictional flight in James Sadler's balloon terminated.

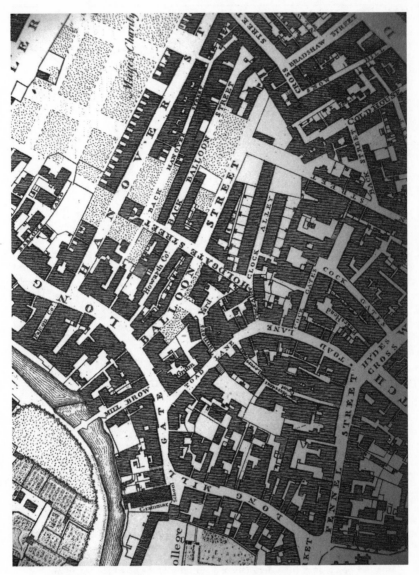

Map D. From 'A Plan of Manchester and Salford' (1794) by William Green, surveyed 1787 to 1794 (reproduced by Falkner and Son, 1902).

Balloon Street and Back Balloon Street were named in recognition of the first ever ascents from the city, made by James Sadler on 12 and 19 May 1785 from the premises of John Haworth (note Howarth Court nearby).

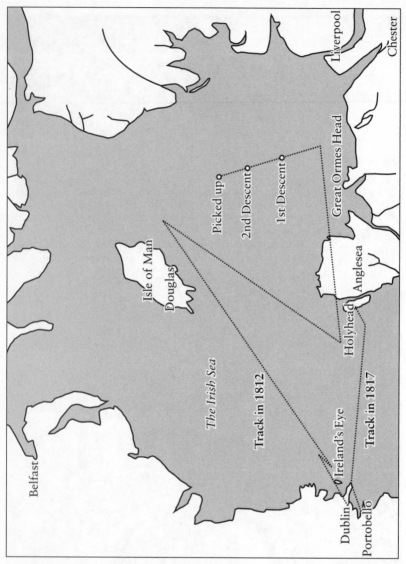

Map E. Copy of map from *Aerostation: a narrative of the aerial voyage, of Mr. Windham Sadler, across the Irish Channel*, showing the courses taken both on this journey of 1817 and that made by James Sadler in 1812.

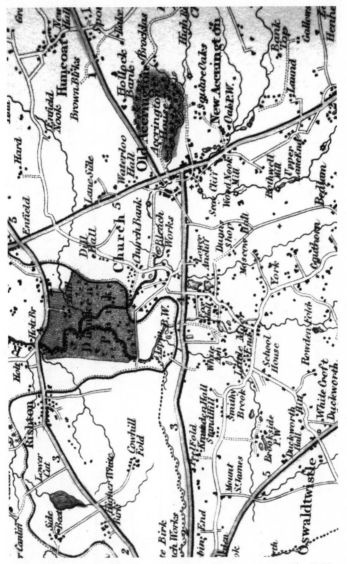

Map F. From 'A Map of the County Palatine of Lancaster' (1830) by G. Hennet, surveyed 1828/29. (Bodleian Library, University of Oxford: Lancs C17:37, 51)

Note Church, where Windham Sadler had his fatal accident in 1824; Accrington, from where medical assistance was summoned; Oswaldtwistle, where the firm of Peel, Haworth and Yates began in 1764; and Peelfold about a mile to the north, which had been the Peels' ancestral home since 1731.

Sadler Family of Oxford (and Liverpool): select genealogy

William (?–1649?) = 1627 Jane Weller
blacksmith, gunsmith

William (1631–1680?) = 1661 Jeane/Jane Marten (1643?–1679?)

?

William (1662?–1720) = (1) Joanna (?–1713) (2) Grace
tailor

John (1694–1749) = Sarah (?–1753)
victualler

James (1718–1791) = Elizabeth ? (c.1718–1802)
cook

Thomas Blakeney (1756–1829) confectioner
= Eleanor ? (c.1752–1807)

| Elizabeth (1782–?) = 1816 Charles Reed | Henry (1784–?) = 1815 Mary Whitchurch | Thomas (1788–1831) = 1808 Jane Cox | Charles James (1792–1872) = 1815 Jane Needle |

Charles James (1817–1882)
= 1840 Elizabeth Reed

James (1753–1828) pastry-cook, aeronaut and chemist
= (1) 1775 Mary Harper
= (2) 1795 Martha Hancock

| Mary Ann (1777–?) | John (1779–1838) = 1802 Mary Long | James (1780–1817) | William Windham (1795–1824) = 1819 Catherine Richards | Martha Sybella (1798–1851+) |

John Coxe Hippisley (1805–1860)

John Muncaster (1823–1912)

Amelia (1831–?)

Harold

PART 1

LAND
1753–84

I

GROWING UPWARDS: CHILDHOOD AND BACKGROUND

The Sadlers of Oxford (*see* Appendix 1 and Family Tree)

James Sadler, the future aeronautical pioneer, engineer and inventor, was baptised in the Oxford church of St Peter-in-the-East on 27 February 1753. His parents, James and Elizabeth, had only one other child, his younger brother, Thomas Blakeney Sadler, who was baptised at the same church in August 1756.

Beyond this, nothing is known of his childhood, though the evidence suggests that his education was minimal, and that he was groomed instead to follow in his father's footsteps as a cook and retailer of food. James Sadler senior had also been the firstborn of his family, according both to a list of births recorded in a family prayer book[1] and the parish records of St Peter-in-the-East. He was born on 16 January 1718, followed by seven siblings, the last of whom was born in 1731. The father's name recorded at all eight of these baptisms is John (1694–1749), who had been made a freeman of Oxford on 23 February 1718,[2] a matter of a month after James's birth. The Sadlers had been present in Oxford since at least the early seventeenth century, but John seems to have been the first to prepare or sell food for a living: in 1732 he was working at Queen's College as an 'under butler',[3] but by 1737 he was an independent 'victualler'.[4] One of a very large family, John had chosen a different career from that of his father William (1662?–1720), who had been a tailor of some repute.

In the seventeenth century there were gunsmiths in the family, perhaps influencing the younger James's later interest in this area, when during his employment with the Navy his improvements to guns and cannons attracted much praise. At about the same time, in the 1650s and 1660s, Robert Boyle (1627–91), an instigator of modern chemistry, had been a tenant of Deep Hall, the High Street house that Sadler's great-grandfather, William, would later occupy. 'Boyle's Law' defined the relationship between the pressure, volume and temperature of gases, something that James Sadler would have cause to ponder often enough during his life. Perhaps it may be fanciful to conjecture that James might have been inspired a little by this association with Boyle to pursue the career he did, but with virtually no facts to rely on, some degree of speculation becomes necessary. Whatever, when James Sadler the aeronaut fell on hard times in his fifties, his supporters' attempts to solicit local sympathy by underlining the long Oxford pedigree of his family was therefore genuinely founded. A detailed account of his antecedents, taken from parish, municipal and university records appears in Appendix 1.

James Sadler Senior (1718–91) and Elizabeth Sadler (*c.* 1718–1801)

No record of Sadler's parents' marriage has been found, but it is possible that the maiden name of his mother, Elizabeth, may have been Blakeney, the middle name given to his brother Thomas, who was baptised at St Peter-in-the-East on 6 or 8 August 1756. On the basis of her newspaper obituary[5] Elizabeth had been born in about 1718. Another possibility is that she was from Blakeney in Gloucestershire (where several eighteenth-century generations of a family named Sadler are apparent).

James senior seems likely to have been the unspecified Sadler who, along with others, was required on 8 June 1744 to answer charges by agents of the Cooks' Company that they were 'neither matriculated nor entered a member of the cooks company', yet undertook 'the business of a Cook within the precincts of this University'.[6] The university was understandably keen to regulate the provision of food on its premises, and it may be that Sadler's relatively recent status as a freeman (since 9 April 1743)[7] proved sufficient dispensation, as no further action was taken: 'warrant not gone forth' was noted against his name on 19 October 1744.[8]

By 1764, James Sadler had acquired his own premises, having newly 'taken and entered on the House called LEMON HALL, near Carfax' according to his advertisement in *Jackson's Oxford Journal* of 15 December 1764. The sophisticated range of products and services on offer were:

Dressing and Cutting out various Sorts of Meat, ready every Day from Twelve till Two – Sausages fresh made every Day; Alamode Beef; Potted and Collared ditto; Collared Eels; Broths and Soups always ready; Neats Tongues, Boiled or Green; Pickles of all Sorts; Best Durharm [*sic*] Flour of Mustard, and Mustard ready made. Likewise sells Morells, Truffles, Hartshorn Shavings, Vermicelli and Anchovies. Neat Wine, Brandy, Rum &c. Dinners &c. drest and sent off in the neatest Manner.[9]

Carfax is at the very centre of old Oxford, the ancient junction of north–south and east–west routes. The location also loosely marked the geographical boundary between the two rather different aspects of Oxford, the university and the city. To the west, the houses and shops of residential Oxford sloped gradually down towards the braiding streams of the River Thames and the dark alleys and insanitary environs of the adjacent flood-prone suburbs of St Thomas' and St Ebbe's. To the south of Carfax, on the eastern side of the main road leading eventually to Southampton, was the college of Christ Church, with its extensive meadowland bordering the main branch of the Thames. To the east of Carfax lay the two dozen or so colleges and halls which held almost exclusive sway over the tracts of land on either side of Oxford's architecturally famous High Street, which curved gently down to the city's other river, the Cherwell. Beyond that lay the suburb of St Clement's, where the two main roads from London converged. The university, partly through geography, partly through opportunistic acquisition, was thus fairly neatly defined. Oxford Gown was, so to speak, hemmed in on the east and west by Oxford Town, and on the south by the Thames. To the north was open meadowland, awaiting the university's rapid academic and domestic expansion of the late nineteenth century.

Being so central, a location near Carfax was ideal for any tradesman, so James Sadler might have expected custom from both townspeople and university men, both staff and scholars. The young James Sadler would almost certainly have helped in the shop from an early age, and it is tempting to imagine that growing up in the environment of a cook's shop might also have inspired his later passion. He would, presumably, have had more opportunity than most to become familiar from an early age with the tendency of smoke to rise and to have observed the elevating effect of heat on the dough, cake mix and pastry cooked by his parents.[10]

Yet if Carfax represented a convergence of Oxford 'Town and Gown', it was also a symbol of division, the marshalling point for the bloody disputes in which the two different Oxfords had engaged for centuries. The bells of the church at Carfax had long been used to summon the men of the town, whenever the perpetual tensions with the scholars of the university erupted into mass pugilism. It was an accepted aspect of Oxford life. Indeed, these 'rows' appear to have been positively relished, being recalled in innumerable Oxford memoirs and almost *de rigeur* for every novel set in Oxford. One of the earliest, *The Adventures of Oxymel Classic Esq.*, published in 1768, sets the scene for one of these violent clashes with: 'The townsmen themselves, who are chiefly dependent on the students for their very existence, take every opportunity of treating them with contumely, and there has been, from time immemorial, a perpetual war carried on.'[11] This antipathy between the university and its interdependent neighbours was something that the younger James Sadler would experience first-hand later that century.

It would seem that the Lemon Hall venture was relatively short-lived. No further advertisements appeared in *Jackson's*,[12] and by 1768, when a poll of the freemen of Oxford was taken, and still in 1772 when a citywide survey of Oxford properties was made,[13] Sadler resided in the parish of St Peter-in-the-East, too far down the High to be classed as 'near Carfax'. It would be unusual not to live above the business, so it seems safe to assume that the shop referred to often over the next twenty years or so was located at the property identified in 1772 as what is now 84 High Street (appropriately enough, nowadays a café). The survey shows that Sadler shared the ground floor with a Mr Dickinson, however, with a frontage of only 3 yards, 1 foot and 9 inches (Dickinson's being 4 yards, 1 foot and 4 inches). It must therefore have had a very small capacity, and was probably not especially profitable: the leases of University College, owners of the property, show that Sadler was never the main tenant, but sublet from the leaseholder.[14]

Nonetheless, the house was strategically placed within the long, narrow 'town' intrusion into the collegiate quarter, one of many businesses occupying premises on either side of the High Street which were largely dependent on the university and its visitors for their custom. Still more helpfully, it was adjacent to Oxford's most prestigious coaching inn, the Angel Hotel. By 1781, and probably earlier, the Angel had even expanded into No. 83 next door.

James Sadler continued to provide outside catering, as had been offered in 1764, albeit not always successfully, as the Oxford Corporation minutes of 8 September 1778 show: 'Five guineas is to be taken off Mr. Sadler, the cook's, bill at the venison feast, he having charged many of the articles on the said bill far too highly and carelessly lost many of the things committed to his care.' A sufficient quantity of what might very appropriately be called humble pie had evidently been consumed by the following year, however, as on 2 July 1779 James, the eldest son of James Sadler, cook, was admitted by the corporation into the ranks of the freemen of Oxford.[15]

The Brothers James (1753–1828) and Thomas Blakeney Sadler (1756–1829)

Prior to this, time the younger James had been living in Abingdon, where, designated as a 'cook', he married Mary Harper (*c.* 1756–91+) on 5 November 1775 at Abingdon's main church of St Helen's. Mary's father, Matthew Harper, was also a vendor of food, a baker (as stated at the baptisms of all six of his children at St Helen's between 1756 and 1772, and also when listed among freemen eligible to vote in 1768).[16] Both men were among the very long list of 'Gentry, Clergy, Freeholders, and other Inhabitants of Berkshire' who, as a result of the first stirrings of revolt in America in 1775, presented their 'strongest Assurances of our ready Attachment to your Majesty's and this Nation's united Cause, in opposition to the insolent Efforts of all the Enemies of Peace, Order, and good Government'.[17] Coincidentally or not, the names of Sadler and Harper would also be united in a ballooning context soon after James's first ascents at the end of 1784 (*see* Appendix 5).

James and Mary were still residing in Abingdon when their first child was born, Mary Ann, who was baptised at St Helen's on 23 November 1777, but had moved to Oxford by the time of the birth of their second child, John. He was baptised at All Saints Church on 9 March 1779. This change from the traditional family church of St Peter-in-the-East to one a little farther up the High, closer to Carfax, seems to suggest that James had returned to run an outlet in his own right while his father continued to operate from No. 84 next to the Angel.[18] With a frontage of less than 11 feet, that shop was, in all probability, too small to admit of either son taking an active part: James's younger brother, Thomas, had also gone to work elsewhere, as a notice that he placed in *Jackson's* of 9 November 1782 reveals.

Under the headline 'Oxford Sausages' he emphasised the expertise that he had acquired as a cook at the long-established and well-respected Star Inn in Cornmarket[19] and announced the availability at his own new food outlet in St Clement's of 'the very best sausages, fresh made every day, likewise potted beef'.

On the face of it, St Clement's represented a retrograde step. This suburb, separated from the most easterly of the Oxford colleges, Magdalen, by the River Cherwell, suffered from a slightly dubious reputation as the haunt of 'herds of the lowest rabble ... the bargees, and butchers, and labourers, and scum of the suburbians'.[20] But then, there was no such thing as an Oxford suburb which failed to exhibit some barely imaginable depravity or other, according to the hypocritical standards of those who stalked the cloisters and lecture halls of the university colleges. A university proclamation at the time prohibited scholars from frequenting 'Coffee Houses, Cook's shops, and victualling houses',[21] within which definition Thomas' establishment would certainly have fallen. Nonetheless, as St Clement's spanned both of the roads to London (via either High Wycombe or Henley) the suburb was no doubt an excellent one from which to pick up passing trade – albeit of a less affluent and sophisticated nature than the clientele which might frequent the High Street. The business acumen which would establish Thomas Sadler as a leading Oxford tradesman – a sense in which, experience would show, his older brother appears to have been largely deficient – was apparent in that he followed his father's example of offering outside catering: 'Dinners dressed at any Distance from Oxford.'

Around this time, on the city side of Magdalen, the nature of the family business was changing a little, one or other James Sadler having identified himself for the first time as a 'confectioner and pastry cook' at the very beginning of 1784.[22] Specifically on offer was a 'large assortment of Twelfth Cakes', popular confections made especially to mark the twelfth day of Christmas. While it is not clear if this advertisement refers to the older or younger James Sadler, one can only assume that at least one of the parents continued to play a major role in the catering business, because, little more than a month later, their son would find time to construct and launch his first air balloon; before the end of the year he would be famed as the first English aeronaut; and all too soon after that, elements of the fickle national press would be making reference to these same 'Twelfth Cakes' in the context of implying that Sadler would be far better advised to concentrate on producing such dainties, and to leave ballooning to men rather better qualified to undertake the task.

The fact is, though, that there *was* no one better suited to the new science of ballooning than James Sadler, at least, not in England, and while his brother Thomas and his descendants went on to prosper in the confectionary trade, James experimented with 'confections' of a far more permanent and mechanical nature. To do so, the poorly educated pastry cook, son of a cook, grandson of a victualler, great-grandson of a tailor, needed some help to realise his ambitions. Fortunately, he found it within the precincts of nearby academia …

2

'SOARING CURIOSITY': JAMES SADLER'S FIRST TRIAL OF FEBRUARY 1784

James Sadler appears to have found two principal allies within Oxford University. One was the former University College graduate William Windham (1750–1810), whose support would be sustained over many years. The other was a noted botanist, John Sibthorp (1758–96), whose association, albeit much shorter, was critical at the very beginning of Sadler's experimental endeavours. Sibthorp was born in Oxford on 28 October 1758, the only son of Humphrey Sibthorp (c. 1712–97), Sherardian Professor of Botany at Oxford. The story goes that as holder of that post from 1747 to 1783, Humphrey Sibthorp suffered the inconvenience of presenting a lecture on only one occasion, and even then to a decided lack of acclaim.[1] Indeed, Humphrey Sibthorp's ineffectiveness was such that it was unkindly whispered that his sole notable contribution to the advancement of botany was to father a son who added immensely to the advancement of botany!

It is not John Sibthorp's contribution to botanical knowledge that is important to the story of James Sadler, however, but his role in facilitating Sadler's earliest experiments with flight. It was an incidental role, no doubt, in that he probably merely provided Sadler initially with a place where he could discreetly build his first experimental balloon, prior to its launch from his premises, and then work on improving its design. In central Oxford, where so many properties were owned by the colleges or the corporation, for a tradesman to find such a location, away from prying eyes and interfering hands, would otherwise have been a very tall order.

*

John Sibthorp took his degree at Lincoln College in 1777, studied medicine in Edinburgh in 1778–79, and passed his MA in 1780. His mother died the same year, leaving him a considerable legacy. Between 1781 and 1783, he studied in Paris and Montpellier. For anyone of a scientific bent, there could have been few better places to be in the summer of 1783 than France. On 5 June 1783, the Montgolfier brothers, Joseph (1740–1810) and Étienne (1745–99), launched the world's first hot-air balloon, at Annonay, to the south of Lyon. The concept of the Montgolfière, as it came to be known, relies on the simple physics that warm air will expand and become lighter, and that it will therefore rise, with the potential to elevate any restraining fabric within which it is contained.

A manufacturer of paper by trade, Joseph Montgolfier claimed to have realised the *potential* of elevation by this means long before he and his brother put it to the test, when he saw his wife's chemise inflate when left over the hearth to dry.[2] Another story is that the brothers' inspiration came when their mother 'took the conical paper wrapping of a sugar loaf and threw it on the fire, whereupon Joseph observed that it filled with hot air and flew up the chimney'.[3] The idea that a youthful James Sadler might have been similarly inspired in his father's cook's shop is perhaps therefore not so fanciful.

Like many other pioneers of early ballooning, the Montgolfier brothers acknowledged their debt to the Scottish chemist and physician Joseph Black (1728–99).[4] Black had commenced his work in Edinburgh in the 1750s, and proceeded to show that gases – what he called 'fixed air' – can be differentiated in the same way as solids and liquids. The Montgolfiers took practical measures to prove the feasibility of hot-air propulsion only once they had learned of Black's experiments.

Later on (in October 1784), Black generously deferred to the French-born British scientist, Henry Cavendish (1731–1810), as 'the person who first discovered with exactness the specific gravity of inflammable air'.[5] This had been in 1766, and at the time Cavendish had identified what he called 'phlogiston' or 'inflammable air' (that is, hydrogen, though the name had not then been coined). Black had swiftly realised the potential of this gas to inflate balloons, and had conducted some early experiments using a calf's bladder, but 'certainly never thought of making large artificial bladders, and making these lift heavy weights, and carry men up into the air'.[6] The Montgolfier brothers also acknowledged the work of another British scientist, Joseph Priestley (1733–1804), and particularly his discovery in 1774 of what would come to be called oxygen, a gas he termed 'dephlogisticated air'.[7]

The realisation that the French had pre-empted all others in seeing the practical possibilities of these British discoveries did not go down well at the Royal Society, the oldest and most prestigious scientific organisation in Britain. Sir Joseph Banks (1743–1820), the President, first learned of the Montgolfiers' achievement in one of the regular letters sent to him from France by the physician and fellow of the society, Dr Charles Blagden (1748–1820). His letter of 4 July 1783 outlined how the Montgolfiers had elevated 'a huge sack 40 feet in diameter of canvas' through filling it with smoke, and he concluded that 'we are much nearer flying than I expected'.[8] An exchange of letters between Banks and Benjamin Franklin (1706–90) – in France as one of the commissioners of the newly recognised United States of America, and on the point of formally ending the American Revolutionary War by putting his signature to the Treaty of Paris (on 3 September 1783) – shows Banks' ambivalent attitude to the concept. Franklin first touched on the subject on 27 July, and then alerted Banks to the rapidity with which the science was moving, with a detailed account of the successful launch by Jacques Alexandre César Charles (1746–1823) in Paris on 27 August of a balloon powered by inflammable air, in other words, hydrogen.

Franklin had seen the event with his own eyes, and his postscript, dated 30 August 1783, shows how swiftly the concept had captured the imagination:

> Some suppose Flying now to be invented, and ... that a Running Footman or a Horse Flung and suspended under such a Globe ... might with a Fair Wind run in a Straight Line across Countries as fast as that Wind, and over Hedges, Ditches & even Water. It has even been fancied that in time People will keep such Globes anchored in the Air, to which by Pullies they may draw up Game to be preserved in the Cool, & Water to be frozen when Ice is wanted. And that to get Money, it will be contrived to give People an extensive View of the Country, by running them up in an Elbow Chair a Mile high for a Guinea.[9]

In subsequent correspondence, Franklin was consistently enthusiastic about the prospects, especially once the next great breakthrough had been successfully achieved: the safe launch and return of the first living creatures. This was achieved by the Montgolfiers, in front of huge crowds at Versailles on 19 September. The race was truly on to become the first human being to fly.

Banks was either reluctant to disagree with Franklin, or else changed his mind over the coming year, because at almost the same time as conceding to the greatly respected American (on 13 September 1783) that the balloon might be 'greater than anything since the invention of shipping'[10] he nonetheless declined the offer of funds from George III, advising the monarch bluntly in October that 'no good whatever could result' from the activity.[11]

Franklin wrote again on 8 October, but when Banks relayed both of Franklin's letters to the Royal Society he detected 'an inclination in the more respectable part of the R. S. to guard against the Ballomania ... & not to patronise Balloons ... till some experiment likely to prove beneficial either to Society or Science is proposed to be annext to them'.[12] Franklin, who is reputed to have countered initial scepticism about the utility of the balloon with the retort, 'What is the good of a new-born baby?',[13] must have been puzzled by this attitude, and still more by Banks' rejection of royal patronage. Many members of the Society itself might well have been puzzled too. Banks did not command universal respect, being seen by many as a kind of gentleman virtuoso whose credentials, being within the less prestigious plant sciences, lacked true substance.

The frustrations of the collective British scientific mind, constrained as it was in this way, grew with every new revelation of progress from across the Channel. For, on 15, 17 and 19 October 1783, Jean-François Pilâtre de Rozier (1754–85) delighted huge crowds in Paris by ascending in a 'captive' balloon, that is, one anchored to the ground. Soon after, on 21 November, de Rozier made the first ever free hot-air ascent, accompanied by François Laurent, the Marquis d'Arlandes (1742–1809), who had probably financed the venture. The first men ever to fly, the pair are reported to have achieved an altitude of 3,000 feet in their Montgolfière balloon, albeit briefly, in a journey of 9,000 yards (about 5 miles).[14]

Hardly had the scientific world had time to absorb this achievement than, on 1 December, J. A. C. Charles made the first manned hydrogen ascent, also from Paris. He was accompanied by Aîné Robert, but when they landed an impressive 27 miles away, Robert got out, enabling Charles to become the world's first ever solo pilot, on a journey of a further 3 miles. His adrenalin-fuelled exhilaration was apparent in the striking phrase, 'I could hear myself live, so to speak',[15] but so too was his trepidation: 'Never has a man felt so solitary, so sublime – and so utterly terrified.'[16] He never flew again.

*

It wasn't only men of a scientific bent who were swept up in the 'soaring curiosity' of balloons, as Dr Samuel Johnson wittily described the subject.[17] The earliest reference to ballooning in any of Johnson's letters was on 22 September 1783, when writing to his friend and very regular correspondent Hester Thrale. Johnson had always shown an interest in chemistry – indeed Henry and Hester Thrale had even created a laboratory for him on their Streatham estate – and in this letter he demonstrated his understanding of the chemical processes involved in creating the necessary 'vapour', but concluded of balloons in general that 'I know not that they possibly be of use'. This seems a little surprising, a little lacking in imagination for someone who had envisaged human flight (albeit with wings) in his 1759 novel *Rasselas, Prince of Abissinia*. Anticipating the emotions described by the balloonists of a few decades later, Johnson had written then:

> How must it amuse the pendent spectator to see the moving scene of land and ocean, cities and deserts! to survey with equal security the marts of trade, and the fields of battle, mountains infested by barbarians, and fruitful regions gladdened by plenty, and lulled with peace!

By early 1784, however, Johnson felt much the wiser, writing to Hester Thrale that 'The Balloon engages all Mankind, and it is indeed a wonderful and unexpected addition to human knowledge.'[18] A passing reference in another letter to her (13 December 1783) shows the extent to which the topic had captured the public imagination by the end of that first year. Johnson thought it worthy of particular note that during an entire day spent with some friends 'no mention had been made among us of the air balloon, which has taken full possession, with a very good claim of every philosophical mind and mouth'. He then added, 'Do you not wish for the flying coach?' The question was evidently intended jocularly, as an impossible aspiration. Johnson's friend Charles Burney (1726–1814) was apparently less sceptical. An immediate convert, he wrote to his daughter Susan (Phillips) on 7 December 1783 that he thought balloons to be 'the most wild, Romantic, pretty playthings for grown Gentlemen that have ever been invented, & that the subject, as well as the thing, lifts one to the Clouds, whenever one talks of it'.[19] He added with apparent seriousness that he was in no doubt that his granddaughter (then fourteen months old) 'will live to see a regular Balon stage established to all parts of the universe that have ever been heard of', adding whimsically that 'military men might appropriately go to Mars, lechers to Venus, and lunatics to the Moon'. On a similar theme, Burney had written to Thomas Twining (10–12 Nov 1783):

> Barring accidents if no Necks are broken, or lives lost in early experiments a *Diligence* to the moon will ere long be established – I know well enough that your timid & sober Philosophers will tell you that such are the properties of Air that respiration cannot be performed, beyond a certain height in our atmosphere – but that's a difficulty which will be easily obviated – have we not Means of subsisting *under* Water in diving Bells, by supplying fresh air to those who are in them? Lord! Sir, we shall soon have a *Moon* Gazette instead of that published at Noon – How pretty it would be to be carried up to heaven, body and Soul, without the pain of dying![20]

*

The botanist John Sibthorp was no longer in France by the time the first four pioneering Frenchmen went aloft, as he had returned to Oxford to succeed his father as Professor of Botany. It is not clear how enthused he was by the subject of balloons – his own specialism was based very much closer to the ground, of course – but he was interested enough to go to see Joseph Banks in London on 17 October 1783, immediately on his return to England, to give him, as well as some plants, 'the Plates for the Description of the Aerostatique Ballon which makes so much Noise at Paris'.[21] The balloon in question must have been de Rozier's 'captive' one.

Banks was away when Sibthorp called, but if the latter kept to his intention to return in two weeks[22] he might just have coincided with the first balloon to be launched on British soil. This was an unmanned Charlière, as balloons powered by hydrogen came to be known, and was launched in London on 4 November 1783. But even this achievement was not a belated British attempt to emulate French ingenuity; indeed, on the contrary, it represented an additional blow to British prestige: the instigator was an Italian, one Count Francesco Zambeccari (1752–1812), assisted by another Italian, an artificial flower maker called Michael Biaggini. The launch was effected with the minimum of publicity from Biaggini's house in Cheapside. Its success emboldened Zambeccari to repeat the experiment with far greater fanfare on 25 November from the Artillery Ground in

Moorfields. It was the first truly public launch of an air balloon in Britain.

Despite some scepticism in the English press, epitomised by a correspondent to the *Morning Herald* (27 December 1783) who encouraged 'all men to laugh this new folly out of practice as speedily as possible', other similar small-scale experiments, usually employing hydrogen, followed in a dozen or so British locations.[23] The Scot James Dinwiddie (1746–1815) was one such experimenter, becoming probably the first Briton to launch a balloon, in London on 18 December 1783,[24] followed by one from Bath on 10 January 1784 (which travelled about 10 miles to land at what is still today known as Air Balloon Hill). The very same day, in the same city, Charles Henry Parry (1755–1822) launched one from the Royal Crescent, filled with 'inflammable air' derived from 'iron shavings and concentrated vitriolic acid'.[25] He released another balloon of 15 feet circumference from Stoke's Croft in Bristol on 24 January 1784.[26] Also swift to try his hand at this new craze was Erasmus Darwin (1731–1802), who dispatched one from Derby, which travelled about 30 miles, making him 'probably the first Englishman to fly a hydrogen balloon, probably on 26 December 1783'.[27]

*

Meanwhile, in Oxford, the pastry cook James Sadler, by hook or by crook, was developing his own designs. Word first crept out in the middle of January 1784 that he had nearly finished an 'aerostatic globe of a large size'. This was the first mention in *Jackson's Oxford Journal* (17 January 1784) of any ballooning activity in the neighbourhood of Oxford, although the newspaper had, like all newspapers, kept its readers reasonably well informed about developments in France. News of Charles' first hydrogen 'flying globe' of 27 August 1783 was described under the block capital heading of 'The Areostatic Sphere' (sic), for instance, and there was also a belated mention on the front page of the issue of 13 September of the Montgolfiers' very first experiment the previous June: 'a Globe made of Linen and Paper, 105 feet in circumference' which 'rose of itself to an Height beyond Calculation'.

Accounts such as these, it can be assumed, were sufficient to inspire James Sadler in his own endeavours, and in *Jackson's* of 7 February 1784 came the announcement that his own first unmanned experiment would be held two days later. The launch was to take place from 'Dr. Sibthorp's in St Clements', meaning the mansion of Cowley House, 'merely separated from the Botanic Gardens by a meadow and a stream',[28] that is, a branch of the River Cherwell. From Sadler's point of view the location would have been ideal: only a few minutes' walk from his own home in the High Street, yet providing sufficient seclusion and space to enable him to work without interruption. How it came about that he was able to engage the assistance of such a powerful ally as John Sibthorp, about to be appointed Sherardian Professor of Botany, is not known, but within the context of Oxford society it was more likely than not that they would have become aware of each other: the one having had direct contact with the first French exponents of ballooning and the other busy devising the means to emulate them only a few hundred yards away.

An account of the launch on Monday 9 February appeared in *Jackson's* the following Saturday (14 February). The means of inflation is not specified, but seems likely to have been hydrogen, given that the 36-foot-circumference balloon (previously noted as holding 'upwards of 4,000 gallons') took only about twenty minutes to inflate. It then 'ascended nearly perpendicular to the Height of about fifty Yards, amidst the repeated Shouts and Acclamations of the surrounding Multitude', and was carried in a north-easterly direction, travelling 'by a Moderate Computation, at the Rate of sixteen Miles in eight Minutes'. It was then assumed to have passed over Buckinghamshire and into Northamptonshire, and was eventually discovered in Kent. A letter of 16 February, sent to Sadler's High Street address from Richard Walter of Stanstead (near Wrotham) in Kent, was printed in *Jackson's* a week later:

> This Day a poor Man in my Neighbourhood found your Air Balloon, which was soon noised about, and finding that the Inhabitants were going to try Projects, I immediately took Possession of it, and it is safe in my House. By Enquiry I find it lighted last Monday about Four o'Clock in the Evening, Distance from Oxford 79 Miles; and all the Damage it has sustained is a small Rent in one of the Seams. It was seen fall by several of my Neighbours, as well as one of my own Workmen. I have spread it open in a large Room to dry, where it shall safely remain till I hear from you.[29]

The balloon was returned from Kent within the week, and the assumed initial course was confirmed in *Jackson's* of 28 February, meaning that the balloon had therefore 'upon a moderate Computation travelled upwards of 200 miles in the Space of two Hours and a half'.

Even before the full extent of this achievement was known to him, Sadler was probably well pleased with his efforts. Certainly, everyone else appears to have been. *Jackson's* (14 February) had 'the Pleasure to inform our Readers' that Sadler had 'received the Approbation of the whole University, to whom in general he gave the utmost satisfaction'. Much encouraged, Sadler lost no time in launching a subscription for a new and larger balloon, being mindful 'to present his most humble Respects to the Noblemen and Gentlemen of the University' and 'his sincere Thanks for the Favours already received'. This is a telling phrase. Clearly, Sadler, a mere food vendor, was very unlikely to have had the means independently to purchase all the materials needed to construct such a specialised piece of apparatus. Fortunately, in a city like Oxford, there were plenty of people who were not nearly so financially constrained. Practically every early balloonist depended on subscribers, who paid for the right to inspect the machine in advance and witness the launch at close quarters. With public interest swiftly aroused, and being able to boast of covering some 200 miles at his first attempt, Sadler was probably able at this stage to attract plenty of support, especially with the respected name of Sibthorp as a reference.

From scattered evidence and deduction, the following Oxford alumni seem likely to have supported Sadler's early efforts, if not on this opening sortie, then certainly soon after: Thomas Burgess, George Croft, Philip Fisher, Davies Giddy, John Ingram Lockhart, Henry Peter Stacy, Thomas Warton and William Windham. Two other important supporters – albeit not Oxford-educated – were the naval commander and naval commissioner Sir Charles Saxton and the newspaper proprietor William Jackson. We shall encounter them all in due course.

One significant Oxford alumnus who remained unconvinced, however, was Joseph Banks.[30] It must surely have been news of Sadler's accomplishment which occasioned what the politician William Windham (a man instantly infatuated by the whole concept of ballooning) described at their club in London as 'conversations about balloons at which Sir Joseph Banks chose to take offence, and exposed himself completely'.[31] To be fair, Banks was possibly merely exhibiting a certain hard-nosed pragmatism: if individual experimenters here, and adventurers in France, were willing to fund their own enterprises, subsidised by a willing public, then he might easily have reasoned that there was little justification for him to risk the Royal Society's resources at this juncture.

Locally, James Sadler had only two rivals deemed worthy of note. On 21 February *Jackson's* recorded a launch on Thursday 19th from Queen's College by Mr Rudge. It may or may not be relevant that Edward Rudge (*c.* 1763–1846) was another near-neighbour of

Sadler's with a particular interest in botany. His balloon was 15 feet in circumference, and came to earth near Watlington, about 12 miles away.

The other exponent emerged a few months later. He was also a university man, but certainly not one who needed to rely on public subscriptions. Indeed, it would be difficult to imagine a more striking contrast between James Sadler's situation and that of George Spencer-Churchill of Blenheim, the Marquis of Blandford! Blandford – later the 5th Duke of Marlborough – who launched his balloon on 4 June. A bound, anonymous diary of notable Oxford events[32] summarised the achievement as:

An air balloon launched from the Garden of Mr Brodrick[33] in St Giles by the Marquis of Blandford. The machine was richly ornamented and during its ascent was very beautiful – visible more than 15 minutes directing its course northwards. Fell at Weston near Stratford-upon-Avon, about 40 miles, from a rent in one of the seams.

Neither Blandford nor Rudge apparently experimented any further.

James Sadler meanwhile, had far greater ambitions. Within days of his successful first trial from the grounds of Sibthorp's house, he announced in *Jackson's* (14 February) that his next balloon would be considerably larger, at 54 feet in circumference, 'if the Subscription will admit'. Contributors would be entitled to inspect the apparatus, and have a personal explanation: 'A Gallery will be fixed round the Machine, and a Method whereby Aerial Journeys are performed, clearly shewn and explained.'

The following week (21 February) *Jackson's* was able to report that Sadler was already at work on this larger balloon, which was calculated to have an impressively precise capacity of 22,842 gallons. This time, however, it would be 'filled with Air extracted from burnt Wood, by a Method entirely new, and which has hitherto been unattempted in the Kingdom'. Clearly Sadler was endeavouring to find a way to reduce the cost, by following the Montgolfiers', rather than Charles', example.

The flames of public curiosity were no doubt fanned by a notice in the same issue of the newspaper placed by a 'Sieur Renad', who proposed to exhibit for a period of three days at the Anchor in Cornmarket the 'Grand Aerostatic Globe of the immortal Monsieur Montgolfier'.[34] In return for a charge of one shilling, Renad hoped that 'the Learned and the Curious will instantly profit'. Clearly it was Renad himself who hoped to profit somewhat more tangibly in what was clearly a scam, and although he did presumably exhibit a balloon of some description, this incident reveals an early justification for the suspicion of fraud with which the public would soon come to treat any failure by a balloonist to meet expectations.

Whether Renad's contribution helped or hindered, Sadler's fundraising evidently went well enough. By 20 March *Jackson's* carried the news that he had increased the original intended circumference from 54 to 63 feet, and the capacity to more than 30,000 gallons. He had also reverted to using what is called both 'inflammable Gas' and 'inflammable Air', though, as time would tell, he had by no means given up on trying to improve upon the Montgolfiers' method. His balloon had that same day been 'set afloat in the Town-Hall, where it will be publickly exhibited every Day'. Tickets to view 'this stupendous and magnificent Machine', with its 'Grand Triumphal Car, double gilt, whereon is represented a variety of ornamental devices, in Artificial Flowers, Festoons &c adorned with a curious Assemblage of Emblematic Figures' could be obtained direct from Sadler in the High Street.

It is interesting to note that this item, although appearing in the column dedicated in each issue of *Jackson's* to local news, begins: 'Mr. Sadler ... begs leave to inform the Gentlemen of the University, and the Publick in general ...', in the style of an advertisement, which would normally, of course, have to be paid for. It suggests that the proprietor of the newspaper, William Jackson (1721–95),[35] was sympathetic to Sadler's cause and wanted to help him alleviate the 'great labour and expence' entailed. It was a gesture which Jackson would repeat often in the following months, although perhaps not entirely out of the goodness of his heart. He was an astute businessman, and would certainly have been aware that balloons were highly newsworthy, and that to have a pioneer of the science on his doorstep could only be good for sales!

The following week (27 March) *Jackson's* local news column announced that the popularity of the 'Grand Air Balloon ... which has given universal Satisfaction to true Lovers of Science' had induced Sadler to extend the exhibition of it at the town hall until the first week of April. In alluring prose the report continued: 'This astonishing Machine is allowed by those who are skilled in Philosophical Enquiries to be the most compleat one of its Kind ever exhibited in Europe'. Its size alone was 'sufficient to strike the Spectator with Admiration and Wonder. It swims, suspended in that secret invisible Fluid which surrounds the Earth, and is totally unsupported by any human Assistance whatsoever.' In *Jackson's* of 3 April the public's last chance to view this magical creation was confirmed as being Monday

5 April. For gentlemen the charge was one shilling, but for 'tradesmen etc.' only six pence.

However, the launch itself was delayed a further month, until Saturday 8 May, and even then it was not a success. The week before, another glowing advertorial for the 'Grand Aerial Machine' had appeared in *Jackson's* (1 May 1784), again prefaced with Sadler's 'humble respects to the Gentlemen of the University and the City'. The balloon was now stated to be 'upwards of 70 Feet in Circumference', and the means of propulsion had reverted to 'inflammable Air, extracted chiefly from burnt Materials, by a Method entirely new'. In language which was which was evidently not the uneducated pastry cook's own composition, the newspaper continued:

This stupendous Machine affords a surprising and extraordinary Spectacle, and the Beholder is struck with Wonder and Admiration, as it is undoubtedly without a Parallel, being both in Magnitude and Splendour far superior to any Thing of the Kind ever exhibited. The external Surface is overlaid with Gold, and adorned with beautiful Decorations; the Whole forming a most superb and magnificent Appearance.

Appearance is one thing – and possibly a thing his main sponsors worried about more than Sadler himself did – but functionality was what really mattered, and on the day it failed the test. Sadler had to account for its limitations in an advertisement – no complimentary column inches this time! – which appeared in *Jackson's* on 15 May. There he professed to be 'very much concerned, that his Friends were disappointed' the previous Saturday 'but it was unavoidable on Account of the Violence of the Wind'. The venture was evidently not a complete failure, however, since the balloon 'was found eight Miles beyond Malden, in Essex. Had it gone Half a Mile farther, it would have fallen in the German Ocean.' Indeed, the man who communicated this information to the *General Evening Post* (11–13 May 1784), a surgeon called Arnold, was of the opinion that, had the gas feeder pipe not become compromised, 'the machine would have reached the Continent very speedily'. Arnold had also discovered a label which showed that 'a dog in a basket was appended when let off', though there was no sign of the animal when he discovered the balloon.

Sadler's enthusiasm and faith in his project was undiminished by this minor setback. Indeed, he was probably encouraged that his efforts had attracted the interest of the London press at all. The balloon was swiftly returned from Essex, repaired by Sadler at 'great Expence to him', and made ready for a relaunch exactly a week later. It is noteworthy that unlike most of his earlier announcements in *Jackson's*, this time Sadler did not include any deferential respects to the 'Gentlemen of the University'. Perhaps relations (which would certainly take a turn for the worse the following year) had already begun to sour. Indeed, the university was never again specifically thanked by him. It is the much less precise 'Friends' and 'the Public in general' at whom this appeal was aimed, with, as always, 'most grateful Acknowledgements for the Favours already received'.[36]

John Sibthorp must still have been counted among those 'Friends', because both the launch of 8 May and the one of a week later took place at the 'Physick Garden' (i.e. the university's Botanic Gardens), where Sibthorp's influence was second to none. He had assumed his father Humphrey's role as Sherardian Professor of Botany, at the age of twenty-five, in March 1784. Given the rare and exotic nature of the medicinal plants collected in the Gardens, the oldest in Britain, surely only someone with his authority could have sanctioned so unorthodox an activity there. It reflects well on Sadler that he was trusted to engage in this untested science, involving potentially hazardous equipment and volatile gases, in such a sensitive location.

On this next occasion, Sadler's backers' confidence was not misplaced. The balloon, 27 feet high, 'with an animal suspended' (a dog presumably, as before, or a cat, as subsequently), ascended vertically from the Botanic Gardens on Saturday 15 May, inclining slightly to the south-east, 'to the Height of three or four Miles'. A rent in the material curtailed progress, however, and within 10 minutes it had come back to earth in a meadow about 400 yards away. Fortunately, 'the little aerial Traveller, though much affected while in the upper Regions, came down without receiving any material Injury'. As a consequence, the 'very numerous and respectable Company of Gentlemen and Ladies' who attended, entertained by a band of musicians, 'greatly approved of the Design, and expressed the highest Satisfaction'.[37]

Sadler had proved his ability to emulate the Montgolfier brothers' achievement of some eight months earlier by building a robust vehicle, capable of transporting a living creature without harm. Before he himself could risk making a journey, and emulate the growing number of Frenchmen who had achieved the feat, Sadler intended to improve on the somewhat haphazard nature of the French prototypes.[38] *Jackson's* of 12 June 1784 advised its readers optimistically that Sadler 'had invented a safe and easy Method of

Aerial Navigation, by which means he will be capable of directing a Machine of this Kind through the Air, to any particular Place'.

Earlier that same week, further salt was rubbed into the wounds of British pride when, with no British man yet prepared to attempt the feat, the French claimed another precedent: the first successful ascent by a woman. Her name was Madame Thible or Tible, who 'was anxious to prove that courage was an attribute of ladies no less than of the sterner sex'.[39] When she accompanied a Monsieur Fleurand at Lyon on 4 June 1784, 'singing like a bird',[40] she became not only the first, but also the only, woman known to have ascended in a Montgolfière balloon.[41] The pair travelled about 2 miles in 45 minutes, and reached an altitude of about 8,000 feet.[42]

The general flavour of opinion since the news had broken of the Montgolfiers' early successes, both in the British press and in private correspondence of the time, reflects a patronisingly ambivalent attitude to the French dominance of aerostation. The prevailing attitude could be summed up as: the French having invented it, it was natural that Frenchmen, and now even Frenchwomen, should also be the first to utilise it – much joy may the pointless and expensive folly bring them!

But despite this British scepticism, as voiced most importantly by Joseph Banks, many of the Royal Society's members were considerably diverted by this new and exciting invention. Later that summer, the first thoroughly British-manned experiment was made by Dr John Sheldon (1752–1808), a leading anatomist and fellow of the Royal Society. He became the first man in Britain to ascend in a captive balloon, on Friday 13 August 1784. The balloon had been built for him, with certain logic, by a London umbrella manufacturer called Allen Keegan. At 150 feet in circumference, it was said to be 'the largest that has been made in this country'.[43] The race was still on for the honour of becoming the first Briton to make a genuine flight, however. James Sadler was primed and ready to attempt to be that person …

PART 2

AIR
1784-85

3

JAMES SADLER: THE FIRST ENGLISH, OR BRITISH, AERONAUT?

Following the successful return of the dog, or cat, in May 1784, James Sadler worked on his next 'Aerial Machine' throughout the summer, and announced its completion in early September, at which time it was on display at the town hall. This time, he boldly announced his intention to ascend in it himself, a few weeks later.[1] This was the first mention of Sadler in *Jackson's* since the issue of 24 July, at which time his plan had been to ascend from Windsor, if sufficient funds were subscribed. The cost then had been estimated at £230,[2] an amount which, quite clearly, a mere pastry cook would find impossible to raise without help. Given that no further appeals were issued in the meantime, it would seem that Sadler had managed to find the necessary financial support, most likely from within a small circle of individually wealthy backers. One of them seems likely to have been a man who would become his most important and influential supporter of all: the statesman William Windham.

William Windham (1750–1810)

Windham had matriculated at Oxford's University College on 10 September 1767, aged seventeen, and graduated in 1771. He retained many friends in the city, and a great affection for it, and returned often. One of these return visits, recorded in his diary, occurred between 5 and 13 September 1784. It was evidently during this week that he got to know Sadler, and, on very short acquaintance, felt prepared to consider making an ascent with him. Certainly, that is the implication of a letter written later to his friend and University College, contemporary George James Cholmondeley (1752–1830), in which he stated that it was

> during my residence at Oxford last September I got acquainted with Sadler; with whom I should then have gone up, but that before I knew him sufficiently to trust him with my intention, he had inserted an advertisement, which ... fixed him, as he thought, to the necessity of going up at Oxford.[3]

In other words, Windham was willing to make a flight with Sadler, but apparently not from Oxford. Windham was prone to indecision and crises of confidence, and it can be assumed that he found the thought of an audience in a place where he was so well known just too stressful to contemplate. A month later James Sadler would find himself subject to precisely the same concerns.

Windham had become almost instantly fascinated by balloons, having recorded in his diary on 7 February 1784, 'Did not rise till past nine; from that time till eleven, did little more than indulge in idle reveries about balloons', and on 16 February, 'Went off into a reverie about an air balloon.' Given the timing of these 'reveries', and Windham's many connections in Oxford, it seems quite possible that it was the announcement of Sadler's first launch from Sibthorp's house on 9 February which inspired these distractions. No other public ballooning event appears to have taken place in England at that time to explain his distraction, and it must have been the realisation that Sadler was about to announce a new subscription which occasioned this further wasted morning on 20 July, 'the greater part of the time, till now, one o'clock, spent in foolish reveries about balloons'. Not so foolish, in fact, since the following year he would turn reverie into reality.

*

Despite the distraction of an accusation of assault heard at the Oxford Quarter Sessions for Michaelmas 1784,[4] Sadler worked diligently through the summer and by 4 September *Jackson's* was able to announce that his new balloon comprised nearly 900 yards of cloth and was 160 feet in circumference. In addition there was a 'Car with the Apparatus for increasing the Velocity of the Machine, with proper Instruments for measuring the Height of the Atmosphere, and for the Purpose of making several other Philosophical Experiments'. This new emphasis on the scientific value of the balloon assuredly reflected Sadler's own genuine intention, rather than simply being a judicious attempt to attract more sponsors. Meanwhile, however, up in Scotland, a kindred spirit was at work, spurred on by a similar combination of intellectual curiosity, practical know-how and courageous determination.

James Tytler (1747–1804) of Edinburgh: Friday 27 August 1784 (*see* Appendix 3)

As he laboured to prepare for his first manned ascent, it is impossible to know how Sadler would have taken the news that the eccentric Scot James Tytler (1747–1804) had succeeded in leaving the ground in a craft of his own design and construction. This occurred in Edinburgh on Friday 27 August, after a trial run on the 25th, and the feat made him, in the words of the *General Evening Post* (31 August–2 September), the 'first person in Great-Britain to have navigated the air'.

This was a claim which was not without dispute, however, and the event received little further attention at the time. Indeed, in subsequent histories of aerial navigation, Tytler has often been omitted completely. One reason was that he reached a height of only about 350 feet, being never out of sight during a journey of only about half a mile. Tytler also did himself no favours through his own self-effacing description of the event as a mere 'leap', and although the *Post* claimed that this was 'to the great satisfaction of those spectators who were present', Tytler's cause was not helped by his dubious local reputation, being frequently in debt, a divorcee and prone to drunkenness. Yet he was a highly ingenious man, earlier designing his own printing press to publish some of his writings and editing the second edition of *Encyclopaedia Britannica* between 1777 and 1784 (writing most of the articles himself, including one on 'Air Balloons').[5] Like Sadler, he built his hot-air balloon to his own designs. When, after two subsequent failures, his final attempt ended in the complete destruction of his creation by a disgruntled mob, it was as a laughable failure, rather than a brilliant pioneer, that he has been remembered. The upbeat reports (for example, in the *Post*) that 'Mr. Tytler is now in high spirits, and ... laughs at those infidels who ridiculed his scheme as visionary and impractical' were sadly not sustained.

This may be a good point at which to underline that the dangers faced by the early balloonists were not solely in the sky. There were hazards of a different kind if they disappointed their paying customers. It seems in retrospect an extreme fickleness of human nature that these pioneers of aeronautics – who were risking so much in attempting the unknown while at the complete mercy of the elements – could find themselves rapidly transformed from objects of wonder and adulation to targets of rage and resentment. Some balloonists almost inevitably failed to live up to their grandiloquent billing, often through absolutely no fault of their own, yet if they failed to make their intentions sound impressive enough to attract large numbers of paying customers, they faced potential financial ruin. It was a delicate balance. As one newspaper put it, 'A person who offers to go up in a balloon for the entertainment of the public, has a double chance of meeting with death' because the hazards of the journey were one thing: if he failed to get off the ground at all 'he must avoid getting knocked on the head by the mob'.[6]

*

Meanwhile, in Oxford, Sadler's balloon was being exhibited at the town hall, 'for the satisfaction of the Curious'.[7] The cost was one shilling. Tickets for the actual ascent, even though no date had been announced, were priced at ten shillings and six pence, five shillings, or two shillings and six pence, obtainable from Sadler's shop in the High Street.

Evidently Sadler was still working on refinements to the design even as it was being displayed, as its circumference was soon after increased by another 10 feet to 170 feet, making a strikingly precise capacity of 38,792 cubic feet.[8] Sadler boasted that with his improvements to 'the Principles of the celebrated Montgolfier at Paris' he would 'render the Performance the most perfect one of its Kind that has ever been exhibited in Publick', and boldly anticipated 'the Approbation of the Nobility and Gentry, and the Attention of People of all Ranks'. All mention of the university was again quite blatantly omitted.

According to *Jackson's* of 11 September, the ascent was expected within days. As it turned out, however – unfortunately for Sadler in terms of a truly indisputable first in aeronautical history – it was delayed. At least, a public launch was. Yet according to a later account by Sadler's oldest son, John, his father, on the 12 September

made an ineffectual attempt to ascend in a *montgolfiére* from a retired spot in the neighbourhood of Shot-over Hill near Oxford, which was frustrated by the accidental combustion of the balloon almost immediately after it had quitted the earth and before it had attained an elevation of twenty yards. Had it not been for this untoward accident a foreigner would not have had to boast the honour of having accomplished the first aerial voyage ever executed in England.[9]

Vincenzo Lunardi and the First Manned Flight in England: Wednesday 15 September 1784

The foreigner in question was an Italian, Vincenzo Lunardi (1759–1806). Having abandoned any thoughts of making an ascent with Sadler, William Windham left Oxford for London on Monday 13 September specifically to witness Lunardi's ascent. En route he stayed the night with his close friend Edmund Burke (1729/30–97), the politician and author, at his home near Beaconsfield. In his diary Windham wrote that when he arrived he found that everyone there was 'going to London the next day on the same errand as myself, viz. to see Lunardi ascend'.

Vincenzo Lunardi was the private secretary to the Neapolitan ambassador in London, described by his biographer, Leslie Gardiner, as 'flamboyant yet fastidious, a disarming mixture of modesty and conceit' with 'romantic good looks, uninhibited Latin gaiety and attractive accent'.[10] In common with both Sadler and Tytler, Lunardi seems to have designed and built his balloon himself, using local carpenters and sailmakers in London.[11] To raise funds he had exhibited it at the Lyceum, on the Strand, during the second week of August, offering for a guinea four advance viewings plus a seat near the machine on the day of the launch, or two viewings and a seat in a stand for half a guinea.[12] According to Lunardi, Joseph Banks was 'among the first persons who have taken notice of my design, and he has honoured my subscription with his name'.[13] There is no apparent evidence of this, and seems unlikely, given Banks' consistent scepticism about balloons both previously and to come. Lunardi was given to wild surges of optimism, followed by feelings of hopeless dejection, and maybe Banks too waxed hot and cold about the issue. Certainly Lunardi was confident enough to put his assertion in print, and indeed selected Banks as one of three individuals to whom news of his flight, if successful, should specifically be conveyed. The other two were his employer, the Neapolitan ambassador in London, the Prince of Caramanico and Dr George Fordyce (to both of whom he acknowledged 'many and great obligations').[14] Fordyce (1736–1802) was the eminent chemist who was Lunardi's technical adviser on the day, responsible for the inflation process.[15]

Lunardi had announced his intended day of ascent well in advance – it was to have been on 11 August from the grounds of a hospital for military invalids at Chelsea[16] – but this enabled an opportunist called Chevalier de Moret, claiming to be a friend and colleague of the Montgolfiers, to announce that he would embark on 'the first English Aerial Journey' the day before. He too would depart from Chelsea, and offered near-identical viewing arrangements for subscribers, that is, tickets at one guinea, half a guinea, five shillings, and half a crown. However, when de Moret failed even to manage to inflate his balloon, using smouldering cork and straw,[17] a riot ensued, during which the balloon and equipment were destroyed. Lunardi wrote (with a hint of smug satisfaction) that when de Moret's 'balloon sunk into the fire which expanded it, the mob rushed in; tore it in a thousand pieces; robbed many of the company; levelled with the ground all the fences of the place and neighbourhood; and spread terror and desolation through the whole district.'[18]

The *Public Advertiser* (13 August) sympathised with de Moret, however, decrying the 'savage ferocity which destroyed that noble piece of aerial architecture, the Grand Balloon of Chelsea', and reasoned that had the crowd been more patient they would have been 'gratified with one of the noblest spectacles in Nature'. The riot had come just days after 'savage ferocity' of a similar nature had destroyed James Tytler's equipment in Edinburgh (*see* Appendix 3).[19]

With de Moret out of the reckoning, Lunardi could breathe again, and plan anew, though the authorities, understandably nervous of any further civil disorder, at first forbade him to proceed. It took a month for them to relent – perhaps influenced by the mild interest of George III[20] – and for Lunardi to regain his nerve, and for subscriptions to pick up. A different location was selected, the same that Zambeccari had used the previous November: the Artillery Ground at Moorfields.

A major contributor to Lunardi's costs was George Biggin (*c.* 1760–1803), a wealthy young man with wide literary and scientific interests. The intention had been that the two of them would make the ascent together on the selected day of 15 September. However, as would prove often to be the case, with many a balloonist in many a location, the combined weight of the human cargo (plus a cat, dog and pigeon)[21] proved technically too challenging, and Biggin was obliged to relinquish his place.[22] Joseph Banks' librarian, Jonas Drylander, attended the launch, and wrote gloatingly to Banks that 'for all Dr

Fordyce's boasting how light inflammable air he would make, the Balloon had not power of levity enough to carry two'.[23]

Consequently, the honour of becoming the first man to fly in England fell solely to Lunardi. The journey, with the testimonies of observers, is described in his swiftly published *Account of the first aërial voyage in England*. He landed at South Mimms in Hertfordshire and was received so cordially by the local villagers that he decided to treat them to an additional demonstration of what the gentry of London had paid a whole guinea to see: a balloon ascent.

He was made less welcome on his second descent, however, at Standon, near Ware 'about half a mile to the northwards of the twenty-four mile stone'.[24] There the labourers 'said they would have nothing to do with one who came in the Devil's house, or on the Devil's horse (I could not distinguish which of the phrases they used)'.[25] Luckily a less suspicious, less superstitious sixteen-year-old maid servant called Elizabeth Brett eventually responded to Lunardi's increasingly desperate pleas for someone to take hold of his trail rope, and helped drag him down to earth. It was by no means the last time that the dashing Italian would find greater sympathy among the opposite sex than his own.

Charles Burney's daughter Charlotte (1761–1837) was instantly captivated, for instance. Her father had watched the ascent in London with, amongst others, Burke, Windham and Sir Joshua Reynolds. Charlotte happened to be staying in Amwell, close to where Lunardi landed. She was therefore able to provide her father with the '1st intelligence of Lunardi's safe arrival on Earth', being 'more delighted than if the Man in the Moon had quitted his satellite to visit the neighbourhood of Amwell'.[26]

Joseph Banks continued to remain unconvinced, however. Notwithstanding that Benjamin Franklin had written to him on 21 August 1784 to say how glad he was 'to find that Experiments with the Balloons begin to be made in England', Banks still did not share his enthusiasm. In a letter to Charles Blagden of 22 September, even after Lunardi's success, Banks wondered if it were really true that 'the King gave him money & the Prince Encouragement' and 'whether we are in danger here of having our turn of Ballon madness'. He also expressed the hope, with apparently unintentional humour, 'for my Countrey men that it will not rise to the Absurd hight [sic] we have seen in France'.[27] Blagden was happy to feed the flames of Banks' scepticism, writing on 3 October that at a dinner the previous Thursday Lunardi 'gave but a poor account of his voyage, dwelling mostly on his feelings, which seem, tho' intrepid enough, to be rather those of intoxicated vanity than manly firmness'. His assessment of Lunardi's written account was even harsher: 'Nothing can be more contemptible; it is difficult to say whether ignorance or vanity be most conspicuous.'[28] The politician and historian Horace Walpole (1717–97) was in Banks' camp. Writing to his friend Horace Mann on 30 September 1784, he thought that

> balloons ... seem to me as childish as the flying of kites by schoolboys. I have not stirred a step to see one; consequently, I have not paid a guinea for gazing at one, which I might have seen by looking up into the air. An Italian, one Lunardi, is the first *Airgonaut*, that has mounted into the Clouds in this country. So far from respecting him as a Jason, I was very angry with him: he had full right to venture his own neck, but none to risk the poor cat's.[29]

In fact Walpole had no need to worry about the cat, which became a minor celebrity in its own right. Jonas Drylander told Joseph Banks on 19 October that 'it is quite the fun now to go to the Pantheon to see Lunardi's dog and cat', and supposed the aeronaut to be earning '100 pounds a day for admissions' to the 'fashionable pleasure'.[30] Walpole's scepticism was fuelled by the flaw he had spotted in any claims that balloonists were venturing into the unknown:

> When I heard how wonderfully he had soared, I concluded he arrived within a stone's throw of the moon – alas! He had not ascended above a mile and half – so pitiful an ascension degraded him totally in my conceit. As there are mountains twice as high, what signifies flying, if you do not rise above the top of the earth? Anyone of foot may walk higher than this man-eagle.[31]

The latter thought had occurred almost simultaneously to Samuel Johnson, who wrote to Richard Brocklesby on 29 September:

> In amusement, mere amusement I am afraid it must end, for I do not find that its course can be directed, so that as it should serve any purposes of communication; and it can give no new intelligence of the state of the air at different heights, till they have ascended above the height of mountains, which they seem never likely to do.

Others took a much less jaundiced view. Once the plucky Elizabeth Brett had facilitated Lunardi's second descent on Wednesday 15 September, it had not been only local people who thronged around the triumphant Lunardi. Several individuals had followed him all the way from Moorfields on horseback. Lunardi himself did not mention him, but several newspapers reported that the anatomist John Sheldon was one of those who had gone in pursuit, the *General Evening Post* (18–21 September) supplying the detail that he had changed his horse three times en route. The *Whitehall Evening Post* spotted Sheldon 'lightly equipped to follow Mr. Lunardi, as well as a *fine hunter* and a balloon could keep company with each other!' Equestrian 'pursuits' such as these became known by some as 'balloon-hunting'.

According to Drylander, Sheldon had 'stood close by me at the launch, and was quite happy at Biggins not going, as he now flattered himself with hopes of being the first Englishman who should mount in a Balloon'.[32] It was no idle hope, since Sheldon had already succeeded in ascending in a captive balloon, of course (on 13 August), and it is a measure of his determination that he had done so only days after de Moret's chastening realisation that the dangers of ballooning lay as much in a failure to rise as in actually succeeding in doing so!

But when Sheldon tried to take the next step, the results were disastrous. On Saturday 25 September his balloon burst;[33] and when he made another attempt on Thursday 30 September the repaired balloon caught fire, luckily for him, just *before* he attempted to get into the basket.[34]

James Sadler's Ascent from Oxford, Monday 4 October 1784

Perhaps it was partly owing to these well-publicised debacles by de Moret, Tytler and Sheldon that Sadler continued to bide his time and refine his designs after his own failed experiment on the hill to the east of Oxford known as Shotover. This failure on 12 September[35] would certainly have given Sadler a compelling reason to delay while repairs and modifications were executed, but he probably also felt the need to wait until the end of the university vacation. All aeronauts needed a paying audience, so there would have been little incentive to schedule anything until the students – who no doubt represented a sizeable proportion of the potential purchasers of the more expensive tickets – had returned. The approach of the new term was therefore the cue for renewed marketing activity. Identical notices appeared in *Jackson's*, under the heading 'Aerial Excursion', for three consecutive weeks (25 September, 2 October and 9 October) and although they continued to be addressed to 'the Nobility and Gentry', both the timing and teasing inclusion that he would ascend 'accompanied by a Gentleman of the University' were clearly intended to attract varsity interest. Probably, as we have seen, William Windham was the intended gentleman in question.

It was also surely with an academic audience in mind that Sadler stressed his intention to ascend high enough to 'discover the state of the Air with respect to its Rareness and Density, at different Elevations from the Earth' and to 'ascend into the Atmosphere, for the Purpose of determining its Height, with a greater Degree of Accuracy than has hitherto been discovered'.[36] Whereas Lunardi's flight had simply added to the growing evidence of the feasibility of a balloon as a vehicle, Sadler hoped to show that he was a serious man of science, not simply an aerial adventurer.

However, by the time the third of these notices had appeared in *Jackson's*, Sadler had jumped the gun and already made his first flight. At least, the newspaper announced that he had, in that same issue of 9 October, yet a tiny element of doubt will always remain. The description of the trip was very detailed and sufficiently self-critical to seem utterly persuasive, yet unfortunately for Sadler, no one actually *saw* him accomplish it! Here we encounter the single greatest puzzle of Sadler's life in respect of the claim that he was the first Englishman, or indeed Briton, to fly.[37] Whereas Lunardi had an audience of thousands for his flight of 15 September, and numerous witnesses to his two descents; whereas William Baker, a Hertfordshire Justice of the Peace, took the precaution of taking down some first-hand accounts in the form of sworn depositions; whereas Lunardi's own first-hand account of the trip was rushed rapidly into print, complete with detailed, annotated diagrams; and whereas a monument was swiftly erected at the exact place of descent, the sole evidence for Sadler's pioneering flight is the unusually long and detailed account in *Jackson's* of 9 October 1784. The gist of it, derived presumably both from Sadler's own meticulous observations and the probing questions of a journalist, quite possibly William Jackson himself, is as follows:

It was at 5.30 in the morning of Monday 4 October that Sadler embarked on his six-mile flight. The stove which would fill the balloon with rarefied, hot air had been lit at three o'clock, and when all was ready he 'with Firmness and Intrepidity ascended into the Atmosphere'. True to the spirit of scientific enquiry that he had previously announced, a barometer and a thermometer were on board. The barometer enabled him to judge his altitude, which he computed as reaching a maximum of about 3,600 feet.

> In this elevated Situation he perceived no Inconvenience; and being disengaged from all terrestrial Things, contemplated a most charming

distant View: With Pleasure and Admiration he beheld the Surface of the Earth like a large and extensive Plain, and he felt himself perfectly agreeable, having experienced no remarkable Change in the Air, except a slight Degree of Cold which was easily supportable.

Sadler reported being able to descend by shutting off the stove, but was unable successfully to test the opposite effect, because as he was engaged in 'enlarging the Fire ... he had the misfortune to drop the Fork; this Loss was irreparable'. As a result he was obliged to abandon his plan to reach Woodstock. Instead – frustrating as it might have been to forego the particular satisfaction of landing in the vicinity of that other local experimenter with balloons, the Marquis of Blandford! – he had to allow the breeze to dictate his course and his place of descent. In another candid admission, he confessed that the thermometer had 'so close a Connection with the Fire in the Grate as to be of no Service for the Purpose of Observation'.

Taken in a northerly direction, as he approached a wood, he resorted to using oars, and (as Lunardi had) convinced himself of their efficacy, stating that he utilised them 'with great Success; and the Force of Ascension being again considerably increased, he had a perfect Command of the whole Machinery, and found it extremely easy to regulate'. The account concludes: 'After floating for near Half an Hour, the Machine descended, and at length came down, upon a small Eminence betwixt Islip and Wood Eaton, about six Miles from this City.'[38]

So ended the historic first flight of the first English aeronaut. Or did it?

Practically every flight, from the Montgolfier brothers' very first unmanned experiment in June 1783 through to Lunardi's in September 1784, was undertaken with the intention of attracting maximum publicity. In part this was deliberate, a financial necessity; in part unavoidable, as the sheer size of the apparatus and the nature of the preparations were difficult to keep hidden. The lead-up to James Sadler's debut was no different. The subscription had been launched as long ago as the end of July, the balloon had been exhibited for several weeks, accompanied by exaggeratedly alluring notices, and expensive tickets were on sale. It all conformed to the idea of attracting as wide a public interest in the performance as possible.

Yet when it came to the great moment, Sadler set off at a time of day guaranteed to be seen by hardly anyone! It would still have been dark at half past five on an October morning, and although the long account in *Jackson's* is phrased as a third-party report, it is clear that much of it could only have been taken from Sadler's own observations. Rather persuasively, in terms of its likely veracity, the account is candid about the novice pilot's mistakes and failures. Most importantly, however, one feels that a highly respected newspaper like *Jackson's Oxford Journal* would not have printed such an account without indisputable verification, no matter how much the proprietor William Jackson himself may have been tempted to stretch his own credulity in the interest of his newspaper's likely increased circulation!

Other newspaper editors were also happy enough to believe the account. It was common practice for the early provincial press to reprint verbatim from the London newspapers, which were understandably usually ahead of the rest in terms of national and international news. This time, however, Jackson had the exclusive, his identical text appearing in the following days, as 'an extract of a letter from Oxford, October 7', in numerous other London and provincial titles.[39]

The reasons for Sadler's sudden decision will never be known, but it is clear that he never craved publicity in the same way that some of his peers did. He was not a natural showman, like Lunardi, nor a thick-skinned eccentric, like Tytler, and faced with attempting something he had never done before, in the full glare of publicity, so soon after his failed experiment at Shotover, one can empathise. Suddenly, perhaps, in the early hours of that October morning, after a sleepless night plagued by thoughts of all the very many things that could so easily go wrong, the full implication struck him, and he dared not face the prospect of either the financial or social repercussions of public failure. Unlike almost all of the other early aeronauts, Sadler had the means to act on a whim. Of the others, only Tytler seems to have possessed the competence to make an ascent without at least some additional technical assistance. Sadler apparently constructed his equipment unaided, understood the physics and chemistry of the operation and also possessed the courage and expertise to launch on his own. According to *Jackson's*, the weather on 4 October was 'calm and serene'. It was therefore perhaps just too good an opportunity to miss.

When Edward Jenner (1749–1823), the pioneer of smallpox vaccination, had dabbled with two far less ambitious launches of small hydrogen balloons in front of friends the previous month,[40] he had been very much of a similarly cautious mind. Having received instructions from his friend Charles Parry in Bath, his undated response included his intention to try his balloon out privately before risking a public exhibition, writing also that 'should it prove unwilling to mount & turn shy before a large Assembly, don't you think I may make my escape under cover of three or four dozen Squib & Crackers?'.[41] In comparison, the pressure on Sadler would have been immeasurably greater. The indecisive William Windham would assuredly have sympathised with both men's caution.

Another puzzle, an inevitable one in view of the circumstances, is the exact spot from which Sadler effected the launch. In Monck Mason's alphabetical list of aeronauts (in *Aeronautica,* 1838) he identified the Botanic Gardens as the location, citing Sadler's son, John, who, 'in reply to my enquiries on the subject, expressly alleges his father's first ascent to have taken place at Oxford, on the 12th of October from the gardens of the botanical establishment belonging to that University'.[42] Oh dear! What a shame that between them they got both the date and site wrong! As James Sadler's *very* much more public *next* ascent definitely *was* from the Botanical Gardens *and* on the 12th – but of *November* – it is, sadly, not a statement that can be relied on.

Nonetheless, as Sadler's previous experiments of 8 and 15 May were also both made from the Gardens, it is logical to suppose that this intervening historic ascent of 4 October was also from there. Evidently Sadler continued to enjoy the ongoing goodwill of the Sherardian Professor of Botany, John Sibthorp, and would surely have needed somewhere spacious, secluded and secure to prepare his bulky vehicle. As the flight was made in complete secrecy, however, and *Jackson's* provides no clues, the exact location can never be verified.[43] Whatever, the date is much more important than the location, in terms of precedent, because between Sadler's two ascents of 4 October and 12 November 1784, another Englishman went aloft. We have encountered him before, in pursuit of Lunardi across the Hertfordshire countryside and in despair at his own two failed attempts: his name was John Sheldon.

John Sheldon and Jean-Pierre Blanchard on 16 October 1784

Sheldon's great moment came on 16 October 1784. Undeterred by the trauma of his near immolation of a fortnight earlier, this time he went up in the company of the Frenchman Jean-Pierre Blanchard (1753–1809), whom Sheldon had invited to come to England specifically to advise him. Blanchard was just a couple of months younger than James Sadler. He had made his own first ascent in Paris earlier that year, on 2 March (having designed a kite-like 'flying machine' two and a half years earlier),[44] and would go on to become one of the most accomplished and famous balloonists of all time. Sheldon was therefore in competent, if not entirely trustworthy, hands once in the air and on the ground they were both able to rely on assistance from the experienced chemist Aimé Argand.[45]

The two men had intended taking an array of scientific equipment with them. Or at least Sheldon had. Unlike the inquisitive Tytler and Sadler, Blanchard probably always saw the expectations of scientists as a bothersome encumbrance to his pursuit of ballooning thrills and fame. So when the equipment proved too heavy there is a hint of satisfaction in Blanchard's comment that Sheldon would have to leave it behind 'if he absolutely resolved to accompany me'.[46] As a result they ended up with only a barometer, a compass, a telescope and a flageolet – but also a bottle of wine. No matter at what sacrifice to science, room could always be found, one gets the impression, for a little Dutch courage! On descending near Sunbury, Sheldon disembarked, after an apparently acrimonious journey. The Frenchman then continued alone, and ended his journey at Romsey, near Southampton. Sheldon followed on horseback, catching up with him only at three o'clock in the morning. The pair returned to London the next day to great acclaim.

The October 1784 *London Magazine* carried an account of their expedition, and it is indicative of the huge interest that the subject was now generating that nearly twelve complete pages were devoted to 'Aerostatics' that month.[47] However, even if aeronautics was a subject on every informed person's lips, Joseph Banks continued to show little enthusiasm. In a letter of 12 October to Blagden he wrote, 'It is wondrous how many people have been tolerably at their Ease in the air without making one observation worth a groat.'[48] On 18 October he called Sheldon's trip a 'foolish voyage';[49] and on 24 October Blagden began a letter to Banks with: 'Sheldon's aerial voyage has turned out as you expected, foolish enough, or rather absolutely good for nothing',[50] to which Banks responded two days later that 'Blanchard & Sheldon seem not an atom better, only somewhat more vain & Idle; their Procession seems very Childish indeed'.

*

Even Banks' sense of patriotism could not be stirred when news of Sadler's success reached him. In that same letter of 12 October he told Blagden: 'I see by the papers an Oxford man has made a little trip already; I fear the rage will prevail in its turn here as much as it has done among our volatile neighbors'.[51] The implication of this comment is that John Sibthorp (who was about to go abroad again, to Germany, if indeed he was not already there) was probably no longer involved in Sadler's endeavours. Otherwise, one feels that he would surely have informed Banks directly. On the other hand it is quite possible that Banks' by now well-known scepticism about the subject might have deterred him from showing any kind of enthusiasm. Sibthorp must also have been aware that some elements within the university were downright antagonistic, apparently rattled that for all their own material and educational advantages they had been outshone by a mere pastry cook.

One man with university connections who did remain staunchly supportive, however, was William Windham. Having made Sadler's acquaintance in September, Windham happened to arrive back in Oxford on 4 October, the very day that Sadler made that first flight.[52] He was still in the city when the momentous event surely became the talk of the town on publication of the account in *Jackson's* on Saturday 9th. A letter sent from Oxford to the actress Mrs Sarah Siddons on 10 October shows that Windham was still in the city then,[53] and indeed he remained there, with occasional trips away, until the end of the following month, having prolonged his stay on account of the arrival of a friend, Thomas Burgess of Corpus Christi College, a man who shared his enthusiasm for the subject which Sadler's achievement ensured was on every Oxonian's lips: ballooning.[54]

On 21 October Windham wrote of being 'still in Oxford'[55] and his diary shows that he was still there on 5 November, possibly longer. He would therefore have been fully aware of Sadler's intentions to make his next skyward venture on 9 November, because this was announced in *Jackson's* of 30 October. The following week, however, this date was amended. The great event, Sadler announced in *Jackson's* of 6 November, the first *public* manned ascent ever seen in Oxford, would now be on Friday 12 November.

4

SADLER'S FIRST PUBLIC ASCENT: OXFORD, FRIDAY 12 NOVEMBER 1784

If James Sadler's first flight of 4 October had been surreptitious, some might say suspicious, his second on Friday 12 November was anything but. In announcing it, Sadler advised in *Jackson's* (6 November) that, 'anxious that no one may lose the sight of so noble an Object, should the Day permit, the Bells of Magdalen College will ring from the Hour of Eight till Ten'. Fortunately, the day did permit, and, even though the actual ascent occurred some three hours later than planned, Sadler 'very amply fulfilled his Engagements with the Publick, by ascending in his Air Balloon from the Physick Garden, in the Presence of a surprising Concourse of People of all Ranks'.[1]

One can get some idea of the huge appeal of the event from this extract from a letter of 8 November 1784 by Mary Noel (1725–1802), writing from Kirby Mallory, near Leicester, some 50 miles away:

> There is an Air Balloon to go off with a man in it from Oxford on Friday next. Some of this family intend going, but I think half a Guinea too much to pay for seeing a man set himself on fire, which will probably be the case, as it is to be fill'd with Straw Smoke, so I fancy I shall be of the stay at home party.[2]

In fact she was mistaken about the 'Straw Smoke', the Montgolfier method, because this time Sadler used 'inflammable Gas' (i.e.

hydrogen), 'which was conducted to the Machine by several large Tubes'. A few minutes before 1 p.m. the balloon 'ascended with such wonderful Velocity that within three Minutes Mr. Sadler was enveloped in the Clouds, and for a few Moments totally disappeared'. Three or four more times he was glimpsed through the clouds, and then was lost to sight.[3]

A witness to the event was Samuel Johnson's black servant, Francis Barber (c. 1742–1801). The two men were en route from Lichfield to London, Johnson having 'passed a few days with his worthy old schoolfellow, Mr. Hector' in Birmingham and 'then proceeded to Oxford, where he was again kindly received by Dr. Adams'.[4] It is not certain if Johnson knew about Sadler's ascent, or if his arrival was coincidental, but either way he definitely did know that it was not something he would be liable to attend, having written on 1 November 1784, shortly before leaving Lichfield: 'You see some balloons succeed and some miscarry, and a thousand strange and a thousand foolish things. But I see nothing.'[5] It is an allusion to the deterioration of his eyesight, and explains why, safely arrived in London, Johnson wrote on 17 November to Edmund Hector that: 'I did not reach Oxford till Friday morning, and then I sent Francis to see the Balloon fly, but could not go myself.' This turned out to be the ailing Johnson's last ever written reference to ballooning. He died a month later, on 13 December.[6]

Soon after the launch James Sadler noticed a rent in the fabric – a subsequent letter to the press made the extraordinary suggestion that it may have been sabotage – which restricted the total distance he was able to travel, but, taken on a south-westerly breeze over Otmoor and Thame, he nonetheless reached the vicinity of Aylesbury, a little over 20 miles, in a matter of only 17 minutes. To maintain altitude he had had to eject all his ballast, provisions and instruments, and landed near Hartwell House, the home of Sir William Lee, where he 'had the Misfortune to be intangled in a Tree, afterwards swept the Ground, and again rebounded to a considerable Distance, till at length he cast Anchor upon a Hedge, and landed safe upon *Terra Firma*, tho' the Balloon was totally demolished'.[7]

After his rough landing Sadler recovered at Thame, and, suitably refreshed, was back in Oxford by 7 p.m. If his first voyage had gone unnoticed, this time it was quite the opposite. On his return, 'the Populace seized the Chaise at the Entrance of the Town, took off the Horses, dragged the Carriage through several of the principal Streets of this City, and were not content till they had compelled the Inhabitants to illuminate their Houses' (a common means of public celebration). More fulsome praise would be heaped on Sadler in the following weeks. This time there could be no doubt; James Sadler, pastry cook, was unquestionably a local hero, *Jackson's* designating him 'the first Person who has been his own Architect, Engineer, Chemist, and Projector'.[8]

Although this statement may be open to debate, as James Tytler had demonstrated the same combination of attributes the previous month, it did certainly set Sadler's achievement above all others in England, and Sadler had now undisputedly managed what Tytler had not: a real journey over a considerable distance. For Sadler, things were looking up, as it were! Whereas his secretive first flight of 4 October had, understandably, created only a little discernible reaction, after this second one of 12 November, the word was well and truly out.

One week after it had been the first to expose intelligence of the flight itself, *Jackson's* devoted considerable space on 20 November to two poems and a letter sent in by readers. These were printed, 'verbatim, as they came to Hand', the newspaper stated, 'to manifest our Impartiality'. This caveat is interesting. One might interpret it to mean that William Jackson had been the recipient of criticism for his unquestioning account of Sadler's earlier success. Given subsequent events, that criticism seems likely to have emanated from the direction of the university. Shrewd businessman that he was, Jackson's printing of the third-party contributions enabled him to fan the flames of Sadler's new-found fame while retaining his own neutrality in the eyes of that section of Oxford society which constituted the majority of his custom.

Comparing French naval antagonism towards Britannia with the temerity of the French aeronaut Blanchard when he 'rode insulting through her subject Sky', the shorter of the two poems concluded that any representative of Britannia would inevitably ultimately triumph:

> Sadler she chose, and in his native Air,
> Bade him assert her just Dominion there.

A much longer poem dated 17 November, penned by 'Elmer' from Northleach (in Gloucestershire), began:

> O HAPPY Sadler! whom the Gods design'd
> To scorn the Terrors of a fearful Mind;
> Enraptur'd Beings! open your sightless Eyes;
> Is that a Mortal who can reach the Skies?

The aeronaut's successful return to earth is greeted with:

Welcome, O Sadler! Sadler, hail once more!
From Heaven's bright Vault to grace the British Shore!

'Elmer' goes on to assert, twice, that this was Sadler's second flight. This was a convenient way for William Jackson to demonstrate his belief that this was the truth, while avoiding the necessity of actually stating it himself:

That second Flight perhaps may prove the last,
When thou (thy worldly Cares and Troubles past)
No more will deign to grace terrestrial Things,
But, staid in Heaven, enjoy celestial Wings.

The final two lines of the poem are:

And may that second Flight exalt thy Fame
And crown thy Courage with a deathless Name!

The future Poet Laureate Henry James Pye (1745–1813) also composed a similarly congratulatory poem in Sadler's honour (*see* Chapter Seven), but withheld publication for several years: another example, plausibly, of varsity peer pressure to refrain from public praise of a representative of that despised Oxford species, the tradesman?

The third contribution by a reader in *Jackson's* of 20 November was a letter. Signed 'T. H.' it exhibited almost as much parochial pride in the *location* of Sadler's feat as it did in the merits of its perpetrator. The writer's purpose was not simply to emphasise just how great an undertaking it was 'for one Man to prepare, make, form, and confine that surprizing Volatile Æther by which he ascended into those Regions almost beyond human Thought'. What T. H. hoped was that Sadler would be rewarded for having 'judiciously preferred Oxford for the Exhibition of his Experiment, as a Place formed for the Encouragement of the Arts; and where Munificence, from every Part, meets the Eye', and where, in addition, 'Liberality and Humanity' abounded. Sadler was, after all, the instigator of 'such a Phenomenon as was never before beheld in the Hemisphere of Oxford! No Mortal ever ascended so rapid, or, perhaps, so high!' Therefore, the writer predicted (wrongly):

Thus will our Adventurer's Fate prove like his noble Balloon, though at first depressed and damped by the heavy Clouds of Expence, yet shortly shall soar above them; or, dispelled by the cheering Gale of generous

Bounty, will pleasingly and gratefully see the warm and clear Sun-shine of Prosperity.

Had any reader inspired by these sentiments allowed his eye to stray slightly to the left, he would have seen in the preceding column a means by which to contribute to Sadler's 'cheering Gale'. A notice stated that 'a Subscription is opened at Mr. Sadler's, in the High Street, for the Purpose of defraying his late great Expence in constructing his Balloon'. This was the story of his life: a man whose incessant curiosity and restless genius always impelled him to financial recklessness. The urge to keep on experimenting, inventing and improving was irrepressible. He was able to recoup some of the cost by charging people one shilling a time to view the balloon afterwards in the town hall – it evidently was not 'totally demolished', as had been reported earlier – but it was probably nowhere near sufficient to balance the books.

Meanwhile, others saw an immediate way of cashing in on Sadler's celebrity for themselves, even if the Oxford man lacked the exotic charisma which inspired the immediate marketing of a range of items and materials decorated with Lunardi's balloon. These included 'a briefly fashionable monstrosity',[9] the Lunardi bonnet, and, more daringly, the Lunardi garter (*see* Appendix 4). Below the poems and letter was an advertisement advising that a portrait of Sadler by a student of the Royal Academy, Mr [James] Roberts (who had previously painted Lunardi), could be viewed at his lodgings in St Aldate's, and that an engraving of it would soon be made available to the public. Of particular significance is that Sadler was described for the first time in print as 'the first English Aerostatist'.[10]

Another panegyric letter appeared in the London *Morning Chronicle* of 20 November 1784. Its writer came from Oxford, but the contents were perhaps just a touch too contentious for William Jackson, in view of the pressure one senses he may have been under from certain influential local sources. Written by 'an Englishman', the letter purported 'to recommend a truly philosophick genius to the patronage and protection of a liberal and discerning publick'. Calling Sadler 'the first Englishman who alone attempted the arduous flight' – a truly indisputable claim, since Sheldon had had Blanchard as company – the writer inadvertently touched on some of the reasons which might have contributed to Sadler's decision to make that first unannounced and apparently spontaneous flight:

Mr. Sadler met with several discouraging circumstances which might have intimidated a confidence less firm, and a mind less vigorous. The care of his business, the delay till the University was full, the slowness of his subscription, the uncertainty of weather etc. were much against the probability of his success. While other adventurers were assisted by the first philosophers of the age, he stood alone, and contrived the figure, constructed the net work, invented the apparatus for filling the balloon, and superintended the whole process, as the only director.[11]

Despite a brisk wind and some rain at about noon, the letter continued, 'our English hero was not disconcerted but exhibited through the whole an astonishing instance of scientifick knowledge, unabating activity, and cool resolution', aware (as all balloonists now were) of the dangers of 'falling sacrifice to the boundless rage of a disappointed populace'. The writer, clearly, was an 'Englishman' whose knowledge could only have been gained from being very much involved on the day, as he went on to praise the speed with which the balloon was filled and the rapidity of its ascent. He also noted several intimate misfortunes which 'conspired to shorten Mr. Sadler's journey, and hasten his descent'. Among these was the observation that 'the balloon burst near the bottom as it was launched' and, chillingly, that 'the balloon was maliciously cut in three places, either with a design of frustrating the expedition, or of endangering his life'. It was a contention which was never repeated, but one which adds significantly to the evidence of local hostility towards Sadler which continued through to the following year.

Harper from Birmingham: Tuesday 4 January 1785

The sequel to this triumph was that Sadler was able to recoup some of his outlay by selling his apparatus. A Birmingham man called Harper paid him £120,[12] with the intention of ascending before the end of the year. Sadler travelled with the balloon in order to supervise its display at the New Theatre, according to a notice in *Aris's Birmingham Gazette,* which promised that both Sadler himself 'and his brother will personally attend'.[13] This rare indication of fraternal togetherness strengthens the possibility that Harper, whose first name is not recorded in any known sources, may have been in some way related to James Sadler's wife (*see* Appendix 5). For once, there was no grumbling about the price of the tickets for entry into the New Theatre. This appeared in the *Gazette* on 6 December:

IMPROMPTU.
On Seeing Mr. Sadler's Balloon
The Stately *Balloon*, that's an Englishman's boast!
(Whilst crowds to the Pantheon drive)
With amazement I view! – but *One Shilling* the cost,
I would not have missed it for *five*.[14]

While in Birmingham, Sadler apparently took the opportunity to visit 'the great Philosopher Dr. Priestly, who had expressed a Desire of becoming acquainted with so extraordinary a Genius'.[15] Priestly was a mainstay of the informal grouping of engineers and scientists known as the Lunar Society, amongst whose number were Erasmus Darwin, Matthew Boulton (1728–1809) and James Watt (1736–1819). Darwin had been among the first to experiment with hydrogen balloons in England a year earlier, of course, and Boulton and Watt were also intrigued by the subject. While an appropriate day and venue were sought for Harper's ascent, they sent up a fire balloon of their own, intending 'to determine whether the growling of thunder is owing to echoes, or to successive explosions'.[16] The experiment proved inconclusive because, at exactly the same time as a controlled explosion was made, the noisy excitement of the crowd reached maximum volume, and, Watt ruminated, 'by means of that ill-timed shout, the question could not be solved'.

It is not clear if it had ever been Sadler's intention to supervise the launch, but had he done so perhaps Harper's venture might have had a happier initial outcome: the *Morning Post* of 4 January 1785 was one of many newspapers which noted the Birmingham man's failed attempt to ascend from the city's tennis court on Wednesday 29 December in 'the balloon purchased of Mr. Sadler, of Oxford, in which Mr. S. lately ascended from the Physic Garden belonging to that University'. The previous day,

> strangers of every denomination, in carriages, upon horses, and on foot, crowded into this town from every part of the country: and on Wednesday morning, the numbers that poured in from break of day till eleven o'clock (the hour fixed for the balloon ascending) surpassed all description.

Eleven o'clock came and went, but 'the populace discovered no kind of impatience' on being assured that the delay, caused when a gas pipe burst, would last no longer than an hour or two. However, Sadler's expertise was evidently sorely missed, because 'the process for filling the balloon had been egregiously erroneous', and it became obvious that no launch would in fact occur that day. The crowd – estimated at

60,000 people – became 'clamorous, and soon proceeded to outrage, throwing sticks, stones, dead dogs, and cats, &c. over the scaffolding erected for the accommodation of such persons as had paid to see the balloon filled'. The violence spread, resulting in four arrests and the need to read the Riot Act, after which the mob dispersed, though one man later died in hospital due to a fractured skull. He was possibly the first, unlikely, and certainly unlucky, British ballooning fatality.[17]

The balloon that Harper had acquired from Sadler was badly damaged during the disturbance, as too, no doubt, was Harper's confidence, but neither so badly that it was not thought possible to make another attempt the following Tuesday (4 January 1785). Noting, however, that some people had come 40 or 50 miles, from places as far away as Stafford, Worcester and Shrewsbury, the newspaper added ominously that if the second launch failed 'the consequences may be dreadful; many of the spectators being greatly chagrined at their disappointment'.

Luckily for Harper, all further chagrin was avoided during his second attempt, and the dead dogs and cats of Birmingham were allowed to rest in peace. Indeed, in travelling 50 miles, the longest distance yet flown in Britain,[18] it represented a remarkable change in the mysterious Harper's fortunes. The contrast was commemorated in verse in an anonymous publication titled *The Ballooniad*, which cryptically attributed to Harper the profession of barber, a clue which has not proved helpful in attempts to identify him (*see* Appendix 5).

*

James Sadler, meanwhile, was far away, having been lured to Dover in pursuance of his own aeronautical aspirations. Tucked away within the other news on the same page as the account of Harper's first aborted ascent of 29 December, the *Morning Post* of 4 January 1785 included this single sentence:

> Mr. Sadler's ascent in his Oxford balloon was made perhaps with a nobler spirit of daring than has yet been shown by any man in France or England, for he dashed into the higher regions with such incredible precipitation, as to be entirely out of sight in three minutes.

Although referring to something which had happened almost two months earlier, it was praise calculated to raise the morale of the Oxford man, as he contended for the most evocative ballooning challenge of the moment: to be the first man to fly across the English Channel …

5

CALAIS OR BURST! THE RACE TO CROSS THE ENGLISH CHANNEL

However dimly it was received by some in Oxford, James Sadler's much-heralded second flight had undoubtedly restored English pride in some small measure. At last the country where Black, Cavendish and Priestley had been the first to investigate the composition of air and the properties of gases, had an aeronautical champion to rival the French. The age-old Franco-British rivalry – so prevalent on both land and sea – manifested itself next in a more pacific objective in the air: the race to be the first to cross the English Channel. This aspiration had more than just symbolic or romantic resonance, of course. It had military connotations too. As early as 1782 Joseph Montgolfier is reported to have considered the means 'to introduce into Gibraltar an entire army, which, borne by the wind, will enter right above the heads of the English'.[1] Benjamin Franklin had immediately seen the obvious advantage of 'elevating an Engineer to take a view of the Enemy's army, works, etc.', pointing out that 'a few months since the idea of witches riding thro' the air upon a broomstick, and that of a philosopher upon a bag of smoke, would have appeared equally impossible and ridiculous'.[2] He expanded on the theme once Jacques Charles had demonstrated the efficacy of hydrogen, foreseeing an invasion scenario of 'ten thousand men descending from the clouds'.[3]

Yet despite the political and military implications of this particular cross-Channel quest, Sadler still found no identifiable assistance from official sources. Nonetheless, pleased no doubt to escape the malicious environs of Oxford, he rose to the challenge, as it were. It was a formidable one, embodied in the slight but highly accomplished form of a single rival, the Frenchman Jean-Pierre Blanchard. Blanchard, a veteran of five flights, had already been in Dover for some days, having arrived on Friday 17 December.[4] He had immediately established himself in the town's castle, ideally located atop the famous white cliffs, having made the arrangements as long ago as early November. A few days later he was joined by his backer, John Jeffries (1744–1819), an American scientist and doctor, who bore the entire £700 cost of the venture.[5]

The two men had already had a successful trial run together from London on 30 November, reaching Stone in Kent after a journey of 21 miles.[6] Almost always, if feasible, balloonists transported their equipment straight back from whence they had come, to receive the plaudits of friends and backers (and no doubt to attend to the important business of reconciling ticket sales), but on this occasion Blanchard and Jeffries stayed put, and exhibited the craft where they had landed. Blanchard had made passing reference to his ambition to cross the Channel in his account of his journey with John Sheldon.[7] Now, with his equipment conveniently already en route to Dover, he made his intention definite, by placing an advertisement for subscriptions in the *Morning Chronicle & London Advertiser* of 4 December.

*

Meanwhile, on the other side of the Channel, two other Frenchmen of undoubted pedigree, Pilâtre de Rozier and Jacques Charles, were awaiting a fair wind to convey them in the opposite direction. At least, that is what the *St James's Chronicle* (18–21 December) stated, though Charles may never have actually intended to go himself. The device they had assembled in Calais was an innovation: a Carolo-Montgolfière (that is, a balloon combining both hot air and hydrogen, to produce in theory the combined advantages of reliable uplift and longevity, with economy). The race was well and truly on! The *Morning Post* of 23 December reported that the bookmakers' favourite was de Rozier, 'as the wind is observed to blow more frequently from Calais than from Dover in the month of December'. On the other hand, the *Post* pointed out, 'Mr. Sadler has already soared higher than either Lunardi or Blanchard, and to the honour of Old England, is the only person who has been his own projector and chymist in this or any other country'. James Tytler's strong identical claim had already been virtually erased from memory. The clock was ticking, anxious eyes on both coasts scoured the skies for signs of favourable weather, and Sadler's equipment was 'expected at any hour', though he himself had still to arrive.

In terms of finance, it would seem probable that William Windham, recently elected as MP for Norwich, had contributed to Sadler's costs, as he had even at one point considered being a participant. Windham's entire diary entry for Christmas Day 1784 was: 'Sat meditating whether I should undertake with Sadler the enterprise of crossing the Channel; I had before determined against it, and now confirmed the determination.' His association with Sadler appears not to have been widely recognised, though clearly some of his friends were aware of it, and also of his desire to make an ascent. The Reverend Thomas Burgess was one. In a letter to Windham dated 21 December 1784[8] he began by giving his apologies for failing to attend Dr Johnson's funeral the previous day, Monday 20th.[9] He then wrote:

> I am anxious to hear something of Sadler. The report in the newspaper of his intention of ascending from Maria Park, Dublin I conclude was a feint. I was sorry to see it mentioned in yesterday's paper that Blanchard was gone down to Dover. You will oblige me very much by sending me three lines to let me know something certain about him. And yet I should wish to increase that number by requesting you to add your account of the application of an included place to the Balloon.[10]

By the beginning of the week commencing 20 December, Blanchard and Jeffries were confident enough to name a day, announcing in an advertisement headed 'Crossing the Channel in a Flying Boat' that they would attempt the journey on Thursday 23rd or Friday 24th, weather permitting.[11]

As it happened, the weather that pre-Christmas week did *not* permit, and the launch was postponed. Therefore, when Sadler, 'our ingenious English aerial traveller', arrived on Christmas Eve,[12] he found that there was still all to play for. Except that, while Sadler himself might have arrived, his balloon still had not, condemning him to an anxious wait, aware that Blanchard, from his superior clifftop position, might go speeding over his head at any moment. Not only did Dover Castle present an advantage in terms of elevation, it was also, as castles tend to be, a place which leant itself well to the exclusion of unwanted intruders. Indeed, the vain and scheming Blanchard found that it even enabled him to exclude his patron and would-be passenger as well! For all was not as it should have been in the Blanchard/Jeffries camp:

Mr. Blanchard, on considering the probable dangers of his intended expedition across the channel, and on examining into the state of the balloon, was induced to think that he could not, consistent with his own safety, add the weight of a fellow-passenger to the ballast which he should necessarily require, and therefore told Dr. Jeffreys that he must of necessity take a solitary excursion. The Doctor, who had set his heart upon the voyage, finding all remonstrances ineffectual, assembled a party of British sailors, whom he headed to the Castle, determining, in case of resistance, to storm it, and force away the balloon, that it might be made a flaming victim to his revenge.[13]

This was easier said than done, and on being repulsed,

a parley ensued between the Superintendent and Jeffreys, which resembled the appearance of King Charles before the gates of Hull. The Castle is at present chiefly manned by invalids, who made a most ludicrous appearance: they all put on their best fighting faces, and were resolved to protect the little Frenchman to the last.[14]

Jeffries, baffled by this turn of events, withdrew, leaving Blanchard as 'undisputed master of the fortress' and poised 'to take leave of a country which, in respect to himself, has not manifested its usual countenance to genius and merit'. In fact, rather to the contrary, the British press seems to have taken a fairly consistently sanguine view of the successes of the foreign pioneers of ballooning, even when obvious chancers such as de Moret failed entirely to live up to expectations. Europe was enjoying a few years of relative military calm, the lull before the Napoleonic storm. French support for the rebellious colonists of America was still fresh in the memory, however, so the Dover farce elicited this mild rebuke:

The situation of this country may indeed be pronounced alarming when one of our principal fortresses is under the entire controul [*sic*] of a *Frenchman*, and the British sailors are disposed to exert all their zeal in executing the designs of an *American*.

The impasse was resolved when Jeffries, notwithstanding that he had financed the whole operation, agreed to enter into

a solemn engagement that in their passage, should they find that the globe would not sustain two persons aloft, he would jump into the sea, and commit himself to the security of his cork-jacket. This is a mighty good sort of bargain to be made on dry land, but in the execution of it, we presume it would be an argument of strength, and in such a contest the tiny Frenchman must yield to the brawny American. Mr. Blanchard wisely anticipated this, and would not hazard the adventure.[15]

More days passed, and the *Morning Post* of 7 January was able to state that while Blanchard was 'waiting impatiently for a fair wind ... the little Oxford Pastry Cook has craftily taken advantage of the fracas between France and America to ship his balloon for Dover'. The report continued: 'Mr Sadler sails in his balloon for France with the next fair wind. It is expected this gentleman's return will greatly reduce the price of *French pies*.'

The newspaper's confidence was misplaced (being not quite 'pie in the sky' perhaps, but close enough to admit of this most tempting of aeronautical allusions at this juncture!). In fact, Sadler was no longer even in Dover. When his balloon arrived there he discovered it to have been damaged. There was nowhere local where repairs could be undertaken, so he was obliged to return to London with it. The very same day of Friday 7 January, the wind changed to north-north-west in the early morning, and Blanchard judged that the moment was right. The inflation was overseen by a Mr Deeker of Berwick Street, Soho.[16] Even at this late stage, according to Jeffries, Blanchard was scheming to exclude him in order to reap all the glory: one of 'various artifices ... to deceive, deter, and prevent me from this enterprize' being Blanchard's plan to increase his weight by wearing 'a concealed heavy girdle'.[17]

The prospect of making an unprecedented journey over 20 miles of wintry sea must have been daunting enough for Jeffries, but to undertake it with someone as duplicitous as Blanchard, a man who was prepared to engage in surely the ultimate in vainglorious deceit, can hardly have soothed his nerves. Yet, his later account is tactfully uncritical,[18] his professed willingness to bail out proved unnecessary, and their cork-jackets were never put to the test. It was nonetheless a very close thing. Jeffries sent Banks a long account from France on 13 January 1785 (the basis of his published *Narrative*) which shows that in order to keep from plunging into the sea they had progressively to discard all their ballast, down to the last morsels of food and even the emptying of their bladders! The *General Evening Post* (8–11 January) summed up the achievement as: 'Mr. Blanchard and Dr. Jeffries have the honour to be the first aerial mariners'. Indeed, they must actually have resembled shipwrecked mariners, because by the time they landed near Calais they had discarded absolutely everything bar their underwear![19]

*

Poor Sadler! He had to live with both the disappointment of being deprived again by a matter of days from a potential notable 'first', and also the financial loss (something he would get used to as an almost inevitable adjunct to even his successful flights). He also had to endure the patronising jibes of some elements of the fickle press. The most complete account of the difficulties Sadler had faced appeared in the *Morning Chronicle* of 17 January where it was reported that his new balloon (the old one having been left with Harper in Birmingham, of course) had apparently been moved to London by barge along the Thames, possibly from Reading (where in 1813 Sadler considered the town hall to be the only place large enough to fabricate a large balloon). Once in London, the balloon, 'together with the apparatus, was put on board a vessel ready to be conveyed to Dover. Unfortunately the late severe weather choked up the river, so that it was more than a fortnight before it was received.'[20] Then, when the consignment did finally reach Dover,

> what was Mr. Sadler's surprise, when on opening it he found the silk (owing to the freshness of the varnish) stuck so close to the envelope, that there was no possibility of disengaging it without injuring the balloon; he therefore immediately repaired with it back to London.

Back in the capital, Sadler 'laboured incessantly night and day' to rectify the damage. Exhausting and frustrating as this must have been, the delay did at least give Sadler the opportunity to meet some like-minded souls:

> The balloon, when inflated in London, was examined by many gentlemen of science, and declared (from the excellence of the materials and the principles of its construction) to be by much the completest ever seen in this country; and capable, when entirely filled, of floating more than twelve hours in the atmosphere without being recruited with gas.

Everything was again in place, he 'had perfectly repaired his balloon, and was going to set off from London to Dover the very morning he had the account of Mr. Blanchard's having made the voyage'.[21] It was devastating news, meaning that not only did 'Mr. Sadler and his friends seem very much disappointed', but so too was the national press. On 11 January 1785 the *Morning Post*, in reporting that 'the *Balloon-mania* is a good deal subsided; the nine days wonder is over', put a brave face on national, hurt pride:

We hear there are great rejoicings at Oxford on account of Mr. Sadler's disappointment as it is generally believed that it will remove his balloon frenzy, and restore his cheese-cakes and apple-puffs to that degree of unrivalled excellence they were once so famed for. Mr. Sadler lost the wind that conveyed Blanchard to France from his conjugal tenderness, which induced him to go post to Oxford to assist Mrs. Sadler in the labours of Twelfth-day – and thus was English Glory sacrificed for Plumb-cake!

Did Sadler really find time to go back to Oxford, given the likely condition of the roads at this time of year? One can imagine that he might have tried, since his wife, with four young children to care for, would surely not have been best pleased that he had absented himself from both his domestic and commercial responsibilities during the festive period. Mary Sadler would have been still less pleased to learn that Sadler, a journalist had been 'credibly informed', had spent more than £500 in his quest.[22] Ouch! The equivalent of more plum cake than the mind can imagine!

The disheartening accounts of Sadler's disappointment probably engendered some quiet satisfaction within the scientific establishment and at Oxford University. Among ballooning enthusiasts, many probably fondly imagined that Sadler would now disappear from the scene and allow men with more appropriate credentials to get on with perfecting the science of aeronautics. Among the sceptics, championed by Joseph Banks, there was undoubtedly a hope that the whole pointless phenomenon of English 'ballomania' had been permanently deflated, in order to allow resources to be concentrated on matters of more serious importance to human understanding. But they all underestimated the determination of 'the little Oxford Pastry Cook' – and also that of his principal, surreptitious backer, William Windham MP.

6

'TO SWEEP THE COBWEBS FROM THE SKY': SADLER'S SIX 1785 ASCENTS

In retrospect at least, William Windham (1750–1810), Whig MP for Norwich since April 1784, regretted his lack of conviction in declining to accompany Sadler in his effort to be the first man to fly across the English Channel. As a man of influence and wealth, he might well have been able to tip the balance in Sadler's favour, and as a politician he would have been more sensitive than most to the ruffled diplomatic feathers of conceding the honour to a citizen of England's age-old enemy. The press was surprisingly sanguine about the foreign successes, in fact, even if some individual aeronauts encountered a degree of antipathy from the public. The sensitive Lunardi, for instance, in one of his habitual moments of depression, noted that 'my name being that of a foreigner' meant that he was tarred with the same brush of 'the national prejudice of the English against France'. More accurately, he also observed that 'every thing respecting Air Balloons has been admitted here with reluctance'.[1]

Having regretted missing at least two opportunities to go up with Sadler, Windham immediately set his mind to fashioning another. On arriving in London from Bury St Edmunds he wrote in his diary on 21 January 1785: 'Read diligently, but with interruptions from question of going with Sadler: called on Sadler as soon as I came; walked much about.' A keen sportsman in his younger days, though beginning in his thirties to show signs of the physical infirmity which would affect him for the rest of his life, Windham probably felt it was now or never. With the new, repaired balloon housed somewhere in London, the auspices were good. That day, or soon after, he confirmed the intention he had first expressed back in Oxford the previous September to accompany Sadler on his next venture.

The two men's collaboration was kept as secret as possible, although someone at William Jackson's newspaper seems to have realised that something was afoot, when this appeared in *Jackson's Oxford Journal* of 19 February 1785: 'the Perseverance and Ingenuity of our *First British Aeronaut*, will probably soon be crowned with that applause and Recompense which his unassuming Genius deserves.' Sadler had been intent on finding a way both to steer the balloon and also to keep it inflated for longer and was 'Determined that his Country shall not yield the Palm to her enterprizing Neighbours'. To test his theories, 'in the course of next week, if the weather permits, the grand Experiment will be made from some Place in the Vicinity of London, before a select Party of Nobility and Gentry, among whom, we hear, considerable Betts are laid'. His efforts, *Jackson's* continued, had been supported by 'the most liberal Encouragement from Characters whose Patronage and Approbation would do Honour to any Cause, and whose Support Mr. Sadler considers as the noblest Reward of his Labours'.[2]

Whether this 'grand Experiment' ever took place is not clear, but Sadler did evidently work on improving his designs over the next few months. It must have come as a great relief that he could do so in the knowledge that finances were not an issue on this occasion. There would, for once, be no necessity for subscriptions, for paying customers to view the contraption in advance, or for effusive advertising or grand proclamations beforehand. Indeed, quite the opposite. Not even Windham's close friends knew, partly because he wanted to save them any undue worry on his behalf. One man who *was* informed, though, was his old school friend, Edward Dodwell (*c.* 1749–1828), but then he *had* to know, because it was from his house in Moulsey (now Molesey) Hurst in Surrey that the ascent was to take place.[3]

Helpfully, Windham provides a clue as to how long the secret had to be kept, by noting in his diary on 28 March that he 'set out at twelve to ride to Moulsey to see the balloon for the first time'. Other than this, there is only one other indication that he and Sadler had met in person over this period, when Sadler visited him in Fulham on 23 April.[4]

Dodwell only occasionally stayed at his house in Moulsey Hurst, having also a London home, and evidently relied on Windham to keep him updated. Writing to him one 'Monday morning', probably early April, he enquired

> whether Mr. Sadler has been down to Moulsey and, if he approves of the Place, about what Time you think he will be ready to begin ... to sweep the Cobwebs out of the Sky, as I will take care to be ready to attend you there. I can give you a Joint of Meat and a Pudding, and an aired Bed, further I can not promise as the House is inhabited only by an Old Baucis of upwards of 80.[5]

A second letter from Dodwell shows that their attempts to keep the matter secret were only partially successful. Writing on 'Saturday night' (presumably 30 April 1785) Dodwell wrote:

> I came this evening from Moulsey where Mr. Sadler has been getting forwards with Expedition, and indeed everything seems to be done with so much skill, and in so good style, that I cannot help flattering myself your Experiment will be accompanied by all the Success you can possibly wish. I find however it is impossible to keep such a Thing a Secret, and was not a little surprized to be accosted at Hampton, as I was going over [on] the Ferry with 'so Sir I hear you have got a Balloon going up in a few days'. On my arrival at Moulsey I found people coming from all quarters to see it. I have however given it out, as much as I could, that it is only to be a private Experiment previous to Mr S. going up.[6]

The ruse was effective. When the ascent took place on Thursday 5 May Windham's own part in the proceedings was kept completely secret – even indeed for some days after details of the flight had found their way into the newspapers. A few invited guests, including 'Dr. Horsley, and many other Fellows of the Royal Society', witnessed the ascent and were 'highly entertained as well as surprized at the various manoeuvres performed by these aeronauts, who were hovering about the spot for nearly an hour and a half before the balloon bore away'.[7] The fellows were there out of respect for Windham, presumably, rather than for Sadler, whose achievements had still not been embraced by the Royal Society.

First with news of the flight itself was the *General Evening Post* (5–7 May), which identified Dodwell's garden as the place of ascent, 'amidst a large number of spectators', and also reported that the balloon 'arose in a majestic manner, and continued in sight a full hour and a half, to the great satisfaction of the company assembled'. Sadler's intention, the newspaper asserted, was to continue 'longer in the atmosphere than any one has yet done, having taken up with him more than 300 weight of ballast' and 'proper instruments for philosophical experiments'.

Windham's pencilled notes,[8] rewritten in ink (apparently by another hand),[9] show that preparations began at 5.58 a.m. and – as the newspapers had reported – that they set off soon after 9 a.m., having generated the hydrogen by dissolving two tons of iron using thirty bottles of vitriol and ten butts of water. Windham's first narrative observation was made at 9.20 a.m. when voices on the ground were clearly audible. At 9.51 a.m. – having passed over Southwark, Dulwich, Blackheath and Dartford[10] – with 'the balloon descending fast much ballast thrown out', and at 11.48 a.m. they espied the Nore, the sandbank at the mouth of the Thames estuary. It was another 2 hours, however, at 1.40 p.m., before Windham found cause to jot down:

> think it necessary to descend – air will not escape fast – working to get down – some chance of being carried out to sea – bellows won't work well – Thames and Medway very near – began to think of pulling off our cloathes – we were descending very fast when Sadler contrary to my desire chose to throw out some ballast.[11]

The dilemma: descend fast to avoid plunging into the sea but with a risk of damage to the balloon and themselves, or attempt a more graceful descent with an increased chance of the different risk of requiring a maritime rescue. Windham prepared for the latter, his last entry being 'can't write for my corkjacket'. It was not needed, however. The discharge of ballast was more effective than Sadler had anticipated, causing them to rise 'too far, and were carried up again with rapidity to a greater height than they had yet attained'.[12]

Sadler's judgement proved sound in the end, however. More gas was released by cutting holes in the silk of the balloon, and they descended gradually towards Essex, a little beyond Gravesend, and then back towards Kent, finally making a safe landing not far from Rochester, near the confluence of the Thames and Medway a mile from the coast (and approximately 35 miles from their starting point). Here they were assisted by a labourer 'who was very much alarmed at the Balloon' but was persuaded to grip the rope which they threw to him. The two men then alighted. However, 'the Balloon pulling rather strong, and the man having no great relish for his employment, let go his hold, when it ascended with great rapidity ... taking the direct course over the German ocean.'[13]

The identity of Sadler's companion remained a mystery for several days, the *Reading Mercury & Oxford Gazette* of 9 May being perhaps the first newspaper to identify Windham by name, followed by the *Whitehall Evening Post* (7–10 May), which related how the pair had arrived at the Crown Inn, Rochester, after having descended in the parish of St Mary (in the hundred of Hoe or Hoo), where, in this version, 'some countrymen, who were desired to hold fast the balloon, which was now lighter than the atmospheric air, let it go'. Another variant of their descent was provided in the next issue of the *Whitehall Evening Post* (10–12 May) which said that 'though the gondola several times touched the ground, it always rebounded, and the wind still driving the balloon forward, they were obliged to jump out, and a little time after it fell quite exhausted in the middle of the waves'. Windham himself made no reference to any assistance from the ground in his notebook, where their time of final landing is noted as 1.50 p.m.

A reward was offered for the return of the balloon, but it was the loss of Windham's headgear which appeared to be of almost equal concern to the *Post*: 'Mr. Wyndham had left his hat in the car, and was obliged to borrow one of a countryman as a substitute.' Appearances were everything, and a hat, even a countryman's hat, was evidently better than none![14]

The balloon was picked up almost immediately by the captain of a vessel, called *Peggy*, who saw it fall and changed course to salvage it. However, it was not until they reached Sunderland, the vessel's next port of call, that the balloon and basket were taken ashore.[15] There were still ballast bags on board, marked 'Sadler, Oxford'; otherwise the only contents were 'a right-hand glove, a pair of scissars, a grappling iron and label, with a sheet or two of writing-paper'. A subsequent letter from Sunderland printed in the *Morning Chronicle & London Advertiser* (19 May) related how the balloon was now at a private house, 'wither great numbers of people resort to see it'.

Tucked away among the columns of the *Morning Post & Daily Advertiser* of 12 May was a short paragraph peppered with typically laboured eighteenth-century puns:

> Mr. *Sadler*, when he alighted, and set his balloon to *graze* in whatever mead it chose, – ought, for his security, to have retained a *bridler* in his service. His balloon would, in that case, have still been in his power, and post-chaise hire been saved.

No doubt it was considered droll at the time! The *London Magazine* took a less flippant line, concluding that the whole venture 'resounds highly to the credit of Mr Sadler, who had the sole management of the business.'

One observer of the passage of the balloon was the author, politician and patron of the arts Horace Walpole, who saw it from his house at Strawberry Hill. In a letter of 7 May to Horace Mann he wrote that it seemed 'not bigger than my snuffbox'. Already better informed than the press about the identity of Sadler's accomplice, he repeated the witty term he had used in his earlier letter about Lunardi, in adding that they 'went higher than any Airgonaut had yet reached – but Mr. Windham and Sadler his pilot were near meeting the fate of Icarus'.[16]

Windham's good friend Edmund Burke lost no time in sending a short congratulatory note, writing on 7 May, 'I think you are the first rational being that has taken flight.' He signed off with: 'Adieu, Star triumphant, and some Pity show On us poor battlers militant below.'[17]

Windham's diary account of the day was simply: 'Went up in balloon' (plus the reference to losing his hat), followed by several lines of self-analysis: 'much satisfied with myself; and in consequence of that satisfaction, dissatisfied rather with my adventure'. These mixed emotions stemmed from his regret at having declined the earlier opportunity to cross the Channel with Sadler: 'Could I have foreseen that danger or apprehension would have made so little impression on me, I would have insured that of which, as it was, we only gave ourselves a chance.' Notoriously indecisive, he went on:

> I begin to suspect, in all cases, the effect by which fear is surmounted is more easily made than I have been apt to suppose. Certainly the experience I have had on this occasion will warrant a degree of confidence more than I have ever hitherto indulged. I would not wish a degree of confidence more than I enjoyed at every moment of the time.[18]

Despite the lack of any serious ballooning accidents to date, Windham had taken the prudent step of writing a letter the day before, intended to be opened only in the eventuality of his death. Addressed to his 'ever dear friend', George James Cholmondeley, Windham excused himself for having withheld his intentions on the basis of wanting to avoid causing undue anxiety, in 'the hope that the news of my landing might, from the precautions of secrecy I have used, be the first notice you would receive of my flight'.[19] Fortunately for him, it was.

Manchester: Thursday 12 May and Thursday 19 May 1785

His confidence and reputation restored, James Sadler embarked on two further ascents within a matter of weeks. These were both from Manchester, from the garden of Jonathan (or John) Haworth (1736–86) in Long Mill Gate.²⁰ Haworth was an entrepreneurial Manchester cotton printer and manufacturer, one of whose initial business partners had been his brother-in-law, Robert Peel (1723–95), grandfather of the future British Prime Minister of the same name.

The first Manchester ascent, on Thursday 12th, was of immense local interest, yet seems largely to have eluded the national press. *Jackson's Oxford Journal* printed a belated account, dated 16 May, in its issue of 21 May, however, in which the ascent was said to have been made 'amidst the Admiration and Plaudits of Thousands of surrounding Spectators'. The day being 'calm and beautiful', Sadler remained in sight for 40 minutes, ensuring that 'the Curious were satisfied, the Doubtful convinced, and the Unbelievers obliged to subscribe to what they had before treated as a Jest.' Sadler then descended to within a hundred yards of the ground, 'conversed for some Time with the astonished Spectators', then 'ascended again with great rapidity nearly a Mile and a Half high'.

One of the few national newspapers to mention the event, the first ever in Manchester, was the *Whitehall Evening Post* (17–19 May). This short account noted that Sadler had reached the vicinity of Warrington, from where 'he plainly saw Liverpool and the sea', before an air current took him towards Bury, within a mile of which he descended, having been aloft an hour and three-quarters. It sounds as if the whole event could hardly have gone more smoothly. Certainly that was the opinion of the *Jackson's* article, which concluded:

> The Manner with which this Business was conducted, from its Regularity, Ease, and Punctuality, does Mr. Sadler the highest Honour; and we can with Justice say that every Person present was warmed with an heart-felt Satisfaction on the Occasion.

With such acclaim, one can see why Sadler decided to go up again a week later. This time the result was not nearly so satisfactory, however. The weather on Thursday 19th was much less kind, being described in *Jackson's* (of 28 May, from which come all the quotations that follow) as 'tempestuous'. Nonetheless, spurred on by the expectations of a crowd estimated at some 100,000 people, Sadler 'contrived, as in the former Instance, to pursue his Process of Preparation without the least Interruption or Confusion'.

Once aloft some naval officers calculated that after 16 minutes he had already reached an altitude of 1¼ miles. Sadler himself calculated that later in the journey he reached an altitude of 2½ miles, 'which was higher than he had ever ascended before'. This was not necessarily of his own volition: the string on the gas release valve had frozen, preventing him from being able to descend even when he wanted to. At this point he 'experienced a disagreeable sensation, short respiration, and a most severe pain in his ears, attended with extreme cold to such a degree that he was obliged to take brandy several times to warm himself'. Unusually, the account also contains some glimpses of Sadler's impressions, rather than being purely a description of the routines undertaken. One can believe that he was, perhaps, beginning to relax and enjoy himself!

> So great was his height that he saw nothing of the earth for three quarters of an hour, and the clouds appeared to him as if rolling on the surface of it. While he was in this situation, a kind of transparent sleet hung around him, which, from the reflection of the sun, made a most beautiful appearance. The shadow of the balloon also appeared upon the clouds, and seemed passing in a different direction.

He had left Manchester at about 11.30 a.m. and descended near Pontefract (a distance of about 50 miles) just before 1 p.m. 'Unfortunately there was not a creature near him but a man on horseback; to whom he called, but the man immediately set off in full speed, and rode from him.' When Sadler's grappling iron failed to restrain the balloon, he tried to ascend again by throwing out everything portable, including the balloon's ornamentation, but soon after became wedged between two trees. On getting out, however, the lightened balloon was caught by a sudden gust of wind and propelled further. Refusing to release his grip, Sadler was dragged some 2 miles 'through and over hedges, and was violently dashed against a cottage', after which, 'overcome by fatigue, and the severe wounds and bruises he had received', he was finally obliged to let go. Despite these injuries, he hired a horse and returned to Manchester the same day, where he 'was received with the greatest demonstrations of joy'.[21]

Despite this exhausting and frightening experience, and a decided lack of acclaim from some quarters – 'Mr. Sadler … rambled through the air till he dropped down near Pontefract. A voyage of no great use' was the *Gentleman's Magazine's* entire assessment[22] – Sadler appears to have contemplated a third Manchester ascent, influenced perhaps by the imminent arrival of one of the major celebrities of the day, the actress Mrs Sarah Siddons (1755–1831), 'the most acclaimed tragic actress of her own age, and ... widely regarded as the greatest female performer in English theatrical history'.[23] As a result,

> the vast concourse of people assembled in that town has greatly increased its usual gaiety; persons from all the neighbouring parts flock in daily to add their portion of applause to an Actress so deserving, and Mr. Sadler has given notice likewise of adding to their gratification by an aerial flight in the course of the week.[24]

A recently established London newspaper called the *Daily Universal Register* (renamed *The Times* in 1788) commented on May 31st: 'The *Siddons* – like *Sadler* – continues to fly her balloon about the country – and rose tolerably high at Manchester considering her spouse went with her as ballast.' There was a poignant topicality in this metaphor, since the first balloon ascent in England by a female – in fact two – had been accomplished only a few weeks earlier. However, it was yet another blow to English pride that both the pilot and females in question were French: Jean-Pierre Blanchard had ascended with Rosine Simonet (*c.* 1770–?), the eldest daughter of the French ballet dancers Louis and Adelaide Simonet, on 3 May. Then on 21 May he went up with Rosine's younger sister, Leonora (1773–?). In between, Rosine also became the first female in Britain to make a solo flight, of sorts, in Blanchard's captive balloon on 7 May (*see* Appendix 6).

Not to be outdone, Vincenzo Lunardi also had his sights set on a female accomplice. He had apparently been content to bask in the glory of his one famous ascent in the months that followed it, but with the onset of summer, and uncomfortably aware that his own fame was being eroded by the well-publicised activities of other exponents, he contemplated a reprise. Always keen to attract maximum publicity, he hit on the idea of taking with him a female companion; but to try to trump Blanchard's all-French affair, and engender greater local enthusiasm, Lunardi's lady would be English. Her name was Mrs Letitia Ann Sage (though her first names were never mentioned at the time), and the date selected was 13 May. The location was the same artillery ground at Moorfields from which he had made his historic first ascent, but in the end Mrs Sage was obliged to relinquish her place on account of her weight, a circumstance which occasioned much spiteful merriment among the less merciful elements of the press (*see* Appendix 7). As a result, Lunardi ascended alone that day, and

Mrs Sage was obliged to wait well over a month before the Italian was ready to present her with another opportunity.

Richard Fitzpatrick's Ascent from Oxford: Friday 24 June 1785

The rumour that Sadler would make a third Manchester ascent proved false, and he prepared himself instead for a third ascent from his home city of Oxford. In fact, circumstances would dictate that he would wait another twenty-five years to achieve this aim. An ascent was made, and it was his balloon and his expertise that facilitated it, but he himself remained on the ground. Yet in a way it became a more significant ascent than any he made himself that year, because of the substantiation that the man who did make the flight provided of the local antagonism that Sadler had had to endure. His name was Colonel Richard Fitzpatrick (1748–1813).[25]

Jackson's Oxford Journal of 25 June was the first newspaper to relay the news of the launch. Cryptically headed 'Alfred Balloon, Oxford', the article recorded that the ascent was made on Friday 24th from 'behind Corpus Christi College', meaning probably the north-western edge of Merton Field.[26] At about 1.30 p.m., Sadler judged that the balloon was sufficiently inflated, and 'the Car for accommodating two Passengers began to be attached'. However, as so often, the combined weight of two people defied the lifting power of the gas generated, and, 'the Colonel being resolved not to quit his seat', Sadler acquiesced.

For Fitzpatrick to embark on such a venture alone, with no training and only hurried guidance, shows immense courage. It also shows that he had immense faith in Sadler – fully justified, as his letter to his friend William Windham demonstrates. Written in London on Monday 27 June, he began, 'I have gratified my curiosity in a flight from Oxford, where your protégé Sadler (who, by the by, I consider as a Phenomenon) behaved very handsomely ... and gave me up his place.' He continued: 'After receiving some hasty instructions I ascended by myself in view of all the University.' In attendance were two of Windham's friends, who had been especially helpful: Mrs Croft (probably the wife of George Croft) and Mrs Burgess (whose husband, Thomas, as a fellow of Corpus Christi, may well have influenced the choice of location for the launch). Both were

particularly civil to me, and did their utmost to keep the spectators in order, but in vain for the curiosity and eagerness of the crowd was not to be restrained. The thermometer was broken, and your barometer had a narrow escape.[27]

Fitzpatrick proceeded to give more details of the flight and landing about 1 hour, and some 20 miles, later (near Kingston Lisle in Berkshire): 'the shock was trifling, but the unevenness of the ground overset the Car, and rolled me gently out.' He was helped by some local people to steady the balloon and to take it to a nearby stable, then waited for two hours in a small public house until Sadler – a 'balloon hunter' himself for once – caught up with him in a post-chaise. The two men were then 'conducted with grand triumph about 5 miles to Wantage in Berkshire where we dined'. After this they went their separate ways. Fitzpatrick continued via Henley to London; Sadler returned to Oxford, which he reached with the balloon at about midnight.[28]

Fitzpatrick's unpremeditated solo adventure was all the more remarkable in that he went ahead with it despite the news a few days earlier of the first ballooning fatalities. Poignantly, one of the men who died was the pre-eminent pioneer Pilâtre de Rozier, while attempting to cross the English Channel from Boulogne on 15 June. De Rozier had been hoping to cross the Channel ever since the previous winter, of course, and even though Blanchard had delivered 'a compleat *coup de grace* to all his aerial competitors'[29] at that time, the goal of becoming the first to travel in the opposite direction, *from* France *to* England, remained dear to de Rozier's heart. Persisting with his belief in the Carolo-Montgolfière design, combining both hot air and hydrogen, he enlisted the help of Jules Romain to construct it and to join him in the adventure. It was tragically short-lived: before they had even crossed the coast the stove ignited the gas, and the two men plunged to their deaths.

There had been many accidents, no doubt, since the Montgolfiers had first sent the world balloon mad, and many bruised bodies and bruised egos, damaged equipment and damaged limbs, but considering the experimental nature of these enterprises, and the enhanced danger of ascending to such dizzying heights while so inescapably close to highly combustible materials, it is quite extraordinary that there had been no actual fatalities until this moment. Horace Walpole referred to both incidents of that month in a postscript to a letter to Horace Mann of 24 June:

Notwithstanding Pilâtrier's [*sic*] miscarriage, balloonation holds up its head. Colonel Fitzpatrick, Lord Ossory's brother, has ascended in one from Oxford, and was alone. Sadler ... was to have been of the voyage, but the vessel not being potent enough for two, the Colonel went alone, had a brush with a high hill in his descent, but landed safe about 15 miles from the University – how posterity will laugh at us, one way or other! if half a dozen break their necks, and balloonism is exploded, we shall be called fools for having imagined it could be brought to use – if it should be turned to account, we shall be ridiculed for having doubted.[30]

Walpole had written in similar vein to Lady Ossory on 20 June 1785, to express the hope that the fatal accident would dissuade her brother-in-law: 'it would be silly to break one's neck in going no whither, don't you think?'[31] The *General Evening Post* (18–21 June) was among the first to draw conclusions from the first aeronautical fatality, suggesting that 'whatever it may convey to the moralist, who is shocked at the presumption of men, the philosopher ought not to throw all the blame on balloons'. This had been a self-induced calamity. No serious disaster had befallen a Montgolfière, nor a Charlière, up until then. It was the combination which had created the hazard. Nonetheless,

it were a happy thing if this accident should put a stop to them altogether. They only disturb industry and collect crowds of pickpockets, and all this for the purpose of breaking a dog's bones, and making a general holiday, without any one good consequence to science.

*

If Fitzpatrick was not deterred by this calamity, neither was Vincenzo Lunardi. More impressively, nor was the woman that Lunardi had invited to become the first English female to fly: Mrs Letitia Ann Sage. She had already had to suffer the disappointment and humiliation of her weight being the cause of her exclusion the previous month, of course, but this time, at St George's Fields in Newington, on 29 June, the launch process was in more capable hands. A long account in the *Morning Post & Daily Advertiser* (30 June) included the comment (perhaps derived from Lunardi himself): 'Too much commendation cannot be given to Mr. Sadleir [*sic*], the celebrated aeronaut of Oxford, for his liberal, active, and sensible assistance on the occasion'. Where or how the two men first met is not clear, but Sadler must have been blissfully unaware that in the preceding months Lunardi had poured scorn on his achievements when writing to his guardian in Italy, Gherardo Compagni.[32]

Even with Sadler's assistance, however, the balloon was still unable to achieve sufficient buoyancy to realise Lunardi's intention of raising himself, Mrs Sage *and* his principal sponsor George Biggin. Having already left the latter behind once when he made his historic first flight the previous September, and again in May, Lunardi was probably under duress not to do so again, so it was the Italian who remained behind on this occasion. As a result the spectacle became an almost entirely home-grown affair, and the *Advertiser* was able to announce that Mrs Sage should be 'respectfully distinguished as the first British female who has thus bravely ventured to traverse the courseless regions of the air'.

At the time, practically all that was revealed about Mrs Sage was that she was the sister of a famous London actress, and subsequent histories of ballooning have not elaborated much beyond that, even though she swiftly published an account of the journey as *Letter addressed to a female friend*. If this biography of James Sadler is long overdue, the same can be said of an assessment of the life of Letitia Ann Sage (*née* Hoare), being, in a sense, Sadler's ballooning 'other half' (*see* Appendix 7).

*

Meanwhile, a very different sort of female was preoccupying James Sadler that summer: a new daughter, Eliza. She was baptised at All Saints in Oxford on 30 May 1785. There were, of course, already four small children to feed, clothe, and educate, *and* there was a business to run, or at least to assist with. Neither Lunardi nor Blanchard had any such distractions. That Sadler was devoting at least a little time that summer to domestic concerns is clear from the observations of John Byng (1743–1813), who was visiting an old friend in Oxford. On 4 July 1785, he 'stopt at Sadlers the pastry cook, to have a sight of that famous balloonist; but was disappointed to find him very unlike his print, which describes him of lofty, animated countenance'.[33] This comment is another of the scattered clues to Sadler's somewhat reticent, undemonstrative nature, but to be fair to him, perhaps the newborn Eliza was keeping him up at nights.

Byng visited the shop at least twice more that month, on 9 July, when he and a friend took 'ice at Sadlers' then 'saunter'd along' until he met another acquaintance and made 'a perambulation with him into the town, to the ice at Sadlers'. Byng made a careful note of his usual breakfasts in Oxford: good buttermilk (from Whey-Hall, 'a fashionable & wholesome resort of the scholers') and 'bad strawberries'. He was also less than content with Oxford's 'brown Georges, a bad, doughy cake ... little better than filthy affectations'.

Whether or not these unappetising 'provincial dainties' were purveyed by Sadler himself is not specified!

Sadler's parents were still both alive and, given his wife's domestic distractions, one or both must be presumed to have still been taking an active role in running the shop, since Sadler was able to find time to make three more balloon ascents before the end of the year. For several weeks it was rumoured that Liverpool was where he would choose to visit next, though there were equally strong suggestions that Lunardi would beat him to it. The concept of the avaricious balloonist was already rife, and in the context of the port's recent loss of trade (due to the disruptive effects of the American War of Independence), and consequent tightening of purse strings, a Liverpool correspondent to the *Morning Chronicle & London Advertiser* (24 June) wrote: 'Lunardi and Sadler flatter themselves of making mints of money here.' On 12 July the same newspaper kept the flames of competition fanned with this single sentence: 'Sadler has got the start of Lunardi, at Manchester and Liverpool. He has been there some time, and is now clearing outwards with a tolerable lading.' In similar vein, the July 1785 *New London Magazine* printed a satirical six-liner, neatly comparing Sadler's culinary profession with Lunardi's propensity for self-publicity:

Extempore on Messrs Sadlier [*sic*] and Lunardi, the rival Aeronauts at Liverpool

Behold a windy competition,
Two puff-makers in opposition,
The whole must end in vapour;
By various means their puffs they utter,
This uses water, flour, and butter,
And that, pen, ink, and paper.

Ultimately, it was Lunardi who won the race, if there ever was such: neither in *Mr. Lunardi's account of his ascension and aerial voyage, from the New Fort, Liverpool, on Wednesday the 20th of July, 1785,* nor in *Mr. Lunardi's Account of his Second Aerial Voyage from Liverpool, on Tuesday the 9th August, 1785,* both published in the form of letters to George Biggin, did Lunardi make any reference to a competitor. Indeed, in the former, his appreciative assessment of Sadler suggests that the whole idea of a rivalry was contrived purely by the newspapers. He had visited Oxford on 10 or 11 July, en route to Liverpool, recording his thanks to 'the Gentlemen of the University, especially those of Trinity College', as well as – in a marked change of attitude to earlier in the year – specifically praising 'Sadler, whose Generosity and Good-Nature I must ever own myself indebted to'.[34]

Worcester: Thursday 25 August 1785 and Saturday 10 September 1785

It was all very well for Lunardi to traipse around the country wherever the whim, or the financial incentive, took him. He had no other particular responsibilities, whereas James Sadler, of course, did. He was obliged to consider the domestic and commercial repercussions of any absence. For a balloon ascent was not simply a question of disappearing for a day or two, far from it, as the drawn-out saga of his ascents from Worcester demonstrates.

The *Whitehall Evening Post* (30 July–2 August) estimated that 20,000 people gathered at Worcester on Friday 22 July 'to see Sadler ascend into the atmosphere in his balloon and flying vis-a-vis'.[35] However, the balloon burst while being filled. As a consequence of this delay, once the hour of 7 p.m. had passed, 'Vollies of Stones, Dirt, &c. were sent into the Garden, and the Tumult increasing, the Gates were forced open, and Numbers rushed in, threatening Destruction to the Balloon and its Proprietor'.[36] The *Post* summarised this public reaction as:

> the lower class of rustics (who are not, like the populace of London, susceptible of reason and open to conviction) vexed at their disappointment, became much irritated against Mr. Sadler, and wanted to duck him in the Severn.

This opinion reflects a decidedly biased metropolitan view, since the London mobs had been equally unforgiving of any aeronautical failure – and would continue to demonstrate a decided *lack* of susceptibility to reason well into the next century! Luckily for Sadler 'some Gentlemen of Respectability and Influence humanely interposed', and persuaded some of the crowd to desist even though 'the Cry of "Down with it; destroy it &c." was repeatedly vociferated by others'.[37] Sadler himself then made an appearance, and 'with a Confidence which conscious Innocence alone could diffuse' explained that 'the Disappointment proceeded from an Accident, occasioned by a Man cutting the Balloon, in loosening the Tarpaulin'. A notice in *Jackson's Oxford Journal* of 6 August provided a fuller explanation: the non-ascent had been due to a combination of heavy rain and the Carelessness of a Man whom Mr. Sadler employed to assist him, and who officiously got upon the Roof of the Building to clear the same of large Quantity of Water which lay thereon, ran his Knife into a Tarpaulin in order to drain off the Water, and by that means cut a large Hole in the Balloon through which the air discharged.

The problem 'was not discovered until Mr. Sadler went to the Top of the Balloon to examine the Valve'. There was obviously nothing more that Sadler could have done at the time, so all he could offer was to try again 'on an early day'. In fact, it would be another month before the vexed rustics of Worcester were given reason to get over their disappointment. On that occasion, Thursday 25 August, Sadler's ascent went without a hitch. The launch was from the garden of a Mr Wheeler,[38] in all likelihood the same location as for the previous month's aborted attempt.

Indeed, if there *were* any complaints this time, they were probably that the whole affair went off rather *too* well, since Sadler was lost to sight within only 4 minutes, the day being a cloudy one. He had departed at 1 p.m., and at 2.37 p.m. he 'approached the earth again so nearly as to converse with the people in the fields' at Burford (near Tenbury, 21 miles from Worcester). He was then carried southwards, landing eventually at Stretton Grandison, approximately midway between Hereford and Worcester, where some forty people were harvesting in the fields, 'but they fled with the utmost precipitation, except an old woman, who with some difficulty was at last persuaded by Mr. Sadler to take hold of the cord'.[39] Sadler dined that evening with Gilbert Nicholett at his nearby mansion of 'Bromtrees'. The family had been eating when he had passed overhead, and they 'immediately ran out to invite him to their hospitable table'. The next day (Friday) he returned to Worcester, where 'the populace took the horses from his carriage, and drew him about the streets in triumph'.

For whatever reason – perhaps because 4 minutes of entertainment was considered poor reward after the earlier debacle – Sadler felt, or was persuaded, that Worcester deserved a second demonstration. So on Saturday 10 September he set off at 3.25 p.m., again from Wheeler's garden. Hindered initially by catching on a large pear tree, the balloon continued for 35 minutes, then descended about 9 miles beyond Lichfield (about 42 miles away). However, having lost his grappling iron in the confusion of the ascent, Sadler, with no means by which to secure himself, was propelled for another 5 miles over 'a rough and extensive heath, and at length thrown out of his car'.[40] The balloon was then carried away on the wind and was eventually found near Durham.[41] Sadler was received by Lord Uxbridge, near whose estate he landed. Whatever its other attractions, ballooning did, it seems, often end up as a way to drop-in, sometimes almost literally, on the gentry and aristocracy.[42]

Stroud: Wednesday 19 October 1785

Sadler made his final ascent of 1785 – and, as it turned out, the last he would make for nearly twenty-five years – on Wednesday 19 October. The location was Stroud, a surprisingly small place to choose, though the short, identical description which appeared in many newspapers implies that this was no impediment, as 'the hills around were covered with people'.[43] Launching from a canal wharf near the town, what followed was the shortest flight he would ever make. Airborne for only 15 minutes, his landing place of Stanley Park at Selsley, the home of Thomas Pettat, was little more than a mile away. It was also a journey which substantiated the earlier gripes of Horace Walpole and Samuel Johnson about the disappointing heights that balloonists reached, since the mansion was situated on a hillside overlooking the town, from where anyone could go higher simply by taking a short walk towards the ridge. Nonetheless, it was reported that all present 'expressed great pleasure at the sight'.

The much reproduced paragraph in the newspapers concluded: 'The hospitality which has ever marked the character of the environs of Stroud was fully displayed upon this occasion. Handsome cold collations were spread on every board to regale their numerous visitors.' However, the *Whitehall Evening Post* (22–25 October) found the means to inject a negative slant to the affair, noting that 'by the imprudent taking the bit from the mouth of a horse in a whiskey, two persons were run away with, and overturned, and very much hurt.'[44] A somewhat suspect calculation of the broader economic hurt followed:

If we consider the taxes which the people impose upon themselves, how much heavier will they be found than those raised by government – What an out-cry would be made against a Minister of State who should levy upon a county in one day, and for no better purpose, the sum expended here on Wednesday last. It is computed that there were no fewer than 40,000 people to view Mr. Sadler's ascent. Calculating the loss, both private and public, sustained by the idleness of the lower class, and the money spent by their superiors, this county cannot suppose to have been taxed by this *Minister of the Air* so little as £6,000 for the *important services* of that day's exhibition.[45]

*

Balloonists were no doubt becoming accustomed to criticisms of the failure of their activities to fulfil the initial promise of scientific advancement; and since the deaths of de Rozier and Romain, there were increasing demands that such a deadly activity – God's response to man's temerity – should cease. This economic argument was a new line of attack, albeit an ill-reasoned one which the shopkeepers, publicans, hoteliers and food vendors of Stroud would surely have been quick to refute! Whether the 'Minister of the Air' himself, that principal stimulus, the balloonist, would have joined them is a matter of doubt. Again and again we find aeronauts bemoaning their losses after an ascent and Sadler's apparent lifelong impoverishment suggests that he was out of pocket more often than most. The newspapers took no consistent line on the financial rewards of ballooning: one moment making snide accusations of profiteering, verging on fraud; the next beseeching the liberality of the public to assist impecunious aeronauts left unfairly out of pocket! There was money to be made, no doubt – these men would not have continued with the activity otherwise – but it was made at considerable risk, both physical and financial. In James Sadler's case, the business side of his beloved occupation seems to have been beyond him.

This would have surprised most people, as James Sadler was pretty much a household name, and with fame came an assumption of riches. Prints of James Roberts' painting of him as 'the first English Aerostatist' had been available since at least May 1785, and a more primitive side profile, 'curiously engraved by Thornton', with the same caption, appeared in the *New London Magazine* of December 1785.[46]

Despite being celebrated in this way – the accompanying article began: 'The abilities of Mr. Sadler in the art of aerostation have justly been acknowledged superior to those of any other that has hitherto engaged the attention of the public' – James Sadler made no further ascents for a quarter of a century. There are many possible reasons for this. Perhaps he was brought down to earth, so to speak, by the deaths of de Rozier and Romain – the first fatalities among a select band of men whose successes were beginning to give them a god-like appearance of invincibility; perhaps the dangers on the ground – the physical toll of uncontrolled landings, such as during the second Manchester and second Worcester descents, and the unpredictable threat posed by vexed mobs such as those at Worcester – became just too psychologically draining; perhaps there was no money in it, as the cost of the war with America continued to take its toll, obliging the British public to tighten their collective financial belts; perhaps his wife persuaded him to consider his responsibilities to his family. Most probably it was a combination of all these factors. With no primary material to rely on, we can never know.

Lunardi continued to make ascents in Britain – a total of seven more from Edinburgh, Kelso, Glasgow and York – until an assistant died at one in Newcastle in September 1786. His name was Ralph Heron, son of the under-sheriff of Northumberland, whose arm somehow became entangled in a trailing rope before Lunardi was able to get into the basket, and he was carried to a height of about 200 feet, at which point the balloon itself caught fire and he fell to his death. The tragedy affirmed the enduring scepticism of the Royal Society. Charles Blagden wrote to Joseph Banks with a certain grim satisfaction to say, 'Unfortunately he was not beat to pieces at once, but lived several hours', adding that 'considering the idleness & many evils this spectacle occasions, it will be a life well sacrificed to the community, however unfortunately for himself & his friends, if it puts a stop to the balloon-show in this country'.[47] The *Gentleman's Magazine* agreed that it 'ought to be a warning to that foolish curiosity which has no real science or utility for its object, but serves only to amuse the gaping croud [sic], and fill the pockets of an audacious adventurer'.[48] Lunardi posted a remorseful notice in the *London Chronicle* of 23–26 September – 'I have never suffered so much since I was born; I am inconsolable, and shall wear deep mourning for him'. His grieving lasted a couple of months, after which he made one last balloon ascent in Leeds in December 1786, then returned to Italy in 1788. An intended London ascent (*Morning Chronicle*, 28 May 1805) did not materialise, and he died in Lisbon the following year.[49] He returned with the intention of making one more ascent from London in 1805 (*Morning Chronicle*, 28 May 1805), but seems to have failed to raise the necessary funds, and died the following year.

In Sadler's own case, another constraint to his ballooning aspirations emanated from within the very institution from which much of his early support had derived: Oxford University. Precisely what form this deterrent took, and the precise reasons for it, we shall probably never know, and indeed the suspicion might never have arisen were it not for a comment in the letter that Richard Fitzpatrick had sent to William Windham on 27 June 1785 after his unexpected solo ascent from Oxford in Sadler's balloon. Having praised Sadler as a 'Phenomenon', Fitzpatrick went on to write:

> I shall endeavour to promote our grand project both for our own amusement, and I hope for the advantage of Sadler, whom I really consider as a prodigy, and who is oppressed, to the disgrace of the University, I believe from pique and jealousy of his superior science.[50]

It is quite an astonishing statement, and one which Fitzpatrick would never have dared to suggest to a loyal Oxford University man, like Windham, without convincing proof. Could the 'pique and jealousy' even have extended to sabotage, as implied in the letter written to the *Morning Chronicle* after Sadler's ascent of November 1784? When the poet Henry James Pye finally published his version of that ascent, in 1787 (*see* Chapter 7), his inclusion of such phrases as a 'sneer of Malice' and of 'poison shafts by scowling Envy thrown' seem to support that possibility.

J. E. Hodgson concluded that the oppression, whatever form it took, 'discouraged Sadler in his aeronautical endeavours'[51] for the next quarter century, although, as outlined above, there were probably a number of other reasons too. Whatever, Sadler's versatility and determination were such that he was not deterred by the peculiar difficulties an uneducated, working man faced in a conservative, class-ridden city like Oxford. He immediately applied himself to other initiatives of a chemical and mechanical nature, and his name gradually faded from popular view. For a few years, though, his fame as a balloonist *was* sustained in works of both fiction and amusement.

7

A LITERARY INTERLUDE: SOARING PROSE AND UPLIFTING AIRS

The mass appeal of ballooning ensured that the activity was rapidly incorporated into works of literature and the performing arts. A farce called *Airostation, or the Templar's Stratagem* opened in Covent Garden in October 1784, the same month that James Sadler and John Sheldon made their first ascents, and at about the same time appeared *London Unmask'd, or the New Town Spy* (printed for William Adlard), 'exhibiting a striking picture of the world as it goes'. The twelfth chapter includes a section on 'Aerial Voyages'. The anonymous author had witnessed the ascents of several foreign balloonists, and pleaded guilty of suspecting beforehand that the whole thing was a con:

> It was my opinion that our good neighbours of the Continent, who exceed us as much in the arts of delusion, as they do in their system of politics, meant to play on the credulity of John Bull, who having so often, poor fellow, run his head against a post before, could hardly be supposed capable of avoiding so capital a stumbling block as they seemed disposed to fix in his way.

Indeed, the writer remained fashionably (for Britain) sceptical, quoting a 'philosophical friend' with whom he had witnessed some of these early ascents as saying: 'There seems to prevail a kind of aerial phrenzy amongst us. The term balloon is not only in the mouth of every one, but all our world seems to be in the clouds.' No aeronauts are actually named in *London Unmask'd*, but it is evidently Lunardi who is meant by the Italian 'second adventurer' of whom it is stated that 'no others have rendered the undertaking so profitable, nor been so generally caressed'. As no British contender is mentioned, the publication must predate Sadler's first undisputed success of November 1784.

The idea of men reaching for the stars appealed to poets too. In April 1785, the Oxford Professor of Poetry Thomas Warton (1728–90) was appointed as Poet Laureate. It is apparently because his first official poem, an ode to George III on his birthday (4 June), was somewhat hurried and weak that *Probationary Odes for the Laureatship* (London: printed for James Ridgeway) was published later that year. The editor of this satirical volume of poems written by a number of supposed laureate candidates was Sir John Hawkins (1719–89), an intimate of Samuel Johnson's, who produced the first substantial biography about him. Within the long introductory section, possibly written by Hawkins himself, comes:

> A full and true Account of the Rev. Thomas Warton's Ascension from Christ Church Meadow, Oxford, (in the Balloon of James Sadler, Pastry-Cook to the said University) on Friday 20th May for the purpose of composing a sublime Ode in honour of His Majesty's Birth-day.[1]

The text commences with Warton's decision on 5 May to write his ode 'at the elevation of one mile above the earth in the Balloon of my ingenious friend, Mr. James Sadler'. On the chosen day ('Friday 28th May', in contradiction to the title) 'I repaired to Christ-church Meadow with my ballast, provisions, cat, Speaking Trumpet and other necessaries'. The provisions consisted of 'a small pot of stewed prunes, and half of a plain diet-bread cake, both prepared and kindly presented by the same ingenious hand which had fabricated the balloon', as well as a loaf's worth of sandwiches, a range of cold meats and alcoholic drinks, and 'a small light barometer'. Having decided to go alone rather than with his brother, Joseph, Warton maintained height by ejecting a considerable quantity of his own compositions and publications, until after about 11 minutes he 'entered a thick black cloud, which I have since found rendered me wholly obscure to all observation'. It was then that he began to compose his ode, which took him four hours and ten seconds of the five and a quarter hours of his total journey. On landing, shortly after striking the weathercock of a church, he wrote: 'They only who have travelled in Balloons can imagine the sincere joy of my heart, at perceiving Dr. Joseph cantering up a turnip-field near Kidlington common'. His brother furnished him with a spare wig, his own having been lost during the earlier collision, and the two brothers returned to Oxford in a dilly, 'the populace most handsomely taking off the horses for something more than the last half mile, in honour of the first Literary Aeronaut of these kingdoms'.[2]

Warton had a reputation for preferring the company of working people to that of his academic peers, most notoriously the bargemen of the River Thames. It seems likely, therefore, that the very suggestion of Sadler being his friend disguises an insult directed at the pastry cook-cum-balloonist, implicitly putting him in his place. Although there is no factual evidence for any association between the two men, it is made more probable by a line in another contemporary satire, in *An asylum for fugitive pieces, in prose and verse, not in any other collection*. The story commences with an imagined petition from Warton to George III, the sarcastic first line of which states that he 'had been for many years a maker of poetry, as his friend Mr. Sadler, the pastry-cook of Oxford, and some other creditable witnesses could well evince'.

Warton, 'a little, thick, squat, red-faced man ... in a very odd dress', had found his way inside Windsor Castle intent on stating in person his grievance at being denied selection as a candidate for the Laureateship. He attributed this omission to the 'vexatious and pertinacious' and 'illegal and oppressive' behaviour of 'several gentlemen'.[3] If Richard Fitzpatrick is to be believed, James Sadler was being subjected to much the same negativity at exactly the same time!

The year 1785 also saw the publication of a two-volume novel entirely based on ballooning. *The Aerostatic Spy, or excursions with an Air Balloon* (London: printed by Edmund Fawcett) published, as the preface explains, by one who had 'ever been an admirer of the Aerostatic Science' and had 'attended all the Expeditions of Messieurs Lunardi, Blanchard, Sheldon, Jeffries, Sadler, &c. And it was on my Return from seeing M. Blanchard's Voyage across the Channel, that Accident threw in my Way the following Sheets'.[4]

The story begins in North America, where the unnamed protagonist was born and where he lived with his British aunt when orphaned at the age of seventeen. At the outbreak of the War of Independence in 1775 he sides with the British, and is captured by pirates while sailing to Lisbon. He escapes and swims to a remote African shore, where he finds an old man called Sagely who had been shipwrecked some years earlier. Sagely has with him 'a variety of philosophical apparatus' with which the two men work together to create a balloon, in which the author travels to some African destinations, and then to India, Lisbon, Spain, Paris and finally across the English Channel.

The second volume of *The Aerostatic Spy* is set in England, where the author witnesses some of the ascents which did truly occur in 1784. The first of these was when de Moret 'escaped with difficulty from the fury of the populace'; the second when 'about 150,000 people were assembled' to see Lunardi on 15 September; and a third when Sheldon became 'the first Briton that ever ascended into the atmosphere' with Blanchard on 16 October. Ignoring his ascent of 4 October, the author continues: 'The ascent of Mr. Sadler with his Aerostatic Machine was the next remarkable. He was the first Englishman who ever constructed an Air Balloon, and alone ventured to try its efficacy'.[5] The novel ends with a short summary of subsequent flights, including Sadler's from Moulsey Hurst, and Blanchard's with Miss Simonet, ending with what is described as Lunardi's 'second experiment' in May 1785. The final line of the novel expresses the optimistic hope that 'Aerostation in this Country ... bids fair, in time, to contribute greatly to the Improvement of the Sciences throughout all Europe'.

Thomas Warton's successor as Poet Laureate, Henry James Pye (1745–1813), published a tribute to Sadler called *Aerophorian,* 'written on seeing Mr. Sadler, the first English aeronaut, ascend from the Physic Garden in Oxford, in November 1784'. It was not published until 1787, in the first volume of a collection called *Poems on Various Subjects* (London: printed for John Stockdale). The delay, as previously suggested, might be interpreted as reflecting Pye's fear of the cool reception that praise of Sadler might engender in Oxford. The poem begins:

> When bold Ambition tempts the ingenious mind
> To leave the beaten paths of life behind,
> Sublime on Glory's pinions to arise,
> Urg'd by the love of manly enterprize;
> Swol'n Indolence and Fear, with envious view
> The radiant track incessant will pursue.[6]

Lines follow on the satisfaction of being able to defy the crowd's 'sneer of Malice', the unwarranted mockery 'of those labors they despair to reach' and 'the poison'd shafts by scowling Envy thrown'. Then Pye praises Sadler's spirit in resisting the criticism of those who were ready to 'damn the Scheme, whose Author can't produce The exact returns of profit and of use'.[7] Pye captures the intrepid nature of venturing into the unknown with:

Hail then ye daring few! who proudly soar
Through paths by mortal eye unview'd before!
From earth and all her humble scenes who rise
To search the extended mansions of the skies.[8]

There follow prescient lines about those

Whose hopes should promise from the improv'd balloon
Planets explor'd, and Empires of the Moon.[9]

Then while the sons of Gallia justly claim
The earliest trophies in this field of fame
Shall Albion's race with impotence of Pride
Not emulate their triumphs, but deride?[10]

The poem concludes with an amplification of this patriotic theme, with passing allusion to Oxford as an appropriate location for such a pioneering feat:

The applauding Muse her garlands shall bestow
To crown the intrepid Youth's successful brow
Who first of Britain's offspring dar'd to rise
Upborne by native Genius to the skies,
New laurels rais'd on Isis' learned plain,
And taught her osier'd brink to rival Seine.[11]

Sadler was clearly more of a scientific than artistic bent, so, flattered though he must have been to be praised with such sympathy and understanding, he might well have appreciated still more this mention in the 1786 *Ladies' Diary, or Woman's Almanack*. In a section called 'New Questions', Richard Donning posed this one:

Supposing Mr. Sadler with his balloon ascend vertically over Oxford to such a height that the city of London just appears in the horizon; it is required to determine his height above the earth, with the direct distance between London and Oxford, supposing the latitude of London to be 51° 31', that of Oxford 51° 45' 38", and its longitude 1° 10' west of London; also the radius of the earth 3979 miles.

As celebrities of the moment, balloonists' names were also eye-catching enough to be used in advertising. Here is one example from the *Morning Chronicle* of 22 September 1785:

Charles and Robert were men of science, as philosophers, as men of adventurous experiment they deserved applause; and so does Mr. Montgolfier, Mr. Blanchard, Mr. Lunardi, Mr. Sadler and many more; but from the number of miscarriages which have lately happened, there appears to be a necessity of some improvement in the art; and this is at length accomplished by the lottery plans of Messrs Hornsby & Co. The balloons constructed by that Society, are free from all the defects which have been hitherto imputable to the invention; instead of inflammable air, they are constructed of such materials as all the sons and daughters of Adam pant after, they are in fact made up of gold, pure gold, and promise a mine of wealth to every subscriber who embarks in them.

Pilâtre de Rozier's name is missing from the list, of course, his death on the ill-fated attempt to cross the English Channel the previous June being the most glaring of those 'miscarriages'. Erasmus Darwin referred to the tragedy in 'The Loves of the Plants', the second part of *The Botanic Garden,* in the couplet:

> Where were ye, Sylphs! When on the ethereal main
> Young Rosiere launch'd, and call'd your aid in vain?[12]

The couplet was an addition to his encapsulation in the first edition of the wonder of the first French balloon successes:

> So on the shoreless air, the intrepid Gaul
> Launch'd the vast concave of his bouyant [*sic*] ball. –
> Journeying on high, the silken castle glides
> Bright as a meteor through the azure tides;
> O'er towns and towers and temples wins its way,
> Or mounts sublime, and gilds the vault of day.
> Silent, with upturn'd eyes unbreathing crouds
> Pursue the floating wonder to the clouds;
> And flush'd with transport or benumb'd with fear
> Watch, as it rises, the diminsh'd sphere.[13]

A later, particularly telling, reference to Sadler came in *The Infernal Quixote* (London: 1801) by Charles Lucas (1769–1854). This novel was published some years after the other works mentioned in this chapter, but as its poignant observation on the contrasting attitudes to the sciences in Oxford and Cambridge is pertinent to the next chapter, it is helpful to refer to it now. The principal character, Rattle, in a conversation arising from mention of a French general using a balloon for reconnaissance purposes[14] says in the context of it being 'the fashion of this country for every fool to laugh at the air-balloon' that:

> James Sadler, a pastry cook at Oxford, had the spirit himself to make the bold experiment in the midst of that learned seminary. For an act which reflected honour on his abilities, as well as his courage, what reward did the sons of Apollo bestow? – A few shillings to gratify their curiosity! Had the circumstance took place at Cambridge, probably he had made his fortune; had it happened in former days, we should have had him among the Stars.[15]

And had that been the case, had Sadler come from Cambridge rather than Oxford, surely his biography would have long since been written, and this current attempt at redress would not have been necessary!

PART 3

LAND
1786–95

8

GROUNDED!

After James Sadler's ascent from Stroud on 19 October 1785, with balloon mania sweeping the nation, his name was known throughout the land, and he could, presumably, have taken his pick of places to continue to elevate his fame, as it were. Some of the possible reasons for causing him to keep his feet firmly on the ground after the Stroud ascent were listed at the end of Chapter 6. Among them, conceivably, was the vindictive 'pique and jealously' of the university, as identified by Richard Fitzpatrick and hinted at elsewhere. It is easy to imagine that unknown forces within that mysterious collation of colleges, cloisters, chapels and common rooms did take it as an affront that a mere pastry cook had outclassed their own scientific credentials with such apparent ease. Certainly, the evidence does suggest an early withdrawal of support from that quarter, but as the the author of *The Infernal Quixote* implied, there was in any case relatively little enthusiasm for chemistry at Oxford, certainly in comparison to Cambridge. Oxford's proud tradition was in classical and theological learning; the sciences posed a challenge to the latter, which was bad enough, but when the men who championed these new disciplines also held politically radical views, tolerance was in short supply. It was Sadler's misfortune that his principal university ally in Oxford – certainly by 1791, but quite possibly as early as 1786 – was himself an unashamed radical. His name was Thomas Beddoes (1760–1808).

Beddoes was one of a handful of notable Oxford chemists who matriculated at Oxford during the late eighteenth century. Another was Davies Giddy, later Gilbert (1767–1839). Both men owed much to the encouragement of William Adams (1706–89), the Master of Pembroke College, and tutor, then friend, of Samuel Johnson. After graduating from Pembroke in 1779, Beddoes chose to work under John Sheldon, the soon-to-be balloonist who was the leading teacher of anatomy in London. Beddoes returned to Oxford to take his MA in the spring of 1783, went home to Shifnal (Shropshire) for the summer,[1] but was back in London when the news of de Rozier's first manned balloon flight of November 1783 reached the Royal Society.[2] It is probable that he was acquainted with Sir Joseph Banks, and as Banks 'held open house each morning and encouraged visitors to his library and museum, there is no reason to suppose that even someone so junior as Beddoes could not have attended'.[3]

Given this combination of factors, with Beddoes on the periphery of the intellectual epicentre of English deliberations on how to respond to the French invention of the balloon, and with Sheldon as his mentor, he could hardly have failed to become interested in the subject of flight. By the autumn of the following year he was in Edinburgh, and even if he did not witness James Tytler's disastrous attempt of October 1784, he must surely have been aware of it, likewise Lunardi's two ascents there in October and December 1785. Beddoes' intention had been to study medicine, but he became increasingly interested in the chemical lectures of Joseph Black – he whose experiments had so enthused the Montgolfier brothers – and especially in the medical and surgical implications of Black's discoveries.

On 13 December 1786 Beddoes returned to Oxford to take his medical examinations. It so happened that there was a vacancy for a chemical lecturer at the time.[4] He applied and was successful. As an Oxford alumnus he would have been fully aware of the challenges he faced in this role. Although the original Ashmolean Museum building (now housing the Museum of the History of Science in Broad Street) had had a chemistry laboratory in its basement since the late seventeenth century (at the instigation of the first Oxford Professor of Chemistry, Dr Robert Plot), the sciences struggled for recognition, for students and for finance.

Given this small enclave of chemical experimentation within a classical academic landscape, it seems probable that Sadler and Beddoes might have become swiftly acquainted on the latter's return to Oxford in 1786. Indeed, Sadler, whether he was constrained from, or merely refraining from, further balloon flights, may well have already found within the university an outlet for his undoubted talents of sufficient obscurity to satisfy those who might otherwise have continued to vilify him. Gerard L'E. Turner (then the Assistant Curator of the Museum of the History of Science) thought so, when noting that Beddoes' predecessor as Professor of Natural Philosophy began on 2 June 1785:

a course of lectures in the Museum on 'The different Kinds of Air, Natural and Factitious'. After three introductory lectures there followed five more on the various types of air, such as 'Fixed Air', or 'Dephlogisticated Air'. Lecture number six was entitled 'Of Inflammable Air – Theory of Balloons'. All these different 'Airs' had 'Their several Properties proved by Experiment', so we can assume, perhaps, that Sadler was kept busy.[5]

Beddoes conducted his own first lectures in chemistry in 1787, and towards the end of that year wrote to Erasmus Darwin: 'I am going through a course of lectures with, I believe, the largest class that ever was assembled in Oxford, at least since the discovery of Justinian's code drew together thirty thousand students.'[6] He repeated the boast in a letter of 23 February 1788 to his old mentor, Black, where he claimed (presumably with no pun intended!) to have convinced his students that chemistry was 'neither a petty branch of medicine, nor one of the black arts'. As a result, he 'had then the largest class that has ever been seen at Oxford, at least within the memory of man, in any department of knowledge'.[7] These grand claims are largely corroborated by an unnamed pupil, who is quoted as saying that

the time of Dr. Beddoes's residence in Oxford was a brilliant one in the annals of the University. Science was cultivated more than it has been since, and I believe that I may say the same of the period that preceded. Dr. Thompson's lectures on anatomy and mineralogy, and Dr. Sibthorp's on botany, were delivering at the same period; and produced a taste for scientific researches which bordered on enthusiasm.[8]

Nonetheless, Beddoes complained to Black of being hampered by 'difficulties in performing demonstration experiments'. This constraint was perhaps the reason why he might have employed Sadler at about this time, to design the sort of apparatus that he had seen during a tour of France.[9] Whilst there he had met Antoine Lavoisier (who coined the terms oxygen and hydrogen in 1790) in Paris. Beddoes became enamoured of the democratic aspirations of the French political activists during this visit.[10]

Beddoes was appointed Reader in Chemistry in the spring of 1788, having already advertised a course of chemical lectures in *Jackson's* in February. Other courses on subjects such as the 'natural history of the earth and atmosphere' and 'chemistry and its application to arts and manufacture' followed over the next four years, all based in the 'elaboratory' (that is, the basement of today's Museum of the History of Science).

*

Sadler was clearly not working for Beddoes in a full time capacity, and another reason to stop ballooning, especially once further refinement of balloons ceased to be a fruitful option, may have been his desire to switch his attentions to the rather different engineering concept of the steam engine. It is not clear where he was able to do this, but wherever it was, he developed his ideas sufficiently for Matthew Boulton and James Watt to consider him a rival to their own patented designs. In a letter to Boulton of 12 September 1786, Watt had written of his regret that William Murdock (1754–1839), whom they employed as their own principal engineer, was wasting his time on attempting improvements to Watt's own patented engine design, because 'if to that you add Symington's and Sadler's patents, it can scarcely be patentable'. Murdock ought, Watt thought, 'to mind the business in hand, and let such as Symington and Sadler throw away their time and money, hunting shadows'.[11]

Sadler continued to interest himself in engines for the next few years, but also found means of earning additional income locally, by applying his chemical knowledge to the field of public entertainment. A suggestion that he was responsible for making Oxford Town Hall the first building in Great Britain to be illuminated using coal gas at about this time seems rather unlikely,[12] though what he certainly *did* do at this time was to illuminate the town hall with demonstrations of what were called 'Philosophical Fireworks'.

The first series of these public events were held every Monday, Wednesday and Friday evening in the early summer of 1789.[13] Despite the high admission fee of two shillings and sixpence the performances were evidently popular. By June he had extended the number of evenings to all except Thursdays and the run continued until early July.[14] It is not clear precisely what form these demonstrations took, but Sadler probably combined the visual impact of ignited gases of various colours with electrical effects. In *Fireworks: pyrotechnic arts and sciences in Europe*, Simon Werrett devotes a whole chapter to 'Philosophical Fireworks', which he defines as 'a collection of variously optical, electrical, hydraulic, mechanical, and chemical imitations of pyrotechnics and fireworks imitating nature's spectacles'.[15] The appeal is not hard to imagine:

> Electric fire was fascinating and hard to comprehend because it could repel and attract bodies, pass through materials invisibly, and produce shocks in the body. Although it might be used to set objects on fire, it did not consume them like pyrotechnic fire.

Given the broad extent of his abilities, Sadler may well have constructed mechanical devices such as those already made on the continent, like, for instance, a Dutch

> cabinet whose interior mechanism sent colourfully painted transparent patterned discs revolving on a spindle. Illuminated from behind by a candle, the whirling spirals and patterns on the discs mimicked the swirling flames of fireworks.

Indeed, one of the discs inside this cabinet of 'optical fireworks' was of a Montgolfière balloon, no less! Sadler's public demonstrations remained clear in the mind of one very small boy of the time. Writing some eighty years later, the New College don G. V. Cox (1786–1875) recalled that in 1789

> and several following years an ingenious native of Oxford, Mr. Sadler (afterwards known as 'the Aëronaut'), gave lectures on what he called 'philosophic fire-works'; the taste for *hard words* of Greek formation had not yet set in, or he would probably have called them 'pyrotechnics'. Mr. Sadler was a clever, practical, and experimental manipulator in chemistry, and as such was patronised by the University, or rather by the few scientific men then in the University; what the University, as such, did or even professed to do in scientific matters at that period it were hard to say.[16]

In 1790, the town hall played host to Sadler's 'improved' 'Philosophical Fireworks'. These ran from early February until early March, stopping only because the premises were required for the county assizes.[17] This, surely, was easy money compared to the manifold uncertainties of the life of a balloonist? There is only one indication that Sadler continued to involve himself with balloons over this period, and it is also the only indication that Thomas Beddoes had any *specific* interest in the subject. The *Public Advertiser* of 16 June 1790 printed this letter from Oxford, dated 10 June:

On Friday last at 10pm at night Dr. Beddoes, Mr. Edwards, a Commoner from Pembroke College, and Mr. Sadler, the famous English aerostatist, (which latter gentleman has invented a very simple and excellent apparatus, with which gas may be collected with the greatest ease and expedition) sent up a balloon from Pembroke College garden, filled with hydrogen gas from marshes, to represent and account for the production of meteors, which it did in a very satisfactory and pleasing manner. When the balloon had gained a certain height it suddenly caught fire; after it was consumed, the air with which it was filled still retained its globular form, and continued rolling about at a great height for a considerable time, and gave such an amazing light, as almost to resemble the sun.[18]

Beddoes' own version of this experiment, also in a letter dated 10 June, was:

Last night I astonished this part of England with sending up an air balloon; filled, partly with light, partly with heavy inflammable air. I was desirous to try whether such a mass of inflammable air, burning at a considerable height in the atmosphere, would produce any imitation of fiery meteors.[19]

Beddoes then described how the gas was ignited by use of touch paper 'at about three miles distant from the place of starting, and probably less than a mile high', and concluded his account with the self-congratulatory: 'It was one of the most perfect and beautiful experiments I have ever seen.' This apparently boastful statement, like those in his letters to Black and Darwin about attracting large attendances at his lectures, may reflect desperation rather than conceit, the plea of a man who feels his true worth is not being recognised – which was almost certainly the case within the unsupportive environs of conservative Oxford. The popularity of his lectures was not just a matter of prestige, as Beddoes had an independent status throughout his appointment, 'and derived no other emolument from his situation, than the fees of such students as voluntarily attended his lectures'.[20]

On 3 January 1791 Beddoes wrote to Joseph Banks (from his family home in Shifnal) to explain the delay in producing a promised report, his excuse being that 'the laboratory at Oxford has been for a considerable time past undergoing a thorough repair, which I hope will render it one of the best in Europe; in the mean time, I have been prevented from making any experiments'.[21] This 'thorough repair' was supervised by James Sadler. The only personal letter of Sadler's known to exist, sent from Oxford on 14 January 1791, shows that

Beddoes had left him in charge while he was away, dealing with a
variety of issues simultaneously:

> I am in greate want of the glass and have been waiting for the glass from
> London for the air pump ever since you left Oxford and cannot get it.
> There is no depending on them. I should therefore be oblige to you for
> the direction to those at Stourbridge. The masons have finished the
> chimneys & the furnaces now answer very well. I have nearly finished a
> very compleate barometer for you.

> Rouse the carpenter has not been to do any thing. Neither can I get him
> to come. If you aprove of it please to send me the estimates and I will
> set someone [else?] about the work. I should be oblige to you for fifteen
> pounds if conveniant. It will be servisable.[22]

Much of the rest of this unique glimpse into Sadler's mindset consists
of his rejection of accusations of breaching the patents of Matthew
Boulton and James Watt. Sadler's expertise had worried the two
Birmingham men sufficiently to cause them to make a legal challenge,
and though convinced that he was in the right at the time, Sadler
had, for undisclosed reasons, deemed it prudent to call a halt to his
endeavours in that respect. His letter goes on to tell Beddoes how, by
a stroke of good fortune, William Windham had happened to be in
Oxford when he received the writ. Windham then 'took the trouble
on his return to town to examin their patent or patents and had the
advice of two or three councelors. Their opinion was I had nothing
to fear.'[23] And their opinion was apparently to be relied on! On 10
June 1791 the patent office granted to 'Mr. James Sadler, of Oxford,
engineer' patent number 1812 'for lessening the consumption of
steam and fuel in steam or fire-engines'.[24]

Beddoes told Joseph Black in a letter of 15 April 1791 that he believed
that Sadler's engine would 'supersede all the water-wheels, steam
engines etc. now in use'.[25] While this was clearly an exaggerated claim,
and one Beddoes was probably not qualified to make, the sheer range of
Sadler's inventiveness is apparent from the impressive list of fabrications
listed. These included 'a very valuable assortment of chemical apparatus
– a gazometer very much improved upon Mr. Lavoisier's – so that I am
able to show any and every experiment in his book' and an

> improved barometer ... by the help of which I can measure the height of
> a room as accurately as by a rule, an air-pump which exhausts perfectly
> & of course is constructed on principles totally new – [and] a balance

which I have seen turn with 1/100 of a grain when loaded with a pound at each arm. I have all these instruments in the Elaboratory.

Interestingly, Beddoes referred to Sadler in this letter as not only 'a perfect prodigy in mechanics' but also still 'a pastry cook of this place'. Sadler was evidently continuing to divide his time between two very different occupations. Only a fortnight later the onus to choose the latter became all the more compelling with the death of his father. James Sadler senior was buried at St Peter-in-the-East on 2 May 1791, but far from tempting his oldest son to assume the mantle of the family business, the death of the head of the family would appear to have enabled him to renounce all responsibilities in that direction. His brother Thomas, clearly far better suited to the catering trade, would assume that responsibility, if not immediately then certainly within two years, leaving James free to concentrate fully on his own preferred vocation. However, the opportunities to do this in Oxford were looking less likely with the increasing isolation of his principal ally, Thomas Beddoes. In his letter to Black, Beddoes complained that science, and especially chemistry, would never flourish in Oxford 'under the shadow of ecclesiastical and scholastic institutions'.[26] He was beginning to experience the ramifications of his democratic principles, first inculcated during his earlier visit to France, as in contrast to a year or two earlier, students were now starting to shun his lectures.

Faced with these reduced opportunities in an increasingly unaccommodating Oxford environment, Sadler now applied his skills to the ever-greater possibilities presented by industrialisation. His letter to Beddoes of 14 January 1791 had contained one other interesting reference, to another target of Watt and Boulton's suspicions, the wealthy iron manufacturer, William Reynolds (1758–1803):

If thay bring their action against Mr Reynolds on account of his condencing in a separate cylinder thay are in the wrong & cannot claim that as their invention for the first leavor engine ever made was condenced in that manner. I should much like to have the particulars of Mr R's engine if agreeable. If it be in my power to communicate any thing that will be servisable I shall be happy to do it.[27]

Later that year Sadler did indeed commune with William Reynolds. Presumably by chance, he happened to become embroiled in the public backlash experienced by those scientists of the period whose support for the ideals of the French Revolution was seen to be unpatriotic. Reynolds was a Quaker, a religious dissenter like many of the prominent scientists and businessmen who formed the informal grouping known as the Lunar Society: men such as James Watt, Matthew Boulton, Joseph Priestley, Erasmus Darwin and Josiah Wedgwood. In Birmingham, the opposition to dissenters was especially strong, becoming assimilated with various other grievances, mostly economic, which were viewed as a kind of conspiracy to gain control of the town. Early in 1790 Priestley's house had been attacked, and worse was to come in the summer of 1791, when mass rioting erupted after a dinner to celebrate the anniversary of the Fall of the Bastille (which had been on 14 July 1789). Priestley, who had helped to arrange the event, was castigated to the extent that his home was ransacked and he was obliged to flee to London (and ultimately to Pennsylvania), never to return. Many other dissenters had property damaged and had to go into hiding. Watt and Boulton took the precaution of providing their workforce with firearms, though they were not in the end put to use.[28]

The rioting in Birmingham lasted four days, and even once it had subsided, dissenters elsewhere understandably remained on their guard. Thomas Beddoes' sister, Rosamund, wrote to him on Sunday 21 August 1791 to describe how William Reynolds' house, at nearby Ketley Bank, had been threatened. Learning that 'a great number of colliers intended to assemble', Reynolds 'in the meantime sent Sadler to Birmingham to purchase firearms'. It appears to have been a worthwhile journey, as when some two thousand men gathered outside on the Monday morning, they 'did not attempt to break in as Mr R. told them that if they did he would immediately fire upon them'. The mob was thereby held at bay until the arrival of a contingent of the horse guards known as 'Oxford Blues', when the men dispersed. Rosamund Beddoes added:

> I have just seen Sadler. He desires me to inform you that he is high spirits as he is now certain his engine will answer exceedingly well. Mrs S went this morning to Oxford. She wishes for Byrne's house very much. Mr Sadler intends going to London in nine days or a fortnight to take out a patent for a pump.[29]

Sadler either remained in the area or returned frequently over the next few years. When Beddoes went home in November 1791, he found his sister drinking tea with Sadler,[30] and Reynolds' sketchbook shows two views of an engine that Sadler erected at Coalbrookdale in 1792 and another dated May 1793, plus one of an incomplete 'engine by Jas. Sadler before he went to London with Dr. Beddoes' (that is, therefore,

1792 or 1793).[31] Some of Beddoes' letters contain the 'somewhat anxious hopes that Sadler should settle down with Reynolds' at this time.[32] It was not to be.

*

In the summer of 1792, John Sibthorp makes a final appearance in this history. Having left Oxford at the end of 1784 to study in Germany, he had then remained abroad until the autumn of 1787, when he returned to Oxford to take up his post as resident Professor of Botany. He had the option to reside in the university accommodation his father had occupied, but wrote to Joseph Banks on 22 December 1787 that the 'Poor Physick Garden looks quite mournfull that I live at present with my Sister Lady Sewall in Cowley House'.[33] He wrote to Banks again on 27 June 1789, still from Cowley House: 'I flatter myself Botany is making some Progress at Oxford.'[34] To try to maintain that progress, Sibthorp petitioned George III in the summer of 1792 (in a letter addressed to Henry Dundas, the Home Secretary, via Lord North) to request that the stipend of £100 payable to the Professor of Botany be restored to its previous £200.[35] The response was swift and positive, though before the matter was concluded, the influential Oxfordshire magistrate Christopher Willoughby (1749?–1808) intervened, after having discussed the situation with 'some of the Heads of the University'.

In a letter to North, Willoughby proposed that because Cambridge had both a Chair of Botany and one of Chemistry, an equitable arrangement would be for the £100 on offer to be allocated to the Oxford Professor of Chemistry rather than to that of Botany.[36] Despite his suspect politics, Beddoes, Oxford's most distinguished chemist, suddenly became valuable to the university as the obvious candidate for this Regius Chair in Chemistry. This was not at all what Willoughby's associates had had in mind, however, and 21 July finds Willoughby at his home in the Oxfordshire village of Marsh Baldon hurriedly writing again to Dundas with the reasons why Beddoes was unworthy of his Majesty's beneficence. Willoughby conceded that there was no disputing Beddoes' 'thorough knowledge of chymistry', nor that he 'reads most able lectures which are well attended', but 'in his political character I am informed, he is a most violent *Democrate* and that he takes great pains to seduce Young Men to the same political principles with himself'. One week later (28 July 1792) Beddoes' name appeared on a Home Office list of 'Disaffected and Seditious persons'.[37] Another name on that list was Joseph Priestley.

*

Understandably, Beddoes immediately began to seek a more welcoming environment; somewhere where he could pursue his overriding interest in the medical application of chemical processes without political constraints. His successor was announced the following April.[38] A disappointed Beddoes wrote to his former student and friend Davies Giddy[39] on 7 April 1793: 'I much wished Stacy to succeed me, as he has a large family, & would, in account of his being able to make apparatus with his own hands, be likely to give as good a course as any body I knew at Oxford'.[40] In the same letter Beddoes wrote of being about to leave Oxford, and of packing up his laboratory equipment.

Sadler was clearly already aware that Beddoes' days in Oxford were numbered and that as a result his own activities and ambitions would need revision. He had a serious choice to make. His father having been dead for two years, he presumably still had the option, as the oldest son, to take over the family business. Indeed, this is probably what he had attempted to do, as his brother Thomas continued to reside, and probably trade, in the suburb of St Clement's until at least the beginning of 1793 (*see* Appendix 2). Whatever, Thomas was clearly better suited to take over, leaving James free to consider more conducive opportunities farther afield. Indeed, he appears to have been tempted to look *very* much farther: Beddoes wrote to Giddy in 1792 that

Sadler meditates no less a design than to gratify old Kien Long & his train of mandarins with an atmospherical excursion & for this purpose he has already bespoke 600 yards of silk. He is to bear the title of Engineer to the Embassy; he has just passed through Oxford on his way from London ... with Sir G. Staunton and the Chinese from Italy to Ranelagh.[41]

Sadler never did demonstrate his ballooning prowess to the Chinese emperor Ch'ien-lung, however. Instead, the Scot James Dinwiddie (1746–1815), that other early experimenter with balloons, sailed on the vessel to China on 26 September 1792 as the embassy's 'experimental scientist'. It is therefore perhaps not surprising to find that it was Dinwiddie's own suggestion to include 'the constructing, filling, and ascending in the balloon' among his duties.[42] There were other similarities between him and Sadler: among the subjects on which Dinwiddie lectured – in addition to his formal courses on chemistry and mechanics – were gunnery, pyrotechnics and aerostatics. However, he also shared some of Sadler's less businesslike traits, and the following assessment, derived from his biographer, W. J. Proudfoot, seems equally applicable to either man:

> Dinwiddie's impressive, expensive apparatus often became a millstone round his neck. It was difficult to store or transport and he was often careless about money; he purchased equipment rather than life's necessities.[43]

*

So, deprived of a place on the expedition to the Far East, Sadler in fact went no farther in that direction than London, accompanying Beddoes there, probably at the beginning of 1793, in a search for suitable premises to test the therapeutic properties of newly discovered gases.[44] Dr William Yonge went with them. He was the Shifnal doctor who had first encouraged Beddoes to study medicine and was also the Reynolds' family doctor, 'highly esteemed by them as a friend as well as for his professional abilities'.[45] Yonge also provided £200 towards the cost of the 'Pneumatic Institute', as the new venture came to be called. Beddoes himself, William Reynolds, and his half-brother Joseph Reynolds each also contributed an equal share.[46]

When Beddoes failed to locate anywhere suitable in London, he tried Bristol instead. This had been Erasmus Darwin's suggestion, which Beddoes narrowed down to the district of Hotwells 'because this resort of invalids seemed more likely than any other situation to furnish patients in all the various gradations of Consumption'.[47] The decision made, Beddoes took his leave of Oxford, having 'previously sent forward Mr. Sadler ... to make some arrangements with reference to his intended pneumatic trials'. However, 'the rumour of a new medical establishment, of which the precise import was unknown, excited some hostility among the inhabitants of Hope-Square', their chosen location.[48] In a letter to his mother from Hotwells (undated but evidently written soon after the move) Beddoes admitted that 'the hammering & noise in the house alarmed the whole neighbourhood'.[49] Delays ensued, and with Beddoes himself often dealing with matters elsewhere, it was fortunate that Richard Lovell Edgeworth (1744–1817) happened to be staying in Clifton with his family at the time. Although not a resident – the family estate was in Ireland – he carried sufficient influence to ease the worries of suspicious neighbours, and Beddoes commended to his mother the 'pains Mr. Edgeworth was obliged to take to pacify them in my absence'.

Edgeworth was a fellow of the Royal Society (his membership having been sponsored by Joseph Banks, who had been his contemporary at

Oxford), and he had always shown an aptitude for mechanics. He was also a founding member of the Lunar Society, and, when introduced to Beddoes in Bristol by another Lunar man, James Keir (1735–1820), he was happy to help.[50] Banks himself was not similarly tempted, despite the repeated entreaties of such influential advocates as the Duchess of Devonshire, Georgiana Cavendish (*née* Spencer), and James Watt. Banks wrote to the former on 2 December 1794, reluctantly declining support for a second time, because he needed 'to be very careful in preventing his name from appearing as an encourager of projects he does not think likely to prove beneficial to Society'. The sentiment has echoes of his attitude to the first balloonists of a decade earlier, as too his peremptory response to Watt of 7 December 1794: 'in the case of Dr. Beddoes's project I do not fully understand it, & from the partial knowledge I have acquired of it I do not expect any beneficial consequences will be derived from its being carried into execution'.[51]

Edgeworth was in any case in Bristol on a medical quest, so Beddoes' endeavours had a personal as well as philosophical interest for him. His daughter Honora had died of tuberculosis in 1790, as too had her mother before her. When Edgeworth's son Lovell (1775–1842) showed signs of the same disease, he decided to move the family away from their estate at Edgeworthstown, near Longford, in central Ireland, and settled on Clifton Spa for its reputed therapeutic qualities. One of his many other children was the novelist Maria Edgeworth (1768–1849), who completed her father's unfinished memoirs after his death. Although their two years in Bristol are barely mentioned, she did say, in respect of Beddoes, that her father 'was, I believe, his first acquaintance there. My father admired his abilities, was eager to cultivate his society; and this intimacy continuing some months, he had opportunities of assisting in establishing the Doctor at Clifton.'[52]

The 'intimacy' was not only with Maria's father! One of the unexpected bonuses of attending the sickly Lovell was that his principal nurse was his half-sister Anna (1773–1824). With the family preparing to return to Ireland in the summer of 1793, Beddoes promptly proposed to her, and they were married at Edgeworthstown on 17 April 1794.[53] The union strengthened Beddoes' ties with the Lunar Society, and also with some of the most celebrated democrats of the time, united in support of the principles of the French Revolution, if not of the bloody carnage which had followed. They were also vociferous against the rising inflation and the harsh taxation which ruined the domestic economy for the poor, provoked riots and intensified class hatreds. Encouraged by the welcoming presence of his new wife, Beddoes' visitors soon included radical poets such as

Robert Southey and Samuel Taylor Coleridge. Beddoes also enjoyed the goodwill of Josiah Wedgwood and James Watt, both of whom entertained the hope that from within the confines of the Pneumatic Institute might emerge a cure for their children's tuberculosis.

Although it took until the end of the decade for Beddoes' Institute to become fully functional, he was able to undertake some private treatments in the meantime, and also operated a small private school, where James Sadler's oldest son, John, albeit aged only fourteen, provided instruction on 'chemistry and pyrotechny' within the first few months of their arrival.[54] James Sadler's role at this time was as a 'machinist'[55] – but also as a guinea pig! He was among those people on whom Beddoes experimented, 'totally free from all irritating and positively deleterious properties'. Whether Sadler himself was also of that opinion seems doubtful, given that:

> I have myself felt the pulse of Mr. Sadler, the English Aeronaut, while he has inspired, for above a minute and a half at a time, pure hydrogene air from steam and iron. From a rate of eighty-four in a minute it increased to an hundred and ten in 15 seconds, and became soft and weak.[56]

That, presumably, was because he was about to pass out! Beddoes continued to seek financial support for his enterprise for several more years. An appeal in the *Star* of 13 July 1796 requested that subscriptions should be paid to Coutts Bank in London, a prospect which no doubt appeared all the more appealing to anyone who might have read in the London *Oracle & Public Advertiser* (26 August 1796) that Miss Coutts 'is happily recovered under the care of Dr. Beddoes at Bristol, whose practice gains much credit'. The Institute was finally opened at No. 6 Dowry Square, Hotwells in 1799.[57] The most notable advance there was made by Humphry Davy (1778–1829), in April 1799, when he discovered nitrous oxide (laughing gas), which led to anaesthesia.

*

James Sadler had parted company with Beddoes long before the Pneumatic Institute opened. In July 1794 Beddoes followed up on a letter of March to ask James Watt if he knew 'one honest workman capable of fabricating a complete apparatus, reservoirs and all, whom it might be charity to introduce to the public as manufacturer'.[58] The implication is that Sadler was not capable of the task, or, more likely, that he wished to find a bigger challenge. At the end of 1795 came a major change in his life: he remarried and acquired stable, well-paid and prestigious employment.

It is not known if James Sadler's first wife Mary accompanied him to Bristol. Certainly, she would seem to have been a prime example of someone whom Beddoes might have felt able to help. She had evidently been in poor health in January 1791, when Sadler had concluded his letter to Beddoes with: 'Mrs Sadlers respects attends you. She as [*sic*] a bad cough which she thinks affects her breath, as it is very bad again at times.'[59] The 'again' shows this ailment was more than a one-off. No record of his wife's death has been found, either in Oxford or Bristol, but whenever it occurred it left Sadler with responsibility by the end of 1795 for a family of four, perhaps five, children between the ages of ten and eighteen. A second marriage was therefore pretty much a necessity.[60] His new bride was Martha Hancock, a spinster of St Augustine the Less, Bristol, where their marriage was held on 24 October 1795.[61]

On the licence, Sadler still identified himself as a resident of All Saints, Oxford, and designated himself somewhat pompously as a 'gentleman'.[62] As for his bride, as her baptism under the name Martha is not apparent anywhere in the Bristol area, it seems possible that she was baptised as Sibylla – a supposition made on the basis that the couple gave their subsequent daughter a slight variant on this unusual name. If so, James's new wife would appear to have been the daughter of the Rev. Benjamin Hancock and Sybilla Smith, and was baptised (as 'Sibylla') at St Augustine's on 23 September 1756.[63]

By the time of the wedding, Sadler's undoubted talents had been drawn to the attention of those with influence over national defence at a time of increasing international tension caused by the rise of revolutionary France. Initially he was recruited to a hugely responsible role at one of England's premier ports, as the Barrack Master of Portsmouth Harbour. His ballooning activities now an increasingly distant memory, he set off for the south coast in order to apply his mind to issues relating to a very different element: the sea.

PART 4

WATER
1795–1809

9

NAVY LARKS AND SPARKS

J. E. Hodgson composed the first comprehensive account of James Sadler's life and ballooning achievements in his 1924 *History of Aeronautics*. Four years later, on the centenary of Sadler's death, Hodgson produced a pamphlet, *The First English Aeronaut: James Sadler of Oxford,* which amended one or two factual errors from the earlier account, and added a few new details. A third contribution by Hodgson, in the *Transactions of the Newcomen Society* for 1927–28, concentrates on Sadler's activities during his twenty-five-year sabbatical away from ballooning.[1] Although it is not the primary purpose of the current publication to appraise Sadler's non-ballooning achievements (nor does the author feel at all competent to do so) the years 1795 to 1810 comprise a period of his life when his contribution to the development of steam engines and of guns of various sorts is too important not to merit some discussion. It was also a period when he came to the attention of a large number of historically significant politicians and industrialists, many of whom would have a major influence on his subsequently resurrected ballooning career.

Engineer

At some point in 1795, Sadler left Bristol to take up brief employment as the Barrack Master at Portsmouth, then the principal English dockyard. It was a responsible, lucrative role, paying an annual salary of £300.[2] It would seem likely that Sir Charles Saxton (1732–1808), the Commissioner for the Navy at Portsmouth between 1789 and 1806, was instrumental in this appointment, since he later made public his familiarity with the 'very ingenious and inventive talents' Sadler had demonstrated while in Oxford.[3]

Sadler's appointment appears also to have been at the behest of Samuel Bentham (1757–1831), Inspector General of Naval Works from 1796 to 1807. He had first been introduced to Sadler by William Windham.[4] Bentham was responsible for enlarging the basin at Portsmouth and building two new deep docks, to enable the Navy's increasingly large vessels to be repaired and refitted. Sadler's engineering skills were essential in accomplishing this, both in order to power the woodworking machines by day and to pump water out of the dry docks during the night.[5] His was 'the first steam engine erected in Portsmouth Dockyard – or indeed in any Naval establishment'.[6]

Sadler also found time to busy himself with furnace design: his printed leaflet 'Description of a Furnace for heating shot' concludes with: 'a plan of these furnaces was communicated to Right Hon. William Windham, and by him to Colonel Mulcaster, then Chief Engineer at Portsmouth' as early as the end of 1794.[7] His designs were then put into practice, as confirmed by Dr Thomas Bradley (one of several individuals who later rallied to Sadler's cause when the effectiveness of his role was questioned by the Admiralty), who attested that 'the furnace erected at Portsmouth was of Mr Sadler's invention' as too the 'improvement in the furnace for heating canon shot, which was tried at Woolwich and Portsmouth'.[8] The implication of the necessity to make this statement is that others were attempting to take credit for the self-effacing and probably less than articulate former pastry cook's efforts. Sadler certainly pointed to this a few years later, in a letter to William Windham,[9] when objecting to being denied credit for the improvements he had made to some boilers and furnaces, which had resulted in lower consumption of coal while at the same time producing alum, a product of huge importance to the Navy for use in purifying water.

Samuel Bentham also appears to have recommended that his brother, the philosopher Jeremy, should consult Sadler in respect of creating a dock on the Thames at Barnes. Writing on 27 May 1796, Bentham wrote of there being 'no doubt of the feasibleness' of applying Sadler's patented engine for 'the extracting of water from holes of variable depths made for docks'.[10]

Whether anything came of this is unlikely, because only the next month Sadler was given a new, wider-ranging role: that of Chemist to the Board of Naval Works, at a still more lucrative £400 a year. Within the first few months of his new appointment, Sadler had erected, or more likely was engaged in completing, another engine. Yet it was built not for the Admiralty but for the commercial firm of Sutton, Keen & Co., mustard makers, on Garlick Hill in the city. A logical explanation is that the Navy saw the advantages and long-term potential benefits, of allowing its brilliant, if sometimes distracted, employee to increase his engineering knowledge at no material cost to itself. However, his endeavours attracted some less than benign attention. The engineer John Rennie (1761–1821) wrote to the ever-watchful Matthew Boulton and James Watt on 12 October 1796 to say that Sadler's engine

> answers exceedingly well. I attempted to get a sight of her, but was foiled. Sadler had been endeavouring to pervert the minds of the good citizens and to persuade them his engine is much better and cheaper than yours, and uses only half the coal; this man should be looked after.[11]

The comment – 'looked after' in the sense of 'watched' rather than 'nurtured' – has slightly sinister overtones, and seems to echo the resentment that the upstart Sadler's ballooning expertise had inspired in Oxford a decade earlier.

Overall, J. E. Hodgson concluded that Sadler 'took a big step in the direction of making the steam-engine direct-acting and self-contained, that is in freeing it from the trammels of the engine-house'.[12] The fact that his skills in this area were little utilised by the Navy in his role as chemist was surely their loss. In 1802 Bentham noted that because he 'never could feel sufficient confidence in Sadler's statements to submit any opinion' he had only 'in very few cases ... applied to him for any assistance'.[13] This was hardly Sadler's fault, but would ultimately count against him when his paymasters asked him to account for his activities a few years later. At that time Thomas Bradley reasoned that the Admiralty were being especially harsh because Sadler had been specifically solicited for the position:

> When Mr. Sadler was first placed in this office, he was taken from a situation in the Barracks, as Master, which afforded him an income of about three hundred a year, including all advantages. This situation he has thus lost, and with it also a share in a business with his brother.[14]

Bradley's allusion to Thomas Sadler and the family business is interesting. It is doubtful if James ever had many doubts about his decision to turn his back on the safe option of a comfortable, if mundane, life of an Oxford shopkeeper. His varied achievements while in the employ of the Navy must surely have satisfied a nature so active, so restless, so inventive, far more than would any amount of confectionary sales. Yet Bradley was right to hint at the remunerative sacrifice he had made on the Navy's behalf; despite the generous salary, the costly nature of his experimental work went largely unrecompensed and he remained apparently perpetually penniless.

Chemist

When Sadler's appointment as Chemist to the Board of Naval Works was first made, several newspapers (such as *St James's Chronicle* 25–28 June and *Jackson's Oxford Journal* 25 June 1796) announced it as: 'Mr. Sadler, Professor of Chemistry, is appointed by his Majesty, one of the new Naval Board.' Professor of Chemistry? How they must have guffawed in the common rooms and coffee houses of Oxford!

The role of Naval Chemist, as defined by Sadler himself in a report of 1806, included 'improvements in relation to the building, fitting out, arming, navigating, and victualing the ships of war; as well as in relation to the docks, basons, slips, buildings, and other matters appertaining to His Majesty's Naval Service'.[15] Specifically, he worked on

> the qualities of Copper-Sheathing; processes of Distillation of Sea-Water; Analysis of Water brought from Springs at the Dock-yards; Improvements in Brewing as practicable on Shipboard in all seasons; Experiments on Seasoning Ship Timber; on the Combustion of Gunpowder for the Purpose of Fire Ships; and various Drawings and Plans for annoying the Enemy's Ships and Boats in the Harbour of Boulogne; the Construction of Signal Lights. etc. etc. etc.[16]

Unfortunately for Sadler, when asked later by his superiors to quantify his achievements from within that long list, he was unable to give a satisfactory account. One major reason was that he had never been provided with an adequate laboratory. Despite repeated assurances he was only ever provided with a single room immediately above the inspector general's office, which was *'wholly inapplicable to the purpose'* (italics in Sadler's original). In the end he had rented a laboratory at his own expense, equating to a third of his net salary of £400 gross.[17] Thomas Bradley substantiated this claim, stating that Sadler was 'obliged successively to turn his house into a Manufactory for Gun carriages, a Brewhouse, or a Chemical Laboratory'.[18] Another contemporary, Thomas Attwood, stated that 'Mr. Sadler's personal expenses were always on the most confined and frugal scale' and that he 'was a witness to the continual distresses of Mr. Sadler, from the great expenses contracted in his experiments and processes for the public service, which produced often law-expenses and arrests of his person'.[19]

Field Guns

One major distraction from James Sadler's main role as chemist, as the Navy saw it, was the improvements that he made to various kinds of weaponry. Yet his endeavours in this area were widely praised and among the first of his activities in his new role to catch the attention of the outside world. Under the headline 'Modern Invention. Experiments on Mr. Sadler's New Theory on Gunnery', the *Morning Post & Fashionable World* of 1 August 1796 announced a second trial at Woolwich Warren of some cannons which, in addition to other improvements, were:

> only of half the weight of any of those now in use, yet will throw a shot much farther, and with greater truth. Their management only requires four men, where ten are otherwise wanted, and the service of charging and firing them is performed with greater ease, and in much less time.[20]

Significantly, the Right Hon. William Windham, by then Secretary of War, was to attend this second demonstration (as he had the first, in August 1795), though there is nothing in Windham's published diary to confirm whether he did or not. Certainly one can imagine that Sadler would have dearly liked to impress the man to whom he owed so much. His continuing appreciation of Windham is clear from the fact that soon after this demonstration, the name given to the newest addition to the Sadler family was William Windham Sadler. The baptism was on 30 March 1797 at St George's Church, Hanover Square, Mayfair. Windham, as he was always known, was born on 17 October 1796.[21] The family home was by then at 10 Stafford Row, Pimlico, very near Buckingham House (later Palace), and was probably accommodation supplied as part of his employment. The family remained there until at least 1807.

During this period Sadler also devised what might be thought of as a prototype of the twentieth-century armoured car. Drawn by two horses, it consisted of a four-wheeled 'war chariot', an image of which was made by Thomas Rowlandson in 1798 with the title 'Sadler's flying artillery'. A brief description of its function appeared in the section on 'Sadler's Sharp Shooters' in Rudolph Ackermann's *Loyal Volunteers of London*, a 1799 publication illustrated by Rowlandson:

> The Corps was partly formed under the direction of Mr. Sadler, of Pimlico, a very ingenious Machinist, inventor of the celebrated War Chariot, in which two persons, advancing or retreating, can manage two Pieces of Ordnance (three-pounders) with alacrity and in safety, so as to do execution at the distance of two furlongs.[22]

When both innovations were first revealed, dubbed as 'flying artillery and a fusee on a new and curious principle', on the king's birthday on 4 June, Sadler presented them in person to the Pimlico Volunteers.[23] Later that year, on 15 August 1798, his handiwork was given still more prestigious exposure:

> Mr. Sadler, Chemist to the Admiralty, had the honour of attending his Royal Highness the Prince of Wales at Carleton House, when a trial was made of his new-invented moving battery of cannon; two of them are mounted on a carriage, which can be fired in all directions, as well advancing and retreating at full gallop; they are loaded without ramming, prime themselves, and can be discharged ten times in a minute. Mr. Sadler also presented the Prince with a musquet on an entirely new construction, acting upon a similar principles, requiring neither ramming nor priming, lighter by far than the common gun, and said to be superior in point of accuracy to the rifle.[24]

Thomas Attwood, who knew Sadler while an officer with the Pimlico Volunteers, later endorsed this view: 'Having made innumerable trials with Mr. Sadler's Musquets I can attest that, for accuracy and facility of charge, they are superior to any Musquet whatever.'[25]

Next we hear of Sadler's artillery being shipped across the English Channel to northern Holland, just days before Napoleon's *coup d'état* of 9 November 1799. Sadler's second son, eighteen-year-old James (it must be presumed, because, although unspecified, he is the only one of his sons known to have had a military career), makes an appearance at this juncture. Having earlier been placed in command of 'two field pieces, 3-pounders ... under the immediate patronage of the Duke of York',[26] the younger James Sadler (1780–1817) embarked from Ramsgate within days of Napoleon's coup. Initially he was thought to have been on board a captured transport vessel,[27] but actually arrived safely back in Ramsgate the next day: 'his capture would have been particularly unfortunate, as most of his father's drawings and plans were with him, at the particular requisition of the Duke of York'.[28]

Amidst the hostilities, the *Oracle* found room to record a brief moment of serendipity, introduced with the phrase 'Tit for Tat!' Again distinguished with the unwarranted designation of 'Chymical Professor', Sadler, after inspecting

> his new-invented guns, which are aboard the *Thames* frigate, prevented a sailor in the Captain's barge from being drowned. On leaving the frigate at night, Mr. Sadler fell into the water, and would inevitably have been drowned, had not the identical sailor jumped in to his rescue.[29]

In July 1800 Sadler's guns were brought not only to the attention of the Prince of Wales, as in 1798, but also to that of King George as well. The inspection of Sadler's 'three-pounder curricle field piece' by the two men, plus the Duke of York, was one of the highlights of a 'Grand Field Day' near Windsor, involving 30,000 or so cavalry and infantry in a 'Sham Fight'.[30] It was held on 17 July. Soon after, on Friday 25 July, Sadler was again in the distinguished company of the duke and the prince who

> attended to some experiments by Mr. Sadler, with his Curricle Flying Artillery. Mr. Windham explained their construction to the Duchess of York, who was particularly pleased with the apparent facility with which the gun was disengaged from the magazine. The quick firing was regulated by her Highness's stop-watch, and fourteen discharges were made with ease within the minute. On Saturday, by the particular command of the Duke, Mr. Sadler, in order to prove the accuracy of the gun, fixed the target at 300 yards, when every shot told. His Royal Highness then ordered Mr. Sadler to fire at an oak tree near the target, the first went through, the diameter being three feet and a half; the next shot lodged in the tree. His Royal Highness expressed the highest satisfaction on both days, at the quickness of firing, accuracy, and the uncommon ease with which the gun was worked and drawn over the ground by two horses, which would be inaccessible to common artillery by four.[31]

This success led to a further trial of Sadler's musketry at Weymouth soon after.[32] Windham was again in evidence, having noted in his diary that he and his wife had arrived there on 18 July, again at the command of the king,[33] and remained for some weeks.

British East India Company

In the years 1798 and 1799, Sadler had a particular connection with the British East India Company. Sir John Coxe Hippisley (1745/6–1825), a former company employee who maintained a keen interest in Sadler's affairs for many years, was no doubt instrumental in this. Hippisley had matriculated from Hertford College, Oxford in 1764, and worked in India throughout the 1780s, returning with a fortune of over £100,000. He then embarked on a political career as a staunch ally of William Windham.[34] Hippisley remained keenly aware of Sadler's inventiveness. The *London Herald & Evening Post* (6–9 February 1799) observed that Sadler's patent musket had been discharged in front of him thirty-eight times in succession, without the necessity for clearing the touch hole. This was an attribute seen worthy of two exclamation marks! Sadler referred to this feat in a fourteen-page printed *Account of Various Improvements in Artillery, Fire-arms etc.*[35] His pamphlet consists mainly of a description, with diagrams, of the advantages of his new ship cannon. Among the merits which Sadler claimed were its lightness and small size; its strength and accuracy; the reduced quantity of charge required; and the swiftness with which it could be reloaded, even when operated by three men rather than the usual twelve.

As for his rifle, Sadler claimed that the improved bore of the inner barrel meant that the discharge was absolute and would avoid the kind of accident that he himself had suffered: 'In an experiment of quick firing with blank cartridges, at Warfield Grove (the seat of Sir J, Hippisley, Bart.) … an accident of this nature occurred to J.S. himself, having his hand much burnt by the powder catching fire from the inflamed remains of the former cartridge'.[36] In the final paragraph of his *Account* (it must be assumed that he was helped considerably with the composition), Sadler appealed to the East India Company directors to consider 'that unfortunately he has had to contend against the influence of that prejudice which is but too frequently opposed to such inventions or improvements as militate against the established usage of a profession *not their own*'. It is a comment, one might well imagine, fuelled by memories of past resistance to the acceptance of his ballooning expertise.

More East India Company demonstrations took place in November 1799, and in April,[37] June – after which it was noted that 'the accuracy with which the gun is pointed is astonishing'[38] – and August 1800.[39] At about the same time, Sadler's interest in the East India Company took a more personal turn when his second son, James, enlisted on 15 July 1800 and soon after departed for Madras (*see* Appendix 8).

Ship Guns

By this time James Sadler senior appears to have been trying to capitalise simultaneously on his Indian connections and his naval ones by offering his guns for the protection of commercial shipping. In an advertisement in the *Oracle & Daily Advertiser* (15 November 1800), carrying his home address of 10 Stafford Row, he claimed that the guaranteed protection afforded by his particular 'Ship Guns' would enable commercial vessels bringing rice from India to Britain to avoid the 'tedious Process of a regular Convoy'. His guns, he announced, 'may be worked by two or three Men with the greatest Facility, and require only one third of the Quantity of Powder used in charging other Artillery'.

In the same way that it is surprising that Sadler continued to work with commercial interests when he first took up his post as Barrack Master at Portsmouth in 1796, this further example of commercial diversion also seems rather strange. It could have been an exploratory attempt to gauge the commercial market, with a view to leaving his Majesty's service. By all accounts, Sadler must have financed the building and development of these guns himself and therefore the incentive would have been strong to try to recoup the cost. Whatever, the advertisement was apparently not repeated.

With the French threat growing ever more apparent, and the Royal Navy therefore all the more crucial to national interests, Sadler's endeavours from 1799 onwards would seem, not unreasonably, to have focussed more on his principal role. It was still guns that interested him most, but they were at least to be used on military rather than commercial vessels. One rare example of the application of his chemical expertise found its way into the newspapers at the end of 1799, when he was said to have 'undergone a number of examinations as to the best method of purifying ships coming from infected ports', then to have 'invented a Plan, by which vessels may be as completely purified in four hours as in forty days'.[40] Otherwise it was weaponry which apparently dominated his working day.

Consequently, he was later able to cite commendations of his ship guns from the officers of HMS *Thames* and HMS *Mars*. These were dated October and November 1799 respectively,[41] while the *Morning Post & Gazetteer* of 29 March 1800 had this to say:

> A very fine East Indiaman, named the *Keighley*, of London, was launched on Wednesday at Greenland Dock. This ship mounts 24 eighteen-pounders, on the principle invented by Mr. Sadler, of the Admiralty, which have lately been used to great advantage on board the *Thames* frigate.

In 1803, as hostilities with France resumed after the short-lived, and always uneasy, armistice of 1 October 1801, which had been ratified at the Peace of Amiens in March 1802, Sadler's gun designs were brought to the attention of Admiral Horatio Nelson, no less. It was Thomas Attwood, the Pimlico Volunteers' officer, who had enthused over Sadler's muskets, and who had been 'a close observer of his indefatigable industry' while at the Admiralty – who showed Nelson a model of Sadler's 'Ship-Gun and carriage'.[42] According to Attwood, Nelson commented that he 'highly approved of the principle, and if again he should be called into service, he certainly would like to take some of the Guns to sea'. Indeed, 'he could wish his upper-deck completely to be mounted with them'.[43] Nelson must have made this comment shortly before he took over command of the British Mediterranean fleet on 14 May 1803. War was declared again two days later, and Nelson spent most of the next fifteen months at sea, arriving back at Portsmouth only on 19 August 1805, in order to rest. Attwood went on to say that Nelson then

> renewed his communications with me on the subject, but upon my going to Mr. Sadler, I found he had been obliged to go into the country, and was otherwise in extreme ill-health, and could not comply with Lord Nelson's wishes, who told me that he would take on board as many Guns as Mr. Sadler could send alongside the *Victory*. His Lordship sailed about a fortnight afterwards, on the Expedition which ultimately terminated his valuable life.

Nelson took charge of HMS *Victory* on 14 September 1805 and sailed almost immediately for Cadiz to fight the conclusively successful, but for Nelson fatal, Battle of Trafalgar. One wonders what might have occasioned Sadler's 'extreme ill-health' towards the end of August and beginning of September. There could of course have been any number of causes, but an element of stress seems to have been involved. Dr Thomas Bradley, thought so, saying that when Sadler had to engage in his various endeavours with no proper laboratory and with his expenditure exceeding his income, 'this distress, together with his incessant activity and natural anxiety of mind in all his pursuits, have greatly impaired his health and disqualified him for very active employments'.[44]

Despite all these many achievements and recommendations, those who counted, mainly Sadler's immediate employers, singularly failed to appreciate his wide-ranging contribution to the national good. The situation came to a head in 1806, when, with the French threat quashed, the Admiralty cast a critical eye over the activities of its maverick chemist.

Sadler's Duties Reviewed: 25 March 1806

When asked to give an account of his responsibilities, it was Simon Goodrich of the Admiralty to whom Sadler reported on 25 March 1806.[45] Unsurprisingly, given the enthusiastic feedback from other quarters, Sadler laid more stress on the 'improvements in Naval and Field Ordnance, in Musquetry, and Gun carriages' than on his work as an experimental chemist. This was unwise, as it turned out, because when Goodrich reported back to Samuel Bentham, he decided to withhold any mention of these gunnery activities on the grounds that such services were not 'performed in an official capacity'. As a result, Sadler's role was deemed superfluous and he was dismissed from his post.

Sadler considered this to be so unfair, albeit due to Goodrich's 'mistaken sense of duty', that (other entreaties having failed) he addressed a three-page printed letter to William Wellesley Pole, Secretary of the Admiralty, in June 1809, pleading for a reconsideration.[46] He pointed out that Bentham had not even seen much of the report, because Goodrich had simply returned many pages on the basis that 'the improvements made by me in Naval and Field Ordnance, in Musquetry and Field Carriages, comprehending observations of the combustion of gunpowder' did not fall within 'the duties enjoined by my appointment'. As well as the use to which Sadler's guns had been put in three East India Company armies, this rejected material seems to have included Sadler's accounts of the new guns and improvements to guns which had been utilised on the *Thames* frigate, the *Hornet* sloop and two other vessels named *Arrow* and *Dart*.

The decision to abolish the post of chemist had been recommended by John Fordyce, a Commissioner of the Board of Naval Revision, as confirmed in a letter from him dated 1 May 1809.[47] John Hippisley and Sadler had gone to talk to him at his house when it became apparent that Sadler was 'the only member of the original Board ... for whom no provision has been made' by way of compensation or pension.[48] At the time, Fordyce had expressed his surprise at this, as confirmed by one J. Spalding:

> I recollect perfectly being present, with Sir J. C. Hippisley, when the conversation ... took place in the house of Mr. Fordyce, who expressed much surprise that Mr. Sadler had been removed from his office without compensation, which had never been in the contemplation of the Board.[49]

Soon after this meeting with Fordyce, Sadler composed his letter of appeal to William Pole. He had moved to 40 Brewer Street, Golden Square by this time and the gist of his complaint was that, despite the lack of a laboratory and a failure to recompense his expenses, Sadler had nonetheless 'attended daily at the office to receive my instructions, *until I was told by the Inspector General that my attendance was no longer necessary*'.[50] In other words, Sadler had been consistently available to undertake any tasks assigned to him, and it was not his own fault if Bentham failed to assign any!

This letter of June 1809 having solicited no response, and a year or more having passed since the talk with Fordyce, Sadler, with the particular backing of Hippisley,[51] tried writing to Pole again. This time he emphasised his impecunious situation by enclosing a copy of a printed letter of appeal. It was dated 25 April 1810,[52] with eight references appended,[53] several of which – from Attwood, Bradley, Saxton and the officers of the *Mars* and *Thames* – have already been referred to above.[54] The others came from John Ingram Lockhart MP, of Tubney Park, near Oxford, who had known Sadler, 'a most ingenious, but unfortunate man', for upwards of twenty years. Lockhart requested compassion be shown to 'the only one of the whole office who has been dismissed uncompensated, unnoticed, friendless, nay absolutely ruined – for I verily believe that he, and his numerous family, cannot command one guinea'. The concept of a 'numerous family' of dependents was somewhat to exaggerate the case, as in fact all the children of his first marriage were now adults. However, two children *were* dependent on him: Windham was then thirteen and Sybella, the second child of his second marriage, was aged eleven (*see* Appendix 8).

Davies Giddy, by then MP for Bodmin, wrote on 20 June 1809: 'I have known Mr. Sadler upwards of twenty years – first as an Aeronaut, then as an Assistant to the Professor of Chemistry at Oxford, then as an Engineer, in the mining sense of that term, and all along with the character of a very ingenious man.' Giddy's reference to mining accords with the eighth reference that Sadler chose to enclose with his appeal to Pole: R. Perkins, Oakhill, Somerset wrote (undated) that 'Mr Sadler's improved method of blasting rock answers beyond expectation', by using a third less gunpowder with increased effect:

> I am the more gratified with the favourable issue of this trial, since it was adopted with no little distrust and reluctance on the part of the owner, who I very well recollect treated the attempt with the most decided contempt. A triumph over ignorance and prejudice, where public good is the object, is ever most cordially relished.

It is not clear how successful this collective appeal to the Admiralty was, but in the interim, as a covering, printed letter, headed Oxford 25 April 1810, stated:[55]

> Some friends of Mr. Sadler, a native and freeman, and, for many years an inhabitant of this city (whose family also has been resident here, with great credit, for many descents), have encouraged him to resort to the liberality of his fellow-citizens and members of the University.

A fund had been opened at three Oxford banks, and Hippisley, Giddy and Lockhart were named as trustees. The reason for this measure was explained as being necessary to discharge Sadler's debts, which, it was casually stated, did not exceed £500. It had been twenty years or so since Sadler had last been a permanent resident in Oxford, so a reminder of why he deserved the city's generosity was thought prudent:

> Mr. Sadler had, among many other objects of science, early directed his attention to the improvement of *Aerostatic Machines*, in the persuasion that they might ultimately be made subservient to many useful purposes – particularly in military service for reconnoitering at a distance – to serve as signals in various circumstances when no other means could be used – the transmission of intelligence from places besieged – from ships in storms – and for many other economical and philosophical purposes. Sadler has made *fourteen aerial voyages* – one of them of much *longer duration* than has been achieved by any other Aeronaut: – his ascent

from the Physic Garden of this University is in the memory of the
greater part of his fellow-citizens.

Two statements in this testimonial are interesting. The flight of
longest duration was presumably that of eight hours made with
William Windham. It may indeed have been the longest in terms of
time up to that date (in Britain, anyway), but if he had really made
fourteen previous flights, six are unaccounted for. It is not impossible
that he did make some surreptitious, unnoticed flights, possibly
even with a military intent, but it is more likely that this inflation
of his flying experience was either a genuine error or a calculated
marketing ploy. The request for charity doubled as an announcement
that Sadler was intent on reviving his ballooning career, and that a
separate subscription for this enterprise had been opened at 'Seales
and Dickesons Coffee Houses'. Probably his sponsors considered that
this exaggeration of his experience would inspire greater interest and
confidence, and consequent higher ticket sales. In so doing, they set a
precedent which others would follow, either cynically or mistakenly,
for the remainder of Sadler's aeronautical career.

Sadler's resurrection was scheduled for the approaching Oxford
Commemoration Week, an annual programme of ceremonies
celebrating the benefactors of the university. Keen to underline that
this was not mere frivolity, but a mission with serious intent, emphasis
was placed on the fact that Sadler would go 'with suitable apparatus
to make experiments on the state of the atmosphere'. It was just like
old times! James Sadler, 'the first English Aerostatist', 'the first British
aeronaut', was back in Oxford and back in business!

PART 5

AIR
1810–24

10

THINGS LOOKING UP AGAIN!
1810–12

Apart from a flurry of ballooning activity occasioned by the optimism generated by the Peace of Amiens in March 1802, there had been very few ascents since Sadler's withdrawal from the activity in 1785. Even in France there had been only sixteen recorded launches between 1786 and 1802.[1] The main constraint was the political situation, where the collapse of the French economy made expensively frivolous pastimes like ballooning increasingly rare, and, with the outbreak of revolution, almost impossible. One Frenchman who managed to overcome these obstacles was André-Jacques Garnerin (1769–1823), who had achieved considerable fame in 1797 as the first man ever to descend from a balloon with a parachute. He went to London especially to make an ascent at the end of June 1802 (with Captain R. C. Sowden); he made two more in July: one with a Mr Brown and one (from Lord's Cricket Ground) with Edward Hawke Locker; and one more in August with his wife Jeanne Geneviève and Duncan Glasford or Glasfurd.[2] For most people, therefore, Sadler's ascent was as novel in 1810 as his first had been in 1784.

Oxford: Saturday 7 July 1810

The city of Oxford, usually a place of sedate and ordered calm, of sombre if not always sober outlook, always presented quite a different appearance during Commemoration Week at the end of the trinity term. The awarding of honorary degrees and the associated ceremonial and social activities attracted visitors in huge numbers, and the normal, somewhat monastic, ambience of the ancient city was, for a week or two, replaced with a more celebratory aura. It was an event which always merited lengthy accounts in both the local and national newspapers, but the Commemoration of 1810 promised to be a bit special. The war with France had reignited, but most actively in the far-off Iberian Pensinsula, and the mood was relaxed enough for the Oxford public to be treated to a sight which had not been seen in the ancient and noble seminary of learning for a quarter of a century. A balloon flight was to be the literal highlight of the week, and to whet the appetite still more, the man who was to ascend beyond the clouds was none other than Oxford's very own celebrated veteran, returning to the scene of his first triumphs: the pastry cook and confectioner, turned engineer-cum-naval chemist and gun inventor, James Sadler.

Sadler was now fifty-seven. Almost all the other balloonists of the previous century had either died or retired.[3] The years of conflict had not permitted much in the way of refinement of either balloon manufacture or technique, and Sadler's retained knowledge was therefore still as relevant as ever. The notice in *Jackson's Oxford Journal* of 30 June 1810 had a familiar ring to it too, harking back to those heady days of 1784 when all Oxford – both Town *and* Gown – could be called upon for support: 'Mr. Sadler respectfully informs the Nobility and Gentry of the University and City of Oxford that on Saturday 7th July he will ascend from Merton Fields in a Magnificent Balloon.' Though William Jackson was long since dead, Oxford's original weekly newspaper still retained the name of its respected founder.

That same Saturday marked the installation as the new University Chancellor of the former Prime Minister (and Christ Church graduate) William Grenville (1759–1834). In the week preceding, a service attended by the new chancellor and other dignitaries was held as usual at the university church of St Mary the Virgin. Less usual was the great crush and unseemly behaviour of those in attendance, as

the gallery in the church was reserved for the Ladies, but their numbers were so great that they were dispersed over the whole of the church, though the rain at the moment poured down in torrents, and many could not gain admittance. The proportion of beautiful women was immense, and the dresses were so various as to surpass the most variegated bed of tulips. On the Tuesday, several hundred Ladies could not enter the Theatre during the commemoration, and the struggle to gain admission was so great that many lost their bracelets, shoes, and other ornaments, and several were considerably bruised. The ball on the same evening was crowded with beauty and fashion, exceeding fifteen hundred Ladies, notwithstanding which the dancing was kept up with great spirit till six o'clock this morning. The dinner was a complete scramble, and little order could be kept.[4]

One reason for the excessive number of visitors seems likely to have been the added allure of Sadler's balloon. No one else had made an ascent from Oxford since Sadler had helped Richard Fitzpatrick to do so in 1785 (nor would anyone else do so for another thirteen years, at another Commemoration, in 1823 – *see* Appendix 9). Only one of Sadler's eight ascents of the 1780s had been made with company, the one with William Windham. On this, his return to the aerial stage, he chose to be accompanied again, taking with him his eldest son, John, then aged twenty-one. A relatively new newspaper, the *Oxford University and City Herald* (14 July 1810), described them as 'our British Dædalus and Icarus'.

John Sadler (1779–1838)

John Sadler had probably remained in Bristol after his father's departure in 1795 or 1796. On 29 December 1802 he married Mary Long (a widow) at St Andrew's, Clifton, designating himself a 'chymist' in both the register and on the licence. By that time he was actually based in London, however, where he worked as a chemical assistant at the Royal Institution and assisted Humphrey Davy (with whom he had probably become acquainted at Beddoes' Bristol Institute) until 1804.[5] It was almost certainly John who was the unnamed son of James Sadler summoned to assist Beddoes with 'chemical inquiries and experiments' when an outbreak of influenza occurred in Bristol in 1803.[6] And also John – by implication a sensible, level-headed individual – who was the subject of the 'only pun Davy is said to have ever made', in the context of Beddoes' tendency for rashness: 'I cannot imagine … why he has engaged Sadler, unless it is that he may be well bridled.'[7]

Before the end of 1805, John and Mary Sadler left London for Northumberland, where John was employed at Thomas Richard Beaumont's Dukesfield lead mill, near Hexham.[8] Their son, John Coxe Hippisley Sadler, was born at Darthope on 27 November, according to the parish register at Slaley (a little south of Hexham), where he was baptised on 23 December 1805.[9] The name chosen for James

Sadler's first grandchild reflects the respect and gratitude the family already had for Sir John Coxe Hippisley, that influential proponent of Sadler's talents and close political ally of William Windham. John Sadler was a member of the Newcastle Literary and Philosophical Society from 1806 to 1809.[10] Soon after this he returned to London, where he arranged for the Beaufoy vinegar works in Lambeth to be supplied with gas lighting.[11] Both he and his father would maintain an association with the Beaufoy family for many years to come (*see* below and Appendix 8).

*

The Oxford Commemoration Week balloon had previously been exhibited at the Pantheon in London's Oxford Street, according to a printed handbill (in which Sadler is again designated the 'first British aeronaut') which was distributed in advance.[12] The balloon was then brought to Oxford, and displayed for four days at John Hardaway's Racket Court in St Mary Hall Lane (now called Oriel Street), just round the corner from Thomas Sadler's thriving confectionary business at No. 104 High Street.[13]

It was reported that 4,500 people each paid one shilling to view the apparatus on the day of the launch alone, and that 50,000 people crammed into Oxford,[14] a city with a normal population of about 13,000.[15] The launch, on Saturday 7 July, was from Merton Field, a meadow lying to the west of Sadler's former preferred launch location of the Botanic Gardens, adjacent to the colleges of Christ Church, Corpus Christi and Merton, the heads of which 'very obligingly consented to block up all access to the Meadow' to anyone not paying the admission charge of five shillings. Inevitably this restriction resulted in numerous people trying to find a vantage point for which they would not have to pay any shillings at all! Taking a ferry across the Thames near Folly Bridge was a popular choice, according to the *Morning Chronicle*, but only disappointment ensued: those who did so 'were prevented from a view by some paling and the numerous large trees' on Christ Church Meadow. Not to be thwarted:

> Some jumped over wide ditches, others pulled off their shoes and stocking and walked through rivulets of water and ditches. At length, the immense multitude became so extremely powerful that they broke down very strong fences, and forced their way in, and it being feared that some mischief might ensue, friends of Mr. S. reduced the price of admission to 1s, notwithstanding several thousands gained admittance without paying.[16]

Those thousands were comprised both 'of the ignorant and vulgar, and of the learned and the great'.[17] Among the former (presumably!) were seven notorious pickpockets from London and Birmingham, who were arrested by two Bow Street officers, and held at Oxford Castle. It was deduced that two of them had intended disguising themselves as students, but they all had to be released when no one came forward to claim the items found in their possession.[18]

The account of the day in the *Morning Post* of 9 July included the text of a handbill which had been circulated on the day of the ascent. It began: 'Mr. Sadler must trust to the liberality of the Public, to be enabled to keep his engagements with those who have kindly given him credit for the expensive materials and preparations for this exhibition'. He reminded people of his financially precarious situation and of the subscriptions which were still open. He also took the opportunity to pay tribute to 'his ever-to-be-lamented friend and patron' William Windham, and to remind people of the flight they had undertaken together in May 1785, claiming it to be, at eight hours, still 'the longest ever known'.[19]

The launch of the 30-foot diameter, 87,000-gallon balloon came at a few minutes after 1 p.m., watched from Corpus Christi by the chancellor and other dignitaries, and to the accompaniment of a military band. Three flags adorned the car, one bearing the university arms, one those of the city and one which stated 'The Conqueror of Bonapart; the hero of Acre: Admiral Sir Sydney Smith'.[20] Smith was one of thirty men who were presented with honorary degrees that year.[21] Twenty five barrels of hydrogen were used to fill the balloon, using about a bushel (3 tons) of iron filings and 2 tons of vitriol.[22]

One can easily believe the behind the scenes glimpse provided by the *Caledonian Mercury* (14 July 1810) that on the Friday evening prior to the ascent, John Sadler, having exhausted himself in preparing for the next day, required medical assistance. He was still unwell at the time of the ascent, 'but found himself much better as soon as he got above the clouds'. The two men took with them 'some cold beef, a bottle of brandy, four bottles of water, and' – Horace Walpole, had he still lived, would *not* have approved! – 'a cat, fastened in a wicker basket'. It was released, complete with parachute, and later 'picked up by a countryman, at a village called Headington'. It was wearing 'a red collar and a direction to Miss Robarts, daughter of the coach proprietor in High-street. The countryman took the cat home as directed. On his way, he made an exhibition of Puss, at a premium.'[23]

John Sadler, who kept a journal of their progress (over Brill,

Wootton, Stow and Woburn), noticed at about 3 p.m. that: 'The *halo* about the shadow of the balloon in a cloud, was rich beyond description; the prismatic colours most vivid, distinct, and complete.' This was immediately followed by a third-party comment that:

> The prospect they enjoyed was beautiful beyond imagination; the finely wooded and watered country, for an immense range – the view of fifteen towns and villages at one moment, and of more than double that number, besides palaces, gentlemen's seats &c. when the eye was permitted to take the range of the circular panorama beneath, was an enjoyment which our confined experience forbids our attempting to describe.[24]

One of James's nephews, either Thomas or Henry (*see* Appendix 2), followed their progress from below: 'Mr. Sadler, a grocer of this city, followed the direction of the Balloon, left it near Buckingham, and returned here about half-past seven o'clock.'[25] His cousin and uncle continued for another 10 miles or so, to land at about 4.30 p.m., near Newport Pagnell, about 30 miles from Oxford.[26] The gas had already begun to run out after about 12 miles, after which their altitude remained fairly low, enabling them in due course to converse with some women 'who at first were much alarmed, but then ran to the balloon' but were unable to reach it. The Sadlers then

> descended and rose again with a rebound on touching the earth in a wheat-field about forty feet, and descended again in a field of barley adjoining, slightly rebounded from that, and threw out the grappling irons; the car entangled in a quick-set hedge.[27]

That hedge marked the border between Buckinghamshire, where the car rested, and Bedfordshire, within which lay the balloon.[28] Some haymakers three fields away came to secure the balloon, and about fifty people then packed everything away on a cart belonging to the man in whose North Crawley field they had landed, a Quaker called Marshall. He arranged for both the equipment and the two Sadlers to be taken to Newport Pagnell, where they were entertained at the house of Dr Hardy, a surgeon.[29] They then spent the night in Buckingham,[30] and returned to Oxford at 3 p.m. the next day in a post-chaise.

What was stated in the advance publicity as being Sadler's fifteenth ascent was commemorated by a Mr Pinkney, who drew on old triumphs as well as new in the third and fourth verses of a six-verse, celebratory 'New Song':

Sadler claims each praise, who can pray rescind 'em?
Who took aloft t'gaze the patriotic Windham.
Garnarein has done Travels to the Moon, Sirs,
But Sadler scales t'Sun, with his Grand Balloon, Sirs.

Now they soar aloft, all the Ladies smitten,
Down comes the parachute and Miss Bobarts Kitten.
Genius ne'er can want Englishmen's best Boons, Sirs,
Here's the English Aëronaut, King of all Balloons, Sirs.

Pinkney then expanded his theme from the very local to the constraints which the international context put on the celebrations, the jingoistic fifth verse being:

Frenchmen let come all, in the air we'll meet 'em,
Phæton like they'll fall, damme there we'll beat 'em,
While British Tars seal below their Doom, Sirs,
We'll wage Aërial Wars with our Grand Balloon, Sirs.[31]

The achievement of the 'King of all Balloons' had not escaped the notice of the real king. On a public appearance at Windsor the same month, the septuagenarian George III conversed 'with cheerfulness' and 'on a variety of topics with the utmost freedom and hilarity' on the evening that John Evans was present. The only one of those topics specifically mentioned by Evans was the installation of the new chancellor of Oxford University, in connection with which the king 'inquired also about the balloon in which Mr. Sadler had ascended on the occasion, and was particularly anxious to know how long it continued in the air, and where it landed'.[32]

The Sadlers, father and son, seem to have been differently affected by the experience. For James it was the beginning of a whole new phase of ballooning fame, but John, who in any case had permanent employment at Beaufoy's factory in London, appears to have been of a more down-to-earth disposition, his preference being to follow in his father's more terrestrial footsteps as a chemist and engineer. John's half-brother Windham, however, inherited an elevation gene or two, as we shall see, and exhibited on the occasion of this Oxford launch the single-minded determination which would characterise his own aeronautical career. Many years later John

related a pathetic circumstance concerning his younger brother William Windham Sadler, then aged 14, who walked the fifty-four miles from

London with only a few coppers in his pocket, in order to see his father ascend, but not arriving in Oxford until several hours after the affair was all over, had perforce to walk home again.[33]

Windham would have had very little chance of a lift that day, as there was always a chronic shortage of transport during even a normal Commemoration Week; Sadler's balloon ensured that this was no normal event, severely exacerbating the problem. According to the *Caledonian Mercury* (14 July 1810) when one coach arrived at the Angel Inn, about one hundred people attempted to press their claim for priority and 'actually fought with one another, and broke the windows of the coach-office, in pressing for their money to be taken'.

As with practically all else concerning the life of the enigmatic James Sadler, who left so few clues to his true personality, his motives for taking the bold step of returning to ballooning can only be surmised. Was it a purely financial necessity? On this one occasion, with the backing of the great and the good, and with the fair wind of publicity generated by the Commemoration, there was every reason to go ahead. He probably did make a reasonable profit, to set against his reputed debts, but why he then continued with the pastime is anyone's guess. Every balloonist, from Lunardi onwards, bemoaned their financial losses, but it is inconceivable that those that persisted would have done so without at least some pecuniary reward. There was money, and certainly fame, to be had, although to acquire the former, a degree of organisational sense and financial probity was essential. As the coming years would show, James Sadler, it seems safe to say, had insufficient of either.

Another factor was probably that Sadler had reached a natural crossroads in life, after redundancy from the Navy, and was keen to take advantage of the unexpected opportunity to revive a passion he had been forced to curtail when younger. Or perhaps it was the irrepressible urge of a pioneer to want to go always higher, farther, longer? Or could it have been the lurking desire of this most scientific of balloonists to confound the hurtful criticism that ballooning – still, after all these years – had failed to deliver any tangible or constructive discoveries, or to contribute any astounding supra-nebulous wisdom?

One such critic was a young University College scholar called Percy Bysshe Shelley. He matriculated on 10 April 1810, and had not yet commenced his Oxford studies at the time of the Sadlers' ascent, but it does seem likely that the comments he made about balloons in his first term that autumn were inspired by it. Indeed, it is quite possible that he contrived to be among the thousands of people who pressed into Oxford that day to watch the first known father-and-son ascent in Britain with his own eyes. According to his biographer and friend, Thomas Jefferson Hogg, Shelley told him in October 1810 (on the very day that the two new undergraduates first met) that 'chemistry was, in truth, the only science that deserved to be studied', while also acknowledging that recent discoveries had been 'rather brilliant than useful'.[34] Shelley also thought that although 'the art of navigating the air is in its first and most helpless infancy' and the balloon

> a mere toy, a feather, in comparison with the splendid anticipations of the philosophical chemist; yet it ought not altogether to be contemned. It promises prodigious faculties for locomotion, and will allow us to traverse vast tracts with ease and rapidity, and to explore unknown countries without difficulty. Why are we still so ignorant of the interior of Africa? – why do we not dispatch intrepid aeronauts to cross it in every direction, and to survey the whole peninsula in a few weeks? The shadow of the first balloon, which a vertical sun would project precisely underneath it, as it glided over a hitherto unhappy country, would virtually emancipate every slave, and would annihilate slavery for ever.[35]

Bristol: Monday 24 September 1810

Having made such a successful comeback, with no damage to the balloon (nor, evidently, to the parachuted cat), it made undeniable economic sense to put it to further use elsewhere. The new location selected was a city with which Sadler was already familiar – Bristol – and in the company of a man with whom he was also probably already familiar, a wine merchant called William Henry Clayfield (c. 1772–1837).[36] Clayfield was 'a gentleman distinguished for his chemical knowledge, and of great respectability'[37] and had at some point been employed by Thomas Beddoes, who had died in 1808. He was also friendly with James Watt and Humphry Davy.[38]

Jackson's Oxford Journal (22 September) was the first with the news that the Bristol flight – 'the grandest spectacle ever witnessed in that city' – would take place on 24 September from 'an inclosed piece of ground near the Full Moon, Stoke's Croft'.[39] A reputed 100,000 people had already paid to inspect the balloon at the Bristol assembly room, and Sadler was reckoned to have had many personal visitors, whom, it was said, he charged three shillings and sixpence each for the privilege. On the day:

The city was all bustle the whole morning, and every house that could command a view of the ascension was crowded. The shops were all shut up, and all business was at a stand during the whole of the forenoon. The Schools poured forth their contents, and made a holiday.[40]

From the very first French accounts of 1783 onwards, every newspaper almost certainly exaggerated the numbers of people who paid in advance of, or during, an ascent. This sustained an impression of aeronauts as wealthy. While that might have been true of one or two, it was hard-earned, and was apparently never the case with Sadler. One commercial spin-off – long since practised by Lunardi, Blanchard and several one-off balloonists – was to publish a first-hand account of the voyage while it was still fresh in the public's mind. Sadler, a man who could 'hardly speak a word of Grammar', according to Hippisley,[41] had never previously resorted to this means of additional income, but on this occasion, his composition no doubt considerably aided by his passenger, that is what he did.

Balloon, an authentic account of the ærial voyage of Messrs. Sadler and Clayfield, who ascended in a most magnificent balloon from a field in the neighbourhood of Stoke's-Croft, Bristol, on Monday, September 24th, 1810 was made swiftly available to the public 'for the benefit of Mr. Sadler'. It is apparent that many of the newspaper accounts of Sadler's earlier ascents – and indeed on this occasion too – contained verbatim accounts taken probably from conversations with him soon after the flight, but this publication – which proved of sufficient interest to extend to a second edition before the year was out – is the first example of anything implicitly sanctioned by him. It is therefore from there that the following account is largely taken.

On the first page Sadler is credited with fifteen previous ascents, reviving the puzzle of the six which are untraced, and in view of his personal association with this publication, one can only assume that this statement had been endorsed by Sadler himself. It was the identical balloon with which he had ascended in Oxford – 'by far the largest, and altogether the most magnificent, ever exhibited in this country', at 30 yards circumference, and comprising 1,900 yards of varnished silk – and it still displayed the dedication to William Grenville, as the new Chancellor of Oxford University. With the Royal Bristol Volunteers preventing 'the intrusion of the populace' onto the field selected for the launch at Stoke's Croft, the balloon was fully inflated by about 1 p.m., when the two men got into the car.

Sadler's daughter (obviously Sybella, then aged about twelve) had intended going too, 'but the wind blowing fresh from the N. E. she was dissuaded from it', as this increased the chances that they would be taken in the perilous direction of the Bristol Channel. This did indeed prove to be the case. Clayfield and Sadler ascended 'amidst the shouts of at least two hundred thousand persons, for even so far as Lansdown in the vicinity of Bath, the hills were thronged with spectators' (or, more evocatively, 'one forest of people'[42]). Sadly, though, spectators who actually paid 'were less numerous than we might have wished'. An account of the launch in a letter by Frances Prideaux to her brother Francis shows why this was, exemplifying the problems faced by organisers who were powerless to prevent many people from taking up good vantage points while paying nothing for the privilege:

> It ascended on Monday a little before two from a field in Stokes Croft. From the top of our house we had a good view of it, but Mr. Wyndowe kindly invited all our party to his house, which commanded the whole field; I never in my life was more delighted with a sight, the ascension was beyond [any]thing grand I ever saw, all the people in Bristol and twenty miles round were assembled in Kingsdown. Mr. William Clayfield accompanied Mr. Sadler; I understand he gave two hundred guineas.[43]

The *Authentic Account* continues with the two men proceeding in a westerly direction. At one point, the shadow of the balloon was observed on the cloud below, 'surrounded with a most resplendent halo or rainbow'. Before passing over the coast, the almost obligatory ritual of forfeiting one of a cat's nine lives was performed, as it was parachuted over the side in a basket (and later found alive and well). Crossing the coast at about 2.15 p.m., they moved rapidly northwards towards Wales, descending so low that 'the shouts of the Cambrians, and the noise of the Breakers between Scilly and Barry Islands, could be distinctly heard'.[44] At this point, 'there being but little chance of being able to reach the main land, and a strong current of air impelling the Balloon towards the open sea, more ballast was thrown out; and, by accident, Mr. Sadler's hat accompanied it'. Still descending, a quantity of sand was shaken from one of the bags, followed by several whole bags. This had the effect of causing 'an ascent so rapid as to bring the balloon in contact with the sand from the first-mentioned bag, which fell into the car in a profuse shower'. Their course continued parallel to the coast as far as St Donat's, then back across the Channel. The island of Lundy appeared in the distance, and soon after, the scene was strikingly grand, the clouds appearing to be nearly a mile below the Balloon, spreading themselves along the horizon over South Wales, in some places faintly shaded, resembling a mountainous country covered with snow, far beneath which in front, and in some few openings in the distance, the country was strongly illuminated, and coloured with all the varied and glowing tints of Autumn. At this elevation, the clearness of the air rendered the respiration of the Aeronauts extremely delightful, the pulse being full and strong, with a slight throbbing of the arteries of the head.

This attempt at injecting some scientific validity into the enterprise was followed at 4.10 p.m. with the complete abandonment of any such purpose, as they attempted to counter a rapid loss of height by ejecting ballast which included 'a great-coat, a valuable barometer and thermometer, a speaking-trumpet, and grapling iron'. It was to no avail, and they plunged into the water about 4 miles from the English shore. Luckily, their 'perilous situation' had been observed, but they were still obliged to drift for about an hour before a rescue boat arrived, and it took another 2 hours to secure the balloon. The 'valuable barometer' was identified in many newspapers – initially the *Morning Chronicle* and *Morning Post* of 28 September – as 'a favourite Barometer given to Mr. Sadler by the famous Dr. Johnson, for which he has been offered two hundred guineas'. Logically it was the same barometer that was mentioned earlier in the account as having 'sustained an injury in the field, after being placed in the Car, which rendered it useless'.[45] Sadler and Clayfield did not get ashore until about 9 p.m., at Lynmouth. From there, they proceeded to Lynton for the night, rested the following day – well, why not indeed! – and returned to Bristol on the Wednesday.

That was the gist of Sadler's twelve-page published *Authentic Account* of probably the first ever flight over Welsh territory, as experienced mainly from the air. The newspapers added the occasional interesting observation from a spectator's point of view. The *Morning Post* (27 September) provided an eye-witness account from Cardiff Castle by J. Bird, who saw the balloon heading 'in a line from Penarth Point to Swansea' at 2.20 p.m., and the *Morning Post* of 29 September gave a full update on the fate of the cat. It had been picked up by a lime-burner near Leigh Down (a little to the west of Bristol, adjacent to the River Avon), and taken, as its label requested, to 'a medical gentleman' in Bristol, where it was given 'a local habitation and name (Balloon) under that gentleman's hospitable roof'. The saturated balloon itself had been taken to 'Pill' (presumably Pyle, in South

Wales). The total distance covered was estimated at about 100 miles, which, if so, was probably the longest distance Sadler had yet travelled.

Frances Prideaux's letter to her brother shows that details of the flight took next to no time to become common knowledge in Bristol, as she was aware within 48 hours that Sadler and Clayfield had had to throw out 'even part of their clothes and valuable glasses ... to prevent them dropping in the sea', and that 'after spending about two hours on the water', once rescued, 'the two balloon gentlemen were too fatigued to walk without assistance'. When they returned at midday on the 26th it was 'in a coach and four amidst the heartfelt cheering of the citizens of Bristol. The bells were ringing ... from their arrival till twelve at night.'[46]

'Mr. Clayfield is the first Bristolian who ever explored the airy regions, in search of scientific knowledge', a broadsheet issued by the Bristol printer Clouter asserted, and there follows an anonymous song, 'The Countryman's Idea of Sadler's Balloon', on the theme of the two men's audacity in ascending high enough to encounter St Peter:

> I zeed um go into a Cloud,
> I thought they were going to heav'n,
> But it plainly appear'd to the croud,
> That St. Peter he would na have em.

The song ends:

> If we're good upon earth till we die,
> And to evil gas are not inclin'd,
> We've no need of Balloons in the sky,
> To bear us to heaven in wind.[47]

Not surprisingly, the fifty-seven-year-old Sadler's health appears to have suffered following his prolonged immersion in the Bristol Channel. The *Ipswich Journal* of 5 January 1811 observed with no preamble or further explanation that 'Mr. Sadler, who descended with his balloon into the sea near Bristol, has been in a dangerous state from a violent cold that he caught then; he had never been well since.'

Cambridge: Wednesday 3 July 1811

By the following summer, however, Sadler was sufficiently recovered to complete an ascent from a location which must surely have long tempted him: Oxford's sister city of Cambridge. Appropriately enough, the occasion was, as in Oxford the previous year, the installation of a new University Chancellor, the Duke of Gloucester. Cambridge had never yet hosted a balloon ascent, explaining perhaps why the account of it was such a lengthy one in the *Morning Post* of 5 July 1811. As the day dawned, the city was so crowded that it seemed 'as if the surrounding Counties had emptied their contents to pour in here', and by nine o'clock people of all ranks had 'all flocked in, big with expectation, and hopeful of gratification!' By 10 a.m., several thousand people had assembled inside Trinity Square. These were stated to be mainly women, and by midday the crush – with the added discomfort of persistent rain – had resulted in many injuries and a necessity for peace officers to intervene.

Again, the newspapers reported that Sadler intended to ascend with his daughter, Sybella, 'an interesting little girl, only fourteen years of age'. Indeed, *Jackson's Oxford Journal* (6 July) reported that his intention was that he would take *two* daughters with him. This is the only slender evidence that Eliza, who would then have been twenty-six, might have still been alive, although it might also refer to his very recently married oldest daughter, thirty-four-year-old Mary Ann (*see* Appendix 8). Whatever, when the weather conditions on the day again proved unfavourable, neither daughter was permitted to go, and a last-minute replacement passenger, described as both Captain and Lieutenant Paget of the Royal Navy, stepped forward.

At 1.30 p.m., with all seemingly ready, the new chancellor and various dignitaries, including Sadler's staunch ally, Sir John Hippisley, were summoned, and at 2 p.m. Sadler prepared to lift off. However, in a scenario familiar to all regular observers, the balloon proved incapable of lifting the combined weight of both men, so Paget was obliged to step down.[48] Sadler's 'interesting little' daughter, Sybella, then

> embraced her parent, who returned the embrace with a parental feeling, to which description is inadequate. The tear of affection bedewed the cheeks of both, and the sentiment communicated itself to the surrounding spectators, who, while they participated in the feelings of the father and the child, almost at the same instance bore testimony to his character as a man, and as the unfortunate father of a large family (for unfortunate he has been!) by a sympathy expressed but by the silent tear.[49]

Was it a tear of emotion, one wonders, or more of regret, at having to eschew a lucrative payload? According to the *Ipswich Journal* (6 July), Paget had offered to pay 300 guineas for his place (or 100 guineas, according to *Jackson's* of the same date). It is an unusually emotive description, and one cannot help but wonder, in view of this further reference to a (non-existent) 'large family', if someone – Sadler's ally Hippisley perhaps? – had had a word with the editor, in order to try to increase public sympathy and generosity!

The ascent finally took place at 2.20 p.m. One hour and thirty-five minutes later Sadler descended near Stanstead, Essex, a distance of 23 miles as the crow flies (although Sadler himself estimated to have travelled about 80 miles in total).[50] He landed in a barley field and was propelled across another field until temporarily arrested by a hedge. There a man got a grip 'but the violence of the wind soon disengaged the car, which was dragged, with the man, to a great distance, until stopped by another hedge', after which more help eventually arrived.[51]

On the way back to Cambridge in a post-chaise and four, Sadler happened to pass the carriage of the newly installed chancellor, the Duke of Gloucester, going in the other direction. On realising this, the duke called a halt and 'sent one of his servants to go after him, and Mr. Sadler directed the boys to turn round, got out of the chaise, and paid his respects to his Highness, who very condescendingly congratulated him on a safe voyage'.[52] Once back in Cambridge, Sadler composed himself at the house of a Mr Nicholson, in Trumpington Street, opposite Trinity College's gate, where, news having spread, he responded to all enquiries 'with a politeness and affability which made a great impression in his favour'. The *Morning Post* concluded its account with Sadler's reappearance at about 9 p.m. at Trinity College, where the remaining dignitaries awaited his return.[53] Not bad for a man who could 'hardly speak a word of Grammar': a 'double first', at Oxford *and* at Cambridge!

Hackney, London: Monday 12 August 1811

Throughout his flying career, Sadler had never endeavoured to ascend from London. Then as now, to attract maximum publicity and maximum revenue, no matter what the nature of the spectacle, London was the obvious location. All the other early aeronauts had increased their fame and fortune – or at least their chances of them – by appearing there at the earliest opportunity. The closest Sadler had come was in 1785 when passing surreptitiously south of the capital with William Windham. Now he addressed the omission, albeit still not from the city centre.

Monday 12 August 1811 marked 'the venerable and intrepid'[54] Sadler's London debut, in Hackney. The *Morning Post* (13 August) thought that at 'no one time within our memory, from the ascent of the first aerial traveller ... did we ever witness curiosity so much on the alert'. The newspaper implied that this interest, guaranteed to be stirred for any balloon ascent, was especially prevalent on account of 'the fame of Mr. Sadler spread wide and near, and being the only English traveller who ever ventured so many times to mount aloft'. This 'occasioned an immense crowd of spectators to flock from all parts of the metropolis and adjacent counties', including everyone 'from the titled peer to the humble cabbage venders [*sic*]'. He ascended from the Mermaid, Hackney 'dressed in black'. His companion that day, in 'a blue coat and nankeen pantaloons', was Charles Paget, whose disappointment at being left behind in Cambridge therefore lasted little more than a month. Likewise Sadler's disappointment at the lost revenue his omission represented, since Paget paid 100 guineas for his place.[55] This was a rare example of Sadler ascending with anyone other than a family member. He was not, one gets the impression, the most sociable, the most companionable of individuals.

The balloon was the same as that used at Cambridge, but with a new carriage, decorated in honour of the Prince Regent's birthday that day. Sadler's son – presumably John – supervised the launch,[56] and when he 'desired all hands to let go'[57] lift-off occurred at 2.42 p.m.[58] The two men were taken in an easterly direction, 'the sound of a piece of ordnance from Woolwich was distinctly heard', and several more guns fired in salute as they progressed. After crossing the Thames, Paget looked down for the first time to see London resembling a small village, 'nor could he be persuaded to the contrary, till the four bridges, namely, London, Westminster, Blackfriars, and Battersea ... were pointed out to him by Mr. Sadler'.[59]

Nearing Gravesend and the sea, they descended low enough to hear voices on some boats, and the question 'Where are you going?' The answer proved to be not very much farther, as they touched down almost immediately, to the north of the river. A rising gale complicated the situation, however, and while being pursued by some men who had been working in a nearby wheat field 'the grappling irons ... caught in the cloaths of a labourer, and he became so completely entangled, that he could not extricate himself, till his shirt was literally torn from his back'. As the balloon continued its bumpy journey, Paget was thrown out, but managed to hold on, and they came to rest within 300 yards of Tilbury Fort and 150 yards from the river, at 3.55 p.m. Tactfully, 'Mr. Sadler, in alluding to the various occurrences of the voyage, pays the highest compliments to Mr. Paget, whose steadiness, intrepidity, and personal courage, he says he cannot sufficiently admire.'[60] Sadler too was accorded due praise: 'In the many ascensions of aeronauts was never witnessed, either in Garnerin or Lunardi (certainly both men of courage and skill), more of self-possession, or of the latter quality, than was evinced by Mr. Saddler.'[61]

Balloon ascents had almost always been notorious for attracting gangs of pickpockets. The situation was ideal, of course. Even the most incompetently ham-fisted thief enjoyed an increased chance of success amongst hundreds of jostling individuals standing with their attention focussed firmly towards the sky. It presented, so to speak, a heaven-sent opportunity! Even when the authorities anticipated such criminality – order was kept by Peace Officers and the Tower Hamlets Militia on this occasion[62] – they were often outwitted. Thus the *Ipswich Journal* (17 August) reported that a Mr W. A. Smith (of Park-street, Westminster), Major A. Gordon and Dr Roberts of St Paul's School all had their pockets picked in Hackney while watching Sadler's balloon ascend. The major was unwise enough to have had the enormous sum of £50 on him. Given such rich pickings, you can understand why criminals might take the risk, capital offence though this was. The *Derby Mercury* (22 August) neatly summed up the situation as:

> *Example is catching.* No sooner did Mr. Sadler's Balloon mount up on Monday, than the purses and watches of sundry Gentlemen *took flight* at the same time, and it is a moot point whether they, or the Balloon, were sooner *out of sight*!

In keeping with a pattern that Sadler had favoured in the past, of making two ascents from a single destination – as in Oxford in 1784, and Worcester and Manchester in 1785 – Hackney was treated to another demonstration before the end of the month. His idea may have been to test local conditions on the lower-key first ascent, before a more demanding public showing, while ensuring that the second one became all the more public as a result of the greatly increased awareness the first one was likely to generate. Indeed, the crowds this time – pickpockets or not – were estimated by *Morning Chronicle* of 30 August to be even larger than had gathered at the first.

Hackney: Thursday 29 August 1811

Sadler's second Hackney launch was also from the Mermaid. His companion this time was Henry Benjamin Hanbury Beaufoy (1786–1851), son of Colonel (Mark) Beaufoy 'of the Tower Hamlets

Militia',[63] which tried, with limited success, to keep order on the day. The departure was delayed because, as the *Morning Post* (30 August) put it:

> Those who were employed to repress the troublesome curiosity of others found it a still more difficult task to subdue their own, and in their eagerness to enjoy the spectacle, they seemed in a great measure to forget their duty.

Then, while the balloon was filling, 'a poor man, employed amongst the apparatus, received a severe wound in the head, by the falling of a piece of timber' and 'the roof of a building adjoining the garden, which was loaded with spectators, also fell in, but no person was much hurt'.[64] Amidst this apparent chaos, a small pilot paper balloon was launched by one of Sadler's sons to ascertain the wind direction.[65] Again one must presume that this was John, who was living in Hackney at this time,[66] and was employed as superintendent of the Beaufoy vinegar works in Lambeth (*see* Appendix 8). Beaufoy published an account of the trip as *Journal kept by H. B. H. B.* in which, while refraining from identifying himself by name, he confirmed the disorderly preparations, stating that by about 2.30 p.m.

> Mr. Sadler and his companion entered the car, with their instruments, &c. But owing to the excessive confusion, caused by the unwillingness of those that held the car to let go; each individual vociferating at the same time "*Let go, Let go*," though each was unwilling to be the first to set the example, it was not till twenty minutes before three that the machine was launched.[67]

Their instruments included a 'watch, barometer, thermometer, Kater's hygrometer, electrometer, a mariner's compass, and a needle compass', with which Beaufoy hoped to counter the long-held criticism that 'few of the aerial voyages that have been performed either in England, or on the Continent, have been undertaken with reference to philosophical investigation'.[68]

The balloon moved eastwards, over Walthamstow and Chelmsford, where, at about 3.30 p.m., they encountered 'a severe storm, which forced the balloon to and fro in a frightful manner, and twirled it about with great rapidity. While in this state they were visited by a hail storm, which rattled against their vehicle with great violence'.[69] During the flight, Sadler released seven carrier pigeons, all of which returned immediately to the balloon, but were later persuaded to desert it and fly back to their roosts. At least, six were; the seventh, however, 'instead of obeying the wishes of its master, flew to the top of the balloon, and there kept its station until the descent, when it flew into a tree, from whence it was driven by a boy sent up for the purpose. It did not arrive at home till yesterday morning.'[70] The *Times* (31 August) thought it worth mentioning that the seventh pigeon was not the only other passenger: when the balloon was at its greatest altitude, stated to be precisely 5,861 feet, 'a fly, which ... was discovered by Mr. Sadler perched on the rim of the car, on being disturbed by him, rose without difficulty, and took its station in the netting of the balloon'. The precision of the altitudinal measurement certainly confirms Beaufoy's desire to make the flight one of scientific importance, even if the *Times*' correspondent did surely fail to understand that it was not a fly but the seventh pigeon which was being described!

When the balloon descended to land at East Thorpe, near Colchester, Sadler advised his passenger to be prepared 'to heave overboard every thing that would admit of it, with a view to breaking the force of the descent'.[71] The precaution proved unnecessary, however, and the landing was, according to Sadler, 'particularly favourable', although they did nonetheless bump along the ground for several hundred yards until restrained by some people on the ground, among them a farmer called Thomas Ely, to whose house both the aeronauts proceeded, along with the equipment. At least, that was one version, that of Beaufoy himself. The *Morning Post* (30 August) produced this very much more colourful account, with the cautious proviso that it was being printed 'just as we received it'. During the descent

one of the grappling-irons unfortunately caught the clothes of an old apple-woman. She had, however, presence of mind enough to cling to her stall, which with herself was dragged after the car with inconceivable rapidity. The other grappling-iron shortly afterwards caught one of the hind legs of a donkey who had come to offer his assistance, attracted it is supposed, by the voice of Mr. S. The animal roared out aloud, and the sound is described by the Aeronauts as having the effect of thunder on those in the Balloon.

The huckstress, however, rendered desperate by her perilous situation, threw one arm franticly over Mr B.'s head, and proceeded to score his face as she would a leg of pork for the spit. By this time a number of persons were endeavouring to assist them, the car often touched the ground, and bounded up again, and the Balloon still continuing in motion, dragged the party through the horse-pond ... and shortly after, passing through a brier hedge, Mr. S.'s hat was torn off his head, and Mr. B.'s body out of the car. Fortunately he kept his hold, and hung dangling between the old woman and the donkey, till the Balloon stopped … against the back door of a little hedge ale-house.

On landing Mr. B. washed his face with brandy. Mr. S. *generously* gave the old woman three-pence for the loss of her apples. She grumbled, but the Aeronauts passed on, and went into the ale-house where they dried themselves. They then returned to the Mermaid. Mr. B. was in excellent spirits, and quite delighted with the voyage. After supper he sang a song with great spirit and effect, to the tune of 'Fools and their money are soon parted'.

Presumably it was not a tune selected with Sadler's mere thruppence compensation in mind! To be fair to the *Post*, this slapstick account appears to have been gleaned from the two men during their celebration back at the Mermaid the same night. An element of alcohol-fuelled exaggeration had, perhaps, infiltrated the facts!

As with the first Hackney ascent, pickpockets were again out in force – perhaps encouraged by the *Morning Post*'s incautious revelation that men like Major Gordon carried in their pockets what was for many working people the equivalent of several years' pay! The same newspaper implied that the thefts had been coordinated by 'some hundred' pickpockets who arrived at the launch 'in coaches, chaises, gigs, &c. which they left at the entrance of the church-yard, bridge &c.; so that after the Balloon had ascended the most systematic scene of confusion was occasioned'. As a result

the villains had the public completely at their command, and emptied their pockets with the most daring audacity. One Gentleman, who was robbed of this pocket-book containing 28*l*. which he saw in the villain's hand, seized him by the collar, calling for Constable and Police Officers in vain, but was at length obliged to let the robber go, having contrived to bite his hand to that degree that his teeth met.[72]

There follows a list of more than thirty named 'Captains of gangs' who the *Morning Post* felt should have been arrested on sight. We shall never know if Conkey Bean, Jack the Baker, Old Pullen, or any others of those named, were really culpable, but one man who *was* brought to account was Abraham Levy, 'a well-known Jew pickpocket', who was later committed for trial at Bow Street for the theft of a pocket book.[73]

Birmingham: Monday 7 October 1811

Sadler's final ascent of 1811 proved to be his most significant since his very first in October 1784, as it turned out to be the fastest journey any human had ever undertaken,[74] an achievement commemorated by the medal referred to in the Preface. He had been discussing the idea of a Birmingham ascent at the time of the Cambridge one in July, and must surely have had it in his mind ever since the end of 1784, when he chose to go to Dover rather than with Harper. To prepare, he had travelled to Birmingham to make arrangements in between his two Hackney flights in August.[75]

The balloon and car were first displayed at Coventry, then taken to Birmingham[76] for what was billed as Sadler's twenty-first ascent,[77] a further increase by one of his true known total (of fourteen). Vauxhall – pleasure gardens named after those in London – was selected for the launch, but when it proved too windy on the day intended, the Saturday, a contingent of Scots Greys assisted by the police escorted the balloon back to its 'former place of exhibition, a temporary building in Cherry-street'.[78]

Indeed, there must surely have been a still more ferocious wind raging on the Monday, in view of what subsequently occurred, but Sadler and his companion, John Burcham of East Dereham in Norfolk,[79] probably felt that they had no option but to risk it rather than test the patience of the crowd a second time. The authorities may well still have been mindful of the last time a balloon failed to launch in Birmingham, and the fatal disturbances which were attributable to Harper at that time.

So, at 2.14 p.m., like it or not, off they went! As the balloon was visible for only 3 minutes before being engulfed by cloud, the Scots Greys probably braced themselves for trouble on account of the brevity of the entertainment, there being 'a greater number of spectators than was ever before known to be assembled' in Birmingham (estimated by Sadler himself as 'not less than 170,000'[80]). Fortunately for all concerned the balloon soon re-emerged, and 'shouts of joy reiterated from all quarters'. As a result, 'no accidents of consequence happened; and the regiment of Scotch Greys performed their duty in keeping the mob from doing mischief to the adjoining plantations'.[81]

About 112 miles away, a mere 80 minutes later, in the parish of Burton Pedwardine in Lincolnshire, near Sleaford, the balloon came to earth – with a bump! Indeed, with many bumps, constituting one of the most hazardous landings Sadler had ever experienced. He himself was thrown out of the car on first impact. As a result he received several contusions to the head, though 'had sufficient presence of mind to call out to Mr. Burcham not to quit his seat'.[82]

The balloon was then carried a further 1½ miles (to Asgarby) where its anchor finally caught in the field of a Mr Godson. With the gale still raging, 'the silk of the balloon clung round an ash tree in a most extraordinary way, insinuating itself amongst the branches, so as to be torn into a thousand pieces'.[83] An undoubtedly traumatised Burcham was escorted to Godson's house to recover. Meanwhile, Sadler

> made his way to the neighbouring house of a miller, where he borrowed a shoe (having lost one of his own); the miller taking care to have his *quid pro quo*, by receiving a pledge of some money, which the aeronaut happily had about him.[84]

The *Morning Chronicle* (11 October) paints a still less sanguine picture of the miller, saying that

> Mr. Sadler losing one of his shoes on his expulsion from the balloon, he made towards a mill, and begged an old one, which the inhuman boor refused under 7s though not worth two pence. He was, however, recognised in the crowd, and forced to refund, amidst the execrations of all present.

In this state of unmatching footwear, Sadler made his way to Heckington, about 2 miles away. There he was reunited with Burcham, 'each, the moment before, fancying the other killed ... they *flew* into each other's arms with ... enraptured expressions of joy'. The balloon had been destroyed, but the car was still intact, and was taken to the Crown Inn at Heckington. The two men rested at Edward Robinson's house until 3 a.m., then set off on the return journey to Birmingham. So, not even a full night's rest, in those days of infrequent transport, despite having so very recently travelled faster, at an average of 84 mph, than any humans ever had before![85] When the two men arrived back in Birmingham at 9.30 p.m. the following evening:

> the bells rang merry peals, and the firing of guns, pistols, &c announced the welcome intelligence. The populace afterwards drew the carriage with Mr. Sadler jnr. in charge of the balloon through the principal streets, surrounded with lighted torches. In a few minutes the crowd before the residence of Mr. Sadler became so great that to satisfy their impatient anxiety the aerial travellers obligingly presented themselves at

the window, and their presence was most rapturously hailed with long and continued *vivas*.[86]

Unsurprisingly, the whole affair seems to have taken its toll on poor old Sadler. The next time we hear of him, the *Morning Chronicle* of 14 March 1812 was informing its readers that: 'In consequence of the accident which happened to him on his last ascension, he has been confined for upwards of three months to his room.' Nonetheless, he was apparently sufficiently recovered to be preparing for another Birmingham ascent that spring, having 'adopted precautions against a similar misfortune', as it was somewhat disparagingly described, with no mention at all of the astonishing achievement of speed and distance. The 'precautions' included a reticulated texture woven into the silk, to prevent bursting. He was also 'engaged in the completion of a magnificent balloon for the entertainment of the people of Dublin, which place he intends visiting in the summer'. No second ascent was ever made from Birmingham, but the *Chronicle* was right about Dublin, from where Sadler embarked on his most ambitious project yet in October. Before that though, he made a return visit to the familiar environs of Manchester, a place where the streets in proximity to the location of his 1785 ascent had been renamed Balloon Street and Back Balloon Street in his honour.

Manchester: Monday 29 June 1812

One of the earliest accounts of Sadler's return to Manchester, from where he ascended on Monday 29 June from St George's Fields (about one mile to the south of the city centre) appeared in the *Derby Mercury* of 2 July 1812. A week later the newspaper carried a fuller account, under the heading 'Narrative of Mr Sadler's 23rd Voyage'. Once again, there had been a miscalculation or a deliberate exaggeration. In view of its detail, mundane though much of it was, the *Mercury*'s account seems to have come from Sadler himself. A pilot balloon – one of the changes in standard procedure that the new century had inspired – was dispatched at 1.30 p.m., to assess the wind direction, and Sadler himself followed it a few minutes later. The journey lasted less than an hour, and seems to have been fairly uneventful, the emptying of a bottle of water, in order to fill it with altitudinal air, being the only noteworthy occurrence. The event, linked to those of May 1785, was later summarised as

> *En passant*, we mention the gay month of June,
> When the town was delighted with Sadler's Balloon
> Which, majestic ascending, the aeronaut bore,
> Almost in the line he had sail'd in before,
> When, twenty-five years gone, he'd gladden'd men's eyes
> By seeing him, leave Howarth's grounds for the skies.[87]

'Majestic ascending' or not, the landing was a different matter, another dramatic affair. *Just* another, one might say, as Sadler must surely by now have come to accept that a few cuts and bruises were an almost inevitable corollary to the experience. In attempting perforce to land on some moorland where there was little hope of the anchor finding purchase, it struck a cart, which Sadler 'considered fortunate, but the horses taking fright, in consequence of the drivers running away in fear, the cart turned round, and the grapple got loose'. Several miles later, after repeatedly striking the ground, which was punctuated by rocks, his progress was finally arrested when he became entangled in a large tree at Oaks Wood (near Bradfield), about 6 miles west of Sheffield. Some men from the Damflask paper mills came immediately to his assistance, along with the proprietor, Mr Hardern.

It had been another undignified, hazardous, and no doubt painful landing – but it had also been another extraordinarily rapid journey. Not quite as remarkable as that from Birmingham the previous year, but to cover 50 miles in 48 minutes was no mean feat, especially as Sadler calculated that he had also at one point climbed to (perhaps his highest ever altitude of) 3 miles and 640 yards.[88] Yet – as with the record-breaking flight from Birmingham – the achievement raised little by way of wider acclaim. Indeed, rather the opposite. This literary flight of fancy (appearing first in the *Manchester Gazette*) was printed in the *Liverpool Mercury* of 7 August. Drawing the stinging conclusion that the 'aërial excursion ... has every thing to recommend it but *Safety and Utility*' it began:

> Imagination can scarcely conceive a more whimsically impressive, and, could we divest it of its danger, ludicrous scene, than that of a human being, rapidly descending from the clouds in a car, appended to an immense balloon, dancing upon the tops of trees, and capering, with no other fiddle than the whistling winds, from hedge to hedge, and thicket to thicket!

Who, then, was this 'ludicrous' human? Why, James Sadler, of course!

Fancy only a man in this perilous pickle, a large fur cap on his head, enveloped besides in several yards of flannel, making his caput as big as a beehive ... dropping upon a team of horses, and throwing out an anchor, grappling one of the wheels – the carter, poor fellow, and his lad, never having seen nor heard of a balloon in their lives – the horses, terror-struck running one way, and their drivers, as full of fear as the balloon was of gas, running another.

All the sins of the affrighted carter – all the blue devils that ever haunted the conscience of a candidate for purgatory, at that dreadful moment, we dare say, rushed into his mind; nor were they dissipated till he found honest Sadler, the heavenly visitant, was a mere mortal, and no more than flesh and blood like himself.[89]

The same issue of the *Liverpool Mercury* carried an advertisement for Sadler's next defiance of 'safety and utility', billed as his twenty-fourth ascension, which was to be from Liverpool itself. This was a city from where it had been rumoured that Sadler would ascend way back in 1785. That had been at a time when attempts were made to raise public interest by trying to suggest that he and Lunardi were competing to be the first to do so. The local advertising this time took a different tack, emphasising Sadler's undoubted celebrity in a rare acknowledgement of his journey of 'upwards of 112 miles in an Hour and 20 Minutes'.[90]

Liverpool: Wednesday 12 August 1812

The location chosen for the Liverpool ascent was the Pilgrim Pleasure Grounds in Everton, in front of St Domingo Church, described as a 'place admirably selected for public gratification, and equally well adapted for securing to the adventurous hero of the scene the liberal remuneration, so naturally to be expected from the spirited inhabitants of Liverpool'.[91]

The date selected, as the previous year at Hackney, was 12 August, the birthday of the Prince Regent. A notice in the *Liverpool Mercury* (7 August) advised that the public would be admitted at 10.30 a.m., and that the ascent would be at 1 p.m., though, as so often, there was a delay and it was not until 2.30 p.m. that Sadler climbed into the car

with a firm step, and a composed, cheerful countenance, notwithstanding the ceremony of shaking hands with the bye-standers, which perhaps might judiciously be dispensed with on such occasions, when self-possession and coolness are so very requisite.[92]

This 90 minute wait was the only mild criticism that the newspaper had of an event about which it was 'so delighted on the whole that we feel no disposition to cavil about trifles'. After a short flight, Sadler descended without incident about 30 minutes later at Derby Chapel, about 4 miles away. The *Mercury* reported that there were some in the crowd who were 'unreasonable enough' to question why Sadler had not spent longer in the air or flown farther. One practical explanation offered was that 'he would thereby have been unable to have availed himself of a sumptuous dinner' provided in his honour by the mayor of Liverpool that same evening!

What a contrast to those many other trips, where the only reward was a rough landing, immersion in the sea, destruction of his equipment or damage to his person, and a bumpy ride home through the night in a draughty carriage! As a further dash of refinement to what was one of his most dignified ascensions yet, Sadler later went to see 'The Beggar's Opera' at the theatre, 'where he was instantly recognized ... and welcomed with thunders of applause' (according to a letter-cum-review on the same page of the *Mercury* of 14 August). As a final tribute from the city which would retain close associations with the Sadler family well into the twentieth century, it was reported that the sculptor, George Bullock (1784/5–1818), intended 'to preserve the recollection of this memorable day' by fashioning a bust of Sadler to be placed in the Liverpool Academy.[93]

Dublin: Thursday 1 October 1812

The ascent from Liverpool seems to have been scheduled as a warm-up for the rather greater temptation of a Liverpool *descent*. Sadler's intention to try to cross the Irish Sea from Dublin had been known to the press in August, and had also been rumoured the previous year. Indeed, there had been talk of it as long ago as 1784. For Sadler, it must have been a tempting idea indeed. Though he had been foiled in his ambition to cross the English Channel all those years ago – and was apparently never tempted to try again, due no doubt to the ongoing political impossibility of such a journey rather than to its physical challenges – no one had yet crossed the Irish Sea, or St George's Channel, as it was then known.

The Irishman Richard Crosbie (1755–1824) had been the first man to attempt to make such a crossing, on 19 January 1785, and although he did become the first man to fly in Ireland, he came nowhere close to making the 70-mile crossing, having succeeded in travelling only a few miles. On a second attempt, on 12 May 1785, the result was still less impressive, in that the balloon failed to get off the ground at all. Consequently, Crosbie, a heavy, thick-set man weighing more than 16 stone, gave up his place to Richard McGuire, a twenty-year-old former student of Trinity College, who was more in the mould of a Blanchard or a Simonet, being half that weight.[94] McGuire ditched in the sea about 8 miles from the coast.[95] This was not a great deal better than Crosbie's first attempt, yet McGuire was honoured with an instant knighthood for his pains.[96] This was all a bit rough on Crosbie, who had borne the entire cost and who, on a final attempt on 19 July 1785, travelled considerably farther than McGuire before plunging into the sea, but received no honour at all.

As it turned out, although James Sadler improved on Crosbie's distance by a substantial margin, he too fell short of his goal on account of his determination to make Merseyside his specific destination. Many newspapers carried reports of the epic journey, but as a twenty-four-page printed account was produced on this occasion – *Balloon: an authentic narrative of the Æerial Voyage of Mr. Sadler across the Irish Channel* – the summary that follows is taken from there, as the presumed most authoritative account.[97]

As with his Bristol publication in 1810, the first section consisted of a third-person account, which implied that Sadler was honing his showmanship. The launch, in a balloon of 55 feet diameter, was from Belvedere House at Drumcondra, to the north of Dublin. Notable among the many distinguished guests were the Duke and Duchess of Richmond and Lady Mary Lennox.[98] As he made the necessary preparations:

> The mind of Mr. Sadler did not rest alone on *personal objects*, but extended itself to whatever could *gratify* or *accommodate* the numerous and splendid assemblage that attended; and ... whether we contemplate the vast Machine with which the Æerial Voyager entered upon his dauntless track – the brilliant and crowded concourse – the appearance of the Military – the process of Inflation – *the sensation of the moment* – all combined to produce an effect which as far *exceeded expectation* as it *baffles description*.[99]

Also in attendance, to posterity's great good fortune, was Richard Edgeworth's daughter, the novelist Maria (1768–1849). In describing

1. 'A View of part of St Mary's Church, All Saints Church, the Conduit, Carfax Church, &c in the University of Oxford' by John Donowell (1765). Joseph Skelton published his own engraving of this exact view in *Oxonia antiqua restaurata* (1823), adding: 'On the right of the print is the "Old Coach House", on the left is that of "King's Coffee House", which is the house now occupied by Sadler, the confectioner, above which, on the same side, is the sign of the "King's Arms Tavern", being the house now belonging to Wyatt, the Carver and Gilder.' (Courtesy of Sanders of Oxford. www.sandersofoxford.com)

2. 'University & Queen's Colleges' by J. Hill after Augustus Pugin in Rudolph Ackermann's *A History of the University of Oxford, its Colleges, Halls and Public Buildings* (1814). The coach on the right is outside the Angel Hotel, which by this time had expanded into the Sadlers' former residence of No. 84. (Courtesy of Sanders of Oxford. www.sandersofoxford.com)

3. The Angel Hotel, incorporating both Nos 83 and 84 High Street, in the 1820s (on the basis that Thomas Gellett was the innkeeper for most of that decade). The coach on the left is labelled 'Oxford / Cheltenham / London'. (Courtesy of Stephanie Jenkins)

4. Nos 83 and 84 High Street. To the left are the university's Examination Schools which replaced the Angel Hotel in 1866. No. 83 is where in 1874 the first batch of 'Frank Cooper's Oxford Marmalade' was made. (Author's collection)

5. 'Dr Sibthorp's House from Christ Church Meadow' (1798) by an unknown pupil of John Malchair. Now part of St Hilda's College, this is where James Sadler's first experimental launch of a balloon was made on 9 February 1784. (Bodleian Library, University of Oxford: MS Top Oxon c475 fol. 72)

6. 'Physic Garden &c.' in 1766, by Joseph Skelton after B. Green, from *Oxonia Antiqua Restaurata* (1823). (Courtesy of Sanders of Oxford: www.sandersofoxford.com)

Ascensione del Lunardi Londra 13-5-1785

7. 'Ascensione del Lunardi Londra 13-5-1785' by V. Cioni. The image of the balloon and its occupants (Mrs Sage, Vincenzo Lunardi and George Biggin) has been copied from a larger print by John Jones, and transferred to a decidedly non-London landscape! The image is doubly misleading in that only Lunardi actually ascended that day. (Courtesy of the Johnson Museum, Lichfield)

Right: 8. James Sadler, 'first English Ærostatist', by Edmund Scott after James Roberts, 2 May 1785.

Below: 9. The first balloon crossing of the English Channel, 7 January 1785, by E. W. Cocks (painted about 1840). Cocks also painted at about the same time *Balloon over Cliffs, Dover*, presumably representing the same event, in which the location of the launch is shown as being to the east of the castle.

10. 'Mr. Sadler: first English Ærostatist' from the *New London Magazine* of December 1785, 'curiously engraved by Thornton'.

11. Motif from the lid of a lady's patch box, copied from a photograph in J. E. Hodgson's *History of Aeronautics in Great Britain* (drawing by Valerie Petts). A similar design features on the lid of a snuffbox in the London Science Museum's Penn-Gaskell Collection, and also (but with two figures in the basket) on the ticket for Harper's first Birmingham ascent (in the Sarah Sophia Banks Collection at the British Museum).

JEAN PIERRE   BLANCHARD.

12. Jean Pierre Blanchard by L. Sewel, 1 July 1785. (Courtesy of Sanders of Oxford www. sandersofoxford.com)

The Right Hon.ble Will.m Windham M.P.

13. William Windham MP, by William Say, after John Hoppner 1803. (Courtesy of the National Portrait Gallery, London)

14. 'The Three Favorite Aerial Travellers' by Francis Bartolozzi after John Rigaud, 25 June 1785, showing the *anticipated* ascent of, left to right, George Biggin, Mrs Sage and Vincenzo Lunardi, though only Biggin and Sage actually ascended (four days later).

15. 'A Sage Lady's Second Experiment' by Thomas Rowlandson, September 1785. (Courtesy of the Royal Aeronautical Society: National Aerospace Library)

16. Mrs Sage, oil painting on canvas by unknown artist. The portrait is about 2.5 feet by 2 feet, and is one of hundreds of aeronautical items donated to the Science Museum in 1949 by Miss Winifred Penn-Gaskell. (Courtesy of the Science Museum / Science & Society Picture Library)

17. 'Fowls of a Feather Flock together' by John Kay (1742–1820) from *Kay's Original Portraits* (1838). The editor, Hugh Paton, with recourse to Kay's own notes and those of other contemporaries, identified the seven individuals as (left to right): John Mitchell, hardware merchant; an anonymous 'ingenious artist'; James Tytler; Vincenzo Lunardi; James Neilson (looking towards the left), a friend of Lunardi's; John Spottiswood, magistrate (looking towards the right); and Myles McPhail, who collected Lunardi's ticket money for at least one of his three Edinburgh ascents of 1785.

18. Thomas Beddoes by Charles Warren after Edward Bird (posthumous, 1810) from *Memoir of the Life of Thomas Beddoes* (1811) by John Edmonds Stock.

19. James Sadler's signature on his letter of 14 January 1791 to Thomas Beddoes. (Courtesy of the University of Oxford, Bodleian Library, and Mrs Tana Fletcher)

Left: 20. No. 6, Dowry Square, Bristol, formerly Thomas Beddoes' 'Pneumatic Institute'. (Author's collection) *Right:* 21. 'Sadler's Sharp Shooter' by Thomas Rowlandson from *Loyal Volunteers of London* (1799). 'A private of this corps defending himself with Sadler's Patent Gun, and long cutting Bayonet.' (Courtesy of the President and Fellows of Trinity College, Oxford)

Above: 22. 'Mr. Sadler's ascent from Merton Fields', July 1810 (with his son John). (Courtesy of Oxford University Museum of the History of Science)

Left: 23. James and John Sadler leaving Oxford, 1810, by R. Havell after E. M. Jones.

24. James Sadler and William Henry Clayfield in the Bristol Channel, 1810, by E. M. Jones. Apparently, the Severn really was as placid on the day as this view suggests.

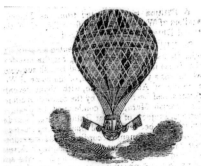

Left: 25. James Sadler leaving Dublin, 1812, by R. Havell. *Right:* 26. Advertisement in the
Oxford University & City Herald of 27 April 1816 for Windham Sadler's lecture in Oxford,
including a very rare depiction of one of his balloons. The lecture was popular enough to
warrant two more the following week.

27 and 28. The medal struck to commemorate Sadler's speed record of 1811, designed by
Peter Wyon. This example was discovered during the demolition of a building in Oxford in
the 1920s. (Courtesy of Oxford University Museum of the History of Science)

29. 'The perilous situation of Mr. Sadler' in the Irish Sea, 1812. (Courtesy of the Trustees of the British Museum)

30. 'The Chinese Pagoda & Bridge' St James's Park, London, 1 August 1814. The view shows John Sadler's balloon soon after its departure from the lawn in front of Buckingham House (in the background, to the right of the Pagoda). (Courtesy of the Science Museum / Science & Society Picture Library)

31. James Sadler possibly by Richard Evans, *c.* 1816. Given the approximate date, could this perhaps have been commissioned as a seventieth-birthday present? The original is nearly 5 feet by nearly 4 feet, so was a considerable undertaking. (Courtesy of the National Portrait Gallery, London)

Left: 32. The gravestone of James Sadler at St Peter-in-the-East (now a part of St Edmund Hall), Oxford. It was refurbished by the Royal Aeronautical Society in 1984. (Author's collection)

Right: 33. Plaque in Deadman's Walk next to Merton Field and near the Botanic Gardens, Oxford, commemorating James Sadler's first flight of 1784. (Author's collection)

the event in a letter to her stepmother, Frances Ann Beaufort
(Edgeworth's fourth wife) she captures the anticipation, novelty and
breathless excitement so eloquently that almost her entire account,
with only slight abridgement, follows.[100] She and her father, two
half-brothers, Sneyd (1786–1864) and William (1794–1829), and
two half-sisters, Harriet (1801–89) and Fanny (1799–1848), had
made the 60-mile journey from Edgeworthstown to Dublin especially.
Evidently, conditions proved unfavourable on the scheduled day,
because 'the first morning was spent in cursing Mr. Sadler for not
going up'. The next day, however, the weather,

to our inexpressible joy, was fine, and the flag, the signal that Sadler
would ascend, was, to the joy of thousands, flying from the top of
Nelson's Pillar. Dressed quickly – breakfasted I don't know how – job
coach punctual: crowds in motion even at nine o'clock in the streets:
tide flowing all one way to Belvidere Gardens, lent by the proprietor for
the occasion: called at Sneyd's lodgings in Anne Street: he and William
gone: drove on; when we came near Belvidere such strings of carriages,
such crowds of people on the road and on the raised footpath, there
was no stirring: troops lined the road at each side: guard with officers
at each entrance to prevent mischief; but unfortunately there were only
two entrances, not nearly enough for such a confluence of people.

Most imprudently we and several others got out of our carriages
upon the raised footpath, in hopes of getting immediately at the garden
door, which was within two yards of us, but nothing I ever felt was
equal to the pressure of the crowd: they closed over our little heads,
I thought we must have been flattened, and the breath squeezed out
of our bodies. My father held Harriet fast, I behind him held Fanny
with such a grasp! and dragged her on with a force I did not know I
possessed. I really thought your children would never see you again
with all their bones whole, and I cannot tell you what I suffered for
ten minutes. My father, quite pale, calling with a stentor voice to the
sentinels. A fat woman nearly separated me from Fanny. My father
fairly kicked off the terrace a man who was intent upon nothing but
an odious bag of cakes which he held close to his breast, swearing
and pushing. Before us were Mrs. Smyley and Mr. Smyley, with a
lady he was protecting. Unable to protect anybody, he looked more
frightened than if he had lost a hundred causes: the lady continually
saying, 'Let me back! let me back! if I could once get to my carriage!'
The tide carried us on to the door. An admirable Scotch officer, who was
mounting guard with a drawn sword, his face dropping perspiration,
exclaimed at the sight of Harriet, 'Oh the child! take care of that child!

she will be crushed to death!' He made a soldier put his musket across the doorway, so as to force a place for her to creep under: quick as lightning in she darted, and Fanny and I and my father after her.

Once inside, the contrast was marked: 'all was serene, uncrowded, and fresh' with; music and the most festive scene in the gardens; the balloon, the beautiful many-coloured balloon, chiefly maroon in colour, with painted eagles, and garlands, and arms of Ireland, hung under the trees, and was filling fast from pipes. Well-dressed groups of people gathered both on the terrace of Belvidere House and 'all over the gardens, mantles, scarves, and feathers floating: all the commonalty outside in fields at half-price'. Soon after 'we made our way behind the heels of the troopers' horses, who guarded a sacred circle round the balloon' and 'got seats on the pedestal of some old statue, and talked and enjoyed ourselves: the balloon filling gradually'.

The drum beats! the flag flies! balloon full! It is moved from under the trees over the heads of the crowd: the car very light and slight – Mr. Sadler's son, a young lad, in the car. How the horses stood the motion of this vast body close to them I can't imagine, but they did. The boy got out. Mr. Sadler, quite composed, this being his twenty-sixth aërial ascent, got into his car: a lady, the Duchess of Richmond, I believe, presented to him a pretty flag: the balloon gave two majestic nods from side to side as the cords were cut. Whether the music continued at this moment to play or not, nobody can tell. No one spoke while the balloon successfully rose, rapidly cleared the trees, and floated above our heads: loud shouts and huzzas, one man close to us exclaiming, as he clasped his hands, 'Ah, musha, musha, GOD bless you! GOD be wid you!' Mr. Sadler, waving his flag and his hat, and bowing to the world below, soon pierced a white cloud, and disappeared; then emerging, the balloon looked like a moon, black on one side, silver on the other; then like a dark bubble; then less and less, and now only a speck is seen; and now the fleeting rack obscures it. Never did I feel the full merit of Darwin's description till then.[101]

The ascent is also described in Sadler's own publication, *Balloon*:

The Balloon was released and the *undaunted voyager* floated from the stage, majestically rising from the Earth on the bosom of the Air, and presenting a spectacle at once awful and sublime, which as it mocks description so was its effect attested by the unbidden tears that stole down many a cheek – for a moment all was *silent extacy* [*sic*] and *tremulous fear* followed by *bursts of applause*, not drawn forth by factitious circumstances, but excited by *real* and *undisguised admiration*.[102]

The rest of the first section of Sadler's *Balloon* is concerned with the technicalities of construction, followed by 'Mr. Sadler's Memoranda ... corrected by himself'. This seems certain to have been ghost-written from his own observations, bearing in mind the rudimentary style of his one and only surviving letter (of January 1791), and also John Coxe Hippisley's opinion (in a scrawled note of 20 September 1812) that Sadler 'has been harshly used ... there is not a better chymist or mechanic in the Universe, yet he can hardly speak a word of Grammar'.[103] Departing at 12.38 p.m., Sadler was soon looking down on Dublin,

> with its Suburbs skirting the Bay, which like a burnished Mirror reflecting the beams of the Sun, exhibited a blaze of Lustre too dazzling for the eye to rest upon – a Grove of Masts marked the course of the River, and passing Vessels animated by their swelling Sails the richness of the scene.[104]

He soon noticed a rent in the fabric, which was allowing gas to escape, and, at some risk, took measures to seal it. After 1 hour, the mountains of Wales became visible, and at 2 p.m. he saw the Isle of Man, 'indistinct and vast, like a broad shield amid the watery waste'.[105] Realising that his trajectory at this point was taking him towards Cumberland, rather than Merseyside, he ascended to try to find an appropriate current. At 3.20 p.m. he was north-west of Anglesey, at an altitude of 3 miles and 652 yards, but after hovering for some time without any lateral progress, he decided at 5.30 p.m., in view of the impending dusk, reluctantly to pitch into the sea, expecting that one of the five vessels in the vicinity would come to his aid.

He was, however, disappointed in his expectation, and when these boats continued on their course, he decided to re-ascend, so that 'the Sun whose parting beams I had already witnessed, again burst on my view, and encompassed me with the full blaze of day; beneath me hung the shadows of Evening; while the clear beams of the Sun glittered on the floating vehicle'. Recalling the pleasure that this double sunset experience had given Jacques Charles on the French chemist's one and only flight in 1783, Sadler duly acknowledged a similar thrill, feeling moved to 'almost feel a sentiment of thankfulness to the Captains of those Vessels who by their *cold* and *unfriendly* conduct *compelled* me to be a witness of this splendid object'.[106]

Sadler descended for the second time 30 minutes later (at 6 p.m.) in sight of two other vessels which had already signalled their awareness of him. However, the wind propelled him across the surface of the water at a greater speed than the boats, so in an attempt to create more drag, he removed some of his clothes, and tied them onto his grapple line, which he then threw into the water. This having little effect, he then reluctantly released some gas, with the result that, with ballast still aboard, he was 'frequently plunged under water by the rolling of the Balloon'. At the same time the loose contents of the basket were released and Sadler was soon 'surrounded by a multitude of small Sea-birds, who boldly approached the Balloon ... attracted to the Car, by fragments of cake and bread which fell upon the water'.[107]

Finally, one of the boats caught up with him, and, following Sadler's suggestion, ran its bowsprit through the balloon, in order to restrain it. The ordeal was still not over, however, as even after having grasped a rope which was thrown to him, Sadler was dragged for some distance, and was finally pulled on board only 'with much difficulty, having been in the water for at least half an hour, being quite exhausted, nearly insensible, and *almost lifeless*; a state in which I remained for a considerable time'.[108]

When he was sufficiently recovered, Sadler learned that he was on a herring boat called the *Victory* (commanded by John Lee from Douglas on the Isle of Man). Conveniently, the vessel was bound for Liverpool, where he disembarked early the next morning. Word of his arrival soon spread, but, 'wet and exhausted, I found myself for the moment unequal to meet their congratulations'.[109] Fortunately he found sanctuary from this unwanted attention aboard a naval vessel, HMS *Princess*, commanded by Lieutenant Roche, who provided him with dry clothes and 'every accommodation that my situation required'. He was, no doubt, disappointed at the way things had turned out, but also encouraged by the great, total distance he had travelled. It was apparent to him that given the quantity of ballast and gas which remained that 'I possessed sufficient power ... to have accomplished at once the passage of the Channel, had not my ardent desire to reach Liverpool operated as a counteracting principle.'[110] This desire had already been stated in the very first paragraph of his 'Memoranda', where he described Liverpool as 'a City to which I was bound by every tie of friendship, and by those feelings which kindness of the most marked and flattering kind excited'.[111]

He returned to Dublin via Holyhead on the evening of Saturday 3rd, quite possibly determined to have another attempt. That is what J. Fellowes, 'Agent of his Majesty's Packets' thought, stating that 'notwithstanding the great fatigue and anxiety he has undergone, he was in good spirits, and intends once more making an attempt to cross from Dublin, when the Moon is sufficiently old to enable him to see his way'.[112] That did not happen, in fact, and this 'most ingenious, but unfortunate man', as John Ingram Lockhart had called him a few years earlier,[113] had been foiled again by circumstance in his attempt to be the first man to cross a second symbolically significant stretch of open water. His consolation would come five years later, when he assisted Windham to succeed where he had narrowly failed.

Father and son were not reunited until the evening of Sunday 4th, a storm having obliged the ship on which Sadler was returning to berth at Skerries, 16 miles from Dublin.[114] The narrative of *Balloon* ends with the self-congratulatory thought that 'Mr. Sadler may with confidence look for that approbation which his talent and perseverance so amply entitle him to'. It was, as time would tell, an unjustifiably optimistic prediction.

11

LIKE FATHER LIKE SON: WINDHAM SADLER, HEIR TO THE AIR

By the end of November 1812, James Sadler was back in England.[1] Contemplating a more sedentary, yet in some ways complementary, means of earning a living, he put his knowledge of the properties of gas into establishing a soda water factory in central London, being listed as 'James Sadler, Soda Water-maker, 40 Brewer Street, Golden-square' in the *Post Office Directories* of 1813–16.

Windham Sadler's First Ascent: Cheltenham, Tuesday 7 September 1813

With this new venture to distract him, and given the exertions, and the immersions, of the Irish Sea crossing, one would have thought that James Sadler might have had enough of all this aerial galavanting by the time he celebrated his sixtieth birthday in 1813. Not a bit of it! Perhaps if his oldest son had shown more enthusiasm he might have been content to remain in a merely advisory role on *terra firma*. John, however, while he inherited much of his father's technical aptitude, evidently had only occasional thoughts of following in his supra-nebulous footsteps. His second son, James (born 1780), was pursuing a military career in India, and the third, Thomas (born 1782) cannot be reliably traced (*see* Appendices 2 *and* 9). James's youngest son

William Windham (1796–1824), however, was a definite chip off the old block in two respects: his enthusiasm for both engineering *and* flying.

Always known as Windham, his first introduction to solo ballooning came at Cheltenham, on Tuesday 7 September 1813, aged sixteen. It was unpremeditated, James having either intended going alone or to have taken his son as co-pilot. The advertised intention had been to go up the day before, in fact, but a 'tremendous hurricane' halted preparations at what was called 'the Iron-railway Company's yard' where the balloon was stationed.[2] As always, any cancellation increased the pressure: 'The storm has caused great dismay and disappointment to appear upon every countenance', the *Morning Chronicle* (9 September) advised, piling on the hyperbole with 'more so than any thing that ever occurred in this country'.

As a precaution against dismay and disappointment turning to disturbance and destruction, James Sadler had swiftly circulated handbills to say that he would now ascend the next day, the Tuesday, weather permitting. However, this decision had apparently been made without consulting the organisers, who, not wishing to clash with the Hereford Music Meeting, which was due to start on the same day, deemed that the launch should be postponed until the Friday. Poor Sadler! All this uncertainty on top of the unfavourable weather and the usual multitude of responsibilities and worries that even a well-planned launch entailed. Yet it was he who got his way, since, while every effort had been made to circulate the news of the second proposed postponement, so many people were already flooding into the town that the Committee felt it wise to accede to Sadler's wishes. Meanwhile, not every Cheltenham countenance exhibited 'dismay and disappointment'. The landlord of the White Hart, for instance, shrewdly acquired an extra 'twelve buttocks of beef' with which to tempt the large numbers of detained visitors, and arranged a sparring exhibition 'by professed pugilists, consisting of the Ruffian, Abrahams, and a man of colour'.[3] At the same time, playing surely to packed audiences, was 'The Mogul Tale, or the Descent of the Balloon', a short play (by Elizabeth Inchbald, first performed in 1784) about three Europeans who float by accident into an Asian seraglio.

At 10 a.m. the next day, Tuesday 7th, the balloon was duly taken from the Assembly Rooms, where it had been on display, to the railway yard on the Gloucester Road. Sadler followed at 11 a.m. With him were his 'Committee', comprising 'twelve gentlemen of the town, distinguished by wearing on their breasts large silver medals, that were presented to Mr. Sadler by the inhabitants of Birmingham after his last ascension from that place'.[4] The wind was still an impediment and it took until 4.20 p.m. for all to be ready. Even then, when Sadler got into the basket his weight proved too great so Windham, 'an interesting youth', replaced him 'with all the composure, fortitude, courage, and indifference which his veteran father possesses'.[5] The wind having by then eased, the balloon ascended without difficulty at about 5 p.m. It remained in sight for several minutes, and Windham could hear the voices of people on the ground for 10 minutes. At one point he 'encountered a thick fall of snow that beat against the balloon with so much force, that it was with the utmost exertion that he could open the valve'.[6] He descended low enough to hear voices again in the vicinity of Wychwood Forest, before throwing out ballast in order to avoid the tops of the trees and to continue on his way.

Down on the ground, James followed his course in a carriage; John did the same on horseback.[7] They discontinued their pursuit on meeting someone who reliably informed them that Windham had descended safely at Chipping Norton. After finding somewhere to stay for the night they returned to Cheltenham early on the Wednesday morning, expecting to find that Windham would already have returned. However, although he had indeed alighted near Chipping Norton (Chadlington, in fact), Windham had made the decision to continue to Oxford for the night, 'accompanied by a cousin'.[8] It was not until 1.45 p.m. the next day that he found his way back to Cheltenham, with the balloon and car, on a post-chaise. What relief his anxious father and half-brother must have felt, *and* what pride! At sixteen years of age, Windham would appear at that moment to have become the youngest ever solo aeronaut.

Newspapers had always vacillated between accusations of avaricious aeronauts fleecing the public or the miserly public failing to adequately remunerate the intrepid aerial adventurers. On this occasion, the *Morning Chronicle* (10 September) took the latter line:

> It is greatly to be lamented, that out of the immense concourse few indeed paid for admission to see the operation of filling the balloon and the ascension; and the ingenious and enterprising artist, Mr. Sadler, the first English aeronaut, will be a loser of several hundred pounds, instead of being a gainer of so much at least, especially as he was invited here by a number of the inhabitants, and from their allurements he was induced to give up a lucrative engagement to ascend from Ireland.

It is impossible to say how true any of this was. It would no doubt be quite tempting for a balloonist to maintain that his costs had exceeded his outgoings whatever the true situation, and it would seem only common sense for Sadler to have got his mysteriously bemedalled committee to underwrite the cost. Yet Sadler seems always to have struggled with the financial and legal aspects of his chosen career, and consistently took all the financial risk himself. This tendency towards a lack of prudence would be shown most clearly a month later – and on this next occasion, he failed even to get anywhere *close* to leaving the ground!

Derby Days

Evidently, when a Mr Wilkes had failed even to inflate his balloon at Derby on 20 September 1813, a section of the crowd responded with the same sort of considerate understanding that citizens throughout the land had exhibited on many previous similar occasions: they 'excited a disposition to tear in pieces the balloon'![9] More often than not a disappointed crowd would be mollified by an undertaking that the pilot would try again within a day or two. On this occasion, one of the individuals who comprised the Derby Committee had the still better idea of offering the crowd the prospect of something far more exciting: rather than risk another attempt by an unknown like Wilkes, they would invite the most famous of all balloonists, the much more dependable James Sadler. A letter was duly dispatched the following day by Dr Richard Forester, the Chairman of the Committee.[10] The date suggested to Sadler was 5 October, but first the Committee needed to know what his fee would be.

Forester's letter was addressed to Sadler's Brewer Street premises at Golden Square, London. However, as Sadler was in Bristol at the time, having arrived there on Saturday 25th,[11] the letter took several more days to reach him. On reading its contents, in which it was 'represented to him that the tranquillity of the town of Derby in some degree depended upon his compliance, Mr. Sadler very handsomely relinquished for the present his Bristol engagement',[12] and, as his balloon was still en route from Cheltenham, diverted it to Derby. He did so despite having to abandon preparations to exhibit in Bristol both this balloon and a second new one, 'the largest that ever was made'.[13] The size of this new balloon was 'so enormous that no place in London could be found so sufficiently large to make it in. The nearest place that could be procured was Reading Town Hall, where several of the first rate artists were employed to ornament it.'[14] No matter how big, the newspaper's claim that it was designed to take twelve people across the Irish Sea was another journalistic fabrication, since not even a lone aeronaut had managed that journey yet.

At this point the two versions of events, Sadler's and the Derby Committee's, differed. Evidently, there had been a misunderstanding of huge proportions, as a very long statement in the *Derby Mercury* of 14 October showed. This was issued by the Committee in response to an assertion by Sadler that he had gone directly to Derby *only* on the basis of absolute assurances that all would be made ready for him to make an ascent on 5 October. The Committee denied having made any such guarantee, citing a letter which Sadler's former flying companion William Clayfield had sent to them from Bristol on 27 September, in which he stated that Sadler was ready to set off for Derby the next day but would *not* be able to comply with the date suggested, 5 October, in view of the repairs required to the balloon.[15] The subsequent correspondence between Sadler (assisted, no doubt, by Windham, or some other more literate advocate) and Forester was presented to the public in the *Derby Mercury* of 14 October. It showed that Sadler arrived, with his balloon and car, on 30 September, that he inspected the proposed site, and that on 2 October confirmed his willingness to ascend on the 5th. His fee would be 500 guineas. No response was received to this demand until the very day of the proposed ascent, the Committee writing only then to say that they were unable to accept his terms, but that they would keep open the subscription which had already been started with a view to inviting him back in the spring.

This unfortunate tale of impetuosity versus indecision continued with a long letter from Sadler to Forester, dated 6 October. In summary, Sadler declined the future invitation on account of 'the very unexpected reception I have been so unfortunate as to experience from the Committee from the first moment of my coming here, and, in particular, my personal reception by yourself, on my first arrival'. Forester's response to this assertion appeared as a letter dated 12 October (the receipt of which was the cue for the *Derby Mercury* to print it and all the preceding correspondence). Forester repeated the Committee's own case, and its honourable intentions, and responded to the personal nature of Sadler's accusations to say that

> whilst he feels regret at the circumstance, he is on a retrospect of every thing which took place at the only two interviews he had any opportunity of have with Mr. S. totally unaware of any thing in his behaviour capable of having given that gentleman the slightest ground for the charges which he has brought against him.

A fortnight later came Sadler's response, the apparent last word, at least in public. The *Derby Mercury* (28 October) allowed him a whole column – perhaps pandering to local resentment against the individuals who had twice now failed to live up to their promises of a balloon ascent, no matter whose fault it was. Sadler set out his own version of events again, with two particular challenges. One was to the Committee: 'to state to the public the name of *any one gentleman of the Committee* that did call on him, to give him or even to offer him, the least assistance in *any respect whatsoever* on his making known to them his arrival at Derby'. The other challenge was specifically aimed at Forester: to 'tell the world' exactly 'the kind of reception he gave Mr. S. when he called upon him at his own house; and the next morning when Mr. S. met with him by accident, in the street'.

In justification of his requested fee of 500 guineas, Sadler also included a helpfully revealing schedule of the 'Expences which would have been incurred, had Mr. S. ascended from Derby', pointing out that had he 'endeavoured to raise his balloon, and unfortunately failed in the attempt, the whole expence must have fallen upon himself'. Ballooning was still a highly risky business – and not just of life and limb!

Balloon, Net, Car, &c	£320
Materials and apparatus for obtaining gas	£200
Expences of bringing the Balloon to Derby, my	
Own expences while there, with Servants, Labour &c	£120

Finding himself unexpectedly in the Midlands with his balloon, it made sense to look for other nearby venues in order to salvage some return on the costly excursion. Given the very public nature of the Derby impasse, very few people would have been unaware of Sadler's presence in the locality, so the moment was ripe to capitalise on this complimentary publicity. To rub Forester's Committee's noses in it, the city which took the initiative to issue an immediate invitation was the neighbouring county town of Nottingham!

Nottingham: Monday 1 November 1813

This opportunistic Nottingham ascent had obviously already been agreed in principle even as the details of the Derby debacle were being made public, as an advertisement appeared in the *Nottingham Journal* of 16 October.[16] No date was specified, because Sadler was at long last getting wise to being left out of pocket. The launch would proceed only 'provided he can be assured of the Disposal of Tickets to the Amount of Five Hundred Guineas; which sum it will absolutely require to indemnify him for the Expenses he must incur'. Tickets were priced at five shillings.

Presumably, the necessary sum was swiftly pledged, because the ascent occurred just two weeks later. It was billed as his 28th (representing another addition of two to the known tally) in the *Morning Chronicle* of 5 November and in *Air Balloons*, a twenty-page pamphlet printed – evidently with great expedition – by E. Hodson of Nottingham in anticipation of Sadler's performance. Several pages are devoted to accounts of the ascents from Bristol, Birmingham, Dublin and Cheltenham, the author emphasising Sadler's scientific merits by saying that 'from the various experiments he has made, we are confirmed, that the air of an high region ... is found to be purer than the air below', and 'the existence of a continual electricity, of the positive kind, in a clear atmosphere, has been further ascertained by the undaunted aeronaut'.[17]

Air Balloons concluded with a description of the balloon, which was made of alternate stripes of crimson and white varnished silk. It was 30 feet in diameter, 98 feet in circumference, with a capacity of 20,540 cubic feet. Sadler's other, more ambitious project, the balloon that he was working on at Bristol when called away, was also described. It was 70 feet in diameter and contained 1,435,220 gallons. The design was as 'a superb temple, floating on the bosom of fleecy, azure, and sable clouds' and embellished with 'various heathen deities' as well as 'the Prince regent's star and feather' and a 'Crown, Thistle, and Shamrock'. Said to be 'the largest ever made in England', the boast that it was reckoned to be 'capable of bearing ... a company of 75 soldiers, perfectly accoutred with arms, ammunition &c.' was, of course, wildly optimistic.

A canal barge was used as the launch platform.[18] People came from all directions – from Newark, Leicester, Mansfield and, of course (and perhaps particularly), from Derby! One can only imagine the emotions of Dr Forester and his associates, on reading of the 'universal delight and satisfaction' given by 'a spectacle which has not occurred in this or the neighbouring counties since the first attempt to navigate the higher regions by balloon'.[19]

The ascent was made at 2.40 p.m., without undue delay. This was perhaps particularly fortunate in the city in which the Luddite movement could trace its birth almost exactly two years earlier, and where therefore one might expect malfunctioning machines to be shown particularly little sympathy! It was additionally fortunate that the day was clear and fine enough for the balloon to remain visible for 37 minutes, constituting what the *Bury & Norwich Post* of 10 November called (with little apparent heed for the facts) 'the longest time which any balloon ever remained in sight from the time of its ascension'. The *Derby Mercury* of 11 November calculated it at even longer; nearly 45 minutes.

Sadler's own account appeared in the *Mercury* of the same day in the form of a letter headed Nottingham, 4 November. The wind took him in a south-easterly direction, and though he had hoped to veer back towards Nottingham, he found himself continuing towards 'the celebrated Thistleton Gap' (where Leicestershire, Lincolnshire and Rutland converged). Soon after, he was about to land when he found himself precipitated towards a windmill and so – wisely! – 'thought it most prudent to re-ascend'. Soon after he crossed the Great North Road:

> I was highly gratified with a second view, from the aerial regions, of Exton Park and its beautiful sheets of water, having before passed over it in my excursion from Birmingham in Oct. 1811. Seeing, between the woods, ploughed and meadow fields where there was a pack of hounds returning from hunting, I deemed it a proper place to descend.

Once he had come to a stop, near Pickworth (Rutland), a country girl helped him to secure the balloon until the arrival of the huntsmen, who had seen him pass, and immediately adjusted their quarry to incorporate an unexpected spot of 'balloon hunting'. The *Caledonian Mercury* (15 November) summarised the situation as: 'The lovers of hunting who had the good fortune to be out with Lord Lonsdale's hounds ... were treated to a new interesting species of *game*.' Sadler was escorted to the Greetham Inn, and was, the newspaper stated, 'obligingly communicative', which probably explains how his personal account appeared soon after in the *Derby Mercury*. Among those who congratulated him at the Inn was the Duke of Montrose, who happened to arrive just as Sadler was preparing to return to Nottingham. The car and balloon were undamaged, and having stowed them away safely at a nearby farmhouse, Sadler spent the night in Grantham before returning to Nottingham 'amidst the cheers and acclamations of the liberal inhabitants' at noon the next day.[20]

Perhaps because E. Hodson beat him to it, Sadler published no separate account on this occasion, so that means of raising a little additional income was denied him. With certain predictability, it would appear that despite the assurances he had sought of a guarantee of 500 guineas, Sadler had once again risked his safety and entertained the masses largely at his own expense. One of his 'obligingly communicative' revelations was that the total cost of the balloon and gas had been £900. Even if, as it was stated, about 2,000 people each paid five shillings to see it, that still left a considerable shortfall. As a result, a handbill was circulated in Nottingham the next day (Wednesday 3 November). Headed 'The Friends of Mr. Sadler', the entire text read:

> The Committee who undertook the Management of the Ascension of Mr. Sadler, are sorry to state, that the Receipts fall short of the Sum actually expended, in consequence of which the Committee earnestly request a Meeting of the Friends of Mr. Sadler at the Town Hall, *this Evening at Six o'Clock*, to take into consideration the propriety of entering into a Subscription, and to remunerate Mr. Sadler.[21]

Whatever the response, there seems little doubt that Sadler was once again left considerably out of pocket. The following summer presented him with one final chance to profit from his profession: it was to prove an appropriate finale, accompanying his youngest son for the first and only time, before an audience as distinguished as any he had ever known. Indeed, it would be a momentous couple of weeks for the flying Sadlers, with son John also taking to the air one final time and Windham – in a Sadler 'first' – ascending with a female companion.

London: Friday 15 July 1814 (James & Windham Sadler)

The date of James Sadler's swansong ascent was Friday 15 July 1814. The venue was Burlington Gardens in Piccadilly, the residence of the Duke of Devonshire, with whom Sadler had an audience earlier in the week.[22] Appropriately enough in terms of succession, he had his youngest son for company on the ascent, Windham being in the opinion of the *Morning Chronicle* (1 August) 'the most undoubted heir to his father's talents'. It was an assessment which would be fully borne out over the next decade. The launch was not without incident, however, since

> a scaffold, carelessly constructed, gave way, with from 20 to 30 persons on it. However, as it was but a few feet from the ground, this catastrophe

produced nothing beyond a general laugh at the sufferers, who were thus suddenly thrown from the best into the worst situation of the assemblage.[23]

The ascent was delayed slightly on account of the anticipated imminent arrival of the dukes of York and Wellington, though it is not clear if they did actually attend. Many newspapers gave brief details of the launch, with general agreement that it occurred at 3.25 p.m. The balloon was made of about 3,000 square yards of 'the finest double-wove silk', and was 74 feet in height. As for the car, 'on each end was painted the Imperial German and Russian Eagles, the crown of Great Britain on one side, and the Prince's Plume on the other side, the whole in silver on a pink ground, a gold border all round'.[24]

Once again, it would seem that few people paid to see the sight, since 'there was a very thin attendance of company in the court-yard of Burlington-house', one reason being that 'the concourse of people in the streets was immense, so as that neither in carriages nor a-foot could persons who were disposed to pay for access get near the entrance'. However, numerous unauthorised people did do so: 'There was no restraining them; and they not only made their way into Burlington-court yard; but into many of the adjoining houses without ceremony.' James Sadler, anticipating just such a situation, had written to the authorities on 12 July 1814 specifically to request 'the Presence of the Police'.[25] As *Bell's Weekly Messenger* of 17 July observed, 'this was intended as a spectacle, not a massacre'. The *Ipswich Journal's* account concluded with a comment which appears to have been extracted from a delusional overheard conversation:

> Mr. Sadler said that he could go to any destination he chose with his balloon as at different heights in the atmosphere he constantly found different currents of wind; so that he could take and keep a favourable gale. It was suggested, that to prove this to the satisfaction of London, he had only to make an excursion into the country for 20 or 30 miles, and return to the place from whence he set out. It would be a great discovery indeed if this could be ascertained!

A week later (30 July) the same newspaper presented Sadler's own account of proceedings. He was in an uncharacteristically lyrical mood. Having cleared the east wing of Burlington House, he thought

> it was not we who seemed to rise, but every thing beneath us to retire; in a few minutes we were perpendicular with Leicester square, and our prospect was at once both grand and awful; the whole of London lay

below us, with its surrounding fields, canals, and parks; the beautiful serpentine form of the river, with its rich shipping, docks, and bridges.

Then, after soaring through a bank of cloud, 'my son observed to me, that from the variegated colour reflected and refracted from the multitudinous congregation of vapours around us, and the effulgence of different lights, he could scarcely see to any great distance'. He continued,

> from the intense cold, and a most violent pain in my ears, which I have never experienced before, our height could not be less, in my calculation, than five miles. The late Right Hon. Mr. Windham, about 30 years ago indeed, experienced a similar attack in his ears though we had not then ascended beyond two miles and a half.

5 miles! More delusion, surely? In no other of his accounts was an altitude of more than 4 miles ever suggested, and even that must of course be treated with caution. Whatever, father and son made a gentle descent in a hayfield at Great Warley Franks, Oakenden, Essex. The descent had been at about 4.35 p.m., making a total distance (via Gravesend) of about 47 miles.[26] The landowner, Mr S. Francis, received them hospitably while they waited for a chaise to come from Brentwood to collect the apparatus, and they were able to return to Burlington House by 11 p.m. So ended the last verifiable flight, the nineteenth *verifiable* one, by James Sadler, first English, perhaps British, aeronaut. It was a far, far less eventful affair than many, with as appropriate a co-pilot, and from as grand a venue, as any he had ever made. In addition, simply by virtue of being in central London, it was also probably witnessed by more people than on any previous occasion. On the face of it, a thoroughly satisfactory end, in his sixty-first year, to a glorious, pioneering, inventive, courageous and record-breaking career.

This, it should be mentioned, is only a retrospective interpretation. The Burlington Gardens ascent was evidently not *intended* to be his last. Throughout the next few years, James would often be named in advance publicity for flights, though always, either through circumstance, contrivance or misunderstanding, it was Windham who actually took to the skies. It is partly for this reason that James Sadler has sometimes been credited with making more flights than he actually did. The tally had already been inflated, as we have seen, and a pattern emerged in the years that followed, that simply the announcement of an intended flight was equated by subsequent promoters to his actually having accomplished it!

An example occurred within days, when – notwithstanding the

apparent problems of crowd control of two weeks earlier – a second ascent was announced from Burlington House on Friday 29 July. In order to avoid the earlier problems, the most expensive tickets (ten shillings and sixpence) permitted 'a seat in Burlington House' itself, with access via a private door. Or for five shillings and sixpence one could do battle, perhaps literally, with others to gain access through the main entrance in Piccadilly. It was billed as James Sadler's thirtieth ascent, but turned out to be Windham's third.[27] The advertised presence of a third individual, however, a female one, did prove correct. Miss T(h)ompson was a name that the newspapers would feature fairly frequently in association with the Sadlers for the next few years, but with frustratingly little biographical detail with which to ascertain her actual identity.

London (Piccadilly): Friday 29 July 1814 (Windham Sadler, with Miss Mary(?) Thompson)

Why James withdrew from this second London flight was not made clear at the time, but much later, it was explained by that commonplace reason, the same as had accelerated Windham's maiden flight from Cheltenham: 'a want of buoyancy in the balloon to carry his superior weight'.[28] So Windham, 'with pleasure and alacrity, took possession of the car'. The *Times* (30 July), having earlier announced that one of the aeronauts was to be an actress, the wife of the actor Henry Johnston (1775?–1845), confessed its ignorance of who actually ascended with Windham on the day, but provided these clues: she was 'a slight and delicate figure, in the common summer dress, a light silk hat, muslin gown, a blue silk mantle, and altogether in a costume which seemed to contemplate none of the vicissitudes to which an aerial voyage is liable'.[29] By the next day (1 August), the *Morning Chronicle* had identified the mystery woman as Miss Thompson, who 'though acquainted with Mr. Sadler's family from earliest life, never ascended before'. The *Caledonian Mercury* (4 August) wrote:

> There is a disposition on the part of the British public to sanction and support every woman of spirit, who throws herself on their protection, and we may say hundreds of thousands attended to bestow their applause and encouragement. Miss Thompson has long been desirous of mounting in a balloon from London, and, it is but justice to say, she availed herself of the opportunity with firmness and resolution not excelled in any example of female courage.

The surely still greater bravery of Letitia Sage and the Simonet sisters having already been expunged from the newspaper's memory, it was nonetheless probably accurate in asserting that Miss Thompson was the first female to ascend in England since Madame Garnerin at Vauxhall (in 1802). It meant she was probably also only the second Englishwoman – if indeed she actually was English – ever to have ascended at that time.[30] Adding 'a lilac silk pelisse, with a neat straw hat and feather' to the *Times*' description of her costume, the *Caledonian Mercury* continued that after she had entered the car

> the balloon, under the direction of Mr. Sadler sen. was conveyed to a platform where the car rested. A pause ensued, during which friends of the adventurers took a farewell; a person at the same moment exclaimed among the crowd round the balloon – 'God bless you, Mary,' then addressing his companion, 'I have known her,' said he, 'ever since she was an infant.'

This possibly revealing, possibly misleading, clue to Miss Thompson's identity has proved unhelpful in trying to ascertain more about her. Hodgson was, for once, mistaken when he suggested that she was 'renowned in the Dramatic Corps'.[31] The *Morning Chronicle* (30 July 1814) chipped in, describing her as appearing to be 'about 20 years of age, rather fresh coloured; she wore an orange-coloured silk spencer, white beaver hat and feather'. As the pair prepared to launch, the conditions were so very far from ideal that numerous spectators 'clung to the car, and were very loath to permit either of the voyagers, especially the Lady, "To tempt the uncertain air mid-way," in its perturbed state'.[32] Tempt it they did, however:

> The gale, which occasioned the Balloon to move notwithstanding its confinement, with considerable agitation, had no effect on the intention of the female aeronaut; she refused to hear any observation to alter her resolution, exclaiming to her companion, 'Can you go up?' 'Certainly,' was his answer. 'Then' said the Lady with a smile – 'What man dare, I dare!'[33]

The unknown person who identified her as 'Mary' is also quoted as adding, 'I am sure there is not another woman in England would do this.' No one on the ground could have been more aware of the danger the pair were facing than James Sadler, who made his way to Burlington House several times in the course of the morning, in a state of considerable anxiety and alarm. He expressed his fears that the violence of the wind might have carried the balloon with unexpected rapidity towards the German Ocean, at the same time having the fullest confidence in the skill and dexterity of his son.[34]

James's confidence in his son was justified, and the couple descended safely 45 miles away near Coggeshall, Essex only 40 minutes or so later. With a certain irony, considering they had made this very swift journey in such dangerously boisterous weather without mishap, their chaise overturned on the journey back to London, and they were 'much, though not materially bruised'. The incident led the *Morning Chronicle* (1 August) to surmise that 'Miss T. though she may not openly express herself, would doubtless recommend her fair friends who would travel to Gretna or elsewhere to prefer the safety of a Balloon to the hazards of a chaise'.[35]

Soon after, their achievement was commemorated on the ceiling of (the now demolished) John Tatum's Theatre of Science at No. 53 Dorset Street, off Fleet Street, where the City Philosophical Society met from 1808 to the mid-1820s. The scene consisted of 'bulging clouds, a large eagle, and two figures negotiating a balloon across the skies'.[36] A likely instigator would seem to have been Robert Cocking (1776–1837), an early experimenter with parachutes and Secretary of the Society from 1817–24.[37] The evidence for this lost design is a poem by some unknown hand which was transcribed by the chemist and physicist Michael Faraday (1791–1867), then working at the Royal Institution as a colleague of Humphrey Davy. Dated 2 October 1816, the long descriptive poem includes reference to:

> A small balloon that seems to pierce the skies
> And two strange forms the whole to supervise.

This duo are identified inside

> The car where venal Sadler rides
> And coarse Miss Thompson mounts with manly strides.[38]

Oh dear! Windham, like his father, seemingly able only to induce sneers from his philosophical peers, while the misogynistic disdain for female aeronauts was maintained with unrelenting vigour!

London (St James's Park): Monday 1 August 1814 (John Sadler)

Not to be outdone by his younger half-brother, next to take the London aerial stage was John, to make his second known (and definitely final) ascent.[39] It was also his first as a soloist, demonstrating truly remarkable bravura in that his was by far the most public of the ascents which were undertaken by the three Sadlers in such quick succession. For not only were the celebrations to commemorate both the accession of the House of Brunswick and the victorious Battle of the Nile[40] on Monday 1 August of enormous general interest, the balloon ascent from St James's Park was considered to be 'the first object of attraction' among the array of entertainments provided. The *Caledonian Mercury* (4 August), pointedly ignoring the Hanoverian jubilee, interpreted the holiday as being 'set apart by the British Government for a public and national rejoicing to celebrate the restoration of a solid and honourable peace'.[41]

The filling of the balloon, which was positioned immediately in front of Queen Charlotte's residence of Buckingham House, had begun at 9 a.m., but it took until 5 p.m. before it was deemed sufficiently full to be inspected by the queen, who was accompanied by 'the Duke of Wellington, Lord Liverpool, Lord Castlereagh, Lord Rivers, Lord Burghersh, Lord Buckinghamshire, the Marquis Wellesley, the Princesses and several Peeresses'.[42] Queen Charlotte and her daughters then stationed themselves at a window of Buckingham House, ready to enjoy the spectacle.

Like Windham, John too had intended taking a female escort. It was to be (as the *Times* had earlier rumoured) the actress, Mrs Henry Johnston, but though ready with 'a dove in her hand, that emblem of peace and charity, which she had intended to send down to the earth on her celestial ascension',[43] she was dissuaded by, amongst others, the Duke of Wellington.[44] Indeed the duke also tried to persuade John Sadler himself to abandon the attempt, but that was never likely, given such august scrutiny and widespread anticipation, and despite detecting a problem with the valve at the top of the balloon, John, 'feeling for the disappointment of the public, and for his own honour', went alone. Given his want of experience, it was a decision as courageous in some ways as any his father had made. Evidently, he had inherited some of his father's sangfroid, as well as his practical skills, because when over Woolwich the string which fastened the protective net broke, and the main body of the balloon was forced quickly through the aperture, nearly eighteen feet. Mr. Sadler, to prevent the danger which threatened him, caught the pipe at the bottom of the balloon, and by hanging on it and the valve line, he prevented the balloon from farther escaping. The valve, which had for some time resisted every attempt to open it, in consequence of being frozen, at this time gave way, and suffered the gas to escape.[45]

The *Morning Chronicle* (3 August) took up the story:

Owing to some derangement of the valve, Mr. Sadler was under the necessity of making an incision in the Balloon; that so much precipitated his descent, that had there been two persons in the car, the termination of their excursion must have been fatal.

It is to be hoped that Mrs Henry Johnston was duly thankful that she stayed behind! As John lost altitude 'he experienced much difficulty in preventing a descent in the river Thames, to which the balloon had a decided tendency', but ultimately landed it on dry land, albeit at high speed, at Mucking Marshes, on the Essex coast, about 15 miles beyond Gravesend. He had been in the air for 40 minutes.[46] Luckily, two fishermen had followed his course for 10 miles, took the balloon on board their boat, and conveyed it and him to Gravesend. John Sadler had survived the near-fatal adventure with nothing worse than a sprained foot, and, after a short rest and some refreshment, he returned to London at about 3 a.m. Despite the hour, his return 'was hailed by the throng with the loudest cheers, who would scarcely permit him to touch the earth from which he had soared so high'.[47]

The following evening, according to the *Morning Post* (3 August), John Sadler was introduced to Queen Charlotte and her daughters at 'the Queen's Palace ... and gave a full account of his aerial voyage, sixteen miles beyond Gravesend, and exhibited to them the Car in which he travelled and explained to them its operations with the Balloon.' What an honour! It was thoroughly deserved, of course, though seems harsh on James and Windham – the country's oldest and youngest aeronauts respectively – if they too were not invited. It was a truly remarkable, surely unprecedented, achievement for three members of the same family to ascend in three separate flights within three weeks! Neither James nor John would ever make another flight; Windham, however, would go on to make nearly another thirty ...

12

THE 'INHERITOR OF HIS FATHER'S GENIUS AND INTREPIDITY': WINDHAM SADLER'S ASCENTS FROM 1814 TO 1823

The main purpose of this book is to celebrate the life and achievements of James Sadler, Oxford pastry cook and first English aeronaut. James may never have taken to the air again after the display with Windham in London on 15 July 1814, but he was certainly present as a guiding hand at many of the ascents made by his youngest son over the next few years. Indeed, he lived long enough to know about every one of the thirty-one aerial adventures of Windham's action-packed but tragically short life.

York: Wednesday 24 August 1814

In the pre-publicity for Windham's fourth ascent, at York, it was actually billed as being the thirty-first of Sadler senior, 'late member of the Board of Local Works and Inspector of Chemistry to the Admiralty'.[1] This was the first of many occasions that such erroneous advertisements would appear, though whether out of unfulfilled genuine intentions, misunderstanding or as a deliberate marketing ploy is not clear. Sadler senior was the most famous name in ballooning at the time, after all, a curiosity as the last of the eighteenth-century pioneers and likely therefore to attract greater numbers of spectators than his son.

Using the same car and finely decorated 70-foot diameter balloon which all the Sadlers had used in London, Windham went up from Kettlewell's Orchard, behind the cathedral. This was exactly the same location from which Lunardi had ascended twenty-eight years earlier,[2] on indeed, the very same day of 24 August. Windham landed only 12 miles away, near Craike, although in travelling a total of 63 miles, after being visible for a gratifying 45 minutes, this was farther than on any of his previous trips.[3]

Pontefract: Thursday 15 September 1814 (with Miss Thompson)

Windham's next ascent, from Pontefract, was described in detail in the *Leeds Mercury* of 17 September, which stated that 'the Corporation patronized the intrepid aeronaut by every possible act of kindness', this being in 'striking contrast to the parsimonious and frigid reception he has experienced in some other places'. Miss Thompson accompanied him again in the 'magnificent Temple', and James was present to supervise the preparations for an ascent which he 'considered equal in grandeur to any he had ever witnessed', on account of the balloon remaining visible for 48 minutes. They landed near Tadcaster, having covered 14 miles in 50 minutes and risen to about 2 miles.

Doncaster: Thursday 29 September 1814

The last of Windham's three Yorkshire ascents was another uneventful affair, lasting only about 1 hour. He landed near Barnsley, where he 'was ably assisted in his descent by two men, who appeared highly pleased with their office'.[4] Balloon-mania was still prevalent, evidently, as soon after 'they were joined by at least one thousand, who conducted themselves in the most orderly manner'.[5] He returned to Doncaster the same evening and almost immediately set off on a long journey to the south coast.

Exeter: Saturday 22 October 1814

There is no mention of James Sadler being present at Doncaster, though it would seem highly likely, and father and son were certainly together again a month later, at the opposite end of the country, when Windham ascended from Exeter Castle. *Trewman's Exeter Flying Post* of 27 October carried the longest account, and is notable for its unusually detailed coverage of the preparatory phase. As so often with balloon ascents, the momentous nature of the day was stressed in hyperbolic terms: 'so great was the attraction that the concourse of people continued to flock through the streets the whole of the morning, greatly exceeding any thing ever remembered on any former occasion'. The balloon, which had been on public display the previous week, was transferred to the castle, where

> in the ground had been sunk a large lead cistern for containing the materials necessary for the production of the hydrogen gas, and fitted with tubes for conveying it to the Balloon, which was now suspended over the cistern by cords and poles. When the process of filling was completed the vast globe was conveyed to the platform erected for the purpose near the centre of the Castle-yard; here Mr. Sadler, jun. affixed the car to it.

Windham ascended at 1.23 p.m., 'after taking an affectionate leave of his father'. Windham's own account is appended to the *Post's* version, and includes reference to a cutter firing a gun in salute. Landing in an orchard, some 3 miles from Sidmouth, a little after 2 p.m., he wrote that

> the countryman who first approached the Balloon, seemed frightened, retired, and hid himself behind a tree ... until a second came up, ... also at first much frightened ... 'thinking it was full of men' ... from seeing the transparent paintings on it.

To be fair to the countryman, the inhabitants of the south coast had more reason than most to be wary of unexpected airborne arrivals, given that the long-standing potential of French invasion had eased only earlier that year, with Napoleon's abdication in April. By 10 p.m. Windham was back in Exeter having ridden the 10 miles or so on horseback. A band was waiting to provide a musical tribute, and 'he was carried on men's shoulders to his lodgings in the high-street, amidst the exulting shouts of the multitude'.

(Plymouth: 24 November 1814)

Another attempt from a south coast port the next month proved much less successful. Indeed, it was as *un*successful, and probably as embarrassing, as any that James Sadler had experienced in his long career. This time the intention did match the advertising, and it really was James – 'late Member of the Board of Naval Works and Inspector of Chemistry to the Admiralty' – who intended to ascend from The Citadel at Plymouth on Thursday 24 November.[6] The 'superb temple and car with which Miss Thompson and Mr. Sadler jun. ascended' in London the previous July could be viewed beforehand at the Royal Hotel where the Sadlers were staying.[7]

The apparent main reason for accepting the invitations to ascend from the south coast towns had been to try to resolve James's very long-standing desire to cross the English Channel. Windham had been in Portsmouth as long ago as May to discuss that possibility,[8] but James had already realised that the opportunity had once more been denied him because

> in consequence of the damage which the large Balloon received after its Ascent from Exeter, it is unfit for an Aerial Voyage, and there not being time to construct one of sufficient capacity to carry him across the Channel to the French Coast, the Ascent will not take place as he originally intended.

In view of this reduced capacity, he was only prepared to ascend if the wind was blowing landward; if it was towards the sea, he would postpone; if calm, giving an equal chance of descending on land or water, he would 'take the Chance of any Vessel being at Sea to pick him up'.[9]

In the event, none of these three scenarios transpired. A balloon did ascend, but unfortunately neither James *nor* Windham went with it! Despite all their combined experience, the two men failed to judge the strength of the wind that Thursday, and the balloon was blown onto some iron railings before either had got in. With the main valve damaged and the gas escaping 'it only remained for Mr. Sadler, who had gone into the car to adjust the ballast, to quit it, or remain at the imminent hazard of his life', *Trewman's Exeter Flying Post* (1 December) reported. Hardly had he been 'dragged from the car ... when the Balloon being quite unmanageable, rushed into the air' (to be retrieved later on Dartmoor). It was a disappointing end to a momentous year. As usual on such occasions, 'when it was generally known that Mr. Sadler had not ascended, different emotions arose among the spectators, some of whom shewed strong marks of disapprobation'. However, 'others, convinced that every thing possible had been done by him to fulfil his promise, applauded'. It is doubtful if the Sadlers gained much consolation from this, given that the reported value of the balloon, made of 500 yards of 'the best Italian silk', was several hundred pounds.

One more flight was contemplated that year, from Norwich,[10] William Windham's former constituency, but was postponed until the following summer. In between, a man called Steward attempted to pre-empt the Sadlers, by becoming the first person to ascend from Norwich since James Deeker in 1785, but his failure occasioned scenes reminiscent of the unforgiving days of the 1780s, when, after he had 'skimmed and skimmed and skimmed and skimmed' for no more than 500 yards, the crowd found better entertainment in tearing the balloon to pieces.[11] His failure meant that the way was still clear for the Sadlers to raise the first balloon in Norwich for thirty years, though, wary of Steward's fate, they must surely have approached the task with above average trepidation.

Norwich: Saturday 29 July 1815

In the months prior to the Norwich ascent, James and Windham had been busy making enforced cosmetic changes to a new craft as a result of the resumption of hostilities with France after Napoleon escaped from Elba in February, having

> been engaged for several months in constructing a balloon, at the express desire of Louis the Eighteenth, to ascend with at his late expected Coronation, but from the later circumstances of France, he has been obliged to change the ornaments appropriate to that country ... and also a most splendid car formed similar to the state bed made for the Emperor of Russia when in London, with national trophies and other superb decorations, upon which several eminent artists have been employed for some time past, at an expense of several hundred pounds for the car only.[12]

The Norwich balloon, however, was to be the same as had ascended the previous year at Burlington House in London. It was announced in advance as the '46th ascension' of the former 'Member of the Board of Naval Works'[13] and suggested that James would be accompanied by Miss Thompson, for what would have been her third flight. In the end, however, neither she nor James went, and, with a certain misleading inevitability, it was Windham who took to the skies on 29 July, from what was known as Harper's Ranelagh Gardens.[14] Conditions were so perfect that Windham was able to make a controlled landing after travelling only about 3 miles in an hour. This meant that many people were able to witness both the ascent and the descent, 'a novelty often wished,' as Windham himself observed in his own account of the voyage, 'but seldom performed, the velocity of the wind in general preventing the possibility of it'.[15]

Newcastle: Friday 1 September 1815

A month later, with further disregard for the facts, Windham's next flight, from Newcastle's Bowling Green in Northumberland Street (later renamed Prudhoe Street) on Friday 1 September, was advertised and described as Mr Sadler's forty-seventh. The first detailed account to appear, in the *Caledonian Mercury* of 9 September, did nothing to disabuse its readers of the idea that James had made this ascent, but many other accounts reveal it to have been Windham. An eyewitness, James Losh, noted in his diary that his family watched from a nearby house, while he himself joined 'from 1,000 to 1,100 well dressed people'[16] on the green, from where he closely observed the ascent with 'a kind of enthusiasm and pleasing anxiety which I cannot describe'.[17] Losh's sentiments are mirrored to some extent in these extracts from local songs. 'A Ramble to see Sadler's Balloon'[18] begins

> It was upon our pay Friday, thou may depend I'se reet,
> When we ware washt, away we set to see that wonderous seet:
> A man went up most to the sky, ty'd to a tartain bag,
> But I thought he wad a cowpt his creels, he went with sic a swag.[19]

The second verse (of twelve) in William Mitford's song, 'Bob Cranky's account of the ascent of Mr. Sadler's balloon, from Newcastle, Sept. 1, 1815' (in *Newcastle Songster,* published about 1815) is:

> And a man, mun, there means in this verra balloon
> Above, 'mang the stars to fly.
> And to haud a converse wi' the man i' the moon,
> And cobwebs tae sweep frae the sky.
> So we started frae heame by eight i' the morn,

Baith faither and mother and son,
But fand a' wor neibors had started before,
To get in gude time for the fun.

Sadler is mentioned by name once, in verse nine:

Another said Sadler, (for that is the nyame
Of the man) may pay dear for his frolic,
When he's up in the clouds (a stree for his fame!)
His guts may hev twangs of the cholic.

And finally, in verse twelve:

The ropes were then cut, and upwards he went,
A waven his flag i' the air;
Every head was turn'd up, and a' eyes wur intent
On this comical new flying chair.

The Newcastle trip was another short but swift one for Windham, of about 10 miles in a little over a quarter of an hour. Before the end of the year, the Sadlers (for it would seem that both Windham and James remained together throughout this period) made their first ever venture north of the border.

Glasgow: Thursday 19 October 1815

The first of two Scottish ascents was made 'under very unfavourable circumstances' from above the Grammar School in Glasgow on 19 October. The incessant rain and wet ground may have deterred many spectators, but not 'Mr. Sadler the younger' himself, who covered about 7½ miles in just over half an hour, landing in Milngavie, where 'he was met with every assistance by the good people'.[20] Well, all the people bar one, it would seem, since 'the servant of the occupier of the land where he lighted insisted on removing the balloon immediately or he would put his knife into it.' When Windham produced a knife of his own, however, the man thought better of his threat,[21] and the young aeronaut was otherwise 'hospitably entertained'. He arrived back in Glasgow the same evening, 'after which he made his appearance at the theatre, and was received by three hearty cheers'.[22] Be that as it may, the event could not really have been all that cheering: in announcing his subsequent arrival in Edinburgh, it was revealed that, in true Sadler style, the Glasgow ascent had incurred a personal loss of £160.[23]

Edinburgh: Friday 3 November 1815

The newspapers' confusion about which Sadler was which continued north of the border. Notices placed in the *Caledonian Mercury* (28 October, 30 October and 2 November) promised that the ascent from Edinburgh would be the '49th ascension' of the 'late Member of the Board of Naval Works and Inspector of Chemistry to the Army and Navy'.[24] Once again, however, when the moment came, it was Windham who ascended, being, as the *Caledonian Mercury* (4 November) stated, the first person to do so since 1785, 'when Lunardi ascended from the garden in Herriot's Hospital'.

The launch was made from what was called the 'Court-yard of the College' (known today as the Old College, on South Bridge). Tickets were five shillings for a view of the whole process of inflation and lift off, and three shillings to witness simply the ascent. Filling commenced at 12 p.m., and took longer than planned because the water that was needed to create the hydrogen had to be carried to the launch site in buckets. It was not until about 3 p.m. that all was ready. 'Mr. Wyndham Sadler was already in the car, and having fastened on his life preserver, in case of immersion in the sea, he took leave of his father and his friends.' They were not parted for long, as he landed less than 10 minutes later! Short though the journey was, Windham having sufficient control of his vehicle to bring it down before reaching the open sea, the balloon and car were nonetheless inadvertently destroyed by the misplaced enthusiasm of the excited crowd which raced to assist. In Windham's own words,

> from the extreme pressure of the crowd, the balloon was totally destroyed, and, after extreme difficulty, was packed up and forwarded to Edinburgh. The car, and remaining part, which the crowd had in their possession, was carried away by them, and likewise demolished in their parading of it.[25]

This was the same car and balloon as had been used since the Burlington House ascents the previous year, so it had seen good service – small consolation though that probably was for the once again out-of-pocket Sadlers. Some of the crowd were themselves saved from being out of pocket, literally, when 'Mr. Sadler detected a well-known pickpocket among the crowd, and had him immediately turned out'. This shows that balloonists were still attracting a following of an unwelcome kind, given that the man must presumably have been familiar to the Sadlers from south of the border.

The choice of venue and brevity of the spectacle gave rise to some local discontent, but when several people wrote to the *Caledonian Mercury* to complain, the newspaper declined to print their letters, and instead issued a stern rebuke (on 6 November): as these correspondents had evidently not even paid for a ticket, it was pointed out, they had no right whatsoever to criticise. However, another newspaper evidently *had* printed a letter of complaint from a 'Disappointed Spectator', since on 11 November the *Mercury* printed James Sadler's response. Making no reference at all to Windham, while also (carefully, to sustain the mystique?) avoiding specific identification of who the actual pilot had been, James laid out both the reasons for the change of location – their original choice of Piershill having been 'so much overlooked, and ... so far distant from town'[26] – and also for the unavoidably cursory nature of the flight due to the weather.

He also denied that he would profit by the £500 which had been insinuated. After deducting the cost of the hall where the balloon had been displayed, he expected to receive no more than £200 for the exhibition, and less than £220 from the sale of tickets on the day. Sizeable sums, of course, approaching that figure of £500, but against that margin had to be set the cost of his expenses and the 'total destruction' of the balloon. All in all, therefore, it was a letter which would have done much to persuade any neutral reader that 'the ungenerous remarks' of the 'Disappointed Spectator' were – as James had stated with unintended humour at the beginning of his letter – 'totally groundless'.

So, Windham had gone one better than his father in emulating Lunardi by making some ascents in Scotland. Over the next two years, he would also exceed his father's achievements in another country: Ireland. Before that, though, Windham made an apparently rare visit to his father's birthplace to give three lectures on the 'Practice of Aerostation' in May 1816. The venue was the Sun & Chequer Inn, conveniently close to his uncle's confectionary shop on Oxford's High Street, from where tickets could be purchased (and also from Mr Wyatt, the bootmaker, probably Windham's brother-in-law – *see* Appendix 8). The cost of three shillings, three times the standard charge to inspect an actual balloon, reflects either a false sense of his own appeal or the public fascination that balloonists continued to exert. For James, who must surely also have been present, the event cannot have failed to revive memories of some of the shows he had himself arranged in Oxford in 1789 and 1790, since

> the Lecture will be illustrated by a variety of brilliant and striking experiments on the nature and properties of the Gasses [*sic*]. Philosophical Fire Works will be exhibited; and small Balloons, on the principle of Montgolfiers, and with inflammable Air, will be made to ascend in the Lecture Room.[27]

Cork: Monday 2 September 1816

Perhaps being back in Oxford enlivened James Sadler's determination yet again, because when he and Windham travelled to Cork later in the year, it was evidently James who intended making the ascent, though, once again, it was Windham who ultimately did so 'in place of his father'.[28] At least one of them had arrived in the city as early as 21 June, when their highly ornate balloon and carriage, diplomatically embellished with 'shamrocks in gold … the Irish harp … and … the badge and star of the order of St. Patrick' was assessed as 'one of the most splendid and elegant vehicles fancy could picture'.[29] It was another two months before any launch took place, however, and they had evidently spent time elsewhere in the interim, since as the time of the launch approached the *Caledonian Mercury* (24 August) reported that they had arrived only the previous week, intentionally to coincide with the additional allure of the Cork assizes.

The launch was effected from what were called the 'new barracks' (towards the top of St Patrick's Hill), 'amidst an immense assemblage of persons, amongst whom were some of the most distinguished characters of the nobility and gentry'.[30] (For personal reasons, I would like to think that among the 'distinguished characters' of Cork who attended that day might have been Charles Henry Leslie (*c.* 1762–1842), who established the Ballincollig Gunpowder Mills a few miles from Cork in 1794. With time on his hands, and his expertise in guns and explosives, James would surely not have missed the opportunity to visit this impressive operation, where materials were transported through each stage of manufacture via a purpose-built canal. The mills were fundamental to English military resistance to Napoleon, becoming the largest in Ireland, and second largest in Britain, after Leslie – the brother of my ancestor Matthew Leslie – sold the site to the Board of Ordnance in 1805.)

An account of the flight, including Windham's own version of it, appeared in *Ramsey's Waterford Chronicle* of 7 September 1816. Once the balloon had been attached to the basket, Windham got in and 'was conducted from the place of inflation to a stage ... by the gentlemen who were formed into a Committee for that purpose, and among whom we were gratified to see some of the first characters in the country'. Then, as 'universal silence reigned', Windham was presented with a banner from the Countess of Shannon, and 'having bade adieu to his venerable father' the ascent began at 4.40 p.m.;

> whilst cheering acclamations, mingled with prayers and blessings, resounded on every side, reverberating from hill to hill, where thousands had placed themselves, in various groups, to witness what may indeed be estimated as one of the most daring efforts of human enterprise.

The day being 'exceedingly propitious, and the wind being moderate' Windham progressed gently beyond the hills to the south-east and descended near Ringabella, about 14 miles away, soon after 5 p.m. He had already secured the balloon through use of a grappling iron when

> the first person to appear was, I believe, the owner of the farm, who was not a little alarmed, for, although he had run in a direction towards it, he made a full stop at some distance, inquiring where I came from, and it was not without a great deal of exertion on my part in calling, that he was induced to come nearer.

Others soon arrived to help, however, and Windham was taken to stay the night with Mr Hodder, from where he wrote a short note to his father

> I am happy to say, I had an excellent descent within a quarter of a mile of the beach at Robert's Cove. I shall be at Mr Hodder's, at Fountainstown, where the balloon and car are. Send directly some conveyance for my return.[31]

Dublin: Tuesday 5 November 1816 (with Edmund Livingston)

Windham's next two ascents were also made in Ireland, both from Dublin, where his father, of course, had unfinished aeronautical business. The intention of the first, perhaps both, of these flights was clearly for James to improve on his effort of four years earlier. The balloon was put on display at the Dublin Society House in Hawkins Street, the advertisement in the *Freeman's Journal* of 24 September stating that the pilot would be the 'Late Member of the Board of Naval Works, and Inspector of Chemistry to the Army and Navy'. To enhance this impression, an image was included of the 'Descent of Mr. Sadler in the Irish Channel, after passing over 237 Miles of Water, and 43 by Land'.[32] Yet once again it was not the advertised Sadler who made the flight. Instead, it was Windham, taking with him on this occasion Edmund Livingston, a mysterious individual about whom the *Belfast Newsletter* of 8 November merely stated was 'a young gentleman connected with a mercantile house' in Dublin.[33]

The British press had barely noticed the Cork ascent; nor did this Dublin one, from Richmond Barracks on 5 November, attract much in the way of attention. The *Caledonian Mercury* (11 November) did report it, however, observing that the two men descended as darkness was falling about 50 minutes later in the Bog of Allen, about 30 miles from Dublin. In this remote and precarious situation, their salvation came in the guise of 'the cheering sound of the barking of a dog, guided by which, after wandering about an hour and a half, they reached a cottage'. This was how the *Belfast Newsletter* (12 November) described their escape, but it was apparently not until after Windham's death that his own account of their canine saviour was made public. On approaching the bog, Windham dispatched some ballast in order to retain height, since it was clear that to land in such terrain in the dark could easily be fatal. Soon after, on

> perceiving a small patch of vivid green, on which it seemed practicable to descend, I again opened the valve, cast out the grapnel irons, and, at a quarter past four o'clock, once more touched the earth; the grapnel tore up the earth for some distance, and unfortunately came in contact with a horse, which was racing about, alarmed at the appearance of the balloon. The horse was dragged by the leg, when, fortunately, the iron slipped its hold.[34]

On releasing more gas, the balloon became stationary, and though able to disembark, the ground was 'so soft as to sink under the slightest pressure, threatening to ingulph us in ruin at every step'. In the dark, with not even a star to guide them, they tried to find their way to safety, 'sinking at every step, and dreading the almost inevitable consequences of our alarming situation'. Then they discerned a hopeful sound: the barking of a dog. 'Wet, wearied, and exhausted', they made their way in its direction and reached a small cabin. It was now about 7 p.m. The cabin was too small to admit them both, however, so the dog's owner directed them to the home of William Smith of Ballybrack, about a mile away. Even now, the perils of the day were not over. Having survived journeys through both the air and the bog, a different danger presented itself when

> we were taken by the residents of Mr. Smith's house for robbers, with which of late this country has been dreadfully afflicted. We could hear them call for their fire arms and other weapons to protect themselves: we presently saw them opening the window, and having the banners with us, we forced one through the opening of the window, which they instantly seized, and inspecting it somewhat satisfied them, with the addition of our entreaties. They then allowed admission for one, but on our both seeing the fire so comfortable in appearance we both entered on the door being opened, and our wretched appearance soon excited pity; I may say we were the first persons who ever walked a bog in full dress.

After only a few hours' rest, Windham, concerned for the security of the balloon, got up again at 2 a.m., in order to fetch it by the light of a now risen moon, with the help of some local men recruited by Smith. He and Livingston then returned with it to Dublin. Windham concluded that as 'the dog was the chief instrument of our preservation … I obtained him from his master, and shall preserve him as a friend to whom I am so much indebted'.[35]

Undignified, unpleasant and unnerving though landing in a bog might have been, at least the touchdown was a soft one! Windham's next, across the Irish Sea, promised to be still softer unless he could go one better than his father had in 1812. And that, in what would prove to be the crowning achievement of his ballooning career, is exactly what he did do!

Dublin: Tuesday 22 July 1817

There were contradictory predictions about who would make this especially intrepid journey in the weeks preceding. An imminent ascent was initially announced in the *Freeman's Journal* of 18 June, but it was another month before there was any more news. The implication of the *Journal* of 18 July and a similar one the following day, with an image of Sadler's 1812 descent into the sea, is that James would make the journey. The departure time was fixed as being at 2 p.m.

on 22 July, but if one, or both, of the Sadlers felt for whatever reason unable to ascend themselves, Edmund Livingston would go instead.[36] The identical notice in the *Journal* of 21 July carried an additional clarification that a rumour that Livingston had refused to accompany Windham across the Channel was false, and that, on the contrary, 'his Friend' Livingston was 'exceedingly anxious to make the voyage', even though he had accepted that it would not be possible in view of the weight of ballast that would be needed. It was further rumoured that if neither Sadler went, Livingston might make the journey with Miss Thompson.[37]

In the end, it was Windham who went, alone, and slightly ahead of the announced time for once. The British press seemed less than engrossed by this hugely significant achievement, the *Caledonian Mercury*, as consistently interested in and supportive of the exploits of balloonists as any of the newspapers, being one of the few to announce over the next week both his departure and arrival on Anglesey. That being the case, Windham took the opportunity to capitalise, by swiftly publishing his own version of events, 'sold for the benefit of Mr. Sadler', under the title of *Aerostation: a narrative of the aerial voyage, of Mr. Windham Sadler, across the Irish Channel … on Tuesday, July 22nd*.

Eleven of the twenty-five pages of *Aerostation* are devoted to a justification of the utility of ballooning as a means of scientific advancement, the account of the voyage itself beginning with a third-person description of the launch from the Cavalry Barracks at Portabello. James was present at his son's launch for the last verifiable time as Windham, 'aided by his venerable father',

> poised the Machine, adjusting the weight of ballast, and judging of the power of ascent by the elasticity of the Balloon, he evinced that degree of knowledge of the science of Aerostation, which proved that his experiments were not confined to the mere practical part of the operation, but embraced whatever might ultimately tend to render the discoveries useful.[38]

The departure was at 1.20 p.m. Windham was

> at once astonished and delighted with the dazzling and almost unbounded view which burst upon the sight, embracing all the rich variety of Land and Sea, Mountain and Valley, City and Hamlet, together with the winding Coast and projecting Promontories, affording a feast almost too varied to be brought into one field of vision.

At about 4 p.m., as he approached the Welsh coast, he noticed that two vessels had set off in the direction of Dublin. It was a sight at which he 'exceedingly rejoiced', not only because his journey was nearing a successful conclusion, but because 'they would not only see my then state of security, but most probably my safe descent, and be the means of early communication of the facts, so as to remove all anxiety from the bosom of my father and friends'.[39]

Expertly, a 'safe descent' is what he contrived: 'at five minutes after seven o'clock I trod on the shores of Wales', landing about 1½ miles from Holyhead, being about 50 miles from Dublin as the crow flies. 'The first visitors Mr. Sadler had, on returning to Terra firma, were two ladies, one Miss R—, of this city [that is, Dublin], who had arrived a short time before in the packet, and the other Mrs. S—, the Lady of Captain S—, of the packet establishment' (identified in *Aerostation* as Captain Skinner, Captain and Mrs Stevens, and Miss Rogers). The two women were reported to have followed the balloon for 2 miles 'without regarding the impediments of ditch, fence, swamp etc.'[40]

For a significant first in aviation history, it had apparently all been fairly straightforward and uneventful, one reason perhaps why the press failed to give this airborne triumph the fanfare it surely warranted. Indeed, Windham himself gives the impression that what he had done was little more exciting than a ride in a fairground by occupying himself in the spare moments he had in Holyhead with a journey to the opposite extreme: a descent towards the bottom of the sea. At the time of his flight, the harbour at Holyhead was undergoing considerable improvements under the supervision of the engineer John Rennie. It is therefore unsurprising that Windham, 'the inheritor of his father's genius and intrepidity',[41] took the opportunity to examine a pier which was then under construction. On seeing the diving bell which was being used to accomplish some of the underwater work, he then expressed 'his anxious desire to go down in it, exclaiming "I am just come from the clouds, I should now wish to visit the deep"'.[42] He descended several fathoms, in the company of a Mr Foote, the chief diver, who much later recalled that on experiencing, as many people did, a slight pain in his ears, 'Mr. Sadler … described his sensations similar to those he experiences when descending in his balloon'.[43]

Windham lost little time in returning to Dublin. When the *Chichester* packet departed at 1 a.m. the next morning, he was on board, and arrived back in Dublin by 6 a.m.[44] Later that day, Wednesday 23rd, the inhabitants of Dublin 'had the gratification of seeing him pass through the city' at about 2 p.m. on his way 'to pay his respects to his Excellency the Lord Lieutenant, at the Phoenix Park, in a carriage accompanied by the venerable aeronaut his father'.[45] The *Liverpool Mercury,* recalling perhaps that James Sadler's own determination to reach the city of which he was so fond had denied him the honour of this aerial first in 1812, included these laudatory lines with its account of Windham's historic journey in its issue of 1 August:

> Now the bold Aeronaut, ascending far,
> Launch'd in the *azure void* his air-borne car;
> High on the winds, with silken sails unfurld,
> He waved his pennons o'er the admiring world;
> And looming far beneath his eager eyes,
> Saw Nature, mighty Panorama, rise!

This was a rare example of public praise, an omission which the *Literary Gazette* of 29 November highlighted on the front page, when reviewing *Aerostation.* The opening comment was: 'We do not think that this extraordinary voyage has received enough of public attention'; the final one was: 'To the Messrs. Sadlers science is much indebted for their exertions, and it is a pity that enlarged public encouragement has not more amply aided their individual labours'.

(Miss Thompson and Edmund Livingston – Dublin Wednesday 20 August 1817)

As the newspapers had intimated, Windham had apparently considered making his pioneering Anglo-Irish crossing in the familiar company of both or either of Miss Thompson and Edmund Livingston, 'but after consulting his father, he decided that he must carry the maximum of ballast and must go alone'.[46] To assuage their disappointment, however, before leaving Ireland to take up, for the time being, a more sedentary career in Liverpool, Windham assisted his two friends to ascend together on Wednesday 20 August.[47]

A notice in the *Freeman's Journal* (15 August) announced that the balloon was on display at the Dublin Society House and that Livingston and Miss Thompson would ascend on Monday 18th. As with earlier advertisements, the address from which tickets could be obtained, direct from Windham Sadler, was 85 Marlborough Street. The launch was delayed by two days, for reasons which were probably not, on this occasion, due to the weather. A long account in the *Freeman's Journal* (23 August) began:

We have been informed that the disappointments and inconveniences to the public, which attended the ascent of the Balloon on Wednesday, were not at all attributable to Mr. Livingston. – That gentleman was himself, as we understand a participator, and in no small degree in the *chagrin* which generally prevailed.

The problem was considered to be the fault of the 'the elder Mr. Sadler', who, on the Monday evening,

for the first time, objected to Mr. Livingston's ascending. Mr. Livingston conceiving himself bound to the performance of the promise made in the advertisements, declared his intention to persevere, and accordingly appeared upon the ground at the proper time. Here Mr. Sadler renewed his opposition, but was induced ultimately to allow Mr. Livingston to ascend, first however, exacting from him a solemn promise that the moment Miss Thompson should signify her wish to come down, Mr. L. would indulge her.

On this basis, the ascent went ahead. Before any great height had been attained, Miss Thompson released a tortoise with a parachute, and very soon after the balloon was seen to make a rapid descent. According to the *Journal*, the reason was that James Sadler had imposed a second condition: that Miss Thompson would

give her word that she would under no circumstances whatsoever permit Mr. L. to cross the mountain, but insist on coming down as near its base as possible. Mr. L. was not aware of such an arrangement, but on their approaching the mountain the lady insisted on descending, and Mr. L. was of course, compelled to comply.

Despite these additional pressures, Livingston made a safe and controlled landing on the edge of the estate of Mr (David) Latouche at Marlay (a distance of about 5 miles). Quite what caused James Sadler's intervention is not known, but most likely he was concerned for the safety of the balloon if entrusted to a novice like Livingston as well as for that of their family friend, Miss Thompson, who, having disembarked, 'expressed her conviction it would offend Mr. Sadler' if Livingston determined to reascend alone.

The *Journal*, less than impressed by the whole affair, continued its long report of 23 August with a lengthy criticism of the negative ramifications of balloon ascents. While emphasising that 'we are by no means unfriendly to Aeronautic pursuits' the newspaper concurred with many an editor of the previous century:

Whenever a Balloon is to ascend the town is literally emptied into the country. The great majority of the spectators are those industrous and working persons whose time is the most valuable, and they are called off from their employments at the hour of the day that they could labour most effectually.

A somewhat surprising and original additional complaint was that any delay in effecting an ascent necessitated 'remaining exposed to the air for several hours, and standing inactively upon damp ground', this being 'highly injurious to the constitution'. The article then asserted hysterically – apparently alluding to Windham and Livingston's ascent of November 1816 – that 'not less than fifteen hundred persons caught disease of which they died by going to see the ascent which took place near this city about twelve months ago'.

In respect of the Livingston–Thompson ascent, the lack of arrangements to observe the inflation process and the behaviour of the military was thought cause for further criticism, all of which led to the *Journal* finding it 'impossible to avoid saying, that a great mismanagement occurred, and it is to be hoped, that when an exhibition of the kind shall again take place, proper means may be used to ensure the public convenience and satisfaction'.

Poor Mary Thompson! Her feat of becoming the first woman ever to ascend in Ireland, on what was her last known ascent, was entirely ignored amidst this verbose criticism![48] It is not clear if Windham himself remained in Dublin to supervise the flight, but probably not, in view of James Sadler's prominent involvement. One feels Windham would have kept these frictions more private if he had been there. Quite possibly he was in Liverpool, preparing for a less adventurous phase of his life. Since his first experience at Cheltenham in 1813, when he was probably the youngest solo pilot then known, Windham had made ascents in England, Scotland and Ireland, and had touched down in Wales;[49] he had provided the inhabitants of several English towns and cities with their first ever view of a balloon ascent; he had probably been only the second English aeronaut to ascend with a female; he had enabled the first ascent by any woman in Ireland; and he had been the first person ever to cross the Irish Sea by air. At this point he seems to have decided that these achievements were sufficiently numerous and satisfying for any twenty-year-old, and that it was time to pursue a less invigorating, but more financially secure occupation with his feet planted firmly on the ground.

Windham Sadler, Liverpool Gas Light Company Engineer, 1817 to 1822

For details of the next few years of Windham Sadler's life, a principal source is S. A. Harris, who had access to Windham's diary – which cannot now be traced – when writing in the 1950s *The development of gas supply on north Merseyside, 1815–1949*. On 29 August 1817, little more than a week after his friends' Dublin flight, Windham attended a meeting of the committee of the newly formed Liverpool Gas Light Company. It was a job interview of sorts. The company's founding chief engineer had just departed, and on 3 September Windham made a note to himself to solicit 'letters from persons who can judge my abilitys'.[50] Despite having to do so from Dublin, whence he sailed on the *Alert* packet the very next day, his efforts were successful and he received notification of his appointment as the company's engineer on 21 September 1817, at a salary of £100 a year.

It is possible that he already had some experience in this line, as 'tradition has it that he was, at that time, engaged upon the erection of gas retorts at Dublin, but his name does not appear in any extant record of the Alliance and Dublin Consumers' Gas Company'.[51] On 26 September he left Dublin again for London, going via Holyhead on the *Pelham* packet. From there he took the 'Prince Regent' coach, at a cost of 'two guineas outside'. The whole journey to London took four days. Harris provides no clue as to Windham's reason for visiting London, but the capital was still ostensibly his home, and he no doubt had matters to deal with prior to his relocation. Where James Sadler was at this time is not clear. Windham left London again for Liverpool on 5 October, travelling via Oxford, Birmingham, Shrewsbury and Chester.[52]

In Liverpool, Windham found lodgings at 13 Great Crosshall St, 5 minutes' walk from the gasworks in Dale Street. He set to with a will that first week, being 'up before six in the morn and employed generally till my rest at 10'. He was mainly concerned with obtaining gas from retorted coal to meet the insatiable demand for gas lighting. Even on Christmas Day 1817 he went in to the works early to erect some hydraulic cylinders, and on 11 January 1818 he noted that he had 'put on so many lights in the course of 8 days as to increase the income of the company £500 more each year'. Later that month, he noted being 'busy nearly every evening this week until 2 or 3 in the morn'.[53]

These diary entries give no reason to doubt Harris' view that the rapid success enjoyed by the Liverpool Gas Light Company 'was undoubtedly due to Sadler's skill, energy, and enterprise', as a reward for which his salary was increased to £130 from July 1819. This was the same month that the first contract was signed for street lighting in Liverpool. Until then it had only been individual buildings – the town hall, clubs and theatres as well as some commercial properties – which constituted the company's customer base. The rise in salary was recompense for the increased workload – 220 lamps were installed by the end of the year – and in 1820 his salary rose again to £150. High though this remuneration was, it was a sum he could earn in a matter of days as a balloonist, of course – yet could equally easily lose it! In true Sadler style, that is exactly what appears to have happened on the one foray he did make into the skies while still an employee of the gas company.

Liverpool: Tuesday 28 Sept 1819 (with Edmund Livingston)

As it was from Liverpool that Windham Sadler made this aerial excursion, his only one in a period of six years, it was probably the easiest he ever had to organise. For company he took his friend Edmund Livingston, whose idea it seems mainly to have been. The *Lancaster Gazette* (2 October), first to provide a full report of the flight, stated that the balloon had been made – 32 feet in diameter, 38 feet high, and containing 31,880 cubic feet of gas – 'for the express purpose of crossing the Channel to Ireland'. It is not clear if that actually *was* the intention of the two men on this particular Tuesday, but if so, the result could hardly have been less satisfactory, since they very nearly found themselves well over a hundred miles in the opposite direction, just short of the North Sea!

The ascent was made from Liverpool's House of Industry at Brownlow Hill, the inflation having been conducted 'under the able and scientific direction of Dr. Traill', a notable Liverpool scientist. Lift off, in front of an estimated 80,000 spectators, was at a little after 2 p.m. Windham's own account of the journey was published in two parts in the *Lancaster Gazette*. Of note, he specified that it was friends (rather than family) who helped him with the ascent. Once beyond Blackburn, the two men

passed over many small villages and manufactories, from which numbers of people crowded; and at one particular place, unanimously invited us to descend. To gratify them, and amuse ourselves, we opened the valve and descended, making every appearance of acceding to their wishes by waving our banners, and standing up in the car. A general shout announced their conviction that their wishes were about to be gratified, and numbers hastened to where they expected we would alight; but we had approached too near the earth to carry on the deception any longer, and the expending of a bag of ballast terminated their hopes, and in a short time carried us to other scenes; good humour, however, prevailed, for we could plainly hear the huzzas, and see the waving of hats and handkerchiefs.[54]

Windham claimed to have reached a maximum altitude of more than 4 miles and endured temperatures well below freezing in order to cross the Pennines, after which:

Never was there a finer or more sublime spectacle witnessed than now presented itself; the dark and barren tract of that mountain country which we had just passed, partially buried by huge masses of dark vapour, and clouds rolling along their summits, contrasted with the highly cultivated and magnificent prospect, which, though faintly discovered, was every instant presenting new objects, and delighting us by their variety.[55]

They had gas and ballast to have gone farther, but decided to stop on account of approaching the coast. It was a rough landing, at Norton, 3½ miles from Stockton-on-Tees, in a strong wind. First their grappling iron broke under the strain and then Livingston was hurt when he was nearly thrown out of the car. He managed to stay on board, which was very fortunate, because, as Windham observed, he was thereby 'securing our mutual safety, as, by the balloon being released of his weight, it would immediately have re-ascended and carried me out to sea'.[56]

In terms of the distance travelled, and speed, Windham deduced they had gone 150 miles in 2 hours and 50 minutes, statistics which the *Liverpool Mercury* printed on 8 October. The *Lancaster Gazette* (2 October) had been quick to pronounce this as 'a distance and with a velocity never before accomplished with a balloon', but the *Caledonian Mercury* (7 October) modified this (more accurately) to merely 'the longest aerial voyage ever made in Great Britain'. Certainly, it was not the longest ever because, as the *Liverpool Mercury* (8 October) pointed out, 'Blanchard, upon one occasion, traversed 300 miles without alighting' (on his fourteenth flight, from Lille on 26 August 1785).[57] Strangely, for a newspaper able to recall this feat of a Frenchman from nearly thirty-five years earlier, however, it failed to mention the 84 mph journey of Windham's own father in 1811, in pronouncing that by travelling at over 50 mph for 3 consecutive hours, Windham's 'astonishing speed has never ... been surpassed'. The 237 miles of Sadler's total journey from Dublin in 1812 had also not registered.

The *Liverpool Mercury's* account included extracts from Windham's notebook. This exclusive insight enabled the newspaper to utilise probably the best ballooning pun to emerge in the entire thirty plus years of the activity, in claiming that theirs were 'particulars which may be literally said to proceed from the HIGHEST AUTHORITY'! Record-breaking or not, the pair were reckoned to have made an estimated loss of £400 on the whole adventure, although the *Mercury* was confident that the Liverpool public would more than cover this loss as

> it would be contrary to the character of the inhabitants to have it said, that they rewarded gentlemen who risked their personal safety in contributing to their rational gratification, by suffering them to pay the greatest proportion of the cost out of their own pockets.

The Liverpool periodical *Kaleidoscope* also bemoaned the financial outcome, but pointed out that many people had not deliberately avoided payment, but had merely chosen the most conducive locations on realising that 'the view of the balloon would be intercepted by the lofty roof and chimney of the workhouse'.[58] Subsequent newspaper reports suggested that this optimism about Scouse generosity was not misplaced, and no doubt some additional recompense was realised at a lecture Windham planned to give the following week.

*

The day after Windham's triumphant return to Liverpool from Stockton on Friday 1 October 1819, it would seem that a new generation of Sadlers was being drawn into the world of ballooning. At least, his nephew, John Coxe Hippisley Sadler (1805–60), son of John Sadler, seems the most obvious interpretation of the individual called 'Mr. Sadler, jnr.' who reluctantly came to the defence of a certain Mr S. Dean when public expectations were disappointed in Belvidere Gardens in Pentonville on 2 October.[59] When the crowd inside the gardens started to protest, suspecting, in an ever-familiar scene, that the 'evil genius' (as the *Morning Post* was harsh enough to call Dean) was attempting to defraud them, he delegated the responsibility to address the crowd to the teenaged Sadler, who began,

> I am a very poor orator, having never had occasion to address a public company before, but Mr. Dean has wished that some person acquainted

with the subject should inform you that it is impossible that the ascent can take place this day.[60]

The main problem was the very strong wind. Sadler went on to assure people that they could either have an immediate refund, or use their tickets on whichever day the ascent was rescheduled. This caused still greater unrest, as some people had lost or destroyed their tickets, and, inevitably, 'some described themselves to have done this, who had had none to lose or destroy'. Predictably also

> a detachment of the light-fingered gentry took advantage of the disorder thus created, and the crowd without, which was most numerous, and which had amused themselves for some hours by peaceably pelting each other with turfs and turnip tops, now tore down part of the fence, and invaded the garden.

Dean placed an apology-cum-explanation in the *Morning Post* the same day (4 October), promising to ascend when 'a more favourable opportunity' occurred. However, it would seem that in Mr Dean's opinion there was nonesuch for another four years![61]

These two events, in Liverpool and London, occurring within days of each other, represent the only known associations of the Sadler family with ballooning since Windham's historic Dublin flight of 22 July 1817. In London, the soda water factory having closed probably in 1816, the last year that it was listed in the *P.O. Directory*, James was probably coming to terms with enforced retirement. John Sadler, meanwhile, was seemingly pursuing his career with Beaufoy's. He also had new domestic responsibilities. The register of St Mary's, Lambeth shows that he had remarried, and with his new wife Elizabeth (*see* Appendix 8) now had three young daughters to consider: Eliza, Charlotte Rebecca, and Frances, apparently born between 1816 and 1822. At the baptisms of these girls, in 1821 and 1822, John described himself as a 'vinegar merchant', residing in Lambeth. He was evidently still pursuing former interests too, however, as he patented a method of smelting white lead in 1821.[62]

Irrespective of generation, the Sadler name remained firmly inseparable in the public mind from the very concept of flight. A tongue-in-cheek letter in praise of a still relatively new style of book, the novel, is a case in point. The writer, 'Bridgetina Adair', compared the beneficial effect of reading these 'romances' with numerous other exhilarating experiences, including 'the bracing health acquired by your aerial voyage through the Sadler balloonarian (allow me to coin a phrase) regions of azure sky and fanciful improbability'.[63]

*

Meanwhile, for a couple of years, Windham's career as a gas engineer in Liverpool continued on its successful path, as his salary increased in relation to demand for the product his company supplied. On 27 June 1820 he firmly cemented his Liverpool ties by marrying Catherine Richards (*c.* 1794–1832), eldest daughter of Thomas Richards Esq. of Liverpool[64] at St Anne's Church.

Towards the end of 1821, however, Windham fell out with the Liverpool Gas Light Company's sub-treasurer, John King, who criticised his professionalism. Sadler in return accused King of self-interest in the awarding of contracts (although a note in the Company's Committee of Works Book for 16 November states: 'Mr. Sadler having been called up, denied having attributed to Mr. King motives of interest'). The two men's enmity spilled out publicly at the end of October, King acknowledging on 2 November 1821 that 'the language used by myself as well as by Mr. Sadler on Saturday last in the presence of Mr. Lowry and Mr. Muncaster will bear any name but that of Gentlemanly'.[65] The dispute was ended only with Windham's departure, whether by desire or under duress. He received his last pay on 3 June 1822, Harris suggesting that

> it is possible that 'nerves' and lack of tact touched off the clash. Sadler, ... intrepid, impulsive, anxious that 'make' should keep pace with ever-growing demand, and King, in his early thirties, cautious, the infant company's financial watchdog, provided in their conflicting temperaments fruitful ground for seeds of discord.[66]

*

Suddenly finding himself with time on his hands, Windham twice acted as groundstaff for his friend Edmund Livingston, who still nurtured ambitions to cross the Irish Sea in one direction or other. Livingston never did succeed in his quest, however, his flight from Dublin on 4 August 1822 taking him only as far as Dunleary, a few miles south of Dublin; and when he set off from Preston in Lancashire on 9 September he reached only a little north-west of Blackburn, where he was knocked unconscious during the landing.[67]

The means of inflation for the Preston ascent was described as 'carbonated hydrogen gas, which was supplied gratuitously from the town's works'. This appears to be a misnomer, in combining the names of the type of gas favoured by aeronauts from the earliest years with that from a new source: coal. The use of coal gas in a balloon had first been demonstrated by Charles Green (1785–1870) the previous year, on his maiden flight in London in July 1821.[68] As a much cheaper source of fuel, this marked a key moment in ballooning history, and was no doubt one reason why Windham felt encouraged to make a return to the skies himself, once his application of 3 October 1822 for an engineering post at the newly founded Liverpool Oil Gas Company was rejected.[69]

Yet it would seem that the unquenchable curiosity of James Sadler, that irrepressible drive of his to always want to experiment and improve, may have led him to investigate the properties of coal-derived gas several years earlier. In its issue of 20 December 1817 *Jackson's Oxford Journal* claimed within a fairly technical paragraph on the derivation of gas from coal that:

> He has lately much improved the apparatus employed, and has so far succeeded in his endeavours as to have materially shortened the process: he has much increased the production of gas, and has lessened the objectionable part of the operation by decomposing the whole use of the tar, and getting rid of the sulphurated hydrogen.

However, still uncertain of the efficiency of coal gas for use with balloons, Livingston and Sadler made contingencies for the Preston ascent 'to create an instant supply of pure hydrogen gas, if the balloon should not, upon trial, be found sufficiently buoyant'.[70] It appears to have passed the test without the need for any such backup.

The Sadlers and George Graham (August and September 1823)

Meanwhile, at least two of the Sadler family became associated with another of the more celebrated aeronauts of the period: George Graham (*c.* 1785–1868?). He and his wife Margaret (*c.* 1804–64?) became renowned for their immense good fortune in avoiding serious injury despite many near misses over several decades. George Graham's first ascent was in London on 5 September 1823. It followed an aborted attempt the previous month which left the London citizenry in their usual state of destructive disappointment. Some of this negativity was aimed at the Sadlers, whose celebrity names Graham had invoked in his grandiose pre-publicity.

The *Morning Chronicle* (19 August 1823) printed a long account of Graham's failure of the day before, when he had been expected to rise from the White Conduit House in Islington with 'the powerful aid of Messrs. Sadler, the well-known and celebrated Aëronauts'. Once again, which of the Sadlers this meant is open to question. *Jackson's Oxford Journal* (23 August) spoke of 'father and son', which could mean James and John, or James and Windham, or the use of 'Sadler jnr.' in many of the accounts might mean eighteen-year-old John Coxe Hippisley Sadler. He did evidently know a fair bit about balloons, though could hardly be said to be 'well-known and celebrated'.

Whatever, all the accounts of the day agree that one or other Sadler deliberately caused the premature release of the balloon, in order to try to pacify an increasingly restless crowd, after an entire day spent in attempting to inflate it. Some newspapers reported that it was the younger Sadler who 'devoted his whole attention to the scheme, and was to have ascended with Mr. Graham, [and] declared he would mount the car at any time for the gratification of the public, if the balloon would only bear him aloft'.[71] It became increasingly clear that it would not, and 'Mr. Sadler jun. who actively exerted himself throughout the day, began at the latter end to hold out very poor hopes of success'.[72]

The *Times* (19 August) included a long account under the heading 'Balloon Hoax and Riot', which despite extending over two columns still got no nearer to identifying exactly which of the Sadlers were involved. When the crowd, tired of the delay, threatened to force their way into the bowling green where the launch was being prepared, it caused 'Mr Sadler, jnr., as we understood, to cut the ropes of the balloon, and send it by itself without car, parachute etc. on a voyage to the upper regions'. He did so

> in the hopes that the people out of doors would be satisfied, or at least that their irritation would be allayed, by witnessing its ascent even in so unfinished a state; but his hopes with regard to the out-of-doors people were by no means fulfilled, whilst the very mention of them to the in-doors people converted their rage and disappointment into a perfect phrenzy.

As the *Morning Chronicle* put it, 'the balloon, half inflated, without car or Graham, was released and ascended in a slovenly manner' and was then 'wafted ... from the pained view of the spectators' (to land 4 miles away). The unrest increased when Graham himself, who had sought refuge inside the White Conduit House, refused to yield to the clamour for the ticket money (of three shillings and sixpence) to be refunded. As a result 'taunts and reproaches were addressed very plentifully, as well to Mr. Graham as to the two Mr. Sadlers, by whom he was accompanied.'[73] However, as the *Morning Chronicle* (21 August) emphasised, the failure was something in which 'Mr. Sadler had no concern whatever; he having invariably given his opinion to Mr. Graham that neither the form of the balloon, nor the materials of which it was composed, would answer for the purpose of ascension'. Neither was the gas company thought to be at fault – this being coal gas, evidently – but rather the porous nature of the balloon, in the construction of which no Sadler had had any input.

Nonetheless, once the balloon had been liberated, the crowd's discontent was aimed at the younger Sadler, according to the *Ipswich Journal* (23 August), 'who, in reality, was in no respect answerable for the success of the enterprise, to which ... he had done his utmost to contribute', and 'had given his time and attention without remuneration.'[74] All the accounts agree that Graham himself was by this time nowhere to be seen, and another inglorious day in the history of ballooning ended when 'at nine o'clock at night "the curious" growlingly, and ready to quarrel with anybody who might wish it, returned to their homes, not very well pleased with their day's amusement'.[75]

George Graham vindicated himself soon after, by successfully ascending from Soho on Friday 5 September 1823.[76] Graham's own account of this, his first ever ascent shows that he had intended going with 'his friend, Mr. Sadler jnr.', by whom he may have meant either Windham or the younger John. However, owing to some misunderstanding about the date, Graham instead took another friend, Thomas Harris. So, as well as the pressures which faced every balloonist – the weather, the equipment, the landing, the crowd – Graham also had to deal with a particularly heavy weight of expectation after his previous failure and the presence of a novice passenger. In addition, if one account was to be believed, he also had the wrath of an unhappy wife to face on his return: Margaret Graham, who had expected to be his accomplice, and, so it was said, 'did not rest satisfied' at being excluded![77]

With this success under his belt, Graham turned his attention to trying to address the residual resentments, not to mention some potential suits for losses and damage, that his earlier failure at the White Conduit Gardens had caused. So, on Friday 12 September 1823 the crowds again flocked to the same venue, expectant of having their earlier dashed hopes fulfilled. Again, however, they were disappointed – although this time Graham did at least get off the ground. He had again intended going with 'Mr. Sadler jun.', but when a naval officer offered £40, Sadler deferred to him, while still assisting with the preparations amidst 'a scene of confusion which was really disgraceful' on account of a complete lack of crowd control.[78] Once the balloon was inflated

> Mr. Sadler, assisted by some other persons, commenced the work of attaching it to the vehicle. This work was greatly and most vexatiously retarded by the pressure of the crowd, within the railing which inclosed the balloon; they pressed around Mr. Sadler and some of his friends, and completely shut out the modest and most orderly part of the spectators from the possibility of seeing what was going forward.[80]

The *Times* (13 September) was of the opinion that whichever Sadler it was who was there on this occasion then got into the car. When it failed to lift, mainly on account of having lost too much gas when the fabric was accidently ripped, Graham decided to proceed alone (the naval officer having presumably thought better of it anyway by then). He travelled for only half a mile before coming down rapidly, but safely, in a gravel pit. The crowd was satisfied, but Graham nonetheless felt too exhausted, or perhaps wary, to face them, and it was left to Sadler to thank them for their patience and to seek, and receive, their recognition of Graham's 'undaunted courage'.

So, no matter which of the Sadlers were present to advise George Graham, their collective understanding of the advantages and limitations of coal gas can only have been enhanced by these experiences, whether learned first-hand or vicariously. Undeterred by the reminders of the hazards that lay on the ground as well as those of a more expected nature aloft, Windham Sadler relaunched his own aeronautical career at the beginning of that same month of September 1823.

13

'EXPECTATION STOOD ON TIP-TOE': WILLIAM WINDHAM SADLER, 1823–24

Leeds: Thursday 4 September 1823

By some quirk or mismanagement, there were two balloons scheduled to ascend from Leeds in the first week of September 1823. After a gap of nearly forty years, suddenly the city was to experience two flights on consecutive days![1]

Windham Sadler, making his sixteenth ascent, was set to go first and Charles Green the following day. Neither had realised the other's intentions according to the *Leeds Mercury* (6 September), Sadler having been the first to make his plans public, but Green having made the earlier application to the local gas company. As a result, 'it became necessary for Mr. S., at considerable expense, to generate his own gas, for which purpose he erected a large apparatus in the yard of the Coloured Cloth Hall'. The implication of this seems to be that it was hydrogen that Windham Sadler used on this occasion, presumably unexpectedly, certainly expensively, and, by implication, decidedly resourcefully.

Windham was first up, going on Thursday 4th, a day later than planned on account of the weather on the Wednesday. The amicable understanding was that in such an eventuality Green would then also postpone his own flight by a day. It is a gesture which suggests that the general spirit of camaraderie which had distinguished relations between the early aeronautical pioneers – with the possible exception of Blanchard – appears to have been sustained through to the nineteenth century. Perhaps Green, the son of a London fruiterer, found some kind of rapport in their shared tradesmen's background. However, even on the Thursday the wind was sufficiently strong to retard the process of filling Windham's brand new balloon, of 48 feet in height, but as seven o'clock approached he felt obliged to leave, even though the balloon was still only partly filled. As a consequence, he had already had to abandon the idea of taking a companion, and even after removing much of the ballast and inessential equipment, the balloon initially failed to gain any height. Help was at hand, however, and it was 'soon seized by a number of persons in the yard (amongst the first Mr. Green)'[2] and returned to its original position. Much more ballast was then removed, and despite striking the Cloth Hall when released for a second time, and losing more ballast as a result of the collision, this time the balloon did successfully clear the building. Windham landed safely 50 minutes and 36 miles later, near Market Weighton, in the near-dark, then travelled overnight to arrive back in Leeds by the next morning, keen no doubt to be able to return the favour and help with Charles Green's ascent if he could.

In fact, the next day was much finer, and Green ascended from the White Cloth Hall with comparative ease. His landing north of Gainsborough was a rough one, however, in which he was ejected from the balloon, which was carried away on the wind. As it was valued at about £400[3] this was a considerable additional blow to what the *Leeds Mercury* (6 September) had already discerned as: 'a competition unfortunate for the pecuniary interest' of both aeronauts. As Samuel Johnson had perceived many years earlier, the entertainment could in any case easily be had for free:

> A man that had got upon the Cloth-hall, and in that way witnessed the inflation of the balloon, on Thursday, without paying the admission fee, when he saw Mr. Sadler cast out ballast, in order to enable him to clear the buildings, entertained the notion, that he was throwing the sand bags at *him*, to resent his intrusion, and congratulated himself upon the aeronaut having so bad an aim to miss the mark.[4]

Sheffield: Thursday 18 September 1823

If the utilisation of coal gas was indeed an influence on Windham Sadler's decision to return to a career as a professional balloonist, it was more than two years after Green's first demonstration of its use that Windham followed suit. Hydrogen was certainly still the most effective means of elevation, but it was also very much more expensive. It was also much less easily acquired, now that an increasing number of Britain's larger towns and cities were able to offer a ready supply of coal gas from their own works. However, Windham's first known experience of using coal gas was not an unqualified success. Having already had to abandon two attempts to ascend from Sheffield on account of problems with the supply, if a third attempt failed, he announced that he would resort to the tried and tested use of hydrogen.[5] In the end, he used a combination – '9,000 feet of hydrogen and 11,000 feet of carburetted hydrogen' (a misnomer for coal gas) – to travel 17 miles in an easterly direction in 1 hour and 10 minutes. The gas company acknowledged that the initial difficulties had been due to their 'impure gas', and waived any charge.[6]

Spectators' first-hand accounts of balloon ascents are relatively plentiful; those of the end of a journey understandably much less common. This one, written by a resident of the Yorkshire village of Tickhill shows that the superstitious fear caused by the earliest balloons had been replaced by unbridled excitement:

> I just sit down to inform you that I have had a fine race after Mr. Sadler, in his balloon, which descended about a mile south of Tickhill, in a grand style. We had all sorts and sizes after us, and all ages from two years to four score; and such tumbling into the dykes, and squalling of women, as I never heard in my life.[7]

York: Monday 22 September 1823

Windham Sadler's reception on his next Yorkshire descent was rather less satisfactory, as indeed was the ascent in stormy conditions, a reprise of his Leeds experience, as he struck a building on lift off from York. Once clear, he was soon out of sight, carried on the strong wind, and descending with some difficulty at the remote village of Kellington, about 20 miles south of York, about 30 minutes later.[8] Here his arrival attracted only hostility, summarised with a certain metropolitan relish in the *Times* (29 September) as:

> In all his voyages he never received such inhospitable treatment as from the inhabitants of Kellington; their indifference to assist him, and their

rapacity, more resembled a Cornwall wreck-hunter than the general well-known liberality of a Yorkshireman; not a crust of bread nor a draught of water was offered.

Liverpool: Tuesday 30 September 1823

Windham Sadler's fourth and last ascent of the month took him back to familiar territory: Liverpool, a place where he might have expected decidedly greater 'liberality' from the public. Sadly this proved not to be the case here either though, as the familiar woeful tale unfolded of a limited sale of tickets for the launch, while thousands enjoyed the spectacle nearby for free. It would seem that nationally the printed media was losing interest in balloons by this time – except when failures were followed by civic unrest – as this flight was barely commented on elsewhere. However, the *Liverpool Mercury* of 3 October redressed the balance by devoting a very large amount of space, in two separate articles, to this, Windham's second ascent from Liverpool.

The House of Industry at Brownlow Hill was again the chosen location. It had been criticised exactly four years earlier because the height of its walls meant that those inside were very quickly denied a view of the balloon once it had departed. Be that as it may, on this occasion the lack of paying customers was attributed more to the high entrance fee than to the high walls. Outside, for those who had saved themselves three shillings and sixpence, it was quite a different matter:

The heights exhibited a solid mass of individuals of all classes and ages, and even the ledges of the old quarries to the north-east, 'where scarce was footing for a goat,' the wall tops, and lamp-posts, were thick set with adventurous urchins, gazing with eager expectancy at the summit of the balloon, which early appeared above the buildings, undulating to and from as if eager to burst the cords that bound it to the earth. The scene assumed an appearance not unlike that of a fair. Tents and booths, the erections of an hour, served and discharged their thirsty customers. Numbers of carriages, filled with well-dressed individuals studded the ground; and drays and carts bore happy prattling groups of females and children, enlivened by their various expressions of impatience, curiosity, and wonderment. Nor must we forget the see-saws in which the little lads and lasses made their miniature ascents, nor the baskets of tempting gingerbread, and apples and plums, with the noisy and monotonous music of the venders [*sic*].

Conditions inside were praised by the newspaper as 'clean and comfortable' and 'never more healthy than at the present moment', and as a prelude to the launch the resident children 'with drums and fifes, walked round the square, and had a most interesting appearance'. As the preparations neared their conclusion, with gas supplied from the nearby mains, 'expectation stood on tiptoe' until, at about 4.30 p.m., the balloon was released. To initial disappointment, it rose only just beyond the House of Industry, collided with the chimney of a house, scraped over its roof and descended abruptly again in some nearby fields. At this point a passenger who had also been helping with the inflation was obliged to disembark, enabling Windham to achieve the necessary lift to proceed alone. Thus disencumbered, he reached the vicinity of Warrington, 22 miles away, in less than an hour. Here, in contrast to his most recent reception in the village of Kellington, he was warmly received, and transport was found to take him back to Liverpool at no cost to himself.

A celebratory dinner was held at the Globe Tavern, Russell Street, on Thursday 2 October. In response to many toasts in his honour he 'returned thanks in a neat and excellent speech'. A song had been composed (by a Mr Gifford) for the occasion. Based on the theme of Sadler entering Jupiter's realm, it ends:

> Had Jupiter seen the delight of the crowds,
> Who assembled to witness your flight through the clouds,
> He'd have made you immortal; then what should we do?
> This evening our *globe* had been dull without you.
> Come fill up a bumper, my friend, for a toast:
> May this undaunted aëronaut, Liverpool's boast,
> Should he visit Jupiter's palace again,
> Return safe and sound to the regions of men.[9]

The man who had disembarked was later revealed not to have been a wealthy fare-paying passenger or underwriter of the cost, as might have been expected from precedent, but a certain James Donnelly, a lowly nightwatchman operating in the vicinity of Liverpool's St Thomas' Church (where Windham and Catherine Sadler appear to have worshipped). A few months later the *Liverpool Mercury* printed a letter from Donley (as they spelled his name) 'precisely as it reached us', adding sarcastically that it felt unable 'to revise or correct the composition of a soaring genius like the writer'. The purpose of Donnelly's ungrammatical appeal was partly to assert that his rapid departure from Windham's balloon had been out of necessity, not, as some said, through cowardice, but mainly Donnelly wished to advertise through the newspaper's 'widely extended and intilligent columns' his desire 'to become an Airial Voyager' in his own right by navigating from Liverpool to Dublin, from Manchester to Dublin, London to France, and even Scotland to Norway. So confident was he in his 'new plan different to any yet adapted' that he promised that 'those persons who may be inclined to assisted me ... shall have their remittance returned in 12 months'.[10]

Given the range of individuals from whom Windham could have selected a companion, his choice of an evident fantasist like Donnelly is interesting. Evidently he saw some merit in Donnelly's grandiose aspirations as he subsequently provided him with employment and another opportunity to fly. Perhaps he recognised something of his father in the man: someone of limited education who nonetheless exhibited sound, perhaps even inspired, thinking, but without the means to realise his ambitions. Whatever, Windham thought sufficiently highly of him to take him on one more flight. Sadly for both of them, it would prove to be his last and fatal one.

Birmingham: Monday 13 October 1823 (with James Busby)

In the months before Donnelly issued his grandiose plea, 'Liverpool's boast', as Gifford had called him, he made three more flights. The first was within a fortnight. The venue was Birmingham, which was as far south as Windham would take his balloon for the remainder of his life. Although a rapidly expanding city of some 80,000 people, Birmingham had no ideal enclosed place from which to ascend. The Crescent was decided upon, yet this was 300 yards away from the nearest supply of coal gas and entailed the additional cost of erecting fencing to exclude the non-paying public. An additional disincentive was the lack of any single building in Birmingham large enough to display the balloon in advance, thereby further diminishing the overall viability of the enterprise.[11] No doubt already nervous on this score, Windham threatened to pull out when the head of the gasworks wanted to charge him £15 for the gas he had used in tests beforehand. There was a public outcry, for once not aimed at a crestfallen failed aeronaut, and the company agreed to waive its charge.[12] Ultimately, he probably need not have worried unduly. One would imagine that the reported receipts of £235,[13] on what was an uneventful flight of 30 minutes to Stourbridge, would have been sufficient to realise a reasonable profit on this occasion.

A contributor to this income was Sadler's companion on the flight, James Busby (of Edgbaston), who paid twenty guineas.[14] The ascent was scheduled as part of the Birmingham Music Festival, and Sadler's own account appeared in the *Derby Mercury* (22 October). It is unremarkable save for one observation – exactly the sort one might expect from an engineer – on the changing Midlands landscape, namely the 'most beautiful prospect ... of a richly interesting and thickly populated country, so many furnaces &c. the smoke and flames of which had a singular and novel appearance'.

Derby: Tuesday 28 October 1823 (with Charles Brown)

Windham Sadler's next ascent had a particular poignancy. It was to be in Derby, the town in which his father had encountered such frustration and controversy almost exactly ten years earlier. Would those surviving members of the balloon committee still hold a grudge? Dr Forester, with whom James Sadler had conducted his highly public dispute, was still one of the two most prominent physicians and surgeons in Derby, a juror, and well-known subscriber to a variety of charitable causes. It would have been only natural for Windham to be a little more than usually apprehensive.

At least this time, unlike in Birmingham, there was a chance for the public to view the machine beforehand, as a notice in the *Derby Mercury* (22 October) announced. A special building had been erected in the yard of the Old George Inn (where Windham was staying, as his father had done in 1813). Admission was one shilling, and tickets for seats on the day were either two shillings and sixpence or five shillings. Unusually, it was stated that children would be half price, perhaps because the low sales in Liverpool had been partly attributed to the prohibitive cost for anyone with a large family.

An article in the same issue of the *Mercury* observed 'that the public will be gratified with a spectacle never yet exhibited in this town, and which for wonder and interest cannot be surpassed'. Ouch! How Richard Forester must have winced! A more specific reminder of the ten-year-old spat occurred in the account of the ascent itself, printed a week later, when the heightened excitement was attributed to the recollection of 'a failure in a similar attempt ten years ago' (unfairly implying that the failure had been Windham's, as no mention at all was made of James). The balloon was filled using pipes from the nearby gasworks. The comment that this was 'less interesting as a sight than on some occasions where the gas is made on the spot and the busy process can be witnessed' is perhaps indicative of why people felt increasingly disinclined to pay to be close to the point of ascent now that aeronauts were using piped coal gas straight from the mains. Doubtless to be able to witness at close quarters the fizzing, crackling, odorous results of pouring sulphuric acid onto quantities of iron would be deemed by many to be worth a shilling or two extra, even if they were denied ultimately the best view of the machine in motion. With even that incentive now removed, the observation was made once again that 'pecuniary remuneration ... fell far short of what might have been reasonably expected from so large a concourse of people so peculiarly gratified as all seemed to be'.[15]

Windham's own account of the flight, which was made with Charles Brown of Sheffield,[16] was included with the *Mercury*'s report. Again it contained little of note – the Sadlers were not a family given to outbreaks of lyrical whimsy! – except one observation when, at their greatest altitude of about 1¼ miles, 'we were both delighted with the magnificent appearance of the clouds, which appeared like an immense crator [*sic*] beneath us covered with eternal snows'. Sinking then to about 700 yards they conversed with people on the ground. It was separately reported that in coming 'so near that he spoke to the people with his trumpet' at Over Selston (Derbyshire), Sadler had been 'in greater peril than he was aware of' because Samuel Waterall, a farmer's son, 'expressed his regret that he had not had his gun with him, that he might have fetched that huge thing down, for he might as well have had it as any body else! and added, that he threw some stones, but could not hit it!'.[17] Oblivious of having been such a target, the pair landed near Mansfield, after a journey of 22 miles in 45 minutes.

Nottingham: Monday 3 November 1823

The *Derby Mercury* was also the first newspaper to report on Windham Sadler's next ascent, his twenty-second, from Nottingham Castle. In its issue of 5 November it noted that paying spectators were more numerous on this occasion, owing to a reduction in admission price. It was another occasion when Sadler had intended taking a companion, but was unable to gain the necessary uplift and so went alone. En route, he indulged in a rare recorded assessment of his own physiology when, at an altitude of about 2¼ miles, he wrote of having 'examined the state of my pulse, which I found with the aid of the common pulse glass to beat 79 per minute, which previous to my ascending was 75'. Later in the account he also revealed with casual lack of concern that the country below him was 'a vast field of snow'. He landed 5 miles from Lincoln, having covered an estimated 36 miles in total.[18]

*

Seven ascents in two months! It was a literally breathtaking pace, made all the more impressive by the wintry conditions which were evidently prevailing during the last one. Very understandably, Windham Sadler now took a break and turned his attention to matters of a much less risky and more sustainable nature. His idea was to establish 'under the sanction of most of the medical profession of this town' some medicated vapour baths.[19] With this in mind, the *Liverpool Mercury* noted that he was going to London, though with what precise purpose is not stated. His aging father seems certain to have been more or less confined to the capital by this time, and no doubt Windham found time to visit him, to provide him with a first-hand account of his seemingly flawless feats of the autumn. No doubt James could also offer him some advice on his new business venture: the chemistry of water rather than air. Indeed, it can probably be assumed that filial affection and concern was the principal reason for making such a long journey in the depths of winter. Quite possibly it was to make arrangements for his father's immediate care. As no record of his mother Martha's death has been found, and it seems likely to have occurred at about this time, this may also have occasioned the journey.

Windham was not away from Liverpool for long, however. He was back by early December to supervise the installation of his 'vapour and other baths' in his chosen location: the corner of Wood Street and Hanover Street.[20] The *Liverpool Mercury* (12 December) approved:

> The qualifications which Mr. Sadler possesses as a chemist, and the thorough knowledge he has ... of every sort of gaseous combination, point him out as eminently qualified to superintend an establishment of Medicated baths, the want of which the faculty have long lamented.

By the end of the following month, all was ready. Under the name by which he had become recognisable as a balloonist over the previous few years, W. W. Sadler, he announced the opening of his 'Warm, Vapour, Medicated, and Other Baths' in the *Liverpool Mercury* of 30 January 1824. The premises were large enough to include residential apartments, for both men and women.

Manchester (Salford): Friday 23 April 1824

With this water-based business established, come the warmer weather, Windham Sadler turned his attention again to the air and embarked on a rapid succession of ascents, encompassing northern England, Scotland and Ireland. The first was from the Old Cloth Hall, Salford, as part of George IV's birthday celebrations. It was the first ascent anyone had made from this part of Lancashire since that of his father, 'the first, and only, aeronaut known at Manchester'.[21] The day after the ascent, the *Manchester Guardian* (24 April) gave a very long account, including considerable technical detail about the preparations in the days beforehand and on the day itself. Windham's first intention had been to use purely what the newspaper called 'carburetted hydrogen', to ascertain if it was capable of taking two people. However, the gas obtained from both the Manchester and the Salford works proved 'much too ponderous for the purpose', something which 'by the way is pretty conclusive evidence of its good quality'. As a result, Windham was obliged to spend considerable time constructing the means to access a dual supply of both coal gas and hydrogen. Even then, on the day, the combined weight of two men once again proved too much of an impediment.

His intended passenger had been Robert Haworth Peel of the Third Dragoon Guards, who was stationed in Manchester at the time, and was in any case a particularly large man. Via his mother Anne (*née* Haworth), Peel was the grandson of Jonathan Haworth (1736–86), who had hosted James Sadler's two Manchester ascents in 1785. He was also the cousin of Robert Peel (1788–1850), the Home Secretary (and future Prime Minister and founder of the Metropolitan Police). When the balloon failed to rise, a Mr Platt, 'who accompanied Mr. Sadler from Liverpool, being rather lighter than Mr. Peel', took his place. It was still to no avail. Both would-be passengers would in fact get second chances in due course, but on this occasion Sadler had no choice but to go alone. Some further details of the ascent and descent, near Knutsford after a flight of 30 minutes, were supplied by the *Guardian*, but lacked the precision of the *Derby Mercury*'s report of 28 April, which included such specifics as the ratios of 14,000 cubic feet of carbonate of hydrogen to 6,000 feet of pure hydrogen. The *Mercury*'s reporter also (perhaps revelling in the recent acquisition of some state-of-the-art timepiece?) pinned the departure time down to 'nine minutes and forty-five seconds past five o'clock' and the length of time that the balloon remained visible as 'two minutes and fifteen seconds'! Sadler's descent was a safe one as far as the balloon was concerned, but he himself received a severe blow to the head after disembarking. Treated on his return to Manchester the same day, it proved less serious than first feared.

The *Newcastle Courant* (1 May) added that a spectator had had £160 stolen, opining that the thief had 'made a better day's work than Mr. Sadler who received only about £145, out of which he had to defray very considerable expenses'. The *Manchester Guardian* (24 April) had also put the receipts at £145, attributing this low return to people staying away because of the weather, and although an attempt was made 'to collect money from the persons assembled in the streets outside ... a very trifling sum indeed was obtained'. It was the same old story then, of time, labour, expence and risk, for little or no reward. It evidently had a significant bearing on viability if a paying passenger could be accommodated, although it is quite possible that the Sadlers were never exactly in it for the money. One gets the impression that they were rather more interested in getting aloft than getting ahead. Certainly, Windham refused to be deterred and within a fortnight had made preparations to go up again.

Rochdale: Thursday 6 May 1824 (with Mr B. Platt)

Mr B. Platt, the Liverpool man whose lighter weight had proved no advantage in trying to take Peel's place at Salford, got another chance soon enough, on a trip from Rochdale, where the balloon was filled direct from the town's gasometer. At one point, the men heard a cuckoo, and also the voices of villagers 'whose noise fell on our ears like the howling of a distant pack of hounds'.[22] The flight to Bacup was short, covering only 7 miles in 35 minutes, and uneventful, save for some slight damage to the balloon, caused by the curiosity of the crowd once they had landed. A short account in the *Manchester Guardian* (8 May 1824) was repeated with no further expansion in various regional newspapers, the London press apparently deeming this brief and uneventful journey not worthy of any notice at all.

Liverpool: Thursday 27 May 1824 (with Robert Haworth Peel)

Next came Windham's Sadler's third flight from Liverpool, and, as on the previous occasion in September 1823, the *Liverpool Mercury* was eloquent and enthusiastic. Both Platt and Robert Haworth Peel were in attendance again, but this time, the newspaper stated, with little concern for tact, 'gas of a quality sufficiently buoyant to bear up a more than usual weight' was generated and Peel was able to ascend. Indeed, it was on account of Peel's other commitments that the launch had been delayed by a week anyway. This turned out to be somewhat apt, as the day of the launch transpired to be Ascension Day!

Windham had set up the balloon and accompanying equipment in the cattle market in Lime Street, and used both hydrogen and coal gas. As in September 1819, the former was generated with the assistance of Dr Traill, while the latter was obtained from Windham's former employers at Dale Street. In playful mood, the Liverpool Gas Light Company contrived this tribute:

A handsome balloon, of considerable size and painted to resemble that of Mr. Sadler, with a car &c. was let off from the gas-works in Dale Street, and was the cause of much apprehension to some, and of subsequent merriment to others. The car appeared to contain two travellers, and, from its swinging motion, fears were entertained that they would be thrown out.[23]

The real balloon 'in alternate stripes of crimson and yellow' was 34 feet in diameter, 42 feet in height and used 560 square yards of silk, supplied by a Liverpool merchant called Wright. On the day, the usual challenge ensued of providing sufficient gratification for those who had paid by trying to restrict the gratuitous entertainment of those who had not. The cattle market was enclosed using

sails hoisted upon poles to a considerable height above the walls; it having been ascertained that several of those who owned the overlooking property purposed letting off their premises to spectators, and thus defeating in a great measure the exertions of Mr. Sadler's friends to obtain for him an adequate remuneration by the sale of admissions in to the square. Notwithstanding this precaution, numbers of individuals found their way on [sic] the tops of walls, and tore or drew aside several of the sails; and many even mounted to the top of the tent, nor retired till it bent beneath their weight, and they found themselves in danger of being precipitated to the ground. The tops of the adjacent houses that overlooked the scene, upheld masses of spectators, and indeed throughout that part of the town many of the roofs and even the chimney tops were amply tenanted.

Unusually, the two men's 'appropriate' clothing was described on this occasion: Peel wore 'a blue flannel round jacket, and military foraging cap, and white trowsers' and Sadler 'a round jacket, and trowsers, and a fur cap'. Platt was very much involved, and got into the car to test its buoyancy once the additional gas had been supplied from Dale Street. The ascent inspired these loyal words:

> There is an indescribable emotion which arises from the contemplation of so extraordinary a spectacle of human ingenuity and daring, and we know of no gratification in which all classes may more freely and innocently indulge.

The two men landed 4 miles from Chester, between 5 p.m. and 6 p.m., and were back in Liverpool by midnight according to Windham's own account.[24] A banquet at the Globe Tavern in Russell Street followed. Some thirty friends attended, and, as on the previous occasion, many songs, some composed especially for the occasion, were sung throughout the night. Sadler may have been toasted as a returning hero on Merseyside, but down south, the *Morning Post* at least revived its opposition to such exhibitionism. Influenced quite possibly by the death of the balloonist, Thomas Harris, the previous week (*see* Appendix 9), the newspaper covered Sadler's flight in its issue of 31 May in a mere two sentences, the second being: 'This is all that is necessary to be known of so idle and senseless an enterprize.'

Chester: Monday 7 June 1824

The amiable reception that Windham Sadler and Robert Haworth Peel had had in Chester must have influenced Windham's evidently spontaneous commitment to demonstrate to the city the commencement of a journey as well. Probably the offer of free gas also played its part.[25] The *Lancaster Gazette* (12 June) carried a brief account of his short journey from the castle in Chester to Taporley, about 10 miles away. A longer report, including the pilot's own assessment, appeared later that month. It had been a beautiful, calm and clear evening, and he had reached a height of about 3 miles before effecting a very gentle descent, at which point:

> A countryman, whom I induced to get into the car to prevent it again ascending, and to keep the valve open, was considerably alarmed; his good wife coming up soon after, conjectured that her husband was about to take a trip which caused her to manifest considerable agitation, and it required some arguments to remove her fear.[26]

Given the experience of others who had been unexpectedly precipitated into becoming aeronauts, rather than temporary human ballast, her 'agitation' was perhaps fully justified!

Edinburgh: Monday 28 June 1824 (with Mr Campbell)

As befits a publication emanating from a city with such a long scientific pedigree, the *Caledonian Mercury* (1 July) provided a very considered appraisal of Windham Sadler's next ascent, from Edinburgh's Heriot's Green. Within multiple accounts there was a lengthy description of the structure and appearance of his balloon, of the means of inflating it (using coal gas) and of the scientific merits of ballooning. The newspaper's accounts also included a technical analysis of the lifting capacity of the gas in relation to the weight of its load and relative to wind speed and atmospheric pressure, and a separate section on meteorological observations. These details no doubt derived from one or more of the 'scientific characters' among the 'numerous and highly respected assembly' which watched the process of inflation. One was Professor John Leslie (1766–1832) who detected the coal gas generated on the day to be only two-fifths lighter than air, a factor which accounted for the relatively slow nature of the ascent and the low maximum height that Windham achieved. After passing over Leith and the island of Inchkeith, he and his passenger, Mr Campbell of Saddel, landed in a field belonging to a Mr Balfour of Bankhead near Leven, 'about eight miles from the spot where Lunardi descended 37 years before'.[27]

The sequence of related articles in the *Mercury* ended with a familiar appeal to a tight-fisted public, warning that 'it becomes a more imperious duty in this case to adopt some means of levying what is necessary to defray the expences incurred, together with a suitable remuneration to Mr. Sadler for his trouble and risk', otherwise 'we can never again expect any similar exhibition'.[28] Advance tickets had been priced at three shillings and sixpence (and two shillings for children), but takings on the day became compromised when 'an unruly mob broke down the barrier, and rushed in promiscuously, after which no more money was drawn'. The two men returned to Edinburgh by 1 a.m., and Windham set off for Glasgow the following day, the Tuesday, with every intention of ascending from there on the Thursday.

*

However, no Glasgow ascent took place. Windham explained the reasons in a letter printed in the *Caledonian Mercury* of 3 July. Although he had come to an agreement with the Provost of Glasgow when passing through on his way to Edinburgh, and had made arrangements with the local gas company, no venue had been agreed. When the cattle market was proposed he started to make preparations, only to find that the magistrates had suddenly insisted that he would underwrite the cost of any damage the crowd might do to neighbouring properties. This he declined, 'having on no previous occasion ever been called upon for any similar guarantee'. It seems probable that the Glasgow magistrates had got wind of an upcoming compensation claim filed by a resident of Edinburgh's Castle Hill, which overlooked Heriot's Green, even though this had not yet been made public. The gist of the writ against Sadler was 'for damages he alleged to have sustained, in consequence of the railing across the street precluding him from all access to his house'.[29]

The Glasgow authorities reconsidered, however, and the Grammar School, familiar to Windham from 1815, was offered as an alternative venue. So Windham made preparations there on the Friday (2 July) with the intention of ascending the next day, and even offered to pay for the attendance of policemen and watchmen, 'although in no other town from which I have ascended was this ever received'.[30] Then at 8 p.m. that evening he was summoned to speak to a magistrate, James A. Anderson, who told him that, on further deliberation, he would be required to provide a guarantee of compensation after all. When Windham refused, it became clear that no ascent could take place, even if his conditions were met, as he was already committed to visit Dublin, Liverpool and Hull within the next three weeks.

Dublin: Wednesday 14 July 1824 (with Edmund Livingston)

The *Morning Post* had scarcely deigned to notice Windham Sadler's 'idle and senseless' ascent from Liverpool earlier that year, but the newspaper's tone in reporting his Dublin ascent with 'his old companion M. Livingstone' was markedly different.[31] It began: 'In the annals of aerostation, perhaps there never was a more successful and satisfactory display of the art than that of Mr. Sadler, on Wednesday, at the Coburg-gardens in Dublin'.[32] Presumably, as the two men reached only somewhere between Rush and Skerries, no more than (an indisputably *un*successful and *un*satisfactory) 20 miles away, the *Post* was unaware that the intention, announced in all the pre-publicity, had been for Windham, possibly both men, to cross St George's Channel again. The parting words of the mayor of Dublin had been to wish the two men 'a safe, pleasant, and prosperous excursion' and – somewhat damning by faint praise – to hope that 'the example of your enterprising spirit shall be productive hereafter of advantages to your country, by leading to some useful discovery'.

Hull: Wednesday 11 August 1824 (with Reece Davies)

Windham Sadler's seventh flight of the year was the least eventful, or at any rate, the least commented on. Only the *York Herald* and *Leeds Mercury* (14 August) carried short accounts of the journey of about 8 miles to near Preston, which took 25 minutes. Sadler's companion was a surprising choice: no privileged, fare-paying army officer or wealthy, worthy to ease the financial pressures on this occasion, but a mere bookseller's assistant called Reece Davies. Davies was formerly from Liverpool, so perhaps there was some friendly connection, given that Sadler's close ally in Liverpool was the bookseller Thomas Muncaster.

Wigan: Wednesday 22 September 1824 (with George Armstrong)

An ascent from Wigan the next month had apparently been arranged fairly spontaneously, after an invitation from the mayor. Once again, the gasworks was deemed the most appropriate location for what was accurately advertised as Windham Sadler's thirtieth ascent, an offer having again been made to supply gas at no charge. Just as well perhaps, since once again Sadler found that the event had 'not been so profitable as his great exertions to gratify so well deserved'.[33] The journey was made with George Armstrong of Liverpool, in conditions which enabled spectators to have a near-constant view of the machine as it moved south-westwards in the direction of Liverpool to alight 'in a field adjoining Poplar Grove, on the London-road, near the new Iron-works, about two miles and a half from the Town Hall'. Or, in Sadler's own words, 'in a pasture-field about a mile and a half off the town of Liverpool and little more off my own dwelling. Messrs. Muncaster, Platt, Atkinson, and many other friends came up instantly on our descent'. Atkinson accompanied him back to Wigan, where a dinner was held in his honour. In all respects, then, it was a highly appropriate last ever successful flight: uneventful, trouble-free, providing extended visibility for all who cared to watch, descending among friends and able to travel the same day back to his starting point to receive the plaudits of the crowd.

Bolton: Wednesday 29 September 1824 (with James Donnelly)

For Windham Sadler, son of the most famous English pioneer of ballooning, and himself now an accomplished veteran of thirty largely uneventful and fulfilling flights, nothing, it seemed, could go wrong. Over the period of forty years since de Rozier's first ascent into the unknown, the safety record of ballooning had been a remarkably good one, and in Britain, no balloonist had died until Thomas Harris' crash of May 1824 (*see* Appendix 9). With the advances in knowledge, in experience, in technology and in manufacture there appeared to be little risk for anyone like Windham who, to borrow a nautical term, knew the ropes. The one major uncontrollable aspect, however, then as today, was the factor that the *General Evening Post* had proposed in defence of James Tytler's public disasters way back in 1784: the unpredictable British weather.

Even so, the strong wind which blew in Bolton on Wednesday 29 September would not have been of any particular concern to Windham. Certainly, it was brisk when he set about his well-practised routine of preparation, but he had assuredly known worse. By about 2 p.m. all was ready, but when his intended companion felt too unwell to travel, Windham recruited an unidentified substitute, and 'owing to the velocity of the wind he was carried out of sight in a very short time'.[34] As had been widely anticipated, the balloon's course was in the direction of nearby Blackburn, from where it was 'seen rising over the hills on the south-east, and came within a mile' of the town. According to an eyewitness, 15 minutes later, Windham tried to land in the parish known simply as Church (about 4 miles east of Blackburn; 14 miles from Bolton), but struck a chimney, was thrown out of the basket and became entangled in a trailing rope. In this predicament, suspended by one leg, he was impelled into further collisions with the tops of buildings before falling to the ground.

Those were the bald, shocking facts as initially reported.[35] With each subsequent day more details appeared in both the local and national press. The first-hand account of David Aitkin was printed as a letter in the *Morning Post* of 4 October. He and another man were close enough to attempt to grab the rope which was left trailing when the balloon's grapnel was wrenched off, at about 2.30 p.m. From inside the basket Windham shouted to them twice, 'Get hold of the rope', but it was out of their reach. Another eyewitness recalled that Windham shouted, 'For God's sake, catch hold of the cords, and save our lives!'[36] The balloon then struck the chimney of a small house, a collision which resulted in the back of his head being 'completely smashed' as he was thrown out of the basket, and left hanging by one leg for 150 to 200 yards as the balloon skimmed more buildings and a meadow. He then fell to the ground. Aitkin, a clerk at the printing works of Simpson, Haigh & Co. at nearby Foxhill Bank[37] also testified at the inquest held on Friday 1st, and estimated the height of the fall as between 15 and 20 yards.[38] A similar account was presented by Robert Mercer, who told the coroner, John Hargreaves, that he

> distinctly saw the car strike against the chimney of a house near the meadow; a man was then thrown from the car, and was suspended by one foot until he fell; the chimney was thrown down by the shock; whilst the deceased was suspended by the leg, the balloon passed near other buildings, and I think it probable that … he was struck against the chimney of one of those buildings; I think that more probable than that the deceased was hurt by the car striking against the chimney that was thrown down.

James Muir was the first surgeon on the scene, having been summoned from Accrington, about 2 miles away. After the fall, Windham had been carried to a public house at Holyroyds (or Hollytroids) which was later identified as the Greyhound Inn, about 100 yards from where he had hit the ground. Muir observed that 'a large fracture appeared on the right side of the head' and 'the bones were completely driven into the brain'. Immediately, Muir implemented the accepted cure-all for practically every known ailment, even those where copious blood had already been lost, and 'a vein of the right arm was opened, from which no more than four ounces of blood were obtained, without' – one cannot be surprised to learn! – 'any apparent relief'. A specialist surgeon called Barlow then arrived and took over, and applied the only slightly less exacerbating technique of trepanning. Perhaps surprisingly, considering all this, Windham Sadler survived the night, although did not ever regain consciousness. The coroner's verdict was 'accidental death by being struck against a chimney'.

News of the accident was first made public in the *Liverpool Mercury* (1 October), in the form of several letters from individuals who had been at the scene. At this stage, though obviously very seriously injured, Windham Sadler's death had not been confirmed. However, the *Mercury* went to a second edition that Friday, and in a letter from George Armstrong of Church Street, Liverpool (the same man 'who accompanied Mr. Sadler on his ascent from Wigan last week') his demise was confirmed.

Written from Foxhill Bank (Oswaldtwistle), Armstrong's letter imparted the sad news that Windham had died at 8 a.m. on Thursday 30th. Windham's wife Catherine had travelled with Armstrong from Liverpool to be with her dying husband.[39] She had already known to expect the worst, having received via the superintendent of Simpson's printworks[40] a letter from her husband which he always carried, specifically to be delivered to her in the eventuality of any such fatal accident. Because Mrs Sadler was 'far advanced in pregnancy', the coroner had also sent an express letter to Mr Muncaster (stated to be 'the father of that lady') in order 'to prevent the mischief which an incautious disclosure might involve'.[41]

Armstrong also wrote: 'What adds more to this sad misfortune is the death of the person at whose house he now lies, who died yesterday afternoon, from over exertions in assisting Mr. Sadler'.[42] This man's name was Blenkinsop, landlord of the Greyhound Inn, an autopsy concluding that he died in fact from a coincidental apoplectic fit. According to another letter from a resident of Foxhill Bank, Blenkinsop had accompanied the surgeon Muir from Accrington when told of the accident. The writer concluded, with somewhat premature insensitivity, the hope that 'this melancholy affair will deter people in future from venturing up into the air; we are not birds & ought to be content to tread the earth'.[43]

In addition to the details of the inquest, the *Morning Chronicle* (5 October) printed some slightly eerie additional information (taken from the *Bolton Express*). While Sadler was preparing the balloon in Bolton, it reported, a flagstaff on top of the gasometer had snapped, causing him to observe with no sign of apprehension, 'That is an ominous circumstance', yet

> when we witnessed his ascent from Wigan he ... was extremely pale, his step hurried, and his voice and actions seemed to be influenced by a nervous tremour [*sic*] that we should not have expected to find in such a man. But his bearing on this last occasion was characterised by all the firmness that his enteprize demanded ... So much for ominous presentiment!

*

So ended the short, but eventful, life of William Windham Sadler at the age of only twenty-eight. Yet what of his companion on the fatal flight? According to the *Bolton Express*' version of the launch, Windham had 'ordered his assistant (a poor fellow named James Donnelly) to "jump in"'.[44] This of course was the same man who had had to abort his intended ascent with Windham the previous year, the suggestion of compulsion therefore seeming unlikely, in view of Donnelly's avowed enthusiasm to fly even as far as Norway! His identity was not disclosed until 5 October, when both the *Morning Post* and *Morning Chronicle* (albeit also citing the *Bolton Express*) printed the hapless passenger's version of events. The information was no doubt prized from him while he was still in pain and shock, and it is therefore perhaps unsurprising that he presented what the newspapers called 'a very confused idea of what had passed'.

Donnelly's recollection was that just prior to the first collision, Windham had said, 'Jem, we have got in a mist; I don't like this; we will descend a little.' On doing so, and finding better visibility, he then said, 'Come, Jem, we will now drink to our wives and families ... and to our friends in Bolton.' Soon after, they descended a little more, but when Windham cast out the grappling iron, it failed to hold. He tried several times more, then announced, 'It will catch on the next hedge, Jem, hold fast!', followed immediately by, 'Good God, Jem, the grappling is broke!'

Donnelly's account then became muddled. He was probably on the floor of the basket, and unable to see, as he failed to realise that there had been a collision with any building, believing in fact that they had hit the ground, and that Sadler had been thrown out, but was probably safe, while he himself was being propelled onwards at the mercy of the wind. Donnelly realised the awful truth only when there was a sudden increase in buoyancy a few moments later, and 'he heard a terrific shriek from the surrounding spectators'. About 3 miles later he managed to make a descent, but on striking the ground, the car overturned, and his arm was broken in the fall. He found his way to Whalley (about 5 miles from Church), and received medical assistance at the inn there.[45]

The balloon itself was carried all the way to the North Sea. Some idea of the strength of the wind that day can be gained from the time at which it was seen falling into the sea about 100 miles away off Flamborough Head. The captain of a revenue cutter noted this as 4.45 p.m., a little more than 2 hours after the accident. The swell was too great for it to be salvaged.[46]

*

The *Liverpool Mercury* was very swift to acknowledge the passing of a local celebrity. Even by the time of its second edition of 1 October an informative and considered obituary had been composed, which alluded to the many successes of Windham Sadler's father as well as to his own. The newspaper also praised his exceptional engineering skills and observed that in private life 'Mr. Sadler was warm-hearted, gentle, and unassuming; and by his cheerful and agreeable manners he had endeared himself to a large circle of respectable acquaintances'. From somewhere the newspaper had learned that 'the same balloon from which he met his death has, uninjured, borne him aloft in his trips on sixteen occasions' as contributory evidence that 'the fatal catastrophe ... can be deemed one of those accidents which sometimes defy the foresight of the most skilful and wary'.

A subsequent much longer obituary appeared in the Liverpool weekly *Kaleidoscope*.[47] Windham's corpse was brought back to Liverpool via the very pertinent towns of Bolton and Wigan. Having made the journey to Foxhill Bank, his widow Catherine had insisted on a last look at the disfigured corpse, thereby affording her 'a relieving melancholy satisfaction'. A special request had been made to stop outside the Commercial Inn in Bolton, where the committee who had arranged the ascent had gathered to pay their special respects. However, 'owing to Mrs. Sadler's distressed state, it was deemed prudent to proceed' so the hearse continued, followed by 'a large assemblage of individuals, amongst whom were many females'.[48]

In Wigan, the scene of Windham Sadler's last successful ascent, the mayor was present to offer his sincere regrets. The hearse arrived back in Liverpool at 8 a.m. on the Saturday, and the funeral was held on the Monday at Liverpool's Christ Church. Although a private ceremony, some 4,000 people were stated to have attended. Among them, hopefully providing some solace to his widow, was Windham's 'interesting young' sister (evidently Sybella), who had only recently arrived in Liverpool to visit.[49] Some tributes came in the form of verse. 'Nanny Foulds' wrote of Sadler's valedictory journey that 'the Hero rode majestic through the air From cloud to cloud, not thinking death was near' and that 'Death shot his shaft, his rude, relentless dart, And pierc'd the short liv'd victim to the heart'.[50]

A committee was established to raise a subscription for Catherine Sadler. Among its members were Mr Muncaster and Windham Sadler's frequent collaborator, Dr Traill. Two hundred people subscribed within the first week. Separate collections were made in towns such as Bolton, Warrington, Blackburn and Wigan,[51] that in the latter reputedly including a contribution equivalent to the fare anticipated from the passenger whom James Donnelly replaced. Several newspapers reported that some £1,000 had been raised by the end of the month, a figure which can only have increased in the following months, the names of the last subscribers, including a 'Foxhill Bank Subscription, per Mr. G. Armstrong', appearing in the *Mercury* of 4 February 1825. Catherine had by then given birth to a daughter, Catherine Windham Sadler (who was baptised on 17 January 1825 at St Thomas's, Liverpool).[52]

The national periodicals and dailies were generally sympathetic to William Windham Sadler, praising his skill and bravery, but some also felt obliged to highlight the futility of such a death. *The Examiner* (10 October) probably captured the feelings of many:

> We may safely aver, that aërial ascents have contributed to no one beneficial purpose, nor are they ever likely to do, for adventurers are now as much at the mercy of the elements, and as little able to direct their course, as the first who ventured to ascend. We trust that the melancholy fate of one who in thirty ascents had acquired an experience that few others can boast of, and who had, therefore, a more reasonable hope of escape than most others could entertain, will have the effect of rendering such spectacles less frequent. We should be glad if it put an end to them entirely, for we consider the risk of human existence as quite unjustifiable when incurred for no other purpose than to gratify an idle curiosity.

*

Of course, some elements of the press had been issuing discouraging warnings of this kind almost since the creation of the very first Montgolfière, but even the particularly gruesome death of a fellow adventurer was not going to put off the likes of George Graham. It had had no effect in May when he and his wife decided to go ahead with a launch only a week after Thomas Harris' fatal crash, and nor did it now. Graham did apparently think better of an ascent in Canterbury that autumn,[53] but by the spring of next year he was unable to resist any longer.

While there is some doubt about which of the Sadlers were at Graham's London ascents in 1823, there can be no doubt that it was John Coxe Hippisley Sadler, Windham Sadler's nineteen-year-old nephew, who was present when Graham ascended from Kew in April 1825. Far from being deterred by the recent family tragedy, the newspaper noted that 'young Sadler' was 'desirous of treading in the same steps as his father', John Sadler having gained a disproportionate reputation for his mere two ascents, probably on account of that very public, very prestigious St James's Park ascent of August 1814. Displaying the courage, stubbornness or blind faith that was typical of the flying Sadlers, he entered the car with Graham on Easter Monday, 4 April, but had to vacate when their combined weight prevented uplift.[54] It was a very familiar occurrence, as we have seen, and was a circumstance of physics which means that the very last known attempt by any of these three generations of Sadlers to ascend in a balloon ended in something they had very rarely known: earth-bound, flightless disappointment![55]

PART 6

LAND
1824–28

14

'HOW SCHEMING BEGGARS A MAN': JAMES SADLER'S FINAL SHORT DESCENT OF ALL

Since James Sadler's probable last involvement with a ballooning event of any kind – at George Graham's failed launch from Islington in August 1823 – there had been a major change in his domestic situation. To appreciate the circumstances of this last phase of his life, it is necessary to rewind the clock briefly to the spring of 1824, prior to the first of Windham Sadler's seven successful ascents and one fatal one of that year. Presumably as a result of the death of James's second wife Martha, Robert Peel, then Home Secretary, nominated him on 3 April 1824 for a place at the Charterhouse Hospital in London.[1] This charitable institution had been founded in 1613 for the accommodation of eighty 'poore persons as can bringe goode testimonye and certificat of their good behavioure and soundness in Religion',[2] known as 'Brothers'. Alongside was a school for forty similarly meritorious 'Gownboys'.

From his subsequent correspondence it is clear that James Sadler was somewhat incapacitated by this time – unsurprisingly given the life he had led – and may have been dependent on Martha for his daily care. James's son John was still living in Lambeth, but with three young daughters in the house, he presumably felt unable or unwilling to accommodate his father as well. Windham was living several hundred miles away in Liverpool, of course, and James's second son, James, had been killed in action in India in 1817 (*see* Appendix 8). What became of his other children from his first marriage: Mary Ann (born 1777), who married James Wyatt of Oxford, Thomas (born 1782), and Eliza (born 1785) is not known. Sybella (born 1798), his youngest daughter by his second wife, was certainly still alive, coincidentally being in Liverpool when her brother Windham had his fatal accident.

Less than a month after Peel's recommendation, James Sadler was installed at Charterhouse. Indeed, his arrival there can only have been a matter of days before Peel's nephew, Robert Haworth Peel, relinquished his place as passenger on Windham's ascent from Salford on 27 April 1824. A factor in Sadler's favour may have been that the Master of Sutton's Charterhouse Hospital (from 1804 until his death)[3] was Philip Fisher (c. 1751–1842), a graduate of University College.[4] This of course was the Oxford college attended by several Oxford alumni who took a special interest in Sadler: George Croft, George Cholmondeley and especially William Windham. Fisher had been resident in Oxford at the height of James Sadler's first period of public prominence in the 1780s,[5] and the two men evidently knew one another. Fisher's son John (1788–?) wrote to his friend, the artist John Constable, on 31 May 1824:

> Sadler, the Aeronaut is a pensioner at the Charterhouse. How scheming beggars a man. He was a pastry cook in good business at Oxford. He drank tea at the Lodge the other evening: being an old crony of my Father. He says he used all his powers of persuasion with Harris to abandon the voyage, for he knew him to be ignorant of the management of a balloon. Sadler has made 50 voyages.[6]

Sadler was referring to Thomas Harris, of course, who died when his balloon crashed near Croydon on 25 May (*see* Appendix 9). Constable had seen Harris's balloon pass, having written to Fisher that: 'The other day (what is it that this great town does not afford), two people flew over our heads in a balloon – and were knocked on their heads in a park near Croydon.'[7] The two friends also chanced to see another passing balloon the following month. It was one piloted by George Graham, and Constable noted in his journal for Thursday 17 June 1824 that

> on our way from Pall Mall at the top of the Haymarket we had a full view of the balloon – which looked so near that I could see the divisions of colored silk. On its rising higher we saw it on a clear blew sky looking like a golden egg – it then went into a white thin cloud – & then emerged from it with great beauty, one side so very bright – &

the other so clear and dark – looked 'till it was hidden by other clouds. After tea we walked round by Islington to the Charter House. Parted with Fisher at the gates.[8]

Given what they had just witnessed, one might have expected Constable to take the opportunity to go in with Fisher to talk to the great James Sadler, who had actually been at the White Conduit Gardens that day to witness Graham's departure: 'Old Mr. Sadler, the aëronautic veteran, was there, and seemed to observe with a curious eye the gradual inflation of the lion of the day.'[9] This was the last verifiable occasion at which James Sadler witnessed an ascent. No doubt an incentive to make the effort was that Graham's companion that day was a Captain Beaufoy, probably Mark (1793–1854),[10] the younger brother of Henry Beaufoy, who had accompanied Sadler in 1811 (*see* Appendix 8).

From the Charterhouse records[11] it would seem that on admission in April 1824, James Sadler initially received a full quarterly pension, but that this was almost immediately reduced. Possibly this was because it became apparent that, unlike many at Charterhouse, he did in fact have relatives able to support him, because it was only after the death of Windham that James appealed to Robert Peel for an increase in his allowance. Still reeling from the effects of the tragedy of 29 September – 'the shock has affected my feeble frame to the utmost' – he wrote on 21 October 1824 that prior to admission to Charterhouse he had already been 'suffering from long and severe Illness, the Expenses of which led to embarrassments', and that after moving in to Charterhouse even the inadequate 'trifle' on which he had previously subsisted had been denied him. The death of 'poor dear Windham' meant he would no longer be able to rely on 'occasional assistance from him', so he was left with

nothing but what the House allows which is inadequate, having to find my own Cloathes, Washing, Tea, Sugar and a Variety of other Articles out of £20 per ann. – besides paying a Person constantly to attend me, being unable either to dress or undress myself, or even cut my own food.[12]

Whereas other Charterhouse Brothers had some other income or profession to rely on, Sadler claimed that 'unhappily for me the first I have not, & the latter my infirmities preclude me from'. Peel noted on the reverse of this plaintive appeal, on 23 October, that it was 'not in my power' to intervene.

By the last quarter of 1826 or early 1827, Sadler seems no longer to have been resident in Charterhouse itself, as he was in receipt of a lodging allowance rather than a pension. Perhaps his infirmities were just too severe for him to remain in a non-medical establishment. This continued until the first quarter of 1828, at which time his allowance was paid to his nephew Charles James Sadler in Oxford. James Sadler's was a life interlaced with journeys of an almost unimaginably intrepid and dangerous nature. Evidently, arrangements had been made for him to make one final, mundane, lugubrious journey back to the place of his birth.

When he died on 26 or 27 March, Sadler had been living in George Lane (now George Street), some distance from the premises occupied by his relations on either side of the High Street. He was, however, buried where he had been baptised seventy-five years earlier, at the ancestral church of St Peter-in-the-East, on 30 March. It would be pleasing to think that Thomas Beddoes's son, Thomas Lovell Beddoes (1803–49), might have gone to the funeral. He was in Oxford at the time, studying at Pembroke College.[13]

Jackson's Oxford Journal (29 March 1828) gave due prominence to the death of the 'celebrated aeronaut' the previous Wednesday.[14] Within a short summary of his achievements the memorable phrase used in *Jackson's* account of his second ascent of November 1784 – 'the first person in that hazardous profession who might be said to be his own architect, engineer, chemist and projector' – was repeated, along with a reaffirmation of his first flight having been on 4 October 1784. The other highlight mentioned was the 1810 Oxford Commemoration flight, dubbed 'the most splendid ascent ever witnessed'.

So, a fitting tribute from the newspaper which had done so much to espouse his early efforts. The account in the *Oxford University & City Herald* (29 March 1828), however, bizarrely noted his status merely as 'the elder brother of Mr. Sadler of Rose Hill', Oxford with no mention at all of James's airborne triumphs. Could it be that 'pique and jealousy' of the 'little Oxford Pastry Cook' was still simmering in the University city, nearly fifty years later?

CONCLUSION

It was exactly another one hundred years before James Sadler received any further public recognition. J. E. Hodgson, in composing his seminal *History of Aeronautics in Great Britain,* realised that the first English aeronaut deserved much greater recognition – to be praised to the skies, one might say – and it was he who persuaded the Royal Aeronautical Society (RAS) to provide the church of St Peter-in-the-East with a commemorative tablet in 1928. Hodgson was present at the installation, with, of note, Harold Sadler (James Sadler's great-grandson), and Sir Michael Sadler, the Master of University College[1] (though there is no known family connection). Hodgson simultaneously produced his separate booklet *The First English Aeronaut: James Sadler of Oxford* to mark the occasion.

In 1984, the RAS stepped forward again on the bicentenary of Sadler's first flight. The gravestone of the 'first English aeronaut' was refurbished and a commemorative metal plaque supplied. This was affixed to the wall on Deadman's Walk, the path leading from Christ Church towards the Botanic Gardens, on Thursday 4 October, and the occasion was marked by the launch of a balloon from Merton Field from where Sadler's 1810 ascent had been made.[2] Two days later, on 6 October, a grand, multiple balloon launch was planned for the nearby Angel & Greyhound Meadow. In attendance was Mrs Eileen Doran (aged eighty-one) of Cheshire and Roy Sadler, both direct descendants of Windham Sadler. The heading of the report in the *Oxford Times* – 'Weather grounds balloonists' – tells its own tale, a tale as old as ballooning itself. The twentieth-century public did not riot, however, nor were the mortal remains of dead dogs and cats in danger of being used as projectiles, so at least some progress had been made. Indeed, true to the spirit of all the many intrepid individuals mentioned in the preceding chapters, six of the twenty balloonists did eventually brave the conditions.[3]

In November 1986, the gravestone in St Peter-in-the-East churchyard was renewed, at a ceremony attended by Sadler's (unnamed) great-great-great grandson.[4] As this site is now a part of St Edmund Hall, the Deadman's Walk plaque remains Sadler's most public, though even then discreet, memorial. The final sentence of Hodgson's 1928 booklet reads:

> To James Sadler belongs the honour of having set his countrymen, for all time, the initial example of air travel – a method of transportation the full significance of which few have the imagination to conjure up, and the immense importance of which, in terms of the British Empire, no man can yet fully comprehend.[5]

Today, almost a hundred years later, that comprehension is still evolving. The prescient lines of Henry James Pye have come to pass as mankind has, as a result of the inspiration of men like James Sadler, his peers and his sons, 'from the improv'd balloon Planets explor'd, and Empires of the Moon'.[6] Hopefully the preceding pages will help provide a much greater public appreciation of the 'most ingenious, but unfortunate man', James Sadler, the first Englishman to make those fledgling flutters in the direction of the stars.

AFTERWORD

Ballooning is the oldest form of flight. In its basic principles it has changed little since 1784. Balloons are still simple devices – fabric bags containing a light gas or hot air, together with a gondola, usually a basket, for the aeronauts.

The original balloon was lifted by hot air, although the Montgolfier brothers suspected that the fire might be producing a light gas. It was a precarious affair in which bundles of straw and twigs had to be burned. But for most of the next two centuries, hot-air balloons were abandoned and gas (often coal gas) was used. They were controlled by venting gas and throwing out sand.

Around 1960 Ed Yost in the USA devised a modern version of the hot-air balloon made from nylon fabric and using a controllable propane burner. This greatly reduced the cost of owning and operating a balloon and led to the modern ballooning movement.

In this modern age of ballooning there have been many achievements. Balloons made of the thinnest polyethylene have flown to the edge of space where only one third of 1 per cent of the atmosphere remains (and the balloon must be 300 times larger). There has been a balloon race across the Atlantic and, on two occasions, balloons have circumnavigated the Earth.

As the technology continues to evolve, the eighteenth-century pioneers of flight should never be forgotten, and I am very pleased to contribute these few words to this long-overdue tribute to an ingenious and courageous British innovator.

Don Cameron MBE, Founder of Cameron Balloons

APPENDIX 1: SADLER FAMILY IN OXFORD

When James Sadler was dismissed from his post as chemist to the Navy, the printed letter of appeal which his friends and supporters issued on 25 April 1810 included the assertion (without any sense of aeronautical drollery) that his family had been resident in Oxford 'for many descents'.[1] How right they were! James Sadler's ancestry can be traced back with certainty to his great-grandfather, a prominent tailor called William Sadler (1662?–1720), and tentatively to two still earlier generations.

Seventeenth Century

Because of the seventeenth-century Sadler fondness for the name William, it is difficult to separate one from another, but the earliest identifiable William Sadler (?–1649) seems likely to have been the grandfather of William the tailor. The baptisms of three of his children – Elizabeth (1628), Richard (1630, but who died in 1631) and William (1631) – are apparent at St Michael's Church in central Oxford following his marriage there to Jane Weller on 23 May 1627. William senior was a blacksmith, who, when summoned in 1633 by the university for his 'contumacy in not appearing in ye Court being warnd', was noted as having resided in St Michael's parish since about 1613.[2] He served as a constable and on the common council, and died prior to 1650.[3] He seems undoubtedly therefore to be the William Sadler who was buried at All Saints on 18 March 1649. What is interesting in view of James Sadler's later career is that at his burial he is designated a 'gunsmith'. It was no doubt a natural transition for a blacksmith to apply his skills to the manufacture of weapons during the turbulent years of the Civil War, and all the more so in the city that Charles I had made his refuge between 1642 and 1645.

William's son William (1631–80) became a wealthy and successful man, though through what means is never stated. He owned a large house – as shown by its four chimneys – in the central Oxford parish of St Mary Magdalen when the hearth tax register of 1665 was compiled, and in 1667, when he was an assessor for the Poll Tax, he was one of only two dozen householders whose rate was in excess of one pound.[4] Described as a 'gentleman' at that time, he was married with three children, only one of whom appears to feature in the baptism register of St Mary Magdalen: Jeane, daughter of Jeane and 'Mr. William Sadler', on 26 June 1666. His wife seems to have come from Steeple Aston, a village some 10 miles north of Oxford. Certainly that is the implication of the marriage there of Jane Marten[5] to William Sadler of Oxford in the summer of 1661. He was buried at All Saints on 8 June 1680, designated as 'of St Mary's'.

William Sadler (1662?–1720) and (1) Joanna (?–1713); (2) Grace

The firstborn son of William Sadler and Jane/Jeane Marten was baptised on 4 May 1662 at Steeple Aston. It is this William who appears to have become a freeman of the city of Oxford as a tailor on 17 June 1687[6] and whose death the Oxford diarist and Bodleian librarian Thomas Hearne recorded on Tuesday 15 November 1720: 'Some time last night died one Sadler, near University College in Oxford. He was a Taylour of Note, & hath left behind him about 11 children, having had 21 in all.'[7] The parish records of St Peter-in-the-East (the church with which the family would be most closely connected for the next three generations[8]) reveal the baptisms of ten of these children (the oldest in 1689; the youngest in 1704), and it is the early burials of two of them (in 1698 and 1701) that confirm this William's occupation as a tailor.

Three further children were baptised at the nearby university church of St Mary the Virgin, suggestive of William Sadler's growing reputation as a tailor of distinction. At these baptisms, in 1706 (twins) and 1710, the mother's name is revealed as Joanna. When she was buried, 'wife of William, tailor', at St Peter-in-the-East on 4 May 1713, their eleven surviving children were aged between about seven and twenty-four years. It is therefore unsurprising that William remarried, his will revealing that his new wife (and executrix) was named Grace.[9] Hearne's estimate of the size of William Sadler's surviving family is verified in this will: he left bequests of £20 to each of his six daughters, but less to his five sons, and a surely rather insulting one shilling to John, the only one of his children identified as having a child of their own at this time, namely James (that is, the future father of James the balloonist), who was bequeathed £5. William Sadler the tailor was buried not with his wife at the favoured church of St Peter-in-the-East, but in the university church of St Mary the Virgin. This ceremony, which took place on 17 November 1720, represents quite a distinction for a tradesman, especially as he was 'buried in the Church' itself, as Hearne noted.[10]

The family home on the High Street no longer exists, but it was what was known as Deep Hall. Grace Sadler was named as a former tenant there in 1733,[11] and the premises continued to be known as 'Sadler's House' or 'Mrs Sadler's House' in subsequent years.[12] A significant former resident of Deep Hall, 'next on the west side of University Coll.', was one of the founders of modern chemistry, Robert Boyle.[13]

Another contemporary William Sadler (?–1714) is worthy of comment because at the baptisms of his children at St Mary Magdalen, he was described as a gunsmith, like his namesake of the 1640s. Most probably it was he who was made a freeman on 11 October 1675.[14] His younger son Richard (*c.* 1692–?) pursued the same trade, becoming apprenticed to his father in 1710–11[15] and becoming a freeman in 1734. It is tempting to imagine that these further examples of the family's background in the manufacture of guns might have had some influence on the aeronaut James Sadler's later interest in this field.

John Sadler (1694–1749) and Sarah (?–1753)

John, the fourth child and third son of William and Joanna Sadler, was baptised at St Peter-in-the-East on 26 April 1694. He was the earliest of the family known to be a vendor of food, being noted in the University Chancellor's Court records as an under-butler of Queen's College in 1732 and as a victualler in 1737. He was made a freeman of the city on 23 February 1718, though not necessarily at that time as a cook. Almost certainly (because there is no other known candidate in the parish) he was buried at St Peter-in-the-East on 4 January 1749. John Sadler's wife, Sarah, seems likely to have been the woman of that name who was buried at the same church on 6 February 1753. The couple had eight children baptised at St Peter-in-the-East as follows: James (26 January 1718), Mary (6 December 1719), Ann (13 December 1721), John (16 May 1724, who lived only a year, being buried on 30 June 1725), Sarah (7 November 1725), Edward (21 August 1727), Elizabeth (14 October 1728), and William (11 June 1731).

These baptisms correlate precisely with a handwritten list inside the front cover of a 1693 prayer book held by Oxford University's Museum of the History of Science. It was donated, with other materials, in 1990 by Stanley G. S. Alford, via his grandmother, Amelia Alford (*née* Sadler), who was the great-granddaughter of James Sadler, the aeronaut, via his son John. The book is embossed with the name 'I. Sadler' and the year '1746'. James Sadler senior was born on 16 January 1717/18, followed by (even the time of delivery of each birth is noted!) Mary (born 1 December 1719), John (24 April 1724), Sarah (15 October 1725), Elizabeth (24 September 1728) and William (30 May 1731). In addition, the name Edward appears, but with nothing more than 'born ye 5th day'.[16]

As discussed in the main text, James went on to follow his father's profession as a cook. It has not been possible to identify his bride, Elizabeth, but she would appear to have been his second wife, he being the only obvious candidate as the James Sadler of St Peter's, Oxford who married Mary Smith of Minster Lovell in Witney on 23 February 1739. This hypothesis is strengthened by the burial of a Mary Sadler at Minster Lovell on 14 July 1746 (that is, well before the birth of James and Elizabeth's first son, in 1753, and the marriage which must have preceded it).

APPENDIX 2: THOMAS BLAKENEY SADLER AND FAMILY IN OXFORD

The brothers, James and Thomas Sadler, chose very different paths in life. James, as the oldest, could have taken a relatively conventional, secure and comfortable course by assuming prime responsibility for the family business, following in the footsteps of his father James and grandfather John as a vendor of food in a prime Oxford location. From at least 1772 until the death of James senior in 1791, the shop was presumably based at what is now 84 High Street (appropriately enough still a place of refreshment), based on the Oxford Survey of 1772.[17]

As the younger brother, Thomas probably thought that his own destiny would lie in establishing himself independently. Indeed, that is the course he embarked on, by opening his own cook's shop in St Clement's parish in November 1782. At the time he was twenty-six, but would have to wait another two years (until 15 October 1784) to become a freeman sanctioned to operate in his own right within the city itself.[18] This was a momentous time for him and his wife Eleanor (c. 1752–1807),[19] since their first child, Elizabeth, was baptised at St Clement's Church only three days later.

Thomas maintained his St Clement's outlet for at least five years, being specified as a cook of St Clements for the last time in *Jackson's* of 22 September 1787.[20] However, as all six of his children were baptised at St Clement's – the last was on 21 December 1792 – it suggests that he remained in the suburb until at least that year, biding his time until his older brother finally made up his mind to leave Oxford for good. Under Thomas's direction, confectionary became the mainstay of a business which would become a respected feature of the Oxford commercial landscape until well into the next century.

Therefore, it is Thomas who is listed as a 'pastry-cook and confectioner' in the *Universal British Directory* of 1794/5 and who appears among the freemen who voted in the election of May 1796. By this time he was living in All Saints, and in 1801 took over the occupancy of No. 104 High Street,[21] though was still listed as a resident of All Saints at another poll of freemen in July 1802. His brother James was listed as a 'Gent.', and even though he was living at Stafford Row, Pimlico he had retained eligibility to vote. Neither of them voted for the unsuccessful third candidate on this occasion, John Ingram Lockhart, who nonetheless argued James's case for compensation from the Navy in 1810.

Thomas Blakeney Sadler led an apparently uneventful life as a city centre tradesman. His name appears regularly in *Jackson's Oxford Journal* as a subscriber to various charitable causes between 1819 and 1825. Of note these included the rebuilding of Carfax Church; help for the 'distressed Irish'; a lunatic asylum near Oxford; St Clement's Church, where of course all his children had been baptised; and St Thomas's Church (4 June 1825). By this time, Thomas had retired, a notice in *Jackson's* of 23 October 1824 stating that he had passed his confectionary business to his son Charles James Sadler.

Thomas & Henry Sadler, Sons of Thomas Blakeney Sadler

While it was the youngest of Thomas Blakeney Sadler's three sons who assumed the reins of the family business, another son, Thomas (1788–1831), had something of his uncle James about him, as by the summer of 1808 he was described as a 'druggist' when cited at the University Chancellor's Court in a case of debt against an undergraduate of Brasenose College.[22] He combined this interest in medicine and chemistry with that of a general grocer, the latter being his stated occupation at the time of his wedding to Jane Cox (*c.* 1785–1841), the eldest daughter of Charles Cox of the King's Arms Inn, Holywell, on 6 October 1808.[23]

Thomas was made a freeman on 3 September 1810, after which he went into business with his older brother Henry (1784–?), who had gained his own freedom on 23 June 1806. Henry Sadler married Mary Reed Whitchurch, the daughter of Samuel Whitchurch of Bath (and Bristol), on Tuesday 5 June 1815.[24] It was the first of three unions between the Sadlers and the Reeds. A year later, the only marriage of any of Thomas Blakeney Sadler's four daughters took place. This was at St Mary the Virgin Church, when Elizabeth (baptised 1782) married Charles Reed, a widower of Bristol, in April 1816.

As businessmen, the two brothers, Thomas and Henry, seem to have shared another of their uncle James's traits: a lack of financial acumen. They were specified as 'grocers, chemists, and druggists' when named as bankrupts in the *Morning Chronicle* (15 March 1826, citing the *London Gazette* of 14 March).[25] Two weeks later, their entire grocery stock and contents of two dwelling houses in the High Street were listed in an auction notice in *Jackson's* of 1 April 1826, followed later that year by numerous properties owned by Henry in the nearby villages of Marston, Wolvercote, Headington and Wheatley.[26] Henry, who was first noticed as a 'chemist etc' in the summer of 1821, had evidently overstretched himself very badly, but it is hard to understand how the brothers could fail so comprehensively. The two High Street houses, with 'front shops', warehouses and out-buildings, 'for many years occupied by Messrs. Henry and Thomas Sadler', were still unsold the following year.[27]

Charles James Sadler (1792–1872)

Fortunately, while the two older sons' businesses became mired in financial difficulties, the Sadlers' mainstay confectionary business went from strength to strength, under the capable stewardship of the youngest son, Charles James (1792–1872). Thomas Blakeney Sadler had expanded from 104 High Street to acquire the lease on No. 105 next door on 3 April 1807, and renewed it on 10 October 1816.[28]

On 5 September 1815, Charles James married Jane Needle at St James's, Piccadilly, London. He was made a freeman a year later, on 2 September, and the year after that saw the birth of their only child, Charles James Sadler junior, on 26 February 1817. He was baptised at All Saints on 14 March 1817.

It was Charles James Sadler who appears to have taken responsibility for his uncle James's affairs towards the end of his life, being named as the recipient of his final Charterhouse allowance in 1828.[29] When James died in March 1828, the *Oxford University & City Herald* (29 March 1828) chose to identify him not as the country's most famous former aeronaut, not as an ingenious inventor of guns and engines, not as a chemist to the Admiralty, but merely as 'the elder brother of Mr. Sadler of Rose Hill', who was much better known locally despite his brother's achievements. He was also much, much wealthier!

Death of Thomas Blakeney Sadler in 1829 and After

Thomas Blakeney Sadler died at his Rose Hill house aged seventy-two and was buried at All Saints Church on 12 April 1829. In his will dated 8 November 1828 and proved 19 May 1829, he bequeathed a 'house and premises in High St' (in St Mary the Virgin parish) to his son Charles James Sadler, confectioner, this arrangement having been apparently previously agreed on 29 September 1824, which was when Thomas's retirement from business was publicly announced.

All seven of Thomas's children were still living, and it is evident that his sons Thomas and Henry had not been forgiven for their recent financial aberrations, as both were denied a specific legacy. Charles James was bequeathed the High Street property; his daughter Elizabeth, wife of Charles Reed (or Read) of Bristol, received £400, and 'each of my three daughters Mary, Ann and Eleanor' received £1,000. The residue of the evidently considerable estate was then to be divided between the three latter women and Charles James, while his other sons, Thomas and Henry, received nothing other than an oddly precise £19 9s, which was to be paid 'to each of the children of my sons Henry Sadler and Thomas Sadler' on reaching the age of twenty-one.

The Sadler family's mainstay, the High Street confectionary business of Charles James Sadler, is listed under 'Confectioners & Pastrycooks' in *Pigot's Directory* of 1830 and *Vincents* of 1835. In 1836 Sadler was elected Mayor of Oxford for the first of four times, the others being in 1849, 1854 and 1860. During his third mayoralty, in 1855, he had the distinction of commencing the process which led, four years later, to the abandonment of the most resented and divisive of any Oxford tradition: a 650-year-old requirement for every new mayor to swear an oath of subservience to the university.[30] In 1839 he apparently expanded the business to some new premises at the corner of Broad Street and Turl Street (where he is shown in the 1841 census), leaving his son to continue to operate from the High Street (that is, Nos. 104 and 105).

A handwritten annotation to a print of 'King Charley' or 'Rex Oxoniensis', in a catalogue for the Oxford Millenary Exhibition of 1912,[31] states that Charles James Sadler senior was 'commonly called "Lollipop" as he made sweets' and that he had gone blind in later life, needing 'someone to lead him about and always wore a flower in his coat.' Stephen Quelch also knew Sadler as 'King Charlie', and thought him 'an old citizen who stood out prominently before all others', 'a fine old gentlemen, with a noble presence', and an 'excellent speaker, full of life and animation, and a great leader of the Liberal party'.[32] Charles James Sadler died in 1872, aged seventy-nine.[33]

Charles James Sadler's identically named son gained his freedom in 1838 and married in 1840. The marriage constituted a further cementing of ties with the Reeds of Bristol, in the pattern of his uncle Henry and aunt Elizabeth. His bride was Elizabeth, the youngest daughter of Charles Reed Esq of Queen's Square, Bristol.[34] He is noted as a 'confectioner' at 104 High Street in *Pigot's* of 1842, but this is apparently the last trade directory in which the name Sadler is listed, Charles James junior having moved to Bristol by 1849, where he and two of the Reed family traded together as wine merchants.[35]

It is Charles James Sadler senior after whom Sadler Street in Oxford's St Ebbe's parish was named in 1899. It disappeared during the wholesale redevelopment of the suburb which began in the 1950s, but the name Sadler Walk was retained in his honour. His internationally famous uncle has been accorded no such recognition in his native city!

APPENDIX 3: JAMES TYTLER
(1745–1804)

While this book seeks to demonstrate that James Sadler deserves to be known as the first English aeronaut, whether he should also be known as the first *British* aeronaut will forever remain a matter of debate. This will depend on whether the 'leap' of half a mile that James Tytler made in Edinburgh on Friday 27 August 1784 can be considered a genuine ascent or not. Monck Mason, in *Aeronautica*, thought that it could: giving no credence at all to Sadler's first ascent, he wrote that Tytler:

> is entitled to the triple distinction of being the *first* native of Great Britain that ever navigated the skies; of having accomplished the *first* aerial voyage ever executed in these realms; and ... the *only* one upon the principle of the original inventor, in which the agent of the ascension was atmospheric air rarefied by the application of artificial heat.

Whatever, Tytler was such an inventive, eccentric and undoubtedly brave individual – in some respects very much in the mould of James Sadler – that his own endeavours undoubtedly deserve due consideration here. We cannot know how aware Sadler was of this kindred spirit. Like him, Tytler was unusual in experimenting in this new science largely unaided; but unlike him, Tytler was highly literate, enabling his own version of events to be told in his own words.

In the exculpatory summary that Vincenzo Lunardi kindly allowed Tytler to insert in his own *Account of Five Aerial Voyages in Scotland*, he gives Friday 6 August 1784 as the date of his first notable attempt, using the Montgolfier hot-air method. He had, however, been intending to ascend since at least the beginning of May, and had made an aborted attempt in July.[36] Tytler had announced his intentions, timed to coincide with one of the great Edinburgh social events of the year, the Leith Races, in the local press.[37] It was not a success, the *Edinburgh Evening Courant* commenting drily that 'its gravity and affection for the earth cannot be overcome'.[38]

This failure was followed by a more public, though equally ineffective, attempt on Saturday 7 August. On this occasion, the *Caledonian Mercury* observed that 'a gust of whirlwind, as if sent by divine command to blast the hopes of this devoted projector, attacked the Balloon, drove it hither and thither, and by compressing it on all sides, soon reduced it to a state of flaccidity'.[39] Another account referred to the failure of 'our famous fire balloon' being due to 'one of those unlucky accidents, which hitherto has never failed to attend every proposed exhibition of this aerial machine'. This particular failure inspired the first British example of what would become the standard, unforgiving reaction: there was a 'universal clamour from a vast crowd ... the lower ranks of whom seized the basket, and after carrying it through the streets in a sort of triumph, at last burnt it to ashes'.[40] Undeterred by the indignity, scorn, inconvenience and of course cost which accompanied this wanton destruction, Tytler's extraordinary determination and self-belief is apparent in that it took him less than three weeks to prepare a replacement. On 25 August, understandably having little wish to be observed on this occasion, he set off at 6.30 a.m. This time, according to the *Courant*, 'the balloon, together with the projector himself, and basket in which he sat, were fairly floated'.[41]

This low-key success was followed by another early morning launch on the 27 August. Tytler's much improved performance that day – the *Edinburgh Advertiser* acclaimed him as 'the first person in Great Britain to have navigated the air'[42] – caused the London press to take an interest in his personal circumstances. The *Gazetteer & New Daily Advertiser* (2 September) compared the mere half a guinea a week that he was supposedly paid for his editorship of *Encyclopaedia Britannica,* to the £300 or £400 salary he might command for such an endeavour in London, adding that therefore 'we should not be surprised at his taking the advantage of the first fair wind for England'.

Buoyed by this partial success, the resolute Tytler tried again a few days later, on 31 August, observed this time by numerous dignitaries. This was, according to his biographer, Sir James Fergusson, 'his one really public ascent', but because he did not get even as high as the 350 feet of four days earlier,[43] his creation was dismissed by those present as 'a cumbrous toy of little scientific interest'.[44] Another failure followed on 29 September, leading the *General Evening Post* (2–5 October) to propose a possible reason why the British were lagging behind their French counterparts: the weather! These islands, a correspondent wrote, were inappropriate for 'a balloon raised by smoke, or rarefied air' except 'when there is almost a dead calm, which cannot often be expected in this climate'. In other words, success could only be expected by using inflammable gas (hydrogen), which was prohibitively expensive. Consoling words for Tytler, no doubt, in view of the increased hostility he had to endure on account of the injuries suffered by a bystander when a mast broke and the balloon collapsed onto the fire.

Lunardi had already accomplished a successful flight on his very first attempt by then, of course, and by the time Tytler made his final attempt of the year, 11 October, so too had James Sadler. This time even Tytler's staunchest supporters could find no excuses for what turned out to be a costly disaster because 'the day was as fine as could be wished; not a breath of wind stirring'. The *General Evening Post* (October 14–16) began:

> Another attempt was made to raise the Edinburgh Grand fire-balloon. About mid-day the inhabitants of the Good Town, who, to do them justice, are seldom backward when any idle scheme is on foot, left their shops etc. to take care of themselves, and repaired to every eminence near the town from which the enterprising Tytler could be seen.[45]

When the balloon was found not to rise, Tytler got out to investigate, and before he could regain his position, 'the balloon having rolled about for a time like an over-grown porpus, at last rose slowly and heavily to a height of about an hundred yards, but being without any director, it fell sideways to the ground, nearly on the spot from which it rose'. The writer found it 'impossible to describe with what contempt and derision the multitude beheld' this sight. A generally jocular piece ends with a line of thought that would be repeated by many in the coming year, as the initial aeronautical expectations of scientists and laymen alike proved unfounded:

> However such exhibitions may gratify the idle and lounging part of society, it is attended with a very serious loss and inconvenience to people in business. It is scarcely to be conceived what a deal of time has been trifled away, from first to last, by the various exhibitions of this bungling and mis-shapen *smoke-bag*.

Nonetheless, Tytler continued to experiment for another year, but when he suffered yet another humiliating failure in July 1785, he finally admitted defeat. When Lunardi met him in Edinburgh in October 1785, the Italian kindly offered 'the voice of consolation to alleviate his distress'.[46] Lunardi also generously facilitated more tangible consolation: several pages within his own publication, *Account of Five Aerial Voyages in Scotland,* in which Tytler was able to document his woes and provide a fuller version of events than had appeared in the newspapers.[47]

During the attempt he had made on the first Friday of August 1784, Tytler wrote, 'the Gallery took fire, and some of the Chains suspending the Stove broke, which prevented any further attempt at that time'. After many other setbacks over the next day or two, Tytler 'came to the resolution of suffering myself to be projected into the air by inflating the Balloon to the utmost, and being appended to it without any furnace, like a log or piece of Ballast. You will easily see that this was the resolution of a madman, and which nothing but my desperate situation could excuse'. Then, on a subsequent 'fine and favourable morning', that is, the 25 August,

> I suffered myself to be projected upwards, seated in one of the small baskets in which earthen ware is carried, without ballast, or indeed without thinking of any. The Balloon set off from the ground with the swiftness of an arrow, but could not ascend more than a few feet, when it was stopped by a rope belonging to the mast which held it up during the time of inflation. This broke its force very considerably, and even when freed from this, it flew with such rapidity that several of the spectators, terrified at the unusual sight, endeavoured to drag it downwards till the rope was forced from their hands. Thus my career was stopped, and I arose only a very small way, some say 350 feet, some others 500.

He then decided to 'take another *leap* of the same kind a few days later', instructing 'my assistants to break its power as I ascended, that I might only pass over the adjacent trees and houses'. On 29 September he failed to inflate at all, and on 11 October

> I was exceeding anxious to have one private trial made before I exposed myself to public view; but being overruled in this, I retired from the [Comely] Garden with a resolution to do nothing more that day, and indeed I looked upon a private trial to be absolutely necessary.

Unfortunately, and inevitably, word had spread, however, and about a thousand people were drawn to the spot. Poor Tytler saw that he had no option but to make the attempt, even though, as he had predicted, the stove proved too small to create sufficient lift. More public recrimination followed, and

> I was obliged to hear my name called out wherever I went, to bear the insults of every black-guard boy, to hear myself called Cheat, Rascal, Coward and Scoundrel by those who had neither courage, honesty, nor honour ... All this I bore with patience; I knew that Popular Opinion, founded on ignorance, varied as the wind, and that a single instance of success would be sufficient to turn the tide in my favour.

However, a lawsuit and illness prevented any further attempt with a larger stove until 26 July, when, on account of the wind, 'the Balloon was torn from the hands of those who held it, several of them overturned, and their lives endangered; the stove was dashed in pieces, and the Balloon itself very much damaged'.

Lunardi included the sad litany above as an appendix to a poem which Tytler had written in honour of the Italian's first three flights in Scotland, from Edinburgh, Kelso and Glasgow. With generous acceptance of his own shortcomings, the tragic Scot summed up his own thwarted aspirations in the couplet:

> Lost are my wishes, lost is all my care
> And all my projects flutter in the air.[48]

Tytler remained in the public eye, nonetheless, described by Robert Burns in 1788 as the 'obscure, tippling, but extraordinary body who ... drudges about Edinr as a common printer, with leaky shoes, a skylighted hat & knee buckles'.[49] In 1795, the thwarted genius emigrated to America, having been charged with seditious libel in 1792.[50] It is probably as a consequence of this exile, of the inauspicious nature of his flights, of his disreputable character, and of a lack of any creditable champion that Tytler was soon forgotten. The *Scots Magazine* omitted any reference to him in a comprehensive discussion of early aeronautics in its issue of November 1805, as did the *Edinburgh Encyclopaedia*'s article on 'Aeronautics' in 1830 (which also, however, omitted James Sadler). Even the *Encyclopaedia Britannica*, to which Tytler had contributed so much, makes no mention of him in its (admittedly very selective) article on 'Aerostation' in its third edition of 1797.

APPENDIX 4: LUNARDI'S LATIN ALLURE: 'ME GIVE YOU LUNARDI – WHOM ALL THE LADIES LOVE'[49]

The appeal of the dashing, handsome, eligible Vincenzo Lunardi contrasted greatly with the image of the staid, undemonstrative, married Sadler. Lunardi was very much aware of his appeal, claiming to have been visited by two hundred 'Scottish Beauties' in a single morning in Edinburgh, for instance, and being delighted by the thought of female attention in general: 'I love them all … to be the object of their admiration! to have all their eyes turned towards me … to hear their united acclamations! Oh Heaven! my very brain turns giddy with the thought'.[52]

The newspapers were happy to add to this titillation. The *Morning Herald & Daily Advertiser* noted on 20 October 1784 that 'The balloon influenza is very rife among the Ladies. Mr. Lunardi every day receives letters from fair petitioners, requesting to accompany him on his next tour to the regions of bliss!' The salacious implication of this comment reflected the tone of the previous few weeks, a convenient focus being the fashion item which adorned many a female thigh:

On some young Ladies wearing Garters inscribed with the name of
   the aspiring Mr. Lunardi:
When Lunardi, unpinion'd, first soar'd to the skies,
Huzza'd by the foolish, admir'd by the wise,
The Ladies all gaz'd with amazement and fear,
And from many bright eyes dropt the pitying tear;

The pitying tear he had when on high,
　　And from every fair bosom the heart-heaving sigh.
　　Now, clasping the thigh of each beautiful Miss,
　　He has soar'd within sight of the regions of bliss.[53]

A few days later this appeared:

　　And when he came
　　To earth again,
　　Each British dame,
　　To crown his fame,
　　Below her knee, or round her thigh.
　　His dear enchanting name did tie;
　　And shew'd the bold advent'rer more
　　Of Heaven than e'er he saw before.[54]

At the end of that month, the *Morning Post & Daily Advertiser* (28 October 1784) thought fit to mention that 'a Lady at the Pantheon, who would be thought Something, told Mr. Lunardi, that she saw his bagatelle rise (meaning the balloon) with pleasure, for it proved him a man, and much superior to Blanchard in that way'. The idea of Lunardi being imbued, simply by being Italian, with an irresistible sexuality was picked up still more blatantly by the caricaturists. A cartoon called 'Love in a Balloon' appeared in the *Rambler's Magazine* on 1 November 1784. It depicted Lunardi ascending with a female passenger. 'Ah Madame it rises majestically,' he exclaims. 'I feel it does Signor,' is the response, while on the ground male spectators observe, 'Damme he's no Italian but a man every inch of him.'[55]

The risqué joke was recycled still more outrageously in a political satire published the following month, where it is the extrovert Duchess of Devonshire and the Prince of Wales who commune suggestively in the rising balloon.[56] The scene has been transposed to that of Blanchard's second ascent in England, in December 1784, at which the Prince of Wales, the Duke and Duchess of Devonshire and numerous friends were present.[57]

APPENDIX 5: HARPER OF BIRMINGHAM

Despite the riot and near destruction of his balloon when Harper failed to ascend from the Birmingham Tennis Court on Wednesday 29 December 1784, he was bold enough to try again within a week. He may have been deprived of the services of James Sadler, who was at that very moment endeavouring to prepare to cross the English Channel, but apart from London there was no better English city than Birmingham in which to find a comparable replacement. Consequently, on this second occasion, on Tuesday 4 January 1785, 'Dr. Withering, Mr. Southern and other scientific gentlemen had kindly undertaken to superintend the filling',[58] which took only an hour.

On this second attempt, Harper ascended, according to a long article in the *London Chronicle* (6 January), 'with the greatest majesty' even though 'it rained incessantly, and was remarkably foggy and hazy'. 'For the first six minutes the rain increased to an uncommon degree, but in four minutes more he shot above every cloud, enjoying the influence of the sun and pure aether'. Harper seems to have demonstrated more scientific acumen than many by remembering to take with him a barometer and thermometer, which enabled him to observe that the temperature was never less than 28°F, despite climbing to 4,300 feet, compared with a temperature of 40°F on departure.

At Trentham Mr. Harper indulged himself with a view of Lord Gower's, and seeing a person at some distance hailed him with his speaking trumpet, to know how far he was from Birmingham? He was answered, 'About 40 miles, Master, but you are going the wrong way'.

Well, it was true enough! He descended near Newcastle, Staffordshire. A long account in *Aris's Birmingham Gazette* (10 January) contained much of the same detail as that in the *Chronicle*, but with this further testimony to Harper's scientific intent: 'about a mile from the place at which he alighted, several bottles of air, which he had collected in different heights of the atmosphere, for Dr. Priestley's philosophical experiments, were broken by his striking a tree'.[59] After a night at Lichfield, he was received back in Birmingham, in stark contrast to a few days earlier, 'amidst the unbounded plaudits of the inhabitants'.[60] Sadler's workmanship had successfully passed another test.

Harper's literal and emotional highs and lows were commemorated in a fifteen-page poem, *The Ballooniad,* printed locally in two editions. The author is unknown, but was evidently present at both launches, and candidly compares the two very different experiences in two cantos. It is in the very first line that Harper is alluded to as 'noble Strap', being the only clue to his profession as a barber.[61] The extracts which follow, all in respect of the failed first attempt, include the disappointment felt by entire families, an obscure swipe at Sadler, an accusation of profiteering by both men, and Sadler's good fortune to avoid recrimination by being elsewhere than in 'Blest Birmingham, the nursery of parts, Where science dwells, and each mechanic art'. The fifth stanza is:

> Come then plain Truth! and in a downright way,
> Say what thou know'st, and none shall dare gainsay;
> Tell how one fool made many thousands more,
> A simple soul which learned Oxford bore.

The seventh stanza describes how

> Tag-rag and bob-tail grac'd th'appointed day,
> Papa with Miss dress'd up as fine as May;
> Mama, and Cousin too, who all remember
> The first of April happen'd in December.

Stanza twelve and thirteen are:

> But still more bless'd when Strap and Sadler came,
> To ease each pocket, and exalt their fame;
> For this aside did Strap his razor lay,
> For this our Sadler threw his knife away.

Oh happy Sadler, well thou went'st to Dover[62]
> Or else, perchance, thy jaunt had been all over;
> When thro' the air the weighty brickbats flew,
> The vulgar vengeance might have fall'n on you.

The remainder of the first canto of *The Ballooniad* relates how the violence of the crowd erupted, was finally assuaged, and how Harper managed to escape. The second canto, which contains no further allusions to Sadler, reveals little in the way of additional detail, being mainly a homage to 'Strap', and his undaunted courage in daring to make a second, this time successful, attempt. It begins:

> Now better scenes await our noble Strap,
> And gentler fate makes up for each mishap.
> Six days had passed; mean while his courage grew,
> The sev'nth exposed the wond'rous man to view.

A correspondent to *Aris's Gazette* (31 January) cryptically challenged the suggestion that Harper was a barber: 'Strap is not a feature of Mr. Harper's profession, which was not of the honourable order of Puffs; but … the more distinguishing appellation of Ragman: Mr. Harper having served an apprenticeship to Mr. Hayward, Linen Draper, Oxford-street, London'.[63] There was indeed a haberdasher and hosier called William Hayward trading from Oxford Street in the mid-1780s, but it has not been possible to identify any apprentice named Harper within the relevant parish. Similarly, the Birmingham directories fail to reveal any barbers called Harper, though a man who did possess what might be considered an appropriate skill was Robert Harper, described as a Birmingham 'joiner' in 1768, a 'Carpenter, Casting Mould Maker and Mender' in 1770 (and subsequently), and 'carpenter' in 1777 and 1780.[64] In the absence of any other candidate, he does seem the most likely, tentative though the suggestion must be.

Harper made one other known ascent, presumably still using Sadler's original construction. It was made on Tuesday 1 February 1785, again from the tennis court at Birmingham, and was as farcical as any of the period. The launch had actually been planned for the Monday, and the *Gazetteer & New Daily Advertiser* of 8 February observed that given the rioting caused by his failure to ascend a month earlier, the decision to delay on this occasion was a brave one. The decision to launch at all was also evidently brave, because the process of filling the balloon was hampered by the sheer number of people attempting to get a close view of the apparatus. Again, John Southern was there to supervise, along with Aimé Argand, who, *Aris's* reported, had 'had the conduct of filling the balloons of Messrs. Montgolfier, Charles and Roberts, and Blanchard in France'.[65] Fearing the consequences of any further delay, the decision was made to launch even though the balloon had not fully inflated, with the result that it 'was carried against the garret-window of an adjoining house, before Mr. Harper could have time to throw out sufficient quantity of ballast' to rise above it. He was then prevented from offloading any more ballast on account of 'the company at the window seizing the car and detaining him – nor could he even prevail with them to liberate him'.[66] Another account, in *St James's Chronicle* (3–5 February), observed that Harper at this point necessarily 'found himself obliged, though reluctantly, to quit the Car, and was taken in at a Chamber window'. The balloon was then hauled down with some difficulty,

> and a boy, who was a Stander-by, got into the Car as a kind of Ballast, to keep it down, but by some Neglect ... the Balloon rose into the Air with the Boy instead of Mr. Harper, when the Lad behaved to all Appearance with great Courage, waving his Hat to the Populace who saluted him with loud Huzzas.

Having lost much of its, in any case insufficient, gas, the balloon descended safely again nearby. However, as soon as the boy – surely the most unpremeditated aeronaut to date! – got out again, off the balloon sped! It finally dropped near Chippenham, 'where it was found by the country people, who suspended it in a barn, and exhibited to strangers at one penny admittance'.[67] And that, as far as is known, was the last resting place of James Sadler's historic first aeronautical creation, signalling the last known attempt by the strangely anonymous Harper to reach for the skies. Be that as it may, Harper's endeavours were briefly renowned enough to decorate items of merchandise, using the design from the ticket for Harper's first Birmingham ascent (an example of which is in the collection of Joseph Banks's sister, Sophia, at the British Museum). Other known examples are on the lid of a lady's patch-box (*see* Hodgson (1924), Plate 68) and on a snuff-box (in the London Science Museum's Penn-Gaskell Collection). These constitute the only known depictions of Sadler's original balloon and car, since no artist captured Sadler himself in flight during his 1780's phase.

APPENDIX 6: JEAN-PIERRE BLANCHARD AND THE SIMONET SISTERS, MAY 1785

It is surprising that it took the newspapers several days to identify James Sadler's companion on 5 May 1785, given William Windham's political prominence. One reason could be the still more newsworthy distraction which had occurred two days earlier: the first flight in England by any female. It was Jean-Pierre Blanchard who orchestrated the historic moment, going up with Rosine Simonet (c. 1770–?),[68] the eldest daughter of a French ballet master, Louis Simonet, and his wife, Adelaide, who had been living and working in London since 1776,[69] their performance on 2 November that year being billed as their 'first appearance in England'.[70]

Rosine's younger sisters were Leonora (c. 1773–?) and Theresa (c. 1775–?), and although the three girls were hardly ever identified in the newspapers as anything other than Miss or Mlle. Simonet, Blanchard himself made it clear in a letter of 6 May that it was Rosine, since his passenger was 'agée de quatorze ans et demi seulement'.[71] With typical hauteur, Horace Walpole immediately belittled the achievement: 'A French girl, daughter of a dancer, has made a voyage into the clouds, and nobody has yet broken a neck – so neither good nor harm has hitherto been produced from these aerial enterprises.'[72] The pair landed in Walthamstow,[73] and returned by road with the balloon still inflated to their starting point of the Barbican. The young dancer had taken with her a small lap-dog,[74] a rare example of an accompanying animal completing the journey, rather than being ejected en route!

Rosine Simonet also became the first female in Britain to make a solo flight, of sorts, when she ascended in a captive balloon the following Saturday (7 May), while Blanchard supervised from below. This occurred at Whitechapel, where Blanchard firstly went alone to the height of the adjacent houses, as a test, then descended again and

> after having satisfied his numerous subscribers, he got out of the boat, and by the particular desire of several persons of distinction, Miss Simonet (his companion on the last voyage) was elevated alone several times, amidst the acclamations and huzzas of the beholders.[75]

Adhering to much the same account, the *Public Advertiser* (9 May) added that many 'persons of the most distinguished rank; nobles, beauties, patriots and placemen' were in attendance. Among them were Edmund Burke, Richard Fitzpatrick, the former Prime Minster Lord North and the Whig politician Charles Fox. Meanwhile, 'the intrepid Dr. Jeffries, and no less gallant Count Zambeccari, assisted at the ceremonies'. Blanchard then made a solo flight to Hornchurch (16 miles), during which he became the unwitting accessory to an increasingly common crime. With all eyes fixed firmly aloft 'Mr. Burke was robbed of his money and watch, as were many other gentlemen coming from their carriages'. Instant justice was on hand on this occasion, however, and one of several arrested pickpockets had his case heard on the spot by the mayor, who presided for the very first time over a new court held in the repository building adjacent to the site of the launch.

Rosine Simonet would probably not have been intimidated by all the attention, having apparently made her London stage debut when only about eight years old.[76] Before the end of the month, Blanchard would well and truly establish that the flightiest females were French by ascending with Rosine's younger sister. In the interim came Vincenzo Lunardi's failure to emulate him on 13 May, when the distinctly greater weight of his chosen passenger, Mrs Sage, obliged him to leave her behind (*see* Appendix 7). Rosine Simonet weighed only 83 pounds,[77] and Blanchard himself not much more, if the *Morning Chronicle & London Advertiser* (9 May 1785) is to be believed: 'Mr Blanchard's weight is exactly 114; Boat and apparatus 45; Ballast he took with him 70' pounds. Given that even by her own estimation Letitia Sage weighed almost as much as this combined total, one can sympathise with the additional challenge that Lunardi faced.

French ascendancy, so to speak, was confirmed a week later when Blanchard took another Simonet sister, logically Leonora, with him. She weighed more than her older sister, being 'exactly eight and a half stone' (i.e. 119 pounds) according to the *Public Advertiser* (23 May). Leonora had made her stage debut in December 1782[78] and earned this commendation in the *Gazetteer & New Daily Advertiser* (25 May 1784): 'the good-natured countenance of Miss L. Simonet will always recommend her in the comic dance'. At the time, she was performing together with Rosine, who was also much praised: 'the carriage of the elder Miss Simonet is certainly unrivalled by any person of her age in Europe'.[79]

More successful than most of his peers in exploiting the commercial possibilities of ballooning, Blanchard had established what he called an 'Aerostatic Academy' in South Lambeth, and it is from there that he made his ascent with Leonora Simonet on 21 May, still using the same balloon with which he had crossed the Channel. He was 'materially assisted ... in many operations' by his (ill-fated) compatriot Pilâtre de Rozier, who, 'in order to ballast the balloon sufficiently ... while Mr. B. was preparing to manoeuvre over the wall of the ground where he ascended from, stripped to the shirt, and threw his cloaths in the car'.[80] This was for gallantry's sake, one assumes, in case the young girl was in need of warmer clothing, rather than out of sheer macho bravado! She was not the intended original sole passenger:

> Mr. Blanchard seated himself in the car, and a trial was made of the ascending power; which proved not to be great enough to take up Mr. Blanchard and his intended companion, Colonel Thornton. Dr. Jeffries now introduced the two Miss Simonets to Mr. Blanchard, the youngest of whom (the sister of the lady who accompanied Mr Blanchard in his excursion a short time since from Langhorn's Repository in Barbican) stepped into the car.[81]

They reached Deptford without incident, and, still seated in the basket, brought the balloon by road back to their starting point, where a further demonstration of Blanchard's undoubted mastery of his machine was provided. Leonora got out, and Blanchard reinflated the balloon sufficiently to ascend over the academy wall to land again at the exact spot from where they had begun earlier in the day. As an additional aid to identification, the youngest of the three Simonet sisters (therefore Theresa) was specifically identified the same month as being 'hardly ten years old' and 'not by the bye the fair Aeronaute, who first of her sex has dared to "soar above all human kind"'.[82] The Simonets' fame as balloonists was short-lived, but they did evidently try to capitalise a little. At the Haymarket Theatre later that summer, between the two favourite pieces of *The Spanish Barber,* and *Hunt the Slipper,* was introduced a new Dance call'd *The Female Balloonists; or, The Ladies in the Air;* in which Young Byrne was the *Lunardian,* or *Blanchardian,* hero, and the two Miss Simonets, who have themselves been real *Aeronauts,* were the Heroines.[83]

By 1792 Rosine Simonet had married the actor William Wilde, and performed from then on under her married name, at least until 1797,[84] while at about the same time one or other sister was gaining a reputation as an equestrian. Otherwise nothing is known about their subsequent careers or lives.

APPENDIX 7: MRS SAGE (*NÉE* HOARE) AND HER SISTERS

Who, then, was Mrs Sage, the first Englishwoman ever to make a balloon flight? In her own published account – *Letter addressed to a female friend* (1785) – she signed herself as L. A. Sage of 10 Charles Street, Covent Garden. According to the *Morning Herald & Daily Advertiser* of 5 July, announcing that the publication was to be made available that same day, priced one shilling, the letter was a genuine one written to her sister in Liverpool (that is, by deduction, Mrs Sarah Ward). The publication was popular enough to go to three editions, the second appearing on 14 July.[85]

Mrs Sage begins her *Letter*, which was dated 30 June 1785, the day after her historic journey, by refuting the idea that Vincenzo Lunardi's failure to take her with him on 13 May was either always his intention or due to her own lack of courage. Lunardi had created especially high expectations beforehand by emphasising the unprecedented spectacle of an ascent by a British female. In view of the predictable disquiet that her subsequent non-ascent had then occasioned, he inserted a long explanation in several newspapers, to stress that he himself should not be blamed as he had delegated 'the business of filling his Balloon to a gentleman of the first reputation in chemistry, and of unimpeached integrity'. (This is not a reference to James Sadler, it would seem, who is known to have been present only on the successful, second occasion.)

In fact, Lunardi had intended taking not only Mrs Sage but also his friend and sponsor George Biggin. When first one, then both, of the would-be passengers had to vacate the basket in order to permit uplift, and Lunardi went alone, suspicions of fraud and profiteering were aroused. Inevitably so! They always were at the slightest change to any advertised programme! The *Public Advertiser* (16 May 1785) neatly summed up the mood:

> What if Lunardi in his aerial cage,
> Refus'd to take the Biggin and the Sage,
> Tho' broke his Promise – surely was no sin
> To leave out two – and take ten thousand in.

Lunardi had not identified his intended female companion, but the newly established *Daily Universal Register* (13 May 1785) contrived to reveal her as Mrs Sage on the day of the ascent. She was in fact fairly unmistakable. Noting that she was the sister of Mrs Ward, a well-known actress then appearing at Drury Lane Theatre, the newspaper explained that she was 'a lady of considerable magnitude, and of course, considerable philosophical *gravity*'. This was the first of many snide allusions to Mrs Sage's weight. The *Public Advertiser* (17 May 1785), in its regular column of 'Disappointments', gave its own similar observation an appropriately theatrical slant by calling her 'the female Falstaffe'.

The *London Magazine* joined in the fun, writing that 'Mrs. *Sage* … was found to have more *gravity* than what belonged to a *wise* name. Other ladies instantly began to dispute the palm for volatility, but none were deemed sufficient *flighty*.'[86] The *Morning Chronicle & London Advertiser* (17 May) made a more serious point, albeit in the same vein, by noting that Jean-Pierre Blanchard's companion on 3 May (*see* Appendix 6) had been the diminutive Rosine Simonet who 'weighed only eighty-three pounds, and Mr. Lunardi's lady two hundred and fifty'.

In her published *Letter*, Mrs Sage appeared not to be affronted by observations like these (exaggerated though the figure of 250 pounds – nearly 18 stone – was). Indeed she freely acknowledged that her weight was an inescapable impediment to her ballooning aspirations. No, it was her supposed cowardice and disagreement with Lunardi that she refuted, riled no doubt by depictions such as this:

> The fat lady, who had swallowed a few spoonfuls of brandy, to recruit her "*heroism,?*" and to dispose her "*liberal mind for the reflections she intended to make for the benefit of her fair countrywomen,*" finding herself left behind, made a national reproach to Lunardi for his neglect of her, and could she have got at him, would have revenged herself with her nails.[87]

*

Spiteful allusions to would-be female balloonists were nothing new. When Miss Grice of Holborn was obliged to relinquish her place with Francesco Zambeccari and the elderly Admiral Sir Edward Vernon (1723–94) at Tottenham Court Road on Wednesday 23 March 1785,[88] her frustration occasioned a sarcastic and risqué poem in the *Morning Post & Daily Advertiser* (1 April 1785). 'The Lunar Travellers' alludes to the original flight made by Lunardi and also Blanchard's with Sheldon. Next comes the ascent of the 'great Zambeccari, Gay, easy, and airy',

> And V—n the bold,
> Notwithstanding he's old
> Swore his compass he'd box in the air.
> As there's no prohibition,
> He makes a condition,
> A damsel should share in the glory;
> Such inflammable air
> The Balloon would not bear,
> As to carry her more than one story;
> For, alas! she saw plain,
> Her hopes were all vain,
> So flaccid and weak the machine,
> And 'tis not the first time,
> From old age and cold clime,
> A maid disappointed has been.

There is no reference to Sadler in 'The Lunar Travellers', but in view of the poem's concluding attack on the 'wretched spawn of new philosophy' as 'mere men-monkies in mortal shape' perhaps that is just as well! Vernon and Zambeccari reached Horsham without incident, but when another attempt on 3 May ended in fiasco and riot, a disheartened Zambeccari left England for the continent.[89]

A month or so later another female was denied the honour of becoming the first English female aeronaut under similar circumstances. No doubt spurred on by Blanchard's successful ascents with the Simonet sisters in May, the London balloon manufacturer James Deeker contemplated something similar the following month. His companion was intended to be a Miss Weller.[90] On the first ascent from Norwich on 1 June,[91] however, she was prevented from joining him due to a 'slight intermittent fever' and was disappointed again on 22 June when the balloon failed to rise and she had to disembark.[92] Deeker continued alone on both occasions.

Another reported case of enforced removal of excess female ballast earlier that same month of June must have been a hoax. It was stated in the *General Evening Post* (2–4 June 1785) that the companion of the Rev. Peter Routh and Robert Davy of Beccles, in Suffolk, was to have been Miss Fanny Shouldham, but she was obliged to make way for 'Mrs. Hines, who was desirous of accompanying the gentlemen, and less corpulent,' upon which 'the balloon instantly rose'. The balloon was reported to have ditched in the North Sea, but could not have been based on reality, as no other accounts of what would have been a very newsworthy story of the first British ascent of three people, one of them the first British female, and a dramatic rescue near the Dutch coast, were mentioned in any other newspaper.

Mrs Sage and George Biggin: Wednesday 29 June 1785

It was more than a month after Blanchard's successful flight with a second Simonet sister, Leonora, on 21 May, that Lunardi made another attempt to emulate him. In order to avoid the massive public outcry which a second failure was certain to provoke, Lunardi had taken the precaution of first going to Birmingham to arrange for more iron – 'that article being very scarce in consequence of the repeated aerostatic experiments which have been made here within a short time'.[93] He had then visited the addressee in Liverpool, from where he anticipated making a subsequent ascent.[94]

The iron was duly delivered to London from Birmingham on Monday 27 June, and all was ready by Wednesday 29 June. The location was the Rotunda in St George's Fields (Newington Butts), a circus and garden of amusement managed by a retired seaman called Stuart Amos Arnold,[95] a would-be aeronaut in his own right. During the preparations, Mrs Sage remained hidden inside a waiting coach 'as I did not like to be seen, until the very moment of getting into the gallery'. This she did at 1.10 p.m., when she joined Lunardi, George Biggin and two others, one being another female whose name she did not know.[96] James Sadler was on hand to supervise the preparations this time,[97] though probably feeling rather less optimistic than Lunardi – Mrs Sage represented quite a challenge, let alone with another four people – and inevitably there were problems. First one, then both of the latter two intended passengers were obliged to disembark, and though it would seem that a little elevation was then achieved,[98] Lunardi decided to get out too, and at 1.25 p.m. the two utter novices set off alone.

Presumably awestruck and preoccupied during the ascent, it is understandable that neither of them noticed that the gap in the side of the basket had not been secured. This was possibly a modification made especially for Mrs Sage's ease of access, and while attempting to lace the cover back in place, 'I ... unfortunately put my knees upon the barometer and broke it'.[99] It is another frank admission of her weight. Her *Letter* goes on to provide details of the route and the views, as well as some technical references to timed experiments and measurements attempted by Biggin during the journey, which ended safely at Harrow about an hour later.

Relieved of what Mrs Sage candidly described as a 'delivery of *two hundred* pounds of *human weight*',[100] the balloon of course instantly regained much buoyancy, providing Biggin with the opportunity to continue alone. He decided against it, however, when no suitable replacement ballast could be obtained. Another more pressing reason was posed by having to appease a farmer in whose field they had descended and whose crops had been damaged. The timely arrival of a master and boys from Harrow school saved the balloon from being destroyed by the increasingly irate associates of the farmer, who was pacified when the schoolboys collected enough money between them to compensate him for his loss.[101]

So everyone was happy, not least Mrs Sage, who wrote that she was 'infinitely better pleased with my excursion than I ever was at any former event of my life'.[102] But actually, not *everyone* was happy. As Mrs Sage capitalised on her fame by appearing daily at the Pantheon along with the balloon[103] there were some who attempted to belittle her achievement and malign her character. Unlike most, Catharine Maria Sydney did not disguise her scorn in anonymity:

> When first come from the skies
> With a bundle of lies,
> Lunardi would prattle and chat;
> All those that were willing
> To part with their shilling
> Might stroke his dear dog and his cat.

> We now see him again
> In his true puffing strain,
> Attempting the town to engage;
> Inviting all willing
> To part with their shilling,
> To chat with and stroke Mrs. Sage.[104]

The actresses Mrs Sage, Mrs Powell and Mrs Ward – the Three Hoare Sisters

So, again, who was Mrs Sage? At the time, all that was publicly known was that she was the sister of the actress Mrs Ward. The *Daily Universal Register* had revealed this on the day of the first aborted flight and the *General Advertiser* of 30 June 1785 provided cryptic confirmation by saying she was 'much more *en bon point* than her sister, Mrs. Ward of Drury-Lane Theatre, and who consequently dreaded her own weight'. Noted actress though Mrs Ward was, a third sister, Mrs Kate Powell, was still better known, though perhaps less so in London. All three sisters are featured under their married names in the multi-volume *Biographical Dictionary of Actors, Actresses … 1660–1800*, and the summaries below are included as a means of attempting to identify the sisters' collective origins, under their maiden name of Hoare.

*

Mrs Sarah Ward *née* Hoare (*c.* 1753–1838) appears to have been born in about 1753 on the basis that she died in Manchester, 'relict of the late Thomas Ward Esq., for many years manager of the Manchester Theatre', in her eighty-fifth year on 19 May 1838.[105] She had married the actor/manager Thomas Achurch Ward, 'who afterwards became a favourite comedian',[106] at St Philip's Church in Birmingham on 26 August 1775, and performed in Birmingham under her married name for the first time on 1 September 1775.[107]

Catherine or Kate Hoare (*c.* 1762–1807) married the actor Sparks Powell in or before 1782[108] and acted thereafter under her married name. Thomas Gilliland, in 1808, stated that she was 'sister to Mrs. Ward, now of the Manchester theatre, but formerly of Drury-lane' and that she was 'nearly related to Mr. Hoare the banker',[109] by whom he meant:

> Henry Hoare (d. 1828) of Fleet Street and one of the founders of the Church Missionary Society, whose son James Hoare (1781–1865) is noticed in The Dictionary of National Biography. Possibly they were also related to Prince Hoare (1755–1834), the dramatist and painter, who was the son of William Hoare (1707?–1792), a Bath artist.[110]

In 1800, after the death of her husband the year before, Kate Powell moved to London.[111] A real trouper to the last, she had been on stage the evening before she died,[112] and was buried on 16 August 1807, aged forty-five, at St Paul's, Covent Garden. Her obituary in *The*

Athenaeum confirmed her as 'the sister of Mrs. Ward, formerly a respectable actress at Drury-lane, and of Mrs. Sage who some years ago ascended in a balloon with Mr. Biggen'.[113]

Letitia Ann Sage

So, for a third time, who was Mrs Sage, whose ballooning feat was recalled in *The Athenaeum* more than twenty years later? The *Biographical Dictionary*, providing dates no firmer than that she was alive in 1773 and 1817, states that 'sometime before 1773 Letitia Hoare lived as the common-law wife of Mr Sage, a haberdasher in Cheapside'.[114] Her 'husband' must have been Edward Sage (*c.* 1745–1816) of Cheapside (whose death aged seventy-one was noted in the *Morning Post* of 6 December 1816), and whose company was trading from Cheapside in the 1780s, according to various trade directories of that decade.

Mrs Sage made her stage debut at Covent Garden on 24 April 1773 as Lady Townly in 'The Provok'd Husband',[115] although identified only as 'a Lady (being her first appearance)' in the newspapers of the time. It was another seven years before she made her 'second appearance on any stage',[116] again at Covent Garden. This time she was duly identified as Mrs Sage, and played Lady Macbeth. At the time her physical appearance was a cause for admiring rather than disparaging comment, the *Morning Chronicle & London Advertiser* (26 April 1780) anticipating that 'if an opinion may be formed from her person and figure, which are truly graceful, a correspondent thinks she promises fair to become a valuable acquisition to the drama'. It appears that this optimism was unfounded, because she apparently never again performed on stage, although did maintain a behind-the-scenes career.

After her abrupt, and literal, rise to fame in Lunardi's balloon on 29 June 1785, nothing certain is known about Mrs Sage for the next twenty years. A fine portrait of her was commissioned by someone, presumably soon after her balloon flight. Among the notes of James Winston (at the Folger Library in America) is the suggestion that

> she lived for a while with the purser of an Indiaman; he was reported to be the son of the Edinburgh manager David Bate. Winston also noted that in 1791 she went to America with John 'Brush' Collins, the actor and monologuist; but the Collins who performed in America in the 1790s was not John.[117]

More certainly, still maintaining her theatrical links, but now in the guise of Mrs Robinson, 'sister of the late Kate Powel, the well known actress', she was wardrobe keeper to Charles Dibdin junior (1768–1833) at Sadler's Wells until the end of 1805 when she left his employment to work at the Crow Street Theatre in Dublin.[118] She would seem likely to have been the same Mrs Robinson who worked as a woman's dresser at Drury Lane from 1812–13 until 1816–17, at a salary of nine shillings per week,[119] which would mean, just possibly, that she might still have been in Dublin when James Sadler made his ascent in October 1812.

Hoare Genealogy (*see* Family Tree)

So, yet again, who was Mrs Sage? It is her relatively unusual first name of Letitia which provides a very helpful clue to her possible origins, in conjunction with knowing the names of her two sisters. A good match for Letitia and Sarah is found in the parish records of Bucklebury in Berkshire, where the baptisms of the following daughters of Thomas (*c.* 1722–96) and Mary (*c.* 1722–98) Hoare[120] are listed as Mary on 26 June 1752; Elizabeth on 20 July 1753; Letitia on 17 November 1754; and Sarah on 26 September 1756.

There was no daughter named Catherine, but there could be many reasons for that. She might have been baptised elsewhere (as she was several years younger); she might have used a stage name; or another possibility is that the three girls were not actually sisters. This flimsy evidence for Letitia Sage's Bucklebury origins is given marginally more credence by the *Dictionary*'s supposition of a possible family connection with the artist William Hoare of Bath (1707–92) and Gilliland's more confident assertion about her connection to the London banking Hoares.

William Hoare of Bath and Henry Hoare of London

The idea of a family tie between William Hoare and Letitia Hoare may be entirely spurious, but becomes slightly more plausible in light of the lecture notes of a former Bath librarian Reginald Wright.[121] It is generally accepted that William 'was born about 1707, at Eye, near Ipswich, and that his father cultivated a farm of his own property of large extent'.[122] Wright's notes state that his father was called John, and that he moved his whole family from Suffolk to

Berkshire,[123] which does at least bring the focus to the same county: William certainly attended school in Faringdon,[124] which was then in Berkshire, and he could be the William Hoare baptised at nearby Little Coxwell on 9 October 1707.

There is also one link of a more certain nature to consider. Gilliland's assertion that the Hoare sisters were 'nearly related' to Henry Hoare, the banker, whose family history is covered in detail in several publications, leads towards some rather less tentative clues. A Suffolk branch of the Hoare banking dynasty is apparent in the earliest account of the family, in *History & Antiquities of the county of Buckinghamshire* (1847), where a 'Pedigree of Hoare of Walton and Wavendon' appears (on page 390). The relevant branch (with some dates gleaned from other sources) begins with Sir Richard Hoare (1648–1719), under whom the family bank became hugely profitable. One of his eleven sons was Richard (1673–1721), who had a son William, (*c.* 1717–53) who was stated to be a merchant of London and Bury St Edmunds, in Suffolk, a place with which he was still associated at his death.[125] According to Captain E. Hoare, in *Early History and Genealogy of the Families of Hore and Hoare* (1883), one of the sons of this William Hoare was Henry (1750–1828), the individual singled out by Gilliland as being 'nearly related' to the actresses. So, although no link has been proven between the banking Hoares and the artistic Hoares, there is a common thread in the Suffolk and Berkshire associations which sustains the idea that the Letitia Hoare born in Bucklebury, Berkshire might indeed be related to both.

It may also be worthy of note that one of the great-grandsons of Sir Richard Hoare (who died 1719) was Henry (1744–85), who married on 25 June 1765 Mary Hoare (1744–1820), the eldest daughter of William Hoare of Bath, 'the well-known and celebrated portrait artist'.[126] In addition, a possibly pertinent theatrical connection becomes apparent

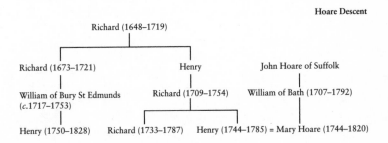

Hoare Descent

Richard (1648–1719)

Richard (1673–1721) — Henry — John Hoare of Suffolk

William of Bury St Edmunds (c.1717–1753) — Richard (1709–1754) — William of Bath (1707–1792)

Henry (1750–1828) — Richard (1733–1787) — Henry (1744–1785) = Mary Hoare (1744–1820)

in that this Henry Hoare, otherwise known as 'Fat Harry', was a great friend of David Garrick, who called him 'sweet-blooded'.[127]

So, to conclude, while it does seem possible that Mrs Sage, the first English female aeronaut, was baptised as Letitia Hoare in the village of Bucklebury in 1754, it is beyond the scope of this book to hypothesise further. It was nonetheless thought worthwhile to lay out information which may possibly prove helpful to any future researcher into this intriguing woman, even though this long appendix must sadly end exactly as it began, with the unresolved question: Who *was* Mrs Sage?

APPENDIX 8: JAMES SADLER'S CHILDREN

Mary Ann Sadler (1777–1811+)

The oldest child of James and Mary (*née* Harper) Sadler was baptised at St Helen's, Abingdon on 23 November 1777. This was the same church in which her parents had married on 5 November 1775. Her own marriage came late in life, at the age of thirty-four, to James Wyatt. The wedding, at All Saints in Oxford on 15 June 1811, was recorded in *Jackson's Oxford Journal* of 22 June 1811 as being between 'Miss Sadler, daughter of Mr. James Sadler formerly of this city' and James Wyatt of the High Street. They were both living in All Saints parish, both signed, and her uncle Thomas was one of the witnesses. There were no apparent children. Mary Ann Sadler's husband seems most likely to have been the James Wyatt baptised at Oxford's St Mary the Virgin Church in 1769. If so he was the nephew of Thomas Wyatt (1738–?), a baker of note, and the son of a baker, John Wyatt (1697–?). Mary Ann Sadler's grandfather, Matthew Harper, had also been a baker, of course. Wyatt's namesake cousin, James (1774–1853), was a gilder and picture dealer, famously painted by the pre-Raphaelite artist John Millais at his home of No. 115 High Street, only a few doors away.

John Sadler (1779–1838)

John Sadler's marriage to Mary Long produced only one child, whom they named John Coxe Hippisley Sadler at his baptism at Slaley, near Hexham, Northumberland in 1805. At some point within the next five years, John moved back to London (where he had assisted Humphrey Davy until 1804). Hodgson cites a letter that John wrote to his sister, Sybella (dated October 1824, and therefore written very soon after Windham's death), in which he refers to having erected in 1810 'a gas light apparatus for the convenience of a Manufactory',[128] namely the vinegar works of the Beaufoy family. According to John it was this which so impressed his half-brother Windham that he decided to become an engineer himself. 1810 is the year that the new Strand (later Waterloo) Bridge was built across the Thames, causing the Beaufoys to move two years later from the original Cuper's Bridge site established by Mark Beaufoy senior (1718–82) to new premises on the South Lambeth Road.[129] Henry Benjamin Hanbury Beaufoy (1786–1851), who flew with James Sadler on 29 August 1811, was a grandson of the founder and inherited the business in 1836.[130]

It was probably due to the Beaufoys' influence that John Sadler became an active member of the Hackney Literary and Philosophical Society. He also contributed to the launch of the *New Agricultural & Commercial Magazine* in 1811.[131] The same year of his one-off return to ballooning (1814) he had a paper, 'On the dislocation of mineral veins', read to the Geological Society and in 1821 patented a new method of making white lead.[132]

It is not clear when or where John Sadler's first wife Mary died, but it would seem that he might have remarried twice, possibly even three times. Certainly by the time of the baptisms of his three daughters – Eliza, Charlotte Rebecca and Augusta (who died in infancy) – at St Mark's, Lambeth on 8 July 1821 the mother's name is shown as Elizabeth.[133] At the baptism of another girl, Frances, on 7 April 1822, at which time her parents were living in Penlington Place (now called Hercules Road) in Lambeth, John's occupation was stated to be a 'vinegar merchant'.

By implication only, he could have been the John Sadler who married Elizabeth Hoar on 17 April 1817, merely on the basis that the venue of St George's in Hanover Square, Mayfair was the same as where his half-brother and half-sister had been baptised many years earlier.

Another possibility is that he is the John Sadler – there are no other obvious local candidates – who married Elizabeth Woodley at Oxford's St Mary the Virgin Church on 14 March 1820, although as both were described as 'of this parish', that is perhaps less likely.

A third candidate is Elizabeth Hulls, a widow, who married John Sadler, widower, at St Mary's, Lambeth on 24 October 1825.[134] His daughters did not necessarily all have the same mother, but that of

Frances survived to old age, and was shown as living in the same household as her daughter in the 1861 census (then aged thirty-nine, and married to Charles Brooks) as the 'wife's mother', then aged eighty.[135]

John Sadler was buried at Clapham on 26 March 1838, and was described as a chemist on his death certificate. John's son from his first marriage, John Coxe Hippisley Sadler (1805–60) sustained his father's and grandfather's inclinations by involving himself in both ballooning (with George Graham) and chemistry. In the 1851 census his occupation is shown as 'chemist'. At the time he was a widower living at 39 Wandsworth Road, Battersea, with six children aged between twelve and twenty-one, including a son John, who was designated a 'student in chemistry' and a daughter Amelia, whose grandson Stanley Alford donated various items of Sadler memorabilia to the Museum of the History of Science in Oxford in 1990.

James Sadler (1780–1817)

After the excitement and responsibility of crossing the English Channel to Holland with his father's guns in September 1799, James Sadler's second son seems to have followed a sporadic military career. His application to join the East India Company forces was made on 18 March 1800[136] and various editions of the *East India Register* from 1803 onwards show that he enlisted as a cadet on 15 July 1800 and was enrolled as a Lieutenant into the 1st Regiment of the Madras Native Infantry on 15 December 1800.

He appears then to have taken the precaution of marrying Ann Barn(e)s at St Peter-in-the-East, Oxford on 9 February 1801, prior to sailing to India. He was promoted to Captain Lieutenant on 11 July 1806, after which he appears to have returned briefly to Oxford, his freedom (as the second son of James Sadler, 'cook') being granted on 3 November 1806.[137] It would seem from this that he might have been contemplating a civilian career in Oxford, because he was shown as 'on furlough' (for at least five months) in both of the half-yearly *Registers* dated 1807.[138] Indeed, he may well have resigned, albeit temporarily, because his length of service was measured subsequently from a new starting date of 11 July 1806. On 1 March 1809 he was promoted to Captain.[139] Both editions of the 1810 *Register* included the announcement that on 1 May 1809 'the lady of Capt. Jas. Sadler' of 24th Native Infantry, Madras, had given birth to a son.

The following year, Sadler was one of approximately twenty

officers given the option of being either tried by court martial or summarily dismissed.[140] There had been a collective revolt or refusal to obey orders – described as 'criminal proceedings' – by a number of battalions prior to the end of September 1809 (the date of the dispatch). Sadler's name is missing from the *Registers* of 1811, 1812 and 1813. He was almost certainly back in Oxford again for at least part of this time, as the All Saints register shows the baptism of the daughter of Captain James and Elizabeth Sadler on 28 July 1811. She was given the possibly Anglo-Indian name of Albinia (Elizabeth was not his first wife, after all, and as the infant was born on 26 May this may have been during the voyage home). One would hope that given the timing of this baptism, James was able to witness some of his resurgent father's balloon ascents and also to attend his older sister's marriage in the same church the month before.

By 1814 it would seem that some measure of exoneration had been applied by the East India Company, because James Sadler's name is again included in the *Register* (second edition, corrected to 8 September 1814), reinstated as a Captain in the 24th Madras Native Infantry Regiment. He served another three years or so, after which the 24th Regiment disappeared from the *Registers*. The reason for this becomes clear from the following, information which seems to have been embargoed for several months, presumably for fear of damaging morale.

Jackson's Oxford Journal (9 May 1818) announced the death of Captain James Sadler, son of the 'celebrated aeronaut', on 26 November 1817. He had died during a 'most brilliant action at Nagpore,' (i.e. Nagpur, Maharashtra) 'in which the British interests in that capital have been gloriously maintained by the undaunted courage and perseverance of a small detachment of the ... Madras Establishment'. Sadler was one of the four named officers who died in facing the numerically superior forces of the Rajah of Berar. The engagement was considered to be an exceptional ordeal for the soldiers in that 'they saw their wives and children exposed and suffering under the same fire that was thinning their own ranks'.[141] Casualties were sufficiently extensive after this encounter for the 24th Native Infantry to be disbanded.

Thomas Sadler (1782–?)

It has not proved possible to identify any references to James Sadler's third son, unless it happens that on occasions it is he rather than his cousin, Thomas Sadler (1788–1831), the son of Thomas Blakeney Sadler, who is named as a chemist, a druggist and/or a grocer in Oxford.

Eliza Sadler (1785–?)

Likewise, no trace of Eliza is apparent, unless, possibly, she was the Sadler 'child' who was buried as Elizabeth at St George's, Hanover Square, in December 1801.

William Windham Sadler (1796–1824)

Windham's wife Catherine (*née* Richards) died on 17 November 1832, aged thirty-eight, and is buried at Christ Church in Liverpool alongside her husband, daughter[142] and brother Thomas, who died 26 May 1865, aged fifty-nine.[143] Windham's son, John Muncaster Sadler (1823–1912), became a railway engineer and worked for many years for the Liverpool Corporation.[144] One of his sons, Harold, is mentioned with his daughter, Eileen Doran (born about 1901), in the Conclusion to this book.

Martha Maria Sybella Sadler (1798–1851+)

Sybella (the name the family knew her by) was born on 27 November 1798 and baptised 23 January 1799 at St George's, Hanover Square, London. She was on the verge of ascending in a balloon with her father on at least two occasions, but never did realise that ambition, as far as is known. In 1851, as Mary S. Sadler, aged fifty, the census shows she was living alone near Bath.

APPENDIX 9: JANE STOCKS AND THE GRAHAMS

The fatal crash of thirty-two-year-old Thomas Harris on 25 May 1824 was covered in some detail in the *Morning Post* of 27 May. His passenger, Miss Stocks, was described as:

> the daughter of a poor man and woman who reside at No. 4, Henry-street, near the Vinegar-yard, City-road, and was a total stranger to Mr. Harris. She paid two shillings and sixpence for admission, and while tendering the money, Mr. Harris observed that he was afraid he should ascend by himself, upon which Miss Stocks replied, 'I'll go, Sir, if you will let me;' to which he instantly assented, and she was introduced to Mrs. Harris.

As well as her first-hand account, until the moment that the balloon burst and she fainted, the *Post*'s reporter had extracted the information that the eighteen-year-old, who was 'of rather a romantic turn of mind', had terminated of her job in a pastry cook's shop only days earlier 'in consequence of a love affair (not in the smallest degree discreditable to either party)'. The *Morning Chronicle* (28 May 1824) carried further particulars about her recovery, saying that notwithstanding her traumatic experience – several early accounts anticipated that she would not survive – she did not hesitate to accept an invitation from George Graham (with whom Harris had made a successful ascent the previous September) to ascend with him the following week. In fact, this did not happen, although Jane Stocks (as her first name was revealed to be) evidently *was* genuinely unfazed by her near-death experience, because she did make another ascent only the week after that! This time she was in the much safer hands of Charles Green, with whom she travelled safely from Leeds to York on 9 June.[145]

George Graham (*c.* 1785–1867) did have a female accomplice for his trip on 2 June 1824, however: his wife, Margaret (*c.* 1804–1864), who had made her first ever ascent with him the previous year. The couple's journey from the White Conduit Gardens, that familiar, though not always conducive, location in Islington, was commemorated in an amusing poem in *Bell's Life* of 6 June. Its theme came from reports in the press like this one: 'The House of Commons which at five o'clock was fully attended, was completely deserted when it was known that the balloon was in sight, and was the cause of the early adjournment of the House'.[146] The poem relates how the few remaining MPs left in the debating chamber resort to discussing the balloon. One says,

> 'Sir, I contend that WE
> Who rule o'er land and sea
> Have only one more element to quell
> And *that*, I tell the Honourable House, is AIR!'

He goes on to suggest a motion,

> 'Which I propose shall be – that England now
> Having command of everything terrestrial,
> Shall take into consideration how
> To conquer other planets call'd celestial;
> That for this purpose Sadler, Graham, and Green
> Shall be examined by a choice Committee, –
> (And be it understood, that by "choice" I mean
> Such as of *buoyant* spirits are – the light and witty).'

Sadly for Margaret Graham (*née* Watson, who was born in Walcot, Bath) her presence went unnoticed in both the poem and most of the newspaper accounts. Another person undeterred by Harris's death was a Mr Rossiter, said to be the uncle of his widow, who demonstrated particular sangfroid by ascending two months later with exactly the same balloon in order to raise funds for her.[147] The artist John Constable witnessed the event, and recorded his observations in his journal of 1 July 1824.[148] Constable had also chanced to see one of George Graham's balloon flights the previous month, as noted in Chapter 13.

Even after Windham Sadler's death in September 1824, and having themselves already had several near-misses, neither of the Grahams were deterred. George Graham made an ascent from Brighton in October

1824[149] and another from Canterbury on 8 November.[150] This made up for two earlier disappointments in the city, which were lampooned in a ballad, 'John Bull and the Balloon at Canterbury'. It began:

> I sing of a bubble, a humbug, and hoax,
> That has lately been played on us poor country folks.
> Who assembled to see – no such wonderful sight –
> A man take our money, and then – take his flight!

The ballad continues:

> Our money we cheerfully paid at the door,
> And one day's delay pretty patiently bore;
> And saw, when another we'd spent in the rain
> Graham get into his car – and then get out again.

> Then Graham, not caring to venture his life,
> Put into the cradle his venturesome wife;
> But scarce had the crowd in the height of their glee
> Applauded her spirit – when out too stept she![151]

Jane Stocks evidently remained friendly with the Grahams, since she was the intended companion of Mrs Graham herself when she ascended from the White Conduit Gardens on 28 June 1826. In the end, for reasons unclear, Margaret Graham went alone on a very short, low-level journey which took her only as far as Stoke Newington.[152] This made her the first British woman ever to fly solo, though the feat went largely unremarked, both then and subsequently.

On 6 June 1837, Margaret Graham became the first woman ever to ascend from Oxford. She followed the example of Richard Fitzpatrick in 1785, James Sadler in 1810 and Charles Green in 1823 by doing so during Commemoration week.[153] She and her husband continued to fly until at least 1851, when, having miraculously escaped serious injury in numerous crashes and collisions, the couple made an ascent as part of the Great Exhibition celebrations. They narrowly avoided a collision with the Crystal Palace before eventually crashing into a house in Piccadilly, leaving the building damaged and the aeronauts badly injured.

In both the 1851 and 1861 censuses, the couple state their occupation to be 'aeronaut', and Margaret's adventurous and injury-prone life is made all the more remarkable in that she also gave birth to six children between about 1823 and 1844, the last when she was about forty years old.

NOTES

Preface

1. Harry Paintin, *Round about Oxford*, No. 253, in *Oxford Journal Illustrated*, 11 April 1928, p. 16.

1. Growing Upwards: Childhood and Background

1. This Sadler family prayer book is in the possession of the University Museum of the History of Science, Oxford.
2. Oxfordshire History Centre OXFO 352 FREE.
3. Oxford University Chancellor's Court papers 1732/66^v to 68^r.
4. Oxford University Chancellor's Court papers 1737/69^v.
5. *Jackson's Oxford Journal*, 7 August 1802.
6. Oxford University Chancellor's Court papers 1744/125^v.
7. Oxfordshire History Centre OXFO 352 FREE.
8. Oxford University Chancellor's Court papers 1744/126^v.
9. Durham was the birthplace of English mustard, first produced there as a relish in 1729; a morel is an edible fungus; hartshorn was used to create smelling salts.
10. *See* footnote 3 of chapter 2 and footnote 1 of chapter 5.
11. *The Adventures of Oxymel Classic Esq.* (printed by William Flexney), vol. 1, p. 113.
12. The only other newspaper reference to Lemon Hall had been in an advertisement in *Jackson's* of 29 October 1757, when it was described as a 'well accustomed publick house near Carfax'. Sadler paid for a St Peter-in-the-East victualler's licence every year from 1745 to 1764, but in 1765, for the only time, it was granted for All Saints' parish (within which, evidently, Lemon Hall was situated). As no further licences at all were issued, it would seem that Sadler ceased to sell alcohol thereafter (Oxfordshire History Centre QSC/A5/5 & 6).
13. Salter, p. 12.
14. Accounts Rolls of University College, UC:E/B2/D3.
15. Oxfordshire History Centre OXFO 352 FREE.
16. Bodleian Library Gough Berks. 3 (27). Mary's mother was Ann Pittaway, who married Matthew Harper at St Helen's on 6 July 1755. It may or may not be relevant that immediately opposite James Sadler's High Street premises, at Nos. 39 and 40, was William Harper's coffee shop. It operated from at least 1759, when he is first mentioned in *Jackson's*, until November 1779, when he retired. The shop had a particular affiliation with Queen's College, where James Sadler senior's father, John, once worked.
17. *London Gazette*, 18–21 November 1775
18. That James and Mary went on to have three more children baptised at All Saints suggests a continuing independence from his father: James on 23 July 1780; Thomas on 1 March 1782; and – right in the midst of her father's first phase of ballooning fame – Eliza on 30 May 1785.
19. The Star was known from 1863 as the Clarendon Hotel, now demolished.
20. 'Bernard Blackmantle', *The English Spy*, vol. 1. (London: Sherwood, Jones & Co., 1825), p. 253.
21. Bodleian Library MS Top. Oxon. d.247, dated 11 April 1784.

22. *Jackson's Oxford Journal*, 3 January 1784.

2. 'Soaring Curiosity': James Sadler's First Trial of February 1784

1. *Dictionary of National Biography:* Sibthorp (and for the subsequent biographical information).
2. Holmes, p. 128, citing 'Dossier Montgolfier', Paris; Gillispie, p. 15, citing memoir of the Montgolfiers' cousin Matthieu Duret, in which he states that Joseph had been musing on this billowing laundry as early as 1777.
3. Rolt, p. 27.
4. This acknowledgement was made to the politician and agriculturalist Sir John Sinclair (1754–1835), who travelled to London with the Swiss (some sources say French) chemist Aimé Argand (1750–1803) and one of the Montgolfier brothers, probably Joseph, towards the end of 1785. In effect, Sinclair wrote, 'had it not been for Dr. Black's discoveries, no experiment would probably have been tried by the two Montgolfiers' (*Correspondence of Sir John Sinclair*, vol. 1. (London: Colburn & Bentley, 1831) p. 434). Argand had demonstrated a hydrogen balloon to George III and his Court at Windsor on 26 November 1783 (Hodgson (1924), p. 103).
5. Black, p. 77.
6. Black, p. 80.
7. One practical result of Priestley's realisation of the implications of gases being lighter than liquids was his invention of soda water in 1772, a product which James Sadler would himself commercially manufacture later in life.
8. Banks, vol. 2, p. 101.
9. Banks, vol. 2, p. 129.
10. Banks, p. 133.
11. Hodgson (1924), p. 103. Banks had been George III's adviser on matters related to science and agriculture since his return from the voyage to Australia on Captain Cook's *Endeavour* in 1771. He was knighted in 1781 (*Dictionary of National Biography:* Banks).
12. Banks, vol. 2, p. 209, in letter dated 7 November 1783.
13. In fact Franklin probably never actually uttered this *bon mot* – see Seymour L. Chapin in *Proceedings of the American Philosophical Society*, September 1985, pp. 278–90.
14. Benjamin Franklin witnessed the ascent and provided Banks with a very detailed description, d'Arlandes and one of the Montgolfiers having visited him the very same evening. (Franklin, pp. 113–121).
15. Rolt, p. 54, from Charles's own account in *La Manche en Ballon* (Paris: Raymonde Fontaine, 1980). On 19 September 1784, Robert's brother, Cadet, flew a quite extraordinary 150 miles from Paris with a Monsieur Collin-Hullin (Rolt, p. 58). Other accounts say both Robert brothers made this journey.
16. Holmes, p. 132, from Charles's own account in *La Manche en Ballon*.
17. Johnson, p. 281, in letter to William Bowles of 3 February 1784.
18. Johnson, p. 272, in letter to Hester Thrale of 12 January 1784.
19. Burney, p. 404 and p. 402.
20. Burney, p. 397.
21. Sibthorp to Banks, 20 October 1783 (Banks, vol. 2, p. 189).
22. Jonas Drylander (1748–1810), Banks' librarian, to Banks, 18 October 1783 (Banks, vol. 2, p. 186).
23. Hodgson (1924), p. 103.
24. *Morning Post & Daily Advertiser,* 17 & 19 December 1783.
25. *Bath Chronicle,* 15 January 1784.
26. *St. James's Chronicle,* 31 January–3 February 1784.
27. Desmond King-Hele in *Collected Letters of Erasmus Darwin* (Cambridge: Cambridge University Press, 2007), p. 223. According to the *Whitehall Evening Post* of 17–20 January 1784 it was on the 27th.
28. The large, plain, three-storey mansion (now part of St Hilda's College) was commissioned by Humphrey Sibthorp between 1775 and 1783 (unpublished text by former St Hilda's Principal, Christine Burrows).
29. *Jackson's Oxford Journal*, 21 February 1784.
30. While studying botany at Christ Church under John Sibthorp's father Humphrey between 1760 and 1764, Banks felt obliged in desperation to arrange, at his own expence, for the Cambridge

botanist Israel Lyons to come to Oxford especially to deliver a course (*Dictionary of National Biography*: Banks).

31. Windham (1886), 17 February 1784.
32. Bodleian Library MS Top. Oxon. d.247.
33. This was presumably Henry Brodrick, shown to be a resident of St Giles in an advertisement in *Jackson's* the following year. Blandford's experiment was also described in *Jackson's* of 5 and 12 June 1784.
34. *Jackson's Oxford Journal*, 21 February 1784, p. 2.
35. The enigmatic William Jackson launched his eponymous weekly title in 1753. Despite his enormous influence within an enormously influential city, very little is known about this great pioneer of the provincial press in Britain. For the fullest published account to date, see Mark Davies, *Oxfordshire Limited Edition*, November 2009, pp. 21–23.
36. *Jackson's Oxford Journal*, 15 May 1784.
37. *Jackson's Oxford Journal*, 22 May 1784.
38. There were some twenty French aeronauts by the end of May 1784 (according to the alphabetical list of balloonists' first ascents published in Monck Mason's generally reliable 1838 *Aeronautica*). These included de Rozier, d'Arlandes, Charles and Robert. Another was Jean-Pierre Blanchard (whose first ascent was on 2 March 1784). The first ascent outside of France was by Paolo Andreani and two brothers called Gerli in Milan on 25 February 1784.
39. Lockwood Marsh, p. 17.
40. Rolt, p. 57.
41. Mason, p. 278.
42. Mrs F. Nevill Jackson, 'Women as Air Travellers' in *Connoisseur*, January 1944, p. 13. Two weeks earlier, on 20 May 1784, in Paris, four women ascended in a captive balloon, under the supervision of one of the Montgolfiers. Quoting from an 'old diary' (the source apparently being the French geologist, Faujas de Saint-Fond, who had swiftly published a very detailed, two volume account of the Montgolfiers' invention in 1783 and 1784), Mrs Jackson identified these women as 'Mesdames La Marquise de Montalambert; La Comtesse de Montalambert; La Comtesse Podenas; Mlle. De Lagarde, accompagnées de MM. Le Marquis de Montalambert et Artand de Bellevue'.
43. *St. James's Chronicle*, 14–17 August 1784. Keegan had been very quick to adapt his existing expertise. Identifying himself as a manufacturer of 'umbrellas, garments, neat cloths for carriages' in an advertisement in the *Morning Herald & Daily Advertiser* (3 January 1784), he also offered to fabricate oiled silk balloons 'to any diameter, warranted, air proof, and at less expence considerably than any hitherto done in this kingdom'.

3. James Sadler: The First English, or British, Aeronaut?

1. *Jackson's Oxford Journal*, 4 September 1784.
2. *Jackson's Oxford Journal*, 24 July 1784.
3. Letter dated 4 May 1785 (British Library add. MS 37914 f27–30) Windham was in Oxford after having visited Samuel Johnson at Ashbourne, as per a letter from Johnson to Richard Brocklesby dated 2 September (Boswell, p. 356). Among the other people whom Windham met in Oxford that week was Joseph Banks (Windham (1866), p. 21).
4. Richard Grove, a servant of the Reverend Dr Bandinell of Oxford, claimed that James Sadler and another 'pastry cook', Richard Marsden, had assaulted him 'with force and arms' on 26 August, and 'did beat wound and ill treat [him] so that his life was greatly despaired of'. Both men pleaded not guilty, and it would seem that the case was dropped. While it is not certain which James Sadler was accused, logic suggests that was unlikely to have been the older man, who would then have been in his mid-sixties (QS Michaelmas Recognisances 24–26, at Oxfordshire History Centre).
5. Fergusson, p. 61.
6. *Independent Chronicle*, 1 September 1785, quoted in Lynn, p. 110. Benjamin Franklin had signalled an early warning of the ramifications for any would-be aeronaut who failed an expectant public, writing on 16 January 1784 that in Bordeaux 'the populace were so exasperated that they pulled down his house, and had like to have killed him' (Franklin, p. 155).
7. *Jackson's Oxford Journal*, 4 September 1784.
8. *Jackson's Oxford Journal*, 11 September 1784.

9. Mason, p. 274.

10. Gardiner, p. 29.

11. Gardiner, p. 31.

12. For example, *Morning Herald & Daily Advertiser,* 4 August 1784, and subsequently.

13. Lunardi (1784), p. 10.

14. Lunardi (1784), p. 50.

15. As long ago as 13 February 1784, four days after James Sadler's first experiment, William Windham had visited Fordyce 'to consult about a balloon' (Windham (1866) p. 5). Fordyce had also been helping John Sheldon with his efforts.

16. Gardiner, p. 29.

17. *St. James's Chronicle,* 10–12 August 1784.

18. Lunardi (1784), p. 15.

19. It was de Moret to whom Samuel Johnson had paid a subscription (mentioned in his letters of 31 January 1784 and 3 February 1784) and whom Johnson accused (although not by name) in a letter of 21 August 1784 of being 'the man that ran away with so much money' (Johnson, p. 279, p. 281 and p. 377). He had not done so in fact, but de Moret's failure that month meant that he might as well have, because, in an almost literal sense, every subscriber's money went up in smoke!

20. Gardiner, p. 30.

21. Lunardi (1784), p. 39.

22. Biggin, of Cosgrove in Northamptonshire, may have missed out on becoming the first Englishman to fly, but did realise his ambition to ascend the following year, and at the same time participated in a different 'first', that of accompanying the first English woman aeronaut (*see* Appendix 7). He invented what became known as the coffee-biggin, a combination of coffee-pot and strainer. His obituary in the *Morning Chronicle* (5 November 1803), which referred to the balloon flight with Mrs Sage, described him as 'about forty-three years of age'.

23. Banks, vol. 2, p. 306, in letter of 16 September 1784.

24. Lunardi (1784), p. 54.

25. Lunardi (1784), p. 37. A labourer in Kent had a similar reaction: when an air balloon descended at his feet, then jumped over his head, he declared that he had seen 'a dancing Devil in the shape of a large meat pudding' (*Public Advertiser,* 13 August 1784). The first Montgolfière of the previous year had inspired a similar reaction among the French peasantry, causing people to think that there was a living animal inside, which they attacked with stones and knives (Benjamin Franklin to Joseph Banks on 30 August 1783 in Banks, vol. 2, p. 128).

26. Burney, p. 443, in a letter to his son of 24 September 1784.

27. Banks, vol. 2, p. 308. Banks had not been able to witness the launch himself, nor would he that of Blanchard and Sheldon in October (Banks, vol. 2, p. 333).

28. Banks, vol. 2, p. 315, in letter of 14 October. This is all decidedly harsh, considering that Lunardi was less than fluent in English (Gardiner, p. 153; letter of January 1785 from G. Talbot at Leicester Record Office DG39/1140).

29. Walpole, vol. 25, pp. 527–28. Samuel Johnson too had realised that 'to pay for seats at the Balloon is not very necessary, because in less than a minute they who gaze at a mile's distance will see all that can be seen' (Johnson, p. 404, in letter to John Hoole of 13 September 1784).

30. Banks, vol. 2, p. 317.

31. Walpole, vol. 25, p. 528, letter to Horace Mann of 30 September 1784.

32. Banks, vol. 2, pp. 306–307, in letter of 16 September 1784.

33. *London Chronicle,* 28–30 September 1784.

34. *Morning Post & Daily Advertiser,* 1 October 1784. Its manufacturer, the umbrella maker Keegan, later unsuccessfully sued Sheldon for the £600 he claimed as its value (*Gazetteer & New Daily Advertiser,* 7 December 1784).

35. Mason, p. 274.

36. *Jackson's Oxford Journal,* 25 September, 2 October, and 9 October 1784. These three identical notices appeared immediately after the column of local news, rather than as a separate advert, again suggesting preferential treatment courtesy of William Jackson.

37. In fact, in no surviving documentation does Sadler himself ever claim to be the first; it is other contemporary commentators who do.

38. Sadler's faith in the oars was obviously misplaced. The Montgolfier brothers had decided against

oars, and while Lunardi attributed his own successful first descent to his dexterity with a single oar (Lunardi (1784), p. 35) he made no further reference to their use in his subsequent ascents.

39. For instance, the 7–9 October issues of the *St James's Chronicle* and *Whitehall Evening Post*; the *Gazetteer & New Daily Advertiser* and *Morning Herald & Daily Advertiser* of 9 October; the *Public Advertiser* of 11 October; the *Bath Chronicle* of 14 October; and *Felix Farley's Bristol Journal* of 16 October.

40. *Gloucester Journal*, 6 September 1784 and 20 September 1784. The arrival of the second balloon near the public house at Birdlip in Gloucestershire is said to be why its name was changed to The Air Balloon. Jenner had helped to process Joseph Banks' specimens on his return from Cook's voyage, and contemplated going on Cook's second expedition. (*Dictionary of National Biography*: Jenner).

41. *Letters of Edward Jenner*, ed. Genevieve Miller (Baltimore: Johns Hopkins University Press, 1983), p. 3.

42. Mason, p. 274. Mason cannot always be relied upon: his identification of John Sadler's own first ascent as being at Worcester on 13 May 1785 is incorrect, for instance.

43. The plaque erected by the Royal Aeronautical Society on the wall to the north of Merton Field states that the flight was made from 'near this place' (*see* Conclusion).

44. Lockwood Marsh, p. 4.

45. Clow & Clow, p. 156.

46. Blanchard, p. 2.

47. The other ascents covered (first names from other sources) were those of Blanchard alone on 23 May and with Monsieur Dominique Boby on 18 July, both from Rouen; of Ainé Robert, his brother Cadet and a Monsieur Hullin from Paris on 19 September; 'Lunardi's Voyage' of 15 September; and Tytler's disastrous failure of 11 October (*see* Appendix 3).

48. Banks, vol. 2, p. 313.

49. Joseph Banks, *Letters*, ed. Warren R. Dawson (London: British Museum, 1958), p. 64.

50. Banks, vol. 2, p. 320.

51. Banks, vol. 2, p. 313.

52. Letter to Samuel Johnson from Oxford on Wednesday 6 October 1784 in Windham (1913), vol. 1, p. 64 – citing British Library add. MSS 37914 f18.

53. Windham (1866), p. 24.

54. Thomas Burgess (1757–1837) matriculated at Corpus Christi College on 14 March 1775, aged eighteen (*Alumni Oxonienses*). He was made a fellow of Corpus Christi in 1783, remaining in Oxford until 1791 (*Dictionary of National Biography*: Burgess).

55. *Works of Samuel Parr*, vol. 7 (London: Longman, Rees, Orme, Brown, and Green, 1828), p. 339.

4. Sadler's First Public Ascent: Oxford, Friday 12 November 1784

1. *Jackson's Oxford Journal*, 13 November 1784. Tickets (*Jackson's* 30 October) were half a guinea, a crown, or half a crown, available from Sadler, High St. As this information appeared in the news column, rather than as a separate notice, it seems a further indication of William Jackson's personal belief in him.

2. *The Noels and the Milbankes*, ed. Malcolm Elwin (London: Macdonald & Co, 1967).

3. *Jackson's Oxford Journal*, 13 November 1784.

4. Boswell, p. 375. William Adams (1706–1789), Master of Johnson's former college of Pembroke from 1775 until his death (*Dictionary of National Biography*: Adams). Johnson had also stayed with him when visiting the previous June. Among other things, the two men had a shared interest in chemistry (*Dictionary of National Biography*: Johnson).

5. Johnson, pp. 432–33 in a letter to Francesco Sastres.

6. Frank Barber had been in Johnson's employment since about 1752, more as a secretary and companion than as a servant. Barber had also accompanied Johnson to Oxford in October 1781, when they stayed at the Angel Inn (Johnson, vol. 3, p. 362).

7. *Jackson's Oxford Journal*, 13 November 1784.

8. The first historian of ballooning, Tiberius Cavallo, in *The History and Practice of Aerostation* (London: 1785), although understandably unable to pronounce on Sadler's precedence, since 'after strict enquiry, it was found that nobody saw him either ascend or descend', did concur with this encapsulation as 'sole projector, architect, workman, and chymist' (pp. 176–77).

9. Gardiner, p. 60.

10. James Roberts (1753–c. 1809) was about to commence a residence in Oxford as a drawing master (*Dictionary of National Biography*: Roberts). The engraving of Sadler's portrait by Edmund Scott was published in May 1785, and very specifically aimed at university clientele, being dedicated exclusively to the Chancellor, Vice-Chancellor, Proctors and Heads of Colleges and Halls.

11. A footnote to this letter specified Banks, Fordyce, and Cavallo. Banks scarcely deserved this plaudit: on 19 November, he wrote to Franklin to say: 'We lament in the R. Soc. that so little addition of Science has yet accrued' and that every traveller in the air 'has constantly hitherto been the abject Slave of that element whenever he has ventured to intrude himself into it' (Banks, vol. 2, pp. 333–34). The newspaper's reference to Sadler's 'business' was a reminder that unlike his peers he had his livelihood to consider, and was unable to concentrate his attention exclusively to ballooning.

12. *Jackson's Oxford Journal*, 27 November 1784.

13. Langford, p. 426, citing a notice dated 25 November 1784.

14. Langford, p. 426. The Pantheon was the favourite London location for the display of balloons, notably Lunardi's.

15. *Jackson's Oxford Journal*, 4 December 1784.

16. Cavallo, pp. 153–154, quoting from a letter of 26 December 1784 from Watt to Dr James Lind.

17. Or, still more tangentially, one might say that a Mrs Saunders, widow of an upholsterer formerly of London's Goodge Street, was the first victim. While watching Lunardi's maiden voyage she was 'so terrified at the downfall of his oar, which she took for a human body, that she was suddenly taken ill' and expired early the following morning, having 'declared that she could not survive the shock' (*Morning Post & Daily Advertiser,* 17 September 1784).

18. Gardiner, p. 66.

5. Calais or Burst! The Race to Cross the English Channel

1. Rolt, p. 29. The story derives from an oration spoken at Joseph Montgolfier's funeral in 1814, when he was said to have contemplated a print of the siege of Gibraltar hanging above an open fire and postulated that 'the force that carried particles of smoke up the flue could be confined and harnessed to lift conveyances and float men' (Gillispie, p. 16).

2. Letter to Joseph Banks of 21 November 1783 (Franklin, p. 116; p. 117).

3. Letter to Jan Ingenhousz of 16 January 1784 (Franklin, p. 156). The notion had occurred to Dr Johnson too, in *Rasselas* (1759): 'If men were all virtuous ... I should with great alacrity teach them all to fly. But what would be the security of the good, if the bad could at pleasure invade them from the sky?' It was an unrealised fear: the only known military use was by the French revolutionary forces at the Battle of Fleurus in Belgium on 26 June 1794.

4. *Whitehall Evening Post*, 16–18 December 1784. *Morning Herald*, 11 November 1784.

5. Hodgson (1926), p. 167.

6. *Morning Chronicle & London Advertiser*, 4 December 1784.

7. Blanchard, p. 12. Both this journey and the pair's subsequent successful crossing of the Channel, are recounted in detail in Jeffries' *Narrative of the two aerial voyages of Doctor Jeffries with Mons. Blanchard* (1786).

8. British Library add. MS 37914 f21–22.

9. Windham, Burke and Banks were pall-bearers at the funeral at St Paul's Cathedral. Johnson had died on the 13th.

10. The 'feint' was quite precise, the *Gazetteer & New Daily Advertiser* of 7 December having stated with great certainty that 'the ingenious English aerial traveller' intended to ascend from Phoenix Park, Dublin, on the 28th, 'accompanied by a Lady'. In fact, it would be another twenty-eight years before Sadler actually made an ascent from Dublin and another thirty-three before he would help the first woman to do so. However, the Irish capital *was* the setting for a successful ascent at about this time, the first in Ireland, made by the Irishman Richard Crosbie on 19 January 1785 (*see* chapter 10).

11. *Morning Herald & Daily Advertiser,* 21 December 1784. Immediately below this advertisement was a similar appeal from Zambeccari, with a very detailed description of his new 'British Balloon', which was on display at the Lyceum. As more days passed, the *Morning Post* suggested (29 December) that Lunardi and Zambeccari, 'whose exploits are to *outwonder wonders*', were both also preparing to join the race, though neither were mentioned again as a candidate.

12. *Morning Post,* 29 December 1784.
13. *Gazetteer & New Daily Advertiser,* 3 January 1785.
14. Charles I had been refused entry to Hull in 1642, after several hours of fruitless negotiation.
15. *Gazetteer & New Daily Advertiser,* 3 January 1785. Rash, desperate and foolhardy though this bargain may seem, Jeffries confirmed his undertaking to leave the car if need be. (Jeffries, p. 41). Blanchard was indeed 'tiny', weighing only a little more than eight stone.
16. *General Evening Post,* 8–11 January 1785. This was James Deeker, a London balloon maker. In a handbill advertising his own intended ascent from Norwich (in June 1785) he referred to himself as 'having constructed, superintended and filled more ærostatic Globes than any other Person in the Kingdom' and that 'he was Mr. Blanchard's Assistant in all his Experiments in this Country, and that the preparatory Measures for that Gentleman's masterly ærial Excursion at Dover was under his sole Management and Direction' (ESTC No13060). It appears that Deeker was inflating the truth, so to speak, as Jeffries makes no mention of him, nor does Blanchard (nor apparently do any other aeronauts). It was not all 'hot air', however, as both he and his son Joseph did make successful ascents of their own. (*see* Appendix 7).
17. Jeffries, p. 40. A retrospective (*c.* 1840) painting by E. W. Cocks (at the Science Museum, London) shows the launch was made a few hundred yards to the east of the castle, which seems plausible. (The location, therefore, was close to the landing place in 1908 of Louis Blériot, after the first powered flight across the English Channel in the opposite direction).
18. Jeffries seems anyway to have been of an affable nature. Samuel Breck (1771–1862) met Blanchard when the latter made the first ever balloon ascent in America from Breck's hometown of Philadelphia in 1793. Breck had listened to Blanchard's version of the Channel crossing 'with feelings of asperity that were not reciprocated in my hearing by the doctor'. Breck retaliated on Jeffries' behalf by designating Blanchard 'a petulant little fellow, not many inches over 5 feet, and weighing about 120 pounds, so physically well suited for vaporish regions' (*Recollections,* ed. H. E. Scudder (London: 1877), p. 69).
19. Inside his underwear Jeffries had managed to retain one or two letters, so facilitating the birth of airmail. The only one known to have survived (in the Franklin papers of the American Philosophical Society) was from William Franklin (son of Benjamin Franklin), who wrote to his son Temple Franklin, 'I dare say you will like to be one of the first who gets a Letter across the English Channel by this kind of aerial Conveyance'.
20. *Jackson's Oxford Journal,* 15 January 1785.
21. *Gazetteer & New Daily Advertiser,* 11 January 1785.
22. *Morning Chronicle,* 17 January 1785.

6 'To Sweep the Cobwebs from the Sky': Sadler's Six 1785 Ascents

1. Lunardi (1784), p. 18.
2. This is the earliest public suggestion that Sadler was not just the first *English* aeronaut, but the first *Briton*. Given that the only other challenger for that particular honour was the unconvincing James Tytler, few then or later would have quibbled.
3. Dodwell had been at school with Windham at Eton, and matriculated at Magdalen College on 20 October 1768, aged nineteen. His house was The Priory (Baker, Rowland G. M., *Book of Molesey,* (Buckingham: Barracuda, 1984) p. 110), a location now apparently occupied by Molesey Football Club.
4. Windham (1866), p. 55. Later the same day, 'at tea I had the company of Liddell', who had also visited him on 3 April. This would seem to be Sir Henry Thomas St George Liddell (1749–91), an ancestor of Alice Liddell of *Wonderland* fame.
5. British Library MS add. 37914 f25. Baucis was an elderly woman from Greek mythology. The words omitted from the extract from Dodwell's letter are the original Greek for the 'Cobwebs' phrase which follows. Ketton-Cremer translated the phrase as being 'more literally, "To walk the air and contemplate the sun", from Aristophanes, Clouds, 225' (Windham (1930) p. 283).
6. British Library add. MS 37914 f26.
7. *Reading Mercury & Oxford Gazette,* 9 May 1785. Samuel Horsley (1733–1806), a Cambridge graduate, became a fellow of the Royal Society (and Christ Church don) in 1767, on account of his mathematical expertise (*Dictionary of National Biography*: Horsley).
8. British Library add. MS 37925.
9. Ketton-Cremer in Windham (1930), p. 291.

10. *London Magazine,* May 1785, p. 373.
11. British Library add. MS 37925.
12. *London Magazine,* May 1785, p. 373, which specified that height as precisely 1 mile, 7 furlongs and 61 yards or '159 yards short of two miles'.
13. *Morning Herald & Daily Advertiser,* 9 May 1785.
14. Within the short observation that Windham transposed from his notebook (British Library add. MS 37925) to his diary, he included the 'circumstance of hat falling' (in other words, it had been blown off or dropped, rather than forgotten). Loss of headgear was a sartorial faux pas to which all balloonists succumbed at their peril. Blanchard too had been embarrassed by the loss of his hat, for instance, on the voyage of 16 October 1784. After Sheldon had disembarked at Sunbury, the Frenchman waited for some time for him to return, but eventually 'I gave way to my impatience' and 'determined, for the second time, to set off without either hat or provisions' (Blanchard, p. 6). At the same time, 'Mr. Sheldon's Hat thrown from the Balloon as it ascended' was considered of sufficient interest to warrant charging one penny when it was exhibited at Covent Garden (*Morning Post & Daily Advertiser,* 30 October 1784, under a heading of 'Cheap Exhibitions').
15. *Whitehall Evening Post,* 17–19 May 1785.
16. Walpole, vol. 25, p. 579.
17. Windham (1930), p. 293. In Burke's *Correspondence,* vol. 5, ed. H. Furber (Cambridge: Cambridge University Press, 1965), p. 211, this is given as 'Adieu, Star triumphant! And some Pity shew On us poor Cobblers militant below', paraphrasing some lines by the seventeenth-century poet, Abraham Cowley.
18. Windham (1866), p. 52.
19. British Library add. MS 37914 f27–30. The letter dated 4 May 1785 is transcribed in full in Windham (1913), vol. 1, pp. 75–80.
20. The streets on either side of Haworth's house were renamed by the time of the publication of William Green's map of Manchester on 1 April 1794 'Balloon Street' and 'Back Balloon Street' in Sadler's honour. Haworth's grandson, Robert Howarth Peel, would make an ascent with Sadler's son Windham in 1824 (*see* chapter 13).
21. The balloon was later found near Gainsborough, Lincolnshire. In the basket was a knife and a handkerchief, and a hat was found nearby. The finder had been offered eight guineas for the balloon, but was holding out for more (*Whitehall Evening Post,* 31 May–2 June 1785).
22. *Gentleman's Magazine's,* May 1785, p. 400.
23. *Dictionary of National Biography:* Siddons. The newspaper's unkind allusion to Siddons' husband, William, reflects his notoriously philandering and feckless reputation.
24. *Public Advertiser,* 2 June 1785.
25. Younger brother of John Fitzpatrick (1745–1818), Lord Ossory. Richard was briefly Minister of War in 1783.
26. The same location from which James Sadler would make his comeback ascent in 1810.
27. British Library add. MS 37914 f32–33. George Croft (*c.* 1747–1809), matriculated at University College 23 November 1762, aged fifteen (*Alumni Oxonienses*). Fitzpatrick does definitely appear to have written 'Mrs', and this is the interpretation in the full transcription of this letter in Windham (1913), vol. 1, pp. 81–82, even though the context might make it more likely to have been their husbands. Could the barometer which Fitzpatrick mentions have once belonged to Samuel Johnson (*see* chapter 10)? Fitzpatrick made one other known ballooning foray, but barely got off the ground, having to leap out when the balloon burst on take-off, according to the *New York Packet* of 29 September 1785 (Lynn, p. 23).
28. *Jackson's Oxford Journal,* 25 June 1785. Many years later (add. MS 37887 f129, dated 7 August 1807) Sadler attempted to exploit Richard Fitzpatrick's favourable opinion of him by asking William Windham to use his influence in the case of a young soldier of whose regiment Fitzpatrick was the Colonel. The political transparency of the time is demonstrated by Sadler's inclusion of 'it may be allowed that the young man in question has a claim on your Compassion having at the Hazard of his personal Safety ventured to Norwich (being a freeman) to give his vote in your Interest'.
29. *Public Advertiser,* 13 January 1785.
30. Walpole, vol. 25, p. 591.
31. Walpole, vol. 33, p. 468. Lady Ossory, *née* Anne Liddell (1737/8–1804), was the only child of Henry Liddell, 1st Baron Ravensworth (1708–84). The peerage was revived in 1821 under

Thomas Liddell (1775–1855), the son of Henry's nephew Henry (1749–91), who was an ancestor of Oxford's Alice (in Wonderland) Liddell.

32. Gardiner, p. 80. Lunardi also disparaged Harper in his letters, and was especially contemptuous of his compatriot Zambeccari, who had himself failed in an attempt to escort a British female skywards in March (*see* Appendix 7).

33. John Byng, *Torrington Diaries,* vol. 1 (London: Eyre & Spottiswoode, 1934), p. 210–211. John Byng (Viscount Torrington) was probably familiar with Sadler's shop from previous visits, since his preferred hotel was the nearby Angel: in June 1781 he wrote 'Oxford has been lately much improv'd in its Inns, (which were so justly complain'd of); and the new stables at the Angel are excellent' (p. 5). He had revised his opinion a little by June 1784, however, when he bracketed the 'tolerable' Angel within a general disapproval of the 'hurry & dirtiness of the Oxford hotels' (p. 120). Byng (whose sister-in-law, Cecilia Forrest, married William Windham in 1798) may have had some influence in dissuading Windham from accompanying Sadler across the English Channel: on 24 December 1784, the day before he made his decision, Windham noted in his diary that he had dined in the city, with Samuel Horsley and others, then 'went home with Horsley, to whom I showed my idea about balloons; afterwards to Byng's'.

34. Lunardi, *Second Aerial Voyage from Liverpool,* p. 4.

35. The *Post* article twice referred to a 'flying vis-a-vis', defined in the *Oxford English Dictionary* as a 'light carriage for two persons sitting face-to-face'. No other example of the noun has been found in a ballooning context.

36. *Jackson's Oxford Journal,* 6 August 1785.

37. *Jackson's Oxford Journal,* 6 August 1785.

38. Presumably William Wheeler, a nurseryman based at Artichoke Fields (1788 *Worcester Directory*). In identifying the approximate location of Wheeler's premises, the website of the Worcester Royal Infirmary (www.wrinl.org.uk) is helpful: 'In July 1765 two acres of land, situated in the "Artichoke Field" at the top of Salt Lane (Castle Street) was acquired'.

39. *Whitehall Evening Post,* 27–30 August 1785.

40. *General Evening Post,* 13–15 September and 15–17 September 1785; *Morning Chronicle & London Advertiser,* 17 September 1785.

41. *Jackson's Oxford Journal,* 1 October 1785.

42. Henry Paget (1744–1812) had assumed the title of Lord Uxbridge only the previous year, and lived at Beaudesert (now demolished), about 4 miles north-west of Lichfield. There was no further balloon ascent from Worcester until that of George Graham in September 1824 (*Berrow's Worcester Journal,* 9 September 1824).

43. For example, *General Evening Post,* 22–25 October 1785.

44. A whiskey is a light two-wheeled one-horse carriage.

45. Earlier in the year, Sadler had been allocated another grandiose nickname. The *Daily Universal Register* (later the *Times*) printed this single sentence about him on 30 May 1785: 'Mr. Sadler, the balloonist, of Oxford, is called by way of distinction, the *flying University*.' It was a comment which might well have caused some in Oxford to scrunch their copies in irritation!

46. *New London Magazine,* December 1785, p. 301. It is presumably Thornton's image which prompted a warning in *Jackson's* of 4 December 1785 that 'a spurious Print ... totally destitute of Likeness' was in circulation, and that genuine engravings of Sadler 'from the Original and authentic Painting by Mr. Roberts' could be obtained only from Roberts himself in St Aldate's or from Sadler's in the High Street.

47. Banks, vol. 3, p. 203, in letter of 26 September 1786.

48. *Gentleman's Magazine,* September 1786, p. 815.

49. Blanchard had departed for the continent rather sooner, to travel an astonishing 300 miles – the longest distance known – from Lille in August 1785. He also made the first ever ascents in Germany, Holland and Belgium that year, followed by the first in Switzerland in 1788, in Poland and Czechoslovakia in 1789, and America in 1793 (Rolt, p. 89).

50. British Library add. MS 37914 f32–33.

51. Hodgson (1928), p. 13.

7. A Literary Interlude: Soaring Prose and Uplifting Airs

1. *Probationary Odes for the Laureatship* was published in several editions. The quotations are

taken from Warton's pretended 'full and true account' of the first edition, pages xxxvii., xxxix.-xl., xliv., and xlv.

2. *Probationary Odes* also includes some actual poems by Warton, who apparently took the lampoon of his balloon flight in good spirit. It was probably through Warton's brother, Joseph, that he first met Samuel Johnson, with whom he became a lifelong friend (*Dictionary of National Biography*: Warton).

3. *An asylum for fugitive pieces, in prose and verse, not in any other collection,* new ed. (London: printed for J. Debrett, 1785), p. 252.

4. *The Aerostatic Spy,* vol. 1, p.v.

5. *The Aerostatic Spy,* vol. 2, p. 204.

6. Pye, p. 153.

7. Pye, p. 154.

8. Pye, p. 157.

9. Pye was not alone in envisioning travel to the moon, of course, but Horace Walpole's similar foresight was tempered with caution. He wrote to Horace Mann on 2 December 1783 that 'I hope these new mechanic meteors will prove only playthings for the learned and idle, and not be converted into new engines of destruction to the human race, as is so often the case of refinements or discoveries in Science'. Furthermore, 'could we reach the moon, we should think of reducing it to a province of some European kingdom.' (Walpole, vol. 25, p. 451)

10. Pye, p. 160.

11. Pye, p. 161. The approval of Oxford mirrors the sentiments of 'T. H.' in *Jackson's Oxford Journal* of 20 November 1784 (*see* chapter 4).

12. Erasmus Darwin, *The Botanic Garden,* part 2 (London: 1791) p. 173.

13. Erasmus Darwin, *The Botanic Garden,* part 2 (Lichfield: 1789), p. 53. In between the two editions, Darwin had written to James Watt on 19 January 1790, 'I feel myself becoming all french both in chemistry and politics' (Erasmus Darwin, *Collected Letters,* ed. Desmond King-Hele (Cambridge: Cambridge University Press, 2007), p. 359).

14. At the Battle of Fleurus in Belgium on 26 June 1794, as previously mentioned.

15. *The Infernal Quixote,* pp. 258/259.

8. Grounded!

1. Stansfield, p. 20.

2. Stansfield, p. 18.

3. Stansfield, p. 17.

4. Stansfield, p. 32.

5. *Oxfordshire Roundabout,* June 1985, p. 23.

6. Stock, Appendix 6, p.xxxvi.

7. Edinburgh University Gen 873 III 71/72.

8. Stock, p. 24. William Thomson (c. 1761–c. 1806) of Worcester, later a specialist in mineralogy, matriculated at Queen's College in 1776, aged 15 (*Alumni Oxonienses*).

9. Stansfield, p. 39.

10. Stansfield, p. 33.

11. Hodgson (1929), p. 73, from the original in Birmingham Reference Library. Although Watt implies that both Sadler and Symington held existing patents, only William Symington (1764–1831), who had studied anatomy, surgery and chemistry at the University of Edinburgh under, among others, Joseph Black (*Dictionary of National Biography*: Symington) seems actually to have applied for one at this date (No. 1610 dated 5 June 1787).

12. *Jackson's Oxford Journal,* 20 December 1817, reporting that the feat was accomplished 'about 32 years since'.

13. *Jackson's Oxford Journal,* 23 May 1789.

14. *Jackson's Oxford Journal,* 13 June 1789 and 4 July 1789.

15. Werrett, p. 201, on which page the subsequent quotations also appear. A good idea of what was on offer at outdoor events, even in the 1770s, may be found in Trevor Fawcett, 'The Norwich Pleasure Gardens', *Norfolk Archaeology,* vol. 35, 1972, pp. 386–87.

16. Cox, p. 3. In fact, the term 'pyrotechnics' *had* already been coined. The *Oxford English Dictionary's* earliest example comes from J. van Rymsdyk's *Museum Britannicum* of 1778, where he wrote that 'those skilful in Pyrotechnics, or the Art of Fireworks, entertain the spectators'.

17. *Jackson's Oxford Journal*, 6 February 1790 and 27 February 1790.
18. The third man seems certain to have been Richard Edwards (*c.* 1770–1827), of Hale, Cornwall, who matriculated at Pembroke College on 5 July 1788, aged eighteen, and later became a 'lecturer in chemical science' at St Bartholomew's Hospital (*Alumni Oxonienses*).
19. Stock, p. 27.
20. Stock, p. 21.
21. Banks, vol. 4, p. 30.
22. Bodleian Library MS Dep. C134/1 (c). A Richard Rouse is named in *Oxford Apprentices 1697–1800* (at Oxfordshire History Centre) as a cabinetmaker in 1794, and seems likely to be the carpenter referred to.
23. Bodleian Library MS Dep. C134/1 (c).
24. *The Repertory of Arts and Manufactures*, vol. 6 (London: 1797), p. 170.
25. University of Edinburgh Gen 873/III 200/201.
26. University of Edinburgh Gen 873/III 200/201.
27. Bodleian Library MS Dep. C134/1 (c). Reynolds studied chemistry under Joseph Black, and in 1777, still only nineteen, supervised the installation of James Watt's new steam engines at the Reynolds' ironworks at Ketley (the fifth largest in Britain by the turn of the century). He subsequently installed similar Watt and Boulton engines at two other locations. One was Coalbrookdale, and it was probably due to his initiative that the first steam railway locomotive was built there by Richard Trevithick in 1802 (*Dictionary of National Biography*: Reynolds).
28. Priestley, p. 211.
29. Cornwall Record Office DG 41/31. Presumably, given her destination, 'Mrs S' was Sadler's wife, Mary; the identity of Byrne is unknown.
30. Jay, p. 44
31. Hodgson (1929), p. 74.
32. Stansfield, p. 62.
33. Banks, vol. 3, p. 363. Sibthorp's birth date in Oxford is given as 28 October 1758 (*Dictionary of National Biography*: Sibthorp). Lady Sewell was his half-sister Mary.
34. Banks, vol. 3, p. 492.
35. Levere (1994), p. 64.
36. Levere (1994), p. 64, citing letter 'Willoughby 11 July 1792' at the National Archives.
37. Levere (1994), p. 65. Joseph Banks presented papers by Beddoes to the Royal Society in 1791 and 1792, but by 1794 rejected outright the idea of supporting a known revolutionary (Stansfield, p. 155).
38. *St. James's Chronicle*, 18–20 April 1793; *Jackson's Oxford Journal*, 20 April 1793.
39. Levere (1994), p. 66. Giddy (who changed his name to Gilbert on marrying in 1808) attended Beddoes' lectures on chemistry while at Pembroke College. The two men became close friends, sharing a mutual sympathy for the aspirations of the French Revolution. Their friendship became strained in later life when Beddoes' wife Anna (*née* Edgeworth) became infatuated with Giddy.
40. Henry Peter Stacy (*c.* 1760–*c.* 1820) matriculated at St Mary Hall on 27 November 1784, aged twenty-four (*Alumni Oxonienses*). His practical skills would come to the fore again when he was 'involved with Sadler in gun boring experiments in London' (*Dictionary of National Biography*: Sadler).
41. L. Cranmer-Byng & Trevor H. Levere: 'A case study in cultural collision: Scientific apparatus in the Macartney embassy to China, 1793' in *Annals of Science*, 38:5, 1981, p. 505. Leading the entourage of nearly 100 people was Lord Macartney, first Great British ambassador to China. Sir George Staunton was the deputy envoy, and 'the Chinese from Italy' were two interpreters recruited from Naples. The letter to Giddy is held at the Cornwall Record Office, M DG 41/17, and is undated other than the year. Ranelagh Gardens, in Vauxhall, were internationally famous as the most fashionable of all of London's eighteenth-century pleasure gardens, where fireworks were one of the main attractions.
42. Proudfoot, p. 27.
43. *Dictionary of National Biography*: Dinwiddie, citing Proudfoot's *Memoir*, and L. Lunney, 'The celebrated Mr Dinwiddie: an eighteenth-century scientist in Ireland', in *Eighteenth-Century Ireland*, 3 (1988), pp. 69–83.
44. Stansfield (p. 97) quotes Beddoes as calling Sadler his 'laboratory genius' at this juncture, though no source is provided.
45. *Reynolds-Rathbone Diaries and Letters*, ed. Emily Greg (Edinburgh: 1905), p. 49.

46. Stansfield, p. 93, citing letter from Beddoes to James Watt of July 1795.
47. Beddoes, p. 40.
48. Stock, p. 92.
49. Bodleian Library MS Dep. c135/2.
50. Uglow, p. 461.
51. Banks, vol. 4, p. 337.
52. Edgeworth & Edgeworth, pp. 132–133.
53. Edgeworth & Edgeworth, p. 133
54. Stock, p. 153.
55. Stock, p. 90.
56. Beddoes, p. 45. The normal rate is between 60 and 100 pulses per minute.
57. *Bristol Gazette*, 21 March 1799.
58. Stansfield, D. A. (1986), pp. 282, 288/289.
59. Bodleian Library MS Dep. C134/1 (c) dated 14 January 1791.
60. His mother was still alive, however, so it is feasible that some or all of his children remained living with her in Oxford. Mrs Elizabeth Sadler died aged eighty-four on Monday 2 August 1802 'after a long life of usefulness' (*Jackson's*, 7 August 1802), and was buried at St Peter-in-the-East on the 5th.
61. Bristol Record Office FCLM 1795/3 dated 22 October 1795.
62. The witnesses were Mary and Joanna Sadler, of unknown relationship, but possibly, in view of the residence of the guarantor of the marriage bond, living in Wiltshire. (Bristol Record Office bond 1719).
63. It is presumably the same Rev. Benjamin Hancock (of Uphill, Somerset) who is mentioned in documentation of 1755 and 1757 in connection with Thomas Hancock, a sail maker of Bristol (Bristol Record Office 28049/41). If so it is tempting to think that this relative's occupation – of potential great relevance to a balloonist, of course – had some part in bringing the couple together.

9. Navy Larks and Sparks

1. Hodgson based much of his paper on documents then in the possession of Sadler's great-grandson, Harold Sadler of Liverpool. Much of this material was evidently the same as that now in the Peel Papers at the British Library (add. MS 40221). L. T. C. Rolt, the only other author who has attempted a substantial summary of Sadler's life, in *The Aeronauts* (1966), evidently derived much of his information about Sadler from Hodgson.
2. *Dictionary of National Biography:* Sadler.
3. Undated letter to Hippisley, British Library add. MS 40221 f475/476. Saxton must have become acquainted with Sadler in the years when his ballooning fame was at its height, or soon after, as he had returned to England at the conclusion of the American War of Independence in the summer of 1783, after some forty years at sea. While he was Commissioner at Portsmouth, the Navy expanded to almost its greatest size (*Dictionary of National Biography:* Saxton).
4. British Library add. MS 40221 f273.
5. *Dictionary of National Biography:* Bentham. In October 1796 Samuel Bentham married the daughter of the chemist George Fordyce, a man much involved in the periphery of many an early balloon flight, including those of Lunardi and Sheldon. He was also a friend of William Windham's.
6. Hodgson (1929), p. 73.
7. British Library RB.23.b.1142(1a).
8. British Library add. MS 40221 f275 (iii), in a letter of 19 June 1809.
9. British Library add. MS 37915 f286/287 & f288/289, in a letter of August 1804.
10. Bentham, p. 209.
11. Hodgson (1929), p. 75.
12. Hodgson (1929), p. 75. As James Sadler Esq., Chemist to the Admiralty, he published a short account of one of his engines, with diagrams, in the January 1798 issue of Nicholson's *Journal of Natural Philosophy, Chemistry & the Arts* (pp. 441–44).
13. Coad, p. 31, citing National Archives ADM 1/3526 of 10 December 1802.
14. British Library add. MS 40221 f275–f276 (iii) in letter of 19 June 1809.
15. British Library add. MS 40221 f273.
16. British Library add. MS 40221 f274.

17. British Library add. MS 40221 f273.

18. British Library add. MS 40221 f275–f276 (iii) in letter of 19 June 1809.

19. British Library add. MS 40221 f275–f276 (vi) in a letter to Sir John Coxe Hippisley dated 23 June 1809. No evidence of any legal proceedings has been found.

20. The first trial appears to have been on 26 August 1795, in the presence of William Windham (Sadler's *Account of Various Improvements in Artillery, Fire-arms, etc.*, p. 2 and pp. 11–14).

21. William Windham had agreed to be the baby's godfather (*Gentleman's Magazine*, November 1824, p. 473) or 'sponsor' (Windham (1913) p. 80). There is nothing specific about this in Windham's published *Diary* and indeed he apparently made no further entries at all about Sadler after the balloon flight of 1785.

22. The illustration by Rowlandson in the publication itself is captioned 'A Light Infantry Man defending himself with Sadler's patent gun &c.', dated September 1798.

23. *Sporting Magazine*, June 1798, p. 167.

24. *St James's Chronicle*, 16–18 August 1798.

25. British Library add. MS 40221 f275/f276 (vi).

26. *Oracle & Daily Advertiser*, 12 September 1799.

27. *Oracle & Daily Advertiser*, 6 November 1799.

28. *Oracle & Daily Advertiser*, 7 November 1799.

29. *Oracle & Daily Advertiser*, 6 Nov 1799. Another near-fatal close call was alluded to in the *London Packet* of 19 July 1800, when an accident caused by a mix-up between live and blank ball cartridges was accounted similar to one that 'had nearly proved fatal to Mr. Sadler, of the Admiralty, at a review near Portsmouth' the previous Thursday, 17 July.

30. *Oracle & Daily Advertiser*, 19 July 1800.

31. *Oracle & Daily Advertiser*, 28 July 1800. William Windham's *Diary* shows he was at Windsor on Sunday 27th, on which day his wife – he had married Cecilia Forrest in 1798 – drank tea with the Queen. The next day he, 'by royal command, went to field-day' and 'rode a great deal with the King.'

32. *General Evening Post*, 23–26 August 1800.

33. Windham (1913), vol. 2, p. 159.

34. *Dictionary of National Biography*: Hippisley. Hippisley was a founder member of the Royal Institution and a Fellow of the Royal Society. James Sadler himself subscribed for life to the Royal Institution on 27 April 1799, very soon after its creation (*Dictionary of National Biography*: Sadler).

35. British Library RB.23.b.1142(1) p. 8. It is dated 6 November 1798, 10 Stafford Row. British Library RB.23.b.1142(2) is an undated companion publication of five pages: *Description of a New and much Improved Rifle Gun*.

36. *Account of Various Improvements in Artillery, Fire-arms etc.* p. 8/9.

37. *True Briton*, 28 November 1799 and *Caledonian Mercury*, 5 May 1800.

38. Report of 7 June 1800 (British Library add. MS 40221 f274).

39. *Oracle*, 16 August 1800.

40. *Lloyds Evening Post*, 18–20 December 1799 and *Oracle & Daily Advertiser*, 21 December 1799.

41. British Library add. MS 40221 f275.

42. Attwood to Hippisley 23 June 1809: British Library add. MS 40221 f276.

43. Ringing endorsement though this is, Hodgson (1929) p. 77 observed that: 'It should be added that further experience proved that there were objections to Sadler's guns which led to their being subsequently discarded'.

44. British Library add. MS 40221 f275-f276 (iii), letter of 19 June 1809, by which time Bradley was working at Westminster Hospital.

45. British Library add. MS 40221 f273.

46. British Library add. MS 40221 f274.

47. British Library add. MS 40221 f278.

48. British Library add. MS 40221 f275/f276.

49. In a printed footnote to British Library add. MS 40221 f273.

50. British Library add. MS 40221 f273.

51. Letter of 16 April 1810: British Library add. MS 40221 f277.

52. British Library add. MS 40221 f272.

53. British Library add. MS 40221 f275–f276.

54. These documents are held collectively as 'the Case of Mr. James Sadler, late Chemist, and a

Member of the Board of Naval Works at the Admiralty' at the British Library within the 'Peel Papers' (add MS 40221 (f272–f279) and a reduced version (add MS 37888 f161–164) is held within the 'Windham Papers'.

55. British Library add. MS 40221 f272.

10. Things Looking Up Again! 1810–12

1. Among these were Madame Garnerin (under the name Labrosse) at Paris on 10 November 1798. In England a Mr. Saint(e)-Croix ascended from Exeter on 19 June (*Morning Chronicle*, 23 June 1786) and at Salisbury on 10 August 1786 (*Whitehall Evening Post*, 12–15 August 1786). An especially remarkable journey was that of George Blake, a naval officer, Major [John] Money, and Mr Lockwood (of the Lyceum) on 3 June 1785 (*General Evening Post*, 2–4 June 1785). On their return from Essex, Blake and Money stopped off to dine with Horace Walpole's nephew, Lord Orford, near Epping Forest. Two other guests were de Rozier and Blanchard, the latter of whom had himself made a solo flight from London the same day (*Whitehall Evening Post*, 4–7 June 1785). Blake also made an ascent with another naval officer, Robert Redmill, on 1 June 1786 (*Morning Chronicle*, 6 June 1786).

2. Hodgson (1924), p. 218–220.

3. Tytler died in America in 1804 and Lunardi in Lisbon in 1806. Blanchard, surprisingly considering his ability and fame, died in penury in 1809. He was outlived by his second wife, Marie-Madeleine Sophie, who died in a ballooning accident involving the use of fireworks in 1819. She had replaced Garnerin as Napoleon's official imperial aeronaut, and succeeded in remaining 'aeronaut of the Restoration' after his fall (Lynn, p. 25, p. 140). Zambeccari was also still flying in Europe, but was destined to die in a balloon accident in 1812 (*Morning Chronicle*, 13 November 1812).

4. *Caledonian Mercury*, 9 July 1810.

5. *Dictionary of National Biography:* Sadler.

6. Stock, p. 303.

7. Paris, p. 73.

8. *Dictionary of National Biography:* Sadler.

9. 1851 census.

10. *Dictionary of National Biography:* Sadler.

11. Hodgson (1929), p. 72.

12. Bodleian Library G.A. Oxon b.111 f126.

13. *Morning Post,* 6 July 1810.

14. *Morning Chronicle,* 9 July 1810.

15. In 1811 the census figure was 13,257 (*Victoria County History of Oxfordshire* (Oxford: Institute of Historical Research, 1979) vol.4, p. 182.

16. *Morning Chronicle,* 9 July 1810.

17. *Hull Packet,* 17 July 1810.

18. *Caledonian Mercury,*14 July 1810.

19. William Windham died on 4 June 1810, having made the last entry in his diary on 13 May 1810. The unreliable nature of newspaper reporting is exemplified in this *Morning Post* account, where, by way of background to the flight Windham made with Sadler, three other quite separate instances are combined in the statement that Sadler's 'first ascension was on 12th October 1784, from the Physic Garden, at Oxford, accompanied by General Fitzpatrick; they descended near Aylesbury'.

20. According to Sadler's report to the Admiralty of 25 March 1806, Smith had joined Nelson in expressing 'the highest approbation' of his improvements to naval cannons (British Library add. MS 40221 f274). Smith subscribed £21 towards the cost of the balloon (*Morning Chronicle*, 9 July 1810) and Davies Giddy gave the same amount (*York Herald,* 21 July 1810). The new chancellor himself gave almost ten times that amount, according to this single sentence reference to the event in the *Mirror of Fashion* (14 July 1810): 'Lord Grenville subscribed £200 to the subscription for Mr. Sadler, after his ascension in the balloon from Oxford.' A long list of mainly local subscribers was published in the *Oxford University & City Herald* of 14 July 1810 and subsequent issues.

21. *Caledonian Mercury,* 9 July 1810.

22. *Morning Post,* 9 July 1810.

23. *Morning Post,* 9 July 1810. Tilleman Bobart (1772–1838) was a famously erudite Oxford

coachman. The daughter who acquired the kitten must have been either Anna (baptised 1802) or Charlotte (born 1804).

24. *Caledonian Mercury*, 14 July 1810.
25. *Morning Chronicle*, 9 July 1810.
26. *Morning Post*, 10 July 1810.
27. *Morning Post*, 10 July 1810.
28. *Caledonian Mercury*, 14 July 1810.
29. *Morning Post*, 10 July 1810.
30. *Caledonian Mercury*, 14 July 1810.
31. Bodleian Library, John Johnson AIR 2.
32. John Evans, *Excursion to Windsor* (London: 1817), p. 203.
33. Hodgson (1928), p. 14.
34. Hogg, p. 51, p. 59.
35. Hogg, p. 63. Jules Verne envisaged just such a journey in *Five Weeks in a Balloon, or, Journeys and Discoveries in Africa by Three Englishmen* (1863), first published in English in 1869.
36. From the evidence of various Bristol trade directories (e.g. *Sketchley's Directory*, 1775) he would seem to have been the son of Michael Clayfield, a tobacconist trading from 71 Castle Street. His mother was probably called Mary, on the basis that the business's name had changed by 1791 to Mary Clayfield & Son, wine-merchant, trading from the same address of 71 Castle St. (*Reed's* 1791 and *Matthew's* 1793/94).
37. *Ipswich Journal*, 29 September 1810.
38. Clayfield was buried at St Andrews, Clifton on 11 March 1837, aged 65. In his obituary in the *Bristol Mercury* (11 March 1837) he was described as 'a gentleman of high philosophic and scientific attainments … chiefly in the several departments of chemistry, botany, mineralogy, and geology'.
39. Stoke's Croft was also where James Dinwiddie had chosen to launch his unmanned balloon in January 1784.
40. *Morning Post*, 26 September 1810.
41. British Library add. MS 40221 f. 270.
42. *Felix Farley's Bristol Journal*, 29 September 1810.
43. Letter dated 26 September 1810, Bristol Record Office 20535/17.
44. The island is not Scilly, of course, but Sully.
45. Sadler (1810), p. 8. Possibly this barometer is the same as that mentioned by Richard Fitzpatrick in 1785, belonging then to William Windham (*see* chapter 6).
46. Letter dated 26 September 1810, Bristol Record Office 20535/17.
47. British Library 74/1880 c.20 (642).
48. Paget is nowhere specifically identified in any contemporary accounts but seems certain to be the officer listed in *Commissioned Sea Officers of the Royal Navy, 1660–1815* (Aldershot: Navy Records Society, 1994): Charles Paget (1778–1839), fifth son of Henry, Lord Uxbridge, at whose home Sadler had been received after his Worcester flight of September 1785.
49. *Morning Post*, 5 July 1811.
50. *Jackson's Oxford Journal*, 6 July 1811.
51. *La Belle Assemblée*, July 1811, p. 53.
52. *Morning Post*, 5 July 1811.
53. The next aircraft to land at Stanstead was in 1942, the year that the first runway was built there by the American air force! There were no further ascents from Cambridge until Charles Green's in July 1824.
54. *Morning Post*, 13 August 1811.
55. *Caledonian Mercury*, 15 August 1811.
56. *Morning Chronicle*, 14 August 1811.
57. *The Times*, 14 August 1811.
58. *Morning Post*, 13 August 1811.
59. *Observer*, 18 August 1811.
60. *Morning Chronicle*, 14 August 1811.
61. *Caledonian Mercury*, 17 August 1811.
62. *Morning Post*, 13 August 1811.
63. *Derby Mercury*, 5 September 1811.
64. *Morning Chronicle*, 30 August 1811.
65. *Morning Post*, 30 August 1811.

66. *Dictionary of National Biography:* Sadler. The founder of the vinegar works was Mark Beaufoy (1718–82), whose son Colonel Mark Beaufoy (1764–1827), an astronomer and physicist, became in 1787 the first Englishman to climb Mont Blanc. Henry (1786–1851) was his oldest son, and the family were living in Hackney by the time of the birth of his third son George in 1796 (Beaufoy, G., p. 163, p. 289). Henry Beaufoy and Sadler had a particular shared interest, as the former was elected a fellow of the Royal Society in 1811 for experiments on the rifling of gun barrels, having published in 1808 (when a 'Corporal of Riflemen') *Scloppetaria: Considerations on the Nature and Use of Rifled Barrel Guns* (Egerton: London), a long and highly technical treatment, in which, while claiming to 'illustrate the talent and ingenuity of every co-labourer in his art' (p.viii), he omitted to include James Sadler!

67. Beaufoy, H., p. 5.

68. Beaufoy, H., p. 1 and p. 3.

69. *Morning Chronicle,* 31 August 1811.

70. *Morning Chronicle,* 31 August 1811.

71. Beaufoy, H., p. 25.

72. *Morning Post,* 31 August 1811.

73. *Morning Chronicle,* 6 September 1811.

74. Hodson, p. 16; Hodgson (1924), p. 151.

75. *Morning Chronicle,* 28 August 1811.

76. *Morning Chronicle,* 24 September 1811.

77. *Morning Chronicle,* 9 October 1811.

78. *Morning Post,* 8 October 1811.

79. *Gentleman's Magazine,* October 1811, p. 375.

80. Hodson, p. 16.

81. *Morning Chronicle,* 9 October 1811.

82. *Morning Chronicle,* 11 October 1811, which carries a long account of the journey, and was the first to specify the distance of 112 miles and time of 80 minutes.

83. *Monthly Magazine & British Register,* November 1811, p. 401.

84. *Morning Post,* 11 October 1811.

85. Garnerin had achieved similar velocities on two of his ascents from London in June 1802. With Sowden he travelled 51 miles in 45 minutes and on another occasion covered about 17 miles in 15 minutes (Hodgson (1924), pp. 220–221). Back in the days when Sadler's was a new name in the annals of aerostation, as he prepared to attempt to cross the English Channel, the *Gazetteer & New Daily Advertiser* of 3 January 1785 had noted that 'a bett of two hundred guineas had lately been placed at a tavern in London, that Mr. Sadler, in a balloon constructed and filled under his own direction, should travel one hundred miles in less time by twenty minutes than any other aerial traveller in England'. Did they collect, one wonders, twenty-six years later!

86. *Morning Chronicle,* 11 October 1811. 'Mr. Sadler jnr.' must mean fifteen-year-old Windham, learning from the best possible tutor available, in preparation for becoming himself the sole flying Sadler from 1815 onwards.

87. Joseph Aston, *Metrical Records of Manchester* (London: Longman, Hurst, Orme, 1822), p. 51. A footnote describes Howarth's premises as 'pleasure-grounds' and the conversion of his former house in Long Millgate into the Manchester Arms Inn (since demolished).

88. *Derby Mercury,* 9 July 1811

89. In a still more whimsical vein, the *Liverpool Mercury* of 10 April 1812 printed a humorous letter from 'Peeping Tom', who proposed that as the Window Tax had brought in less revenue than the government had hoped and that as most skylights were hidden from the view of the 'window-peepers' who assessed the tax, Sadler should be appointed 'to the *high situation* of "ÆRIAL SURVEYOR OF SKY-LIGHTS"'.

90. *Lancaster Gazette & General Advertiser,* 8 August 1811.

91. *Liverpool Mercury,* 14 August 1811.

92. *Liverpool Mercury,* 14 August 1811.

93. It has not proved possible to ascertain if this likeness survives, or indeed was ever made.

94. MacMahon, p. 109.

95. *Freeman's Journal,* 12 May 1812.

96. McGuire (sometimes spelled McGwire) was only the second man ever to be knighted before his majority, the other being King Henry V (MacMahon, p. 113).

97. The publication was advertised for sale at one shilling and eight pence in *Freeman's Journal* of 29 October; the balloon itself, said to be an entirely new one, was displayed in advance at the

Rotunda from 1 September onwards, admission one shilling and three pence (*Freeman's Journal,* 1 September 1812).

98. Indeed, *Freeman's Journal* (26 September 1812), had observed that so great was the interest that 'there is not a noble family, or person of distinction in this city, that Mr. Sadler has not already visited'. Among the guests was Sir Charles Saxton (1773–1838), the son of the man of the same name who had known Sadler at both Oxford and Portsmouth. The younger Saxton had matriculated at University College on 20 October 1792, aged nineteen (*Alumni Oxonienses,* 1888), so may well have crossed paths with Sadler just before the latter moved to Bristol.

99. Sadler, J. (1812), p. 4.

100. Edgeworth, pp. 183–187. Richard Crosbie had hoped to test a machine invented by Richard Edgeworth 'to measure ascent' (Dixon, p. 4) and two of Edgeworth's relevant other inventions were carriages propelled by the wind, one of them based on an idea of Erasmus Darwin's (*Dictionary of National Biography:* Edgeworth).

101. This is a reference to Erasmus Darwin's poetical account in *The Botanic Garden* of watching 'with upturn'd eyes' the progress of 'the floating wonder to the clouds' (*see* chapter 7).

102. Sadler, J. (1812) p. 5.

103. British Library add. MS 40221 f 270.

104. Sadler, J. (1812) p. 9.

105. *Caledonian Mercury,* 19 October 1812.

106. Sadler, J. (1812) p. 14. In a letter to the *Times* (6 October 1812), Mr Fellowes, 'Agent of his Majesty's Packets' in Holyhead, attributed the lack of assistance given by the first ships he encountered to 'the terror his appearance must have occasioned' rather than 'the want of humanity in their crews'. The total distance Sadler was later stated to have covered was 237 miles (on a handbill announcing his flight from Exeter of 22 October 1814, held at the Science Museum, London: reference 10410983).

107. He was later informed by the sailors who rescued him that they were known as 'Mother Cory's Chickens' (or, more usually Mother Carey's, in other words, petrels).

108. The chart (see Map E) which accompanies Windham Sadler's 1817 account of his own similar journey, *Aerostation,* shows his final rescue to have been approximately 40 miles north of the Welsh coast and the same distance from Morecambe Bay, and that he travelled about 10 miles across the water after his second descent. The total distance travelled was later calculated at 237 miles, the direct distance between Dublin and Liverpool being about 100 miles.

109. Sadler, J. (1812) p. 18.

110. Sadler, J. (1812) pp. 16–17.

111. Sadler, J. (1812) p. 8. The chart (see Map E) in Windham Sadler's 1817 *Aerostation* shows that he passed over Anglesey itself, prior to ditching into the sea.

112. The *Times,* 6 October 1812.

113. British Library add. MS 40221 f275-f276 iv.

114. A letter written by John Sadler to his half-sister Sybella soon after Windham's death (in October 1824) mentions him taking an 'active part' during their father's 'balloon speculation' in Dublin in 'a project of lighting the New Post Office with gas' (Hodgson (1929), p. 72. The letter, 'giving particulars of the early life of Windham Sadler', was at that time in the possession of Harold Sadler, James Sadler's great-grandson).

11. Like Father like Son: Windham Sadler, Heir to the Air

1. *Freeman's Journal,* 27 November 1812.

2. The single track railway between Cheltenham and Gloucester had opened in 1811, mainly to facilitate the movement of coal in horse-drawn wagons.

3. *Morning Chronicle,* 9 September 1813.

4. *Morning Chronicle,* 10 September 1813. It is not clear why all twelve men had these medals, nor how many were struck in total. An example is on display at Oxford's Museum of the History of Science.

5. *Morning Chronicle,* 10 September 1813.

6. Hodson, p. 19.

7. *Morning Chronicle,* 10 September 1813.

8. *Morning Chronicle,* 10 September 1813. Windham had several cousins living in Oxford (*see* Appendix 2).

9. *Morning Chronicle,* 25 September 1813. This public reaction was all the more deplorable in

that Wilkes had undertaken the venture to raise funds for the Derby General Infirmary, Richard Forester being one of about fifty named subscribers (*Derby Mercury,* 9 September 1813).

10. Forester's letter was subsequently printed in full in the *Derby Mercury,* 14 October 1813.

11. *Derby Mercury,* 28 October 1813.

12. *Morning Chronicle,* 6 October 1813.

13. Sadler had other business interests in Bristol too. An advertisement in *Felix Farley's Bristol Journal* of 28 September 1813 (p. 3), including the image of a balloon, announced that 'Sadler's Improved Soda-water' was available from William King, 60 Wine Street, sole agent for the soda water and 'other Artificial Mineral Waters: the known excellence of which in London has called for the most unprecedented demand'.

14. *Morning Chronicle,* 6 October 1813.

15. This letter was printed in full in the *Derby Mercury* of 28 October 1813.

16. Nottingham Civic Society Newsletter, January 2014, p. 9.

17. Hodson, p. 13.

18. *Caledonian Mercury,*15 November 1813. The location was where the Fellows, Moreton & Clayton public house now stands (Nottingham Civic Society Newsletter, January 2014, p. 9). Nottingham has led the way in public recognition for James Sadler by fitting a Blue Plaque on the building.

19. *Morning Chronicle,* 5 November 1813.

20. *Derby Mercury,* 11 November 1813.

21. British Library 1888.c. 18/1 (127).

22. *Morning Post,* 16 July 1814. William George Spencer Cavendish (1790–1858), 6th Duke, and the son of Georgiana (1757–1806), who had attempted to persuade Joseph Banks to endorse Thomas Beddoes' Bristol Institute back in the 1790s.

23. *Trewman's Exeter Flying Post,* 21 July 1814.

24. *Ipswich Journal,* 23 July 1814.

25. Hodgson (1924), p. 153. The letter was held at the Patent Office at the time of Hodgson's publication, and is now at the British Library (HS.74/2226 III. 135). It was written from 26 Great Pulteney Street, adjacent to Brewer Street, where the Sadler soda water factory was located.

26. *Morning Post,* 16 July 1814.

27. *Morning Chronicle,* 27 July 1814. When Windham ascended from Edinburgh in 1815, this false aggregation reached its peak with it being billed as James's forty-ninth.

28. *Liverpool Mercury,* 8 October 1824.

29. The *Times* had jumped the gun. In fact Mrs Johnston (*née* Parker, 1782–?) had always intended to go up on a different day, and with John Sadler, but was in any case ultimately dissuaded. The *Times* ended its account by querying the value of such displays, citing Benjamin Franklin's supposed 1783 retort of 'What is the use of a new-born child?' as 'a good answer at the time, but the child should not be still in its infancy' (*see* chapter 2).

30. The reported ascent of a Mrs Hines in October 1785 appears to have been a hoax (*see* Appendix 7).

31. Hodgson (1924), p. 153. The reference, in *Bell's Weekly Messenger* of 17 July 1814, evidently referred to Mrs Henry Johnson.

32. *Morning Chronicle,* 1 August 1814.

33. *Trewman's Exeter Flying Post or Plymouth & Cornish Advertiser,* 4 August 1814.

34. *Caledonian Mercury,* 4 August 1814.

35. Amid a miscellany of other short news items, the *Lancaster Gazette & General Advertiser* (13 August 1815) included this short anecdote about seventeen-year-old Windham: on 'being asked by an antiquary, whether he was *descended* from Sir Ralph Sadler? – "No," replied Mr. S. "from a *Balloon*!" '. (Ralph Sadler was a long-serving sixteenth-century diplomat.)

36. Hamilton, p. 203.

37. Hamilton, p. 194. It is interesting to note that Cocking's membership of the Royal Society of the Arts was proposed by John Cuthbert (p. 196), the man (it is presumed) whose important collection of ballooning memorabilia – now held by the Royal Aeronautical Society – formed much of the source material for J. E. Hodgson's seminal 1924 *History of Aeronautics*.

38. James Hamilton, *Faraday* (London: HarperCollins, 2003), p. 127.

39. Although many newspaper accounts failed to distinguish between the three Sadlers, the *Caledonian Mercury's* account (6 August) appeared under the unequivocal heading of 'Mr. John Sadler's Balloon', and John himself confirmed that his 'last ascent with a Balloon was from St

James's Park on 1st August 1814' in a note dated 22 January 1838 on his own sketch of a Robert Cocking parachute (in the Royal Aeronautical Society collection). As further proof, Windham's obituary in *Kaleidoscope* 5 October 1824 attributes to him only two London ascents.

40. *Morning Chronicle*, 2 August 1814.
41. The festivities commemorated both exactly one hundred years since the accession of George I of Hanover (and Brunswick) and the pivotal defeat of the French Mediterranean fleet by Nelson, between 1 and 3 August 1798. Napoleon had abdicated on 11 April 1814, and was at the time imprisoned on Elba.
42. *La Belle Assemblée; or, Bell's Court and Fashionable Magazine*, August 1814, p. 84.
43. *Caledonian Mercury*, 6 August 1814.
44. *La Belle Assemblée; or, Bell's Court and Fashionable Magazine*, August 1814, p. 84.
45. *La Belle Assemblée; or, Bell's Court and Fashionable Magazine*, August 1814, p. 84.
46. *Lancaster Gazette & General Advertiser*, 6 August 1814.
47. *Caledonian Mercury*, 6 August 1814. A notice in the *Morning Post* (15 August 1814) requested the return of a package which Sadler had mislaid on 1 August 'almost immediately after his return from his Descent in the Balloon'. The package had been the gift of Frederick Thornhill (and the possible contents, therefore, Thornhill's *Poems*, published in London in 1814).

12. The 'Inheritor of His Father's Genius and Intrepidity': Windham Sadler's Ascents from 1814 to 1823

1. *Hull Packet*, 16 August 1814, and described in slightly different format in the *York Herald* (20 August 1814).
2. *Caledonian Mercury*, 27 August 1814.
3. *Bury and Norwich Post*, 7 September 1814.
4. *Caledonian Mercury*, 3 October 1814.
5. *Morning Chronicle*, 4 October 1814.
6. *Royal Cornwall Gazette*, 19 November 1814.
7. *Trewman's Exeter Flying Post*, 24 November 1814.
8. Hodgson (1924), p. 153.
9. *Royal Cornwall Gazette*, 19 November 1814.
10. *Bury & Norwich Post*, 21 December 1814.
11. Fawcett, p. 394, citing *Norwich Mercury*, 11 February 1815.
12. *Morning Chronicle*, 6 July 1815 (being the very day that Louis was reinstated as king, following Napoleon's final defeat at Waterloo on 18 June).
13. *Bury & Norwich Post*, 19 and 26 July 1815.
14. James was in attendance however, as the *Times* (1 August 1815) differentiated between 'Mr. Sadler' and 'Mr. Wyndham Sadler, who ascended with the Balloon'. In the evening one or other 'Mr. Sadler appeared in Mr. Harper's garden, or the Vauxhall of this place ... and was received with the most enthusiastic applause'. These were the same pleasure gardens from which James Deeker had ascended in 1785, when they were known as Quantrell's (Woodforde, James, *Passages from the Five Volumes of the Diary of a Country Parson 1758–1802*, ed. John Beresford (London: Oxford University Press, 1935), p. 204). R[obert] M. Harper had assumed responsibility for the location in 1805, and remained there until 1817 (Fawcett, pp. 393–94), but this reoccurrence of a Harper–Sadler connection is presumably mere coincidence.
15. *Bury & Norwich Post*, 2 August 1815.
16. 1,064 precisely, according to the *Caledonian Mercury*, 9 September 1815.
17. Losh, James, *Diaries & Correspondence*, vol.1 (Durham: Surtees Society, vol. 171, 1956), p. 52. Losh had seen several other ascents 'nearly 30 years ago', and was yet another who found it 'disheartening to consider that during so long a period, no material advantage has been derived from this wonderful invention, nor any very important improvement made'.
18. In *Gateshead Cabinet, being a small collection of songs*, by 'T.R.V.' (Newcastle: printed by J. Marshall, 1816).
19. The *Oxford English Dictionary* defines 'to coup the creels' as 'to fall or tumble over' or 'meet with a mishap'.
20. *Caledonian Mercury*, 21 October 1815.
21. *Caledonian Mercury*, 26 October 1815.
22. *Caledonian Mercury*, 21 October 1815.
23. *Caledonian Mercury*, 23 October 1815.

24. It is intriguing to see the 'Army' mentioned at this late juncture, since officially James Sadler was never in their employ, even though some of the guns he developed while on the Navy's payroll did have land-based utility, this being one of the Navy's gripes, of course.

25. *Caledonian Mercury,* 4 November 1815, and subsequent quotation.

26. *Caledonian Mercury,* 4 November 1815.

27. The *Oxford University & City Herald* (4 May 1816) stated that the first lecture 'gave much satisfaction, particularly the exhibition of Philosophical Fire-works, which were much applauded'.

28. *Freemans Journal,* 5 September 1816.

29. Tuckey, Francis H., *County & City of Cork Remembrancer* (Cork: Osborne, Savage & Son, 1837), p. 251.

30. *Freemans Journal,* 5 September 1816.

31. *Freemans Journal,* 5 September 1816.

32. The same image and caption had been included on a handbill for the Exeter ascent of October 1814 (a copy of which is in the London Science Museum collection).

33. In the *Belfast Newsletter* of 18 May 1822 he was stated to have been born in Belfast. His full name was Edmund D. Livingston (letter to *Freeman's Journal,* 26 May 1826).

34. *Kaleidoscope,* 5 October 1824, p. 116.

35. He was true to his word: 'This dog, we understand, Mr. Sadler kept with much care for several years, and it, at length, to his infinite regret, disappeared.' (*Liverpool Mercury,* 8 October 1824).

36. *Freeman's Journal,* 18 July 1817.

37. MacMahon, p. 199.

38. Sadler, W., p. 5.

39. Sadler, W., p. 12.

40. *Freeman's Journal,* 25 July 1817.

41. *Caledonian Mercury,* 28 July 1817.

42. *Caledonian Mercury,* 28 July 1817.

43. *Morning Chronicle,* 9 August 1824.

44. Sadler, W., p. 14. The remaining eleven pages (of twenty-five) of *Aerostation* consist of a summary of the achievements of the early balloonists and a justification of the scientific value of their endeavours. Also affixed was a chart showing both Windham's route to Holyhead and James's route of 1812. A slightly modified version of Windham Sadler's first-hand account of 'the most memorable aerial feat on record' occupied the front page of the Liverpool *Kaleidoscope* of 26 October 1819.

45. *Caledonian Mercury,* 28 July 1817.

46. Dixon, p. 9, seemingly citing *Faulkner's Dublin Journal.*

47. Prior to this, Windham had arranged 'the ascent of several balloons with Fire-work attached' as part of a benefit event under the patronage of the Duke of Leinster for the 'general Asylum for Orphans, principally the offspring of those Men who have fallen in the Army and Navy' (*Freemans Journal,* 6 August 1817).

48. If, indeed, Mary really was her first name: it is only that reputed comment by a spectator at her first ascent with Windham in London in 1814 which implies this. Otherwise, the press was consistent in its determination to preserve her partial anonymity, and furnish no other details about her.

49. Neither Sadler ever made an ascent *from* Wales, but then nor did any of the early aeronauts. An apothecary called Francis Barrett had made a flight of sorts from Swansea on 15 October 1802, after two well-publicised earlier failures, one at Greenwich and one in Swansea, but he was merely carried over several fields while still close to the ground (Hodgson (1924), p. 223), much in the pattern of James Tytler's disputed first attempts. Barrett's own long account of his Swansea endeavours was printed in the *Morning Chronicle* of 22 October 1802.

50. Harris, p. 18.

51. Harris, p. 18.

52. Harris, p. 18.

53. Harris, p. 19.

54. *Lancaster Gazette,* 6 November 1819. The *Lancaster Gazette* of 16 October had described the 'strange circumstance' earlier in the journey of great numbers of game which flocked into a valley near Blackburn as the balloon passed, 'some entering the houses, and others alighting on the roofs, screaming in a loud and terrified manner'.

55. *Lancaster Gazette,* 13 November 1819.

56. *Lancaster Gazette,* 13 November 1819.

57. *New London Magazine*, September 1785, pp. 159–160.
58. *Kaleidoscope*, 5 October 1819, p. 52.
59. *Morning Post*, 4 October 1819.
60. This strongly suggests that it was the younger John, and not his forty-year-old father, who had spoken often in public.
61. Monck Mason lists the first, and probably only, ascent of presumably the same man as being from London on 23 June 1825, using the 'practically obsolete "Montgolifière" or hot-air principle' (Hodgson (1924) p. 229).
62. *Repertory of Arts, Manufactures and Agriculture*, vol. 38, second series (London: 1821) p. 191 (*see* Appendix 8). The patent was dated 3 January 1821 at which time his address was given as Penlington-place, Lambeth.
63. *Kaleidoscope*, 26 December 1820, p. 208.
64. *Liverpool Mercury*, 30 June 1820.
65. Harris, p. 25. Harris implies that this was Thomas Muncaster, a Liverpool bookseller, after whom Windham Sadler named his son John Muncaster Sadler (1823–1912), who was born on 18 March 1823. At the time of his baptism at St Thomas's Church on 4 May 1823 Windham identified himself as a 'gentleman' residing in Everton.
66. Harris, p. 26.
67. *Morning Post*, 9 August 1822; *Belfast Newsletter*, 9 August 1822; *Caledonian Mercury*, 14 September 1822; and *Lancaster Gazette*, 14 September 1822. On 27 June 1822, while living at Greenmount Cottage, Drumcondra (where he still lived in 1826 as per *Freemans Journal*, 26 May 1826) he made an ascent from Dublin which raised nearly £234 for the starving peasantry of the south of Ireland (*Freemans Journal*, 14 June 1822 and *Freemans Journal*, 4 July 1822), but had to be rescued from the sea.
68. Hodgson (1929), p. 72. When the unknown Charles Green made his daring debut at the celebration of the Coronation of George IV on 19 July 1821 – doubly daring in fact, to do so in front of such a large and prestigious crowd *and* to be the first person ever to use coal gas in public – there was an understandable case of mistaken identity. The *Morning Post* (20 July) reported that: 'The stranger who was to make his first aerial voyage ... was Mr Sadler jun.' Oh no it wasn't! A letter from John Green in the *Morning Chronicle* (21 July) identified the pilot as Charles Green, who was beginning a career which would ultimately see him make an incredible 500 plus aerial excursions.
69. Harris, p. 26.
70. *Caledonian Mercury*,14 September 1822.
71. *Ipswich Journal*, 23 August 1822.
72. *Morning Chronicle*, 19 August 1823.
73. *Caledonian Mercury*, 23 August 1823.
74. *Jackson's Oxford Journal*, 23 August 1823, which attributed the premature launch to the older Sadler.
75. *Bell's Life in London and Sporting Chronicle*, 24 August 1823, under the heading 'Hoax on the Cocknies'.
76. *Morning Post*, 6 September 1823.
77. *Caledonian Mercury*, 11 September 1823. Margaret Graham was obliged to wait until the following year for her first flight. She and her husband ascended on 2 June 1824, only a week after Thomas Harris had become Britain's first ballooning fatality (*see* Appendix 9).
78. *Morning Chronicle*, 13 September 1823.
79. *Bristol Mercury*, 22 September 1823.

13. 'Expectation Stood on Tip-Toe': William Windham Sadler, 1823–24

1. Lunardi had ascended from Leeds on 4 December 1786 (*Public Advertiser*, 12 December 1786).
2. *Leeds Mercury*, 6 September 1823.
3. *Morning Chronicle*, 11 September 1823.
4. *Leeds Mercury*, 6 September 1823. Green's balloon was discovered in Holland, and had still not been returned a month later, the finder wanting £18 plus costs (*Morning Post*, 18 October 1823).
5. *Derby Mercury*, 17 September 1823.
6. *Hull Packet*, 22 September 1823.
7. *Lancaster Gazette*, 27 September 1823.

8. *Leeds Mercury,* 27 September 1823.
9. *Liverpool Mercury,* 3 October 1823. A separate advert encouraged the public to compensate Sadler for his losses. One of the people to whom donations could be made was Sadler's friend, the bookseller Mr Muncaster at Church Street. In the *Catalogue of the Liverpool Library at the Lyceum* (Liverpool: James Smith, 1814) Thomas Muncaster, bookseller, is named as one of the officers of the Liverpool Library in 1813 and 1814 (pp. 40–41). William Muncaster is shown as one of its original subscribers (p. 31).
10. *Liverpool Mercury,* 30 January 1824.
11. *Morning Chronicle,* 10 October 1823.
12. *Morning Chronicle,* 11 October 1823.
13. *Liverpool Mercury,* 17 October 1823.
14. *Berrow's Worcester Journal,* 16 October 1823.
15. *Derby Mercury,* 29 October 1823.
16. Brown later made an ascent of his own from Sheffield (*Morning Post,* 14 August 1824).
17. *Morning Post,* 14 November, quoting from the *Nottingham Review,* and thought worthy of repetition in many other newspapers.
18. Windham's own account of this Nottingham ascent also appeared in *Kaleidoscope* of 18 November 1823.
19. *Liverpool Mercury,* 14 November 1823.
20. In *Baines Directory* of 1824 the address is given as 63 Wood Street.
21. *Derby Mercury,* 21 April 1824.
22. *Kaleidoscope,* 1 June 1824, p. 404.
23. *Liverpool Mercury,* 28 May 1824 (from which account the other passages are also quoted). Sadler called round to the Gas Company two days later but was not charged for the gas. (Harris, p. 26).
24. *Liverpool Mercury,* 4 June 1824.
25. *Liverpool Mercury,* 4 June 1824.
26. *Liverpool Mercury,* 18 June 1824. This was not the first balloon ascent from Chester. That was made on 8 September 1785 by Thomas Baldwin, using Lunardi's balloon and under his supervision. The journey is recounted in great technical detail in Baldwin's *Airopaidia.* Baldwin had witnessed Sadler's first 1785 ascent from Manchester, and, he implies, had also somehow seen his descent (p. 180).
27. *Caledonian Mercury,* 3 July 1824. Indeed, the place of launch, from Heriot's Hospital, had also been exactly the same as that chosen by Lunardi on 5 October 1785. The Italian had made a second ascent from Edinburgh on 20 December 1785 and a third in August 1786, all three being described in his *Account of Five Aerial Voyages in Scotland* (1786).
28. The warning was not heeded; only a further £20 was raised (*Caledonian Mercury,* 16 August 1824).
29. *Caledonian Mercury,* 10 July 1824. The defence was that not only had unencumbered access been preserved for him and his family, they had also been admitted to the Castlehill 'without being charged the small sum which every one, before the barrier was forced, had so cheerfully paid'. The claim was dismissed.
30. *Caledonian Mercury,* 10 July 1824.
31. The intended co-pilot had been Robert Haworth Peel again, as advertisements in the *Dublin Evening Mail* (12 July 1824) and *Freemans Journal* (13 July 1824) show, but he was denied the opportunity 'owing to his Regiment leaving Dublin'.
32. *Morning Post,* 19 July 1824.
33. *Liverpool Mercury,* 24 September 1824.
34. *Liverpool Mercury,* 1 October 1824.
35. *Morning Chronicle,* 2 October 1824.
36. *Jackson's Oxford Journal,* 9 October 1824.
37. *Pigot's Directory* of 1828. By coincidence, the company Simpson, Haigh & Co. had evolved from a three-way partnership between Robert Peel (1723–95), great-grandfather of Robert Haworth Peel; Jonathan Haworth (1736–86), from whose Manchester premises James Sadler made his 1785 ascents; and William Yates (1740–1813). The three men set up a fustian and calico printworks in Oswaldtwistle in 1764 (*Dictionary of National Biography:* Peel). A sketchy account of the early business and matrimonial alliances of the Peel and Haworth families appears

in an 1836 'Memoir of the Peel family' by Miss Jane Haworth in *Sir Robert Peel*, vol. 1. ed. Charles Stuart Parker (1891).

38. The inquest was reported in full in both the *Morning Chronicle* and *Morning Post* of 5 October 1824.
39. *Liverpool Mercury*, 8 October 1824.
40. *Morning Post*, 9 October 1824.
41. *Morning Chronicle*, 5 October 1824. The *Liverpool Mercury* (8 October 1824) also identified Muncaster as her father. As Catherine Sadler's maiden name was Richards, however, perhaps Muncaster was her stepfather, or even grandfather. Whatever, he was evidently considered to be her next of kin.
42. *Liverpool Mercury*, 1 October 1824.
43. *Morning Chronicle*, 4 October 1824. The *Oxford University & City Herald* (2 October 1810) had been informed that Blenkinsop had run 1.5 miles to fetch the surgeon, and on returning 'suddenly fell, to rise no more in this world!' It is a phrase, one feels, which might more aptly have been applied to Windham Sadler!
44. *Jackson's Oxford Journal*, 9 October 1824.
45. Donnelly may have escaped with only a fracture, while poor Windham Sadler lost his life, but the injury had a lasting effect. In an ungrammatical appeal, printed verbatim in the *Liverpool Mercury* (22 July 1825), he stated that the incapacity occasioned by his broken arm eight months earlier meant that he was unable adequately to support his children.
46. *Morning Chronicle* and *Morning Post* of 5 October 1824.
47. *Kaleidoscope*, 5 October 1824, pp. 116–117 and p. 120. This comprehensive obituary listed all the locations of Windham's flights (bar the one made from Nottingham in 1823). The periodical also noted the persistent supposition that James Sadler had 'accomplished, we believe, upwards of fifty ascents' (p. 116).
48. *Kaleidoscope*, 5 October 1824, p. 117.
49. *Liverpool Mercury*, 1 October 1824.
50. From broadsheet in Gimbel collection in America, cited as XC-10-3B (Sad) – 3D in Lynn, p. 66 and p. 153.
51. *Liverpool Mercury*, 8 and 15 October 1824.
52. She maintained the business in Hanover Street until at least the end of the decade, appearing as Catherine Sadler, proprietor of 'warm, vapour, sulphur, and Harrowgate' baths at 63 Hanover Street in *Pigot's National Commercial Directory* for 1828/29 (p. 301).
53. *Berrow's Worcester Journal*, 11 November 1824.
54. *Morning Chronicle*, 5 April 1825.
55. The only subsequent ascent by any of the family, as far as I am aware, was by Roy Sadler in Oxford in October 1984, as part of the bicentennial celebrations of James Sadler's first historic ascent (*see* Conclusion).

14. 'How Scheming Beggars a Man': James Sadler's Final Short Descent of All

1. London Metropolitan Archives, Charterhouse Quarter Book ACC/1876/AR3/192.
2. Davies, Gerald S., *Charterhouse in London* (London: John Murray, 1921), p. 201.
3. Davies, Gerald S., *Charterhouse in London* (London: John Murray, 1921), p. 349.
4. Fisher matriculated 23 April 1766, aged fifteen (*Alumni Oxonienses* 1888).
5. Fisher had been in Oxford during the eventful autumn of 1784, when Sadler made his first two ascents: William Windham's *Diary* shows he was awaiting Fisher's arrival while staying in his old rooms in University College on 27 October 1784.
6. Constable, vol. 6, p. 162. John Fisher had himself been 'admitted a scholar upon the foundation of the Charterhouse ... in 1802' (Constable, vol. 6, p. 12). The figure of fifty flights is, of course, unsubstantiated.
7. Constable, vol. 6, p. 161.
8. Constable, vol. 6, p. 164.
9. *Morning Chronicle*, 18 June 1824.
10. Beaufoy, G., p. 199.
11. London Metropolitan Archives, Charterhouse Quarter Books, ACC/1876/AR3/192–197.
12. British Library add. MS 40369 f.136–7.
13. Beddoes matriculated 1 May 1820, aged sixteen, took his BA in 1825, and MA in 1828 (*Alumni*

Oxonienses, 1888). He had another tangential connection with Sadler too, having previously been a pupil at Charterhouse school, from 1817 to 1820 (*Dictionary of National Biography*: Beddoes).

14. That is, 26 March, though his gravestone in what are now the grounds of St Edmund Hall states 27th.

Conclusion

1. *Times*, p. 13, and *Oxford Times*, p. 17, both 26 October 1928.
2. *Oxford Times*, 5 October 1984, p. 1.
3. *Oxford Times*, 12 October 1984, p. 8. The *Oxford Times* of 5 October 1986 featured two other related articles, on pages 10 and 11, the latter being by Dr Graeme Tytler of Oxford's Warnborough College, a descendant of James Tytler.
4. *Oxford Times*, 7 November 1986, p. 8.
5. Hodgson (1928), p. 18.
6. Pye, p. 160.

Notes to Appendices

1. British Library add. MS 40221 f272.
2. Oxford University Chancellor's Court 1633/62.
3. *Oxford Council Acts 1626–1665*, eds. Grizel, M. G. and Salter, H. E. (Oxford: Oxford University Press, 1933), p. 178.
4. Salter, H. E., *Surveys & Tokens* (Oxford: Oxford Historical Society, vol. 75, 1923), p. 214, p. 274.
5. Jane Marten, daughter of Edward, was baptised at Steeple Aston in 1643.
6. Oxfordshire History Centre OXFO 352 FREE (and for other dates of freedoms here and in Appendix 2).
7. *Hearne's Remarks & Collections*, vol. 7, ed. C. E. Doble, (Oxford: Oxford Historical Society, 1906). Another extract from Hearne from about this time, 17 July 1715, may be of passing interest in the context of this biography: 'Last Night between 7 and 8 Clock a Fellow, who goes by the Name of Cornish Tom, who was lately a Souldier, pretended to fly from Carfax Tower, but had like to have broke his Neck.'
8. St Peter-in-the-East was in Queen's Lane, just off the High Street, and is now the library of St Edmund Hall. The earliest of all Sadler-related events noted at St Peter-in-the-East is the burial of one John Sadler in 1630.
9. Oxfordshire History Centre 207.264 151/1/7, made on 9 December 1719 and proved on 31 December 1720.
10. There is only one example of any possible imprudence, when William Sadler was summoned to answer a charge of debt in 1715 (Oxford University Chancellor's Court 1715/66¹).
11. *Cartulary of Osney Abbey*, vol. 1, ed. H. E. Salter (Oxford: Oxford Historical Society, vol. 89, 1929), p. 198.
12. University College accounts: 'Deep Hall'.
13. *Life & Times of Anthony Wood*, vol.1, ed. Andrew Clark (Oxford: Oxford Historical Society, 1891), p. 290. The demolition of Deep Hall is shown in J. M. W. Turner's 1810 view of the High Street, acquired by the Ashmolean Museum in 2015.
14. Oxfordshire History Centre OXFO 352 FREE.
15. *Oxford Apprentices 1697–1800*, Oxfordshire History Centre.
16. Almost certainly it is Ann's details, in between those of Mary and John in the prayer book, which have been redacted in thick black ink, reflecting, one might surmise, some kind of domestic disgrace and consequent disownment.
17. Salter, p. 12. No. 84 was incorporated into the Angel Hotel in or before 1813, as had No. 83 previously (Account Rolls of University College UC:E/B2/D2 & D3). When the declining hotel was put up for sale in 1855, the lease was purchased by Francis Thomas Cooper (1811–62). He let out No. 83, and used No. 84 as his shop with living accommodation upstairs. Cooper's son Frank (1844–1927) inherited the family business in 1867 and it is at No. 83 that his wife first created the famous Cooper's Oxford marmalade in 1874. (Allen, Brigid, *Cooper's Oxford* (Oxford: Archive Services, 1989), p. 24, p. 35).
18. Oxfordshire History Centre OXFO 352 FREE.

Notes

19. The wedding has not been traced, so Eleanor's origins remain unclear. According to her *Jackson's* obituary of 26 September 1807, she was several years older than Thomas, being then (as the 'wife of Mr. Sadler, Confectioner, High Street') 'in the 56th year of her age'. She died on Monday 21 September and was buried at All Saints on the 25th.

20. The implications of an advertisement placed by 'Mr. Sadler' (that is, probably James senior), confectioner, in *Jackson's* of 18 August 1787 remain unclear. It was for a 'small House, situated in the High Street, Oxford; consisting of four rooms, with an elegant Shop and good cellar'.

21. Shadwell, C. L. and Salter, H. E. *Oriel College Records* (Oxford: Oxford Historical Society, vol. 85, 1926), p. 212. Sadler had secured the property on 26 November 1800 'being a messuage in the occupation of Robert Platt and known as Platt's coffeehouse'. It was re-sold to Oriel College by Emily Jane Sadler for £2,240 on 11 September 1884. The premises are now (2015) occupied by Sanders, a retailer of historical prints.

22. On 24 May 1808: Oxford University Chancellor's Court 1801/92. Although James Sadler also had a son called Thomas, nothing is known of him after his baptism in 1782, and as he did not ever acquire the freedom of the city, it can be safely assumed that all Oxford references are to Thomas's son Thomas.

23. *Jackson's Oxford Journal,* 8 October 1808.

24. *Jackson's Oxford Journal,* 9 June 1810.

25. Thomas' only son Frederick (1811–?) was also described as a 'chemist & druggist' in *Jackson's* of 21 April 1832.

26. *Jackson's Oxford Journal* 20 May 1826 and 15 July 1826. The High Street properties were possibly Nos. 118–19, on which Henry had taken out a lease on 1 November 1814, in association with his relative the cordwainer James Wyatt (Salter, H. E., *Oxford City Properties* (Oxford: Oxford Historical Society, vol. 83, 1926), p. 128).

27. *Jackson's Oxford Journal,* 21 July 1827.

28. Shadwell, C. L. and Salter, H. E., *Oriel College Records,* (Oxford: Oxford Historical Society, vol. 85, 1926), p. 216.

29. London Metropolitan Archives, Charterhouse Quarter Book, ACC/1876/AR3/197.

30. Clark, Andrew (ed.) in *Life & Times of Anthony Wood,* vol. 1 (Oxford: Oxford Historical Society, 1891), p. 374. This demeaning obligation had been in place since the calamitous 'Town and Gown' disturbances of 1209, as atonement for the summary execution by some townsmen of two apparently innocent scholars.

31. Bodleian Library MS Top. Oxon. D.509 (467).

32. 'An Old Freeman', *Early Recollections of Oxford* (Oxford: Oxford Chronicle Co., 1900), p. 13.

33. *Jackson's Oxford Journal,* 20 April 1872.

34. *Jackson's Oxford Journal,* 1 August 1840.

35. *London Gazette,* 20 April 1849.

36. Fergusson, p. 62 and pp. 67–68.

37. Fergusson, p. 68.

38. Fergusson, p. 71.

39. Fergusson, p. 71.

40. *London Chronicle,* 12–14 August 1784. A similar reaction to de Moret's aborted ascent in London followed three days later.

41. Fergusson, p. 75.

42. Fergusson, p. 90.

43. *London Chronicle,* 4–7 September 1784.

44. Fergusson, p. 91.

45. The *Post's* account was plagiarised from the *Edinburgh Evening Courant* (Fergusson, p. 83)

46. Lunardi (1786), p. 104. On one of these five ascents, from Glasgow on 23 November 1785, Lunardi facilitated the first ascent of sorts by a female in Scotland in unusual style. On descending in the vicinity of Hawick, he was spotted by Gilbert Chisholm, whose wife spontaneously took Lunardi's place in the basket and was transported about 3 miles while being restrained from below (Lunardi (1786), pp. 78–80).

47. Lunardi, (1786), pp. 107–112.

48. Lunardi (1786), p. 107.

49. Letter to Mrs Dunlop of Dunlop, 17 November 1788, in *Letters of Robert Burns* (ed. 2), ed. G. Ross Roy (Oxford: Clarendon Press, 1985), vol. 1. It is Burns who dubbed him 'Balloon Tytler' (Fergusson, p. 104).

50. *Dictionary of National Biography*: Tytler.
51. The injudicious toast proposed by Lunardi himself at a ball held in his honour in November 1784 (Gardiner, p. 61).
52. Lunardi (1786), p. 24–25.
53. *London Chronicle*, 9–12 October 1784, written by 'W. de W.'.
54. *Morning Post & Daily Advertiser*, 16 October 1784.
55. Keen, Paul, 'The "Balloonomania": Science and Spectacle in 1780s England' in *Eighteenth-century Studies*, Summer 2006, p. 531.
56. 'British Balloon and – Aerial Yacht', dated 13 December 1784 (British Museum 1868,0808.5390).
57. *London Chronicle*, 30 November–2 December 1784.
58. *Aris's Birmingham Gazette*, 10 January 1785, quoted in Langford, p. 428. William Withering (1741–99) was one of the principal members of Lunar Society; John Southern (*c.* 1758–1815) was the author of the highly technical *Treatise upon Aerostatic Machines* (Birmingham: printed by Pearson & Rollason, 1785), in which Sadler is mentioned in a footnote (p. 51) as being the first person to make use of cisterns instead of casks, appliances which Southern considered less efficient because they were not airtight.
59. Langford, p. 429.
60. *London Chronicle*, 6 January 1785.
61. According to the *Oxford English Dictionary* the term derives from the barber Hugh Strap in Tobias Smollett's *Roderick Random*, 1748.
62. Sadler had travelled to Dover on 24 December, intending to cross the English Channel.
63. Langford, p. 430. William Hayward features in *Bailey's British Directory* of 1784 as a hosier and haberdasher at 368 Oxford Street and at 364 Oxford Street in the 1785 edition, this being clearly in the parish of St James's, Piccadilly, where he was registered to vote in a Poll Book of 1784 (City of Westminster Archive Centre).
64. *Sketchley's Directory*, 1767; *Sketchley & Adams Directory*, 1770; Pearson & Rollason's *Birmingham Directory*, 1777, and their *Birmingham, Wolverhampton, … and Willenhall Directory*, 1780. Could he be the same Robert Harper who was baptised in 1735 at St Helen's in Abingdon, the family church of James Sadler's wife Mary Harper, and therefore related to her? This Robert's father, Abraham Harper, was also a carpenter, and there is no indication that Robert was buried in Abingdon, suggesting that he may well have moved away from the town.
65. Langford, p. 431.
66. *Gazetteer & New Daily Advertiser*, 8 February 1785.
67. *Aris's Birmingham Gazette*, 7 February 1785, in Langford, p. 432.
68. The biographical dates in this Appendix, except where otherwise stated, are taken from the article on the Simonets in Highfill et al., *Biographical Dictionary of Actors, Actresses [etc.] in London* (Carbondale: Southern Illinois University Press, 1991), vol. 14, pp. 76–81.
69. *London Courant & Westminster Chronicle*, 8 January 1780 (when living at 5 Dover Street, Piccadilly).
70. *Gazetteer & New Daily Advertiser*, 1 November 1776.
71. Footnote to Walpole, vol. 25, p. 575, where more biographical detail about the Simonets appears.
72. Walpole, vol. 25, in letter to Horace Mann, 7 May 1785.
73. *General Evening Post*, 3–5 May 1785.
74. *Morning Chronicle & London Advertiser*, 4 May 1785.
75. *Morning Chronicle & London Advertiser*, 9 May 1785.
76. *Morning Post & Daily Advertiser*, 25 November 1778.
77. *Morning Chronicle & London Advertiser*, 17 May 1785.
78. *Biographical Dictionary*, vol. 14, p. 76, which concurs that it was Leonora, not Theresa, who made the second flight.
79. *Morning Herald & Daily Advertiser*, 4 May 1784.
80. *Morning Herald & Daily Advertiser*, 23 May 1785.
81. *Morning Chronicle & London Advertiser*, 23 May 1785.
82. *Morning Herald & Daily Advertiser*, 11 May 1785.
83. *Morning Chronicle & London Advertiser*, 7 July 1785. The comment was immediately followed by: 'Some few, who were unacquainted with the disposition and character of the Manager, seemed to expect an attack on the late laudable exploit of Mrs. Sage; but that idea was soon dissipated' (*see* Appendix 7).

84. *Biographical Dictionary*, vol. 14, p. 80.
85. *Morning Post & Daily Advertiser*, 14 July 1785.
86. *London Magazine*, May 1785, p. 373.
87. *London Advertiser*, 17 May 1785, written quite possibly by a man who would have fled a mile if anyone had suggested that he go up himself!
88. *Whitehall Evening Post*, 22–24 March 1785. William Windham attended the launch (Windham (1866) p. 45–46).
89. Hodgson (1924), p. 176. At Zambeccari's March ascent with Vernon a delay of only two hours had resulted, as at Harper's in Birmingham, in a crowd which amused itself by 'throwing dead-dogs, cats, &c. in each other's faces' while the 'pick-pockets, as usual, made their harvest' (*Public Advertiser*, 25 March 1785). Zambeccari went on to join the Russian navy; he later resumed his aeronautical career, only to perish in a balloon accident in 1812.
90. In his own published account of *Two Aerial Expeditions from the City of Norwich* (Norwich: printed by John Crouse, 1785, p. 13), Deeker identified her as being about fourteen years old. This was also noted by James Woodforde, who witnessed the ascent (*Passages from the Five Volumes of the Diary of a Country Parson 1758–1802*, ed. John Beresford (London: Oxford University Press, 1935), p. 204). Deeker's son Joseph (c1768–1856?), 'an intrepid youth scarcely seventeen years of age', had already become the first man to ascend from Bristol, on 19 April 1785 (*Morning Chronicle & London Advertiser*, 22 April 1785).
91. Confirmed in Monck Mason's *Aeronautica* as Deeker's first ascent.
92. *General Evening Post*, 2–4 June 1785 and *General Evening Post*, 25–28 June 1785.
93. Sage, p. 6.
94. Lunardi did indeed make ascents from Liverpool, in July and August. Mrs Sage accompanied him to Liverpool, according to the *Morning Chronicle & London Advertiser* (18 July 1785), which added cryptically that 'the trip … is under the auspices of the theatrical people – not the best auspices of the place – Mrs. Ward being Mrs. Sage's sister'. Although associated more with Manchester, Sarah Ward had been in Liverpool a year earlier (when her daughter Sally Isabella was baptised at St Peter's), strengthening the notion that Mrs Sage's *Letter* was indeed addressed to her.
95. Hodgson (1924), p. 125.
96. Sage, p. 10.
97. *Morning Post & Daily Advertiser*, 30 June 1785; 2 July 1785; and 24 February 1786.
98. Several illustrators depicted all three of them on board. Lunardi wrote (on 17 July), with no suggestion of it being inaccurate, of having 'just received some Prints one of which, the three Ærial Travellers, lies before me, and I contemplate it with unspeakable Delight!' (Lunardi, *Ascension from Liverpool*, p. 13).
99. Sage, p. 19.
100. Sage, p. 26.
101. Sage, p. 29.
102. Sage, p. 3.
103. *Morning Herald & Daily Advertiser*, 13 July and 16 July 1785.
104. *Daily Universal Register*, 11 July 1785, p. 3.
105. *Manchester Times & Gazette*, 26 May 1838.
106. Gilliland, p. 996.
107. *Biographical Dictionary*, vol. 15, p. 268.
108. *Biographical Dictionary*, vol. 12, p. 127.
109. Gilliland, p. 917.
110. *Biographical Dictionary*, vol. 13, p. 167.
111. Gilliland, p. 917. 'Mr. Ward' was her brother-in-law, of course.
112. *Morning Post*, 17 August 1807, where she is identified as Mrs R. Powell of the Haymarket.
113. *The Athenaeum*, September 1807, p. 302.
114. *Biographical Dictionary*, vol. 13, p. 167. This information derives from a handwritten note in the files of the Folger Shakespeare Library in America (and confirmed in an email from the Library's Head of Reference 11 February 2014).
115. *Biographical Dictionary*, vol. 13, p. 167.
116. *St. James's Chronicle*, 25–27 April 1780.
117. *Biographical Dictionary*, vol. 13, p. 169. Collins (1742–1808) was born, married and often

performed in Bath (*Biographical Dictionary*, vol. 3, pp. 398–402), where, of course, the artist William Hoare resided.

118. *Memoirs of Charles Dibdin, the Younger* (London: Society for Theatre Research, 1956), p. 82.
119. *Biographical Dictionary*, vol. 13, p. 169.
120. Thomas and Mary Hoare were buried at Bucklebury, respectively aged seventy-four on 23 October 1796 and seventy-six on 24 October 1798. In a Tilehurst Overseers examination of entitlement to settlement dated 11 October 1770 (Berkshire Record Office D/P132/13/4 217/3) Thomas Hoare was identified as a 'husbandman'.
121. Confirmed in e:mail dated 20 May 2014 from Local Studies Librarian, Bath Library.
122. Newby, Evelyn, 'The Hoares of Bath' in *Bath History*, vol. 1 (1986), p. 90.
123. Newby, Evelyn, *William Hoare of Bath* (Bath: Bath Museums Service, 1990), p. 9.
124. Newby, Evelyn, *Bath History,* op. cit., p. 90.
125. *Read's Weekly* (19 May 1753) identified him as 'of Bury' and 'a near relation to Sir Richard Hoare' (that is, his cousin, Richard (1709–54), a former Lord Mayor of London).
126. Hoare, Edward, *Early History and Genealogy … of the Families of Hore and Hoare* (London: 1883), p. 56.
127. Hoare, Henry, *Hoare's Bank, a Record 1672–1955,* revised ed., (London: Collins, 1955), p. 41.
128. Hodgson (1929), p. 72.
129. Beaufoy, G., p. 145. T. K. Cromwell identified Beaufoy's earlier location as having been near the famous Coade stone manufactory and contiguous patent shot manufactory, the latter having been established by James Watt in 1789 (*Excursions in the County of Surrey* (London: 1821), p. 92).
130. Beaufoy, G., p. 289.
131. *Dictionary of National Biography*: Sadler.
132. *Repertory of Arts, Manufactures and Agriculture,* vol. 38, second series (London: 1821) p. 191. The patent was dated 3 January 1821 (or 1820 in the 1824 edition, p. 78), at which time his address was given as Penlington-place, Lambeth.
133. Although baptised on the same day, the census of 1841 shows that the three daughters were not triplets.
134. Coincidentally or not, one of only two occurrences of the name Sadler in any of the registers of St Michael's, Oxford is the marriage of a John Sadler to Joan Hulls on 24 September 1792.
135. In 1851 her age was given as 65. In both cases her place of birth was stated to be Cambridge.
136. British Library L/MIL/9/110 f248, which includes proof of his baptism as the son of James and Mary on 23 July 1780.
137. Oxfordshire History Centre OXFO 352 FREE.
138. *East India Registers,* corrected to 15 December 1806 and 26 May 1807.
139. *East India Register,* 1809 (ed. 2).
140. *Morning Post,* 13 March 1810.
141. *Morning Chronicle,* 17 July 1818.
142. The daughter that Windham never saw – Catharine Windham Sadler – was buried at Christ Church, Liverpool on 29 May 1843, aged eighteen years, living then at Great Crosby.
143. Gibson, J., 'Liverpool Epitaphs MSS', vol. 2, p. 132 (from Hugh Torrens' notes for the *Dictionary of National Biography,* Museum of Natural History, Oxford). A Thomas Richards, son of Thomas, was baptised at St Peter's, Liverpool on 28 December 1806.
144. *Dictionary of National Biography*: Sadler.
145. *Morning Post,* 13 June 1824.
146. *Caledonian Mercury,* 5 June 1824.
147. *Liverpool Mercury,* 9 July 1824.
148. Constable, vol. 2, pp. 349–350.
149. *Morning Post,* 12 October 1824.
150. *Globe & Traveller,* 9 November 1824.
151. *Globe & Traveller,* 6 November 1824.
152. *Morning Chronicle,* 29 June 1826.
153. Green ascended on 13 June 1823 with the very aptly named Isaac Earlyman Sparrow, a London ironmonger (Hodgson (1924), p. 244). Another ascent from Oxford during the Commemoration week of 1848 (*Jackson's Oxford Journal,* 8 July 1848) was referred to during a civil action taken by a Mr Hampton, 'an aeronaut of some celebrity', against the Oxford Gas Co., chaired at that time by Alderman [C. J.] Sadler, 'nephew of the distinguished aeronaut' (*Morning Chronicle,* 3 March 1853).

BIBLIOGRAPHY

General

Alumni Oxonienses the members of the University of Oxford, 1715-1886, ed. Joseph Foster, vol. 1 (London: Joseph Foster, 1887), vols. 2 and 3 (London: Joseph Foster, 1888) and vol. 4 (Oxford: Parker & Co, 1888)

Biographical Dictionary of Actors, Actresses [etc.] *in London, 1660–1800,* vols. 12, 13, 14, and 15, eds. Highfill, Philip H., Burnim, Kalman A., Langhans, Edward A. (Carbondale: Southern Illinois University Press, 1987, 1991, 1991, and 1993)

Oxford Dictionary of National Biography online.

Specific

Anon., *The Ballooniad* (ed. 2) (Birmingham: 1785)

Anon., *Aerostatics, or a History of Balloons* (ed. 3) (London: printed by J. Rhynd, 1802)

Baldwin, Thomas, *Airopaidia* (Chester: printed by J. Fletcher, 1786)

Banks, Joseph, *Scientific Correspondence,* vols. 2, 3 and 4 (1782–1784, 1785–1790, 1791–1799) ed. Neil Chambers, (London: Pickering & Chatto, 2007)

Barber, Cedric, *Slaves, Sinners and Saints* (Stoke-on-Trent: Christians for Service, 2008)

Beaufoy, Gwendolyn, *Leaves from a Beech Tree* (Oxford: Blackwell, 1930)

Beaufoy, Henry H. B., *Journal kept by H. B. H. B.* (London: G. Woodfall, 1811)

Beddoes, Thomas, *Letter to Erasmus Darwin, M.D. on a new method of treating pulmonary consumption* (Bristol: printed by Bulgin and Rosser, 1793)

Bentham, Jeremy, *Correspondence,* vol. 5, ed. Alexander Taylor Milne (London: Athlone Press, 1981)

Blanchard, Jean-Pierre, *Journal & certificates on the fourth voyage of Mr. Blanchard, who ascended from the Royal Military Academy, at Chelsea, the 16th of October, 1784* (London: printed by Baker and Galabin, 1784)

Boswell, James, *Life of Johnson,* vol. 4, ed. G. B. Hill (Oxford: Oxford University Press, 1934)

Branson, Richard, *Reach for the Skies* (London: Virgin, 2010)

Burney, Charles, *Letters,* vol. 1, ed. A. Ribeiro (Oxford: Clarendon Press, 1991)

Cavallo, Tiberius, *History and practice of aerostation* (London: 1785)

Clow, Archibald & Clow, Nan L., *The Chemical Revolution* (London: Batchworth, 1952)

Coad, Jonathan G., *The Royal Dockyards 1690–1850* (Aldershot: Royal Commission on Historical Monuments, 1989)

Constable, John, *Correspondence,* ed. R.B. Beckett (Suffolk Records Society, vol. 2, 1964; vol. 6, 1968)

Cox, G. V., *Recollections of Oxford* (ed. 2) (London: Macmillan, 1870)

Dixon, F. E., 'Ballooning in Dublin' *Dublin Historical Record*, June 1955

Edgeworth, R. L. and Edgeworth, M., *Memoirs of Richard Lovell Edgeworth*, vol. 2 (ed. 2) (London: 1821)

Edgeworth, Maria, *Life and Letters*, vol. 1, ed. Augustus J. C. Hare (London: Edward Arnold, 1894)

Fawcett, Trevor, 'The Norwich Pleasure Gardens' in *Norfolk Archaeology*, vol. 35, 1972

Franklin, Benjamin, *Writings*, vol. 9, ed. A. H. Smyth (London: Macmillan, 1906)

Gilliland, Thomas, *Dramatic Mirror*, vol. 2 (London: 1808)

Gillispie, Charles C., *The Montgolfier Brothers and the Invention of Aviation, 1783-1784* (Princeton: Princeton University Press, c. 1983)

Hamilton, James, *Faraday* (London: HarperCollins, 2003)

Hamilton, James, *London Lights* (London: John Murray, 2007)

Harris, S. A., *The development of gas supply on north Merseyside, 1815–1949* (Liverpool: NW Gas Board, 1956)

Hodgson, J. E., *The History of Aeronautics in Great Britain* (Oxford: Oxford University Press, 1924)

Hodgson, J. E., *The First English Aeronaut: James Sadler of Oxford* (London: 1928)

Hodgson, J. E., 'James Sadler, of Oxford'in *Transactions of the Newcomen Society* for 1927–8 (Leamington Spa: Courier Press, 1929)

Hodson, E., *Air Balloons* (Nottingham: printed for Hodson, 1813)

Hogg, T. J., *Life of Percy Bysshe Shelley*, vol. 1, (London: 1858)

Holmes, Richard, *The Age of Wonder* (London: HarperPress, 2008)

Jay, Mike, *The Atmosphere of Heaven* (Yale: Yale University Press, 2009)

Jeffries, John, *Narrative of the two aerial voyages of Doctor Jeffries with Mons. Blanchard* (London: 1786).

Johnson, Samuel, *Letters*, vol. 3 and vol. 4, ed. Bruce Redford (Princeton: Princeton University Press, 1992 & 1994)

Langford, John Alfred, *A Century of Birmingham Life … from 1741 to 1841* vol. 1 (ed. 2) (Birmingham, 1870)

Levere, Trevor H., *Chemists and chemistry in nature and society* (Aldershot: Variorum, 1994), comprising earlier articles in *Notes & Records of Royal Society*: V. 'Dr. Thomas Beddoes at Oxford: Radical politics in 1788–1793 and the fate of the Regius Chair in Chemistry' (1981), VII. 'Dr. Thomas Beddoes and the Establishment of His Pneumatic Institution: A Tale of Three Presidents' (1977); VIII. 'Dr. Thomas Beddoes the interaction of pneumatic and preventative medicine with chemistry' (1982)

Levere, Trevor H., *Dr Thomas Beddoes at Oxford* in *Ambix*, 28 July 1981

Lockwood Marsh, W., *Aeronautical Prints & Drawings* (London: Halton & Trustcott Smith, 1924)

Losh, James, *Diaries and correspondence*, ed. Edward Hughes (Durham: Surtees Society, 1962/63)

Lynn, Michael R., *Sublime Invention* (London: Pickering & Chatto, 2010)

Lunardi, Vincent, *Account of the first aërial voyage in England, in a series of letters to his Guardian, Chevalier Gherardo Compagni*, ed. 2 (London: 1784)

Lunardi, Vincent, *Mr. Lunardi's Account of his Ascension and Aerial Voyage, from the New Fort, Liverpool, on Wednesday the 20th of July, 1785, in three Letters, addressed to George Biggin, Esq.* (London?: 1785?)

Lunardi, Vincent, *Mr Lunardi's Account of his Second Aerial Voyage from Liverpool, on Tuesday the 9th of August, 1785, in two letters to George Biggin, Esq.* (London?: 1785)

Lunardi, Vincent, *Account of Five Aerial Voyages in Scotland in a Series of Letters to his Guardian, Chevalier Gherardo Compagni* (London: 1786)

Bibliography

MacMahon, Bryan, *Ascend or Die: Richard Crosbie* (Dublin: History Press, 2010)

Mason, Monck, *Aeronautica* (London: 1838)

Morris, Peter J. T., 'Eighteenth Century' in *Chemistry at Oxford: a history from 1600 to 2005* eds. R. J. P. Williams, John S. Rowlinson and Allan Chapman (Cambridge: Royal Society of Chemistry, 2009)

Paris, J. A., *Life of Sir Humphrey Davy* (London: Colburn & Bentley, 1831)

Priestley, Joseph, *Scientific Correspondence,* ed. Henry Carrington Bolton (New York: privately printed, 1892),

Proudfoot, W. J., *Biographical Memoir of James Dinwiddie* (Liverpool, 1868)

Pye, Henry James, *Poems on Various Subjects* (London: printed for John Stockdale, 1787)

Ramsay, William, *Life & Letters of Joseph Black, M.D.* (London: Constable, 1918)

Robinson, Eric, 'Thomas Beddoes, M.D., and the reform of science teaching in Oxford' in *Annals of Science,* June 1955

Rolt, L. T. C., *The Balloonists* (Stroud: Sutton, 2006), first published 1966 as *The Aeronauts*

Sadler, James, *Description of a New and much Improved Rifle Gun* (London: printed by A. & J. Black and H. Parry, *c.* 1798), with *Account of Various Improvements in Artillery, Fire-arms etc.* (*c.* 1798)

Sadler, James, *Balloon: an authentic account of the ærial voyage of Messrs. Sadler and Clayfield, who ascended in a most magnificent balloon from a field in the neighbourhood of Stoke's-Croft, Bristol, on Monday, September 24th, 1810* (ed. 2) (Bristol: printed by A. Brown, 1810)

Sadler, James, *Balloon: an authentic narrative of the Ærial Voyage of Mr Sadler across the Irish Channel from Belvedere-House Drumcondra in the Neighbourhood of Dublin, on Thursday October 1st, 1812* (Dublin: printed by W H Tyrell, 1812).

Sadler, William Windham, *Aerostation: A narrative of the aerial voyage, of Mr. Windham Sadler, across the Irish Channel, from Portobello Barracks, in the neighbourhood of Dublin, on Tuesday, July 22d, 1817* (Dublin: printed by William Henry Tyrell, 1817)

Sage, L. A., *Letter addressed to a female Friend* (ed. 3) (London: printed by J. Bell, 1785)

Salter, H. E. (ed.), *Survey of Oxford in 1772* (Oxford: Oxford University Press, 1912)

Simcock, A. V., *The Ashmolean Museum and Oxford Science 1683-1983* (Oxford: Museum of the History of Science, 1984)

Smith, Richard O., *Man with his Head in the Clouds* (Oxford: Signal, 2014)

Stansfield, Dorothy A. and Stansfield, Ronald G., 'Dr Thomas Beddoes and James Watt: preparatory work 1794– 96 for the Bristol Pneumatic Institute', *Medical History* 30 (1986)

Stansfield, Dorothy A., *Thomas Beddoes MD 1760–1808* (Dordrecht: Reidel, 1984)

Stock, John Edmonds, *Memoir of the Life of Thomas Beddoes* (London: 1811)

Turner, Gerard L'E., 'James Sadler, Oxford Engineer, Chemist, and Aeronaut' in *Oxfordshire Roundabout,* June 1965

Uglow, Jennifer S., *The Lunar Men* (London: Faber & Faber, 2002)

Walpole, Horace, *Correspondence,* vol. 25, (with Horace Mann) eds. W. S Lewis et al (New Haven: Yale University Press: 1971)

Walpole, Horace, *Correspondence,* vol. 33, (with Countess of Upper Ossory) eds. W. S Lewis et al (New Haven: Yale University Press, 1965).

Werrett, Simon, *Fireworks: pyrotechnic arts and sciences in Europe* (Chicago: University of Chicago, 2010)

Windham, William, *Diary,* ed. Mrs Henry Baring (London: Longman, Green, 1866)

Windham, William, *Papers,* vol. 1, ed. A. P. P. Rosebery (London: Herbert Jenkins, 1913)

Windham, William, *Early Life and Diaries,* ed. R. W. Ketton-Cremer (London: Faber & Faber, 1930)

INDEX

Index

Index

Peel, Robert Haworth 219–22, 235, 290, 304
Penarth 145
Penn-Gaskell, Winnifred 260; 11, 16
Pennines 202
Pennsylvania 110
Perkins, R. (of Oakhill) 130
Pettat, Thomas 90
Philadelphia 289
Phillips, Susan (*née* Burney) 33
Pickworth (Rutland) 173
Pinkney, Mr (songwriter) 139, 140
Pittaway, Ann 283
Platt, Mr B. 219–22, 225
Platt, Robert 307
Plot, Robert 103
Plymouth 185
Podenas, la Comtesse 285
Poland 291
Pole, William Wellesley 128–30
Pontefract 81, 183
Portsmouth 116, 118, 119, 127, 185, 294, 295
Powell, Kate (*née* Hoare) 270, 309
Powell, Sparks 270
Preston 205, 206, 225
Prideaux, Frances & Francis 144, 146
Priestley, Joseph 31, 67, 110, 111, 258, 284
Pye, Henry James 62, 93, 97, 239, 292
Pyle (Glamorgan) 145
Quantrell's, Norwich 301
Queen Charlotte 180, 181
Ramsgate 124
Ravensworth, Baron 290
Reading 72, 169
Redmill, Robert 296
Reed, Charles (Bristol) 247–49
'Renad, Sieur' 38, 39
Rennie, John 120, 196
Reynolds, Joseph 113
Reynolds, Joshua 50
Reynolds, William 109–11, 113, 293
Richards, Catherine – see Sadler
Richards, Thomas (x 2) 205, 279, 310
Richie, Alex 12
Richmond, Duke & Duchess of 160, 162
Ringabella (Co. Cork) 192
Rivers, Lord 180
Robert, Aîné 32, 99, 260, 289
Robert, Cadet 285, 289
Roberts, Dr (of London) 150
Roberts, James 63, 91; 8
Robinson, Edward 155
Rochdale 220
Roche, Lieutenant 164
Rochester 77, 78
Rogers, Miss (of Dublin) 196
Romain, Jules 84, 91
Romsey (Hants.) 57

Rossiter, Mr (aeronaut) 281
Rouen 287
Rouse, Richard (?) 108, 293
Routh, Peter 268
Rowlandson, Thomas 123, 295; 15, 21
Royal Academy 63
Royal Aeronautical Society 238, 287, 300; 31
Royal Hotel, Plymouth 185
Royal Institution 136, 179, 295
Royal Society 31, 32, 37, 42, 76, 92, 103, 113, 289, 293, 295, 297, 300
Rudge, Edward 37, 38
Russia 175, 186, 309
Rutland 173
Saddel(l) (Argyll & Bute) 223
Sadler, Albinia 278
Sadler, Amelia 277
Sadler, Ann (aunt) 244, 306
Sadler, Ann (niece) 248
Sadler, Catherine (*née* Richards) 205, 214, 228, 230, 231, 279, 305
Sadler, Catherine Windham 231, 279, 310
Sadler, Charles James (great nephew) 247, 249
Sadler, Charles James (nephew) 237, 246–49, 310; 1
Sadler, Charlotte Rebecca 204, 275
Sadler, Edward 244
Sadler, Eleanor (niece) 248
Sadler, Mrs Eleanor (sister-in-law) 245, 307
Sadler, Eliza (daughter) 86, 147, 279
Sadler, Eliza (granddaughter) 204, 275
Sadler, Elizabeth (1628–?) 241
Sadler, Elizabeth (aunt) 244
Sadler, Elizabeth (daughter-in-law) 278
Sadler, Elizabeth (*née* Reed) 249
Sadler, Elizabeth (niece) 245, 247, 248
Sadler, Mrs Elizabeth (mother) 22, 23, 87, 294
Sadler, Emily Jane 307
Sadler, Frances 204, 276, 277
Sadler, Frederick 307
Sadler, Mrs Grace 243
Sadler, Harold 238, 279, 294, 299
Sadler, Henry 139, 246–48, 307
Sadler, James (father) 22–27, 30, 87, 109, 244, 283, 285, 306; 2, 3, 4
Sadler, James (son) 123, 124, 277, 278
Sadler, Jane (*née* Cox) 246
Sadler, Jane (*née* Marten) 242, 306
Sadler, Jane (*née* Needle) 247
Sadler, Jane (*née* Weller) 241
Sadler, Jane 242
Sadler, Mrs Joanna 242
Sadler, John (?–1630) 314

Sadler, John (1694–1749) 22, 243, 283, 306
Sadler, John (great grandson) 277
Sadler, John (son) 47, 56, 115, 136–40, 149, 151, 168, 180, 181, 204, 207, 231, 275–77, 287, 299, 300; 22, 23
Sadler, John Coxe Hippisley 136, 203, 204, 207, 231, 275, 277
Sadler, John Muncaster 279, 303
Sadler, Martha (*née* Hancock) 116, 218, 234
Sadler, Mary (aunt) 244
Sadler, Mary (*née* Harper) 26, 64, 73, 110, 116, 275, 293
Sadler, Mary (*née* Long) 136, 275
Sadler, Mary (*née* Smith) 244
Sadler, Mary (*née* Whitchurch) 246
Sadler, Mary (niece) 248
Sadler, Mary Ann 147, 275
Sadler, Michael 238
Sadler, Ralph 300
Sadler, Richard (1630–?) 241
Sadler, Richard (*c*. 1692–?) 243
Sadler, Roy (descendant) 305
Sadler, Sarah (aunt) 244
Sadler, Mrs Sarah (?–1753) 242
Sadler, Sybella (daughter) 143, 147, 279, 299
Sadler, Thomas (nephew) 139, 246–48, 278, 307
Sadler, Thomas (son) 278, 307
Sadler, Thomas Blakeney 22, 23, 26, 27, 64, 109, 120, 137, 237, 245–49, 275, 278, 306, 307; 1
Sadler, William (?–1649) 241, 242
Sadler, William (?–1714) 243
Sadler, William (1631–1680) 241, 242
Sadler, William (1662?–1720) 23, 241, 242, 306
Sadler, William (uncle) 244
Sadler's Sharp Shooters 123; 21
Sage, Edward 271
Sage, Letitia Ann (*née* Hoare) 9, 82, 83, 85, 86, 262, 265–74, 286, 308, 309; 7, 14, 15, 16
St Donat's (Glamorgan) 144
St George's Channel (Irish Sea) 159, 225
St George's Fields, Manchester 156
St Helen's, Abingdon 26, 275, 283, 308
St Mary's (Kent) 78
St Patrick's Hill, Cork 191
St Philip's, Birmingham 270
Sainte-Croix, Monsieur 296
Salford 219, 235
Salisbury 296
Sastres, Francesco 287
Saunders, Mrs (upholsterer, London) 288
Saxton, Charles (1732–1808) 37, 119, 129, 294, 299
Saxton, Charles (1773–1838) 299
Scots Greys 154